Real-Time Shadows

Real-Time Shadows

Elmar Eisemann
Michael Schwarz
Ulf Assarsson
Michael Wimmer

CRC Press
Taylor & Francis Group
Boca Raton London New York

CRC Press is an imprint of the
Taylor & Francis Group, an **informa** business

AN A K PETERS BOOK

CRC Press
Taylor & Francis Group
6000 Broken Sound Parkway NW, Suite 300
Boca Raton, FL 33487-2742

First issued in paperback 2020

© 2012 by Taylor & Francis Group, LLC
CRC Press is an imprint of Taylor & Francis Group, an Informa business

No claim to original U.S. Government works

ISBN-13: 978-1-56881-438-4 (hbk)
ISBN-13: 978-0-367-65926-4 (pbk)

Library of Congress Cataloging-in-Publication Data

Real-time shadows / Elmar Eisemann ... [et al.].
     p. cm.
  Includes bibliographical references and index.
  ISBN 978-1-56881-438-4 (alk. paper)
    1. Computer animation. 2. Real-time rendering (Computer graphics) 3. Shades and shadows in art. 4. Digital video. I. Eisemann, Elmar.

  TR897.7.R396 2011
  006.6'96--dc22
                                               2011009331

Visit the Taylor & Francis Web site at
http://www.taylorandfrancis.com

and the CRC Press Web site at
http://www.crcpress.com

Dedicated to…

…my family,
including my uncle, who awakened my scientific curiosity.
E.E.

…Ewelina and all the rest of my whole big family.
U.A.

…Romana, Sarah, and Laurenz.
M.W.

Contents

Preface

In recent years, there were several important steps forward in the development of graphics hardware: shaders were introduced, GPUs became more general, and GPU performance increased drastically. In consequence, many new techniques appeared and novel rendering methods, such as deferred shading, became practical. The latter was one of the key factors in enabling a high light count, which added a never-before-seen realism to real-time graphics. The related tech demos were breathtaking, exhibiting enormous amounts of detail and complex surface properties. Skin started to look quite realistic, and even hair rendering reached a new level with image-based shading. Nonetheless, one effect remained very difficult to achieve: realistic shadows.

The cover image demonstrates how versatile shadows can be. The scene exhibits a church hall with a large glass window. The stained glass casts shadows in the form of colored light, scattered by atmospheric effects to yield so-called God rays. Finally, this light produces hard and soft shadows in the very complex scene, where the leaf foliage interacts in complex ways to yield shadows on the detailed grass ground. All these various effects, such as hard, soft, semitransparent, and volumetric shadows, add significantly to the ambiance of the scene. As a whole, the image also provides a good example of how we take the existence of shadows for granted and how crucial they are for creating a pleasing and realistic image—just imagine how dull the image would look like without any shadow.

Due to the importance of shadows for realistic rendering, the topic has received much attention, especially in real-time contexts, where people generally strive for realism but are limited by important performance considerations. These two goals—realism and performance—are difficult to combine in general and, particularly, for shadows. Consequently, in recent years the number of shadow publications and algorithms has exploded. In particular, soft shadows that approach physically plausible results became a major topic, and many approaches appeared.

It was not until 2007, when graphics processing units made another tremendous leap with the introduction of DirectX 10, that the first real-time accurate GPU shadow algorithms appeared. These early algorithms clearly did not exhibit the performance required for games or interactive applications. Ultimately, no algorithm, even today, is capable of delivering an always-convincing result with real-time performance.

In the effort to balance performance and quality, many different tracks appeared that aimed for realistic, plausible, or even fake shadows, each one with its particular advantages and disadvantages. Some of these approaches were even good enough to ensure high quality in many application scenarios at an acceptable performance. However, choosing the right solution for the right context has become increasingly difficult given the wealth of existing possibilities. This was a significant problem because it made it difficult for practitioners to find an appropriate approach for their task. The description of these approaches were spread over various scientific conferences or publications, and no general presentation existed.

It became apparent to us that there was a strong need for an overview, practical guidance, and also theoretical awareness of the remaining challenges and limitations to creating real-time shadows. In this spirit, we developed an overview of the many different shadow techniques that led to this book.

With the PhD theses of two of the authors [Eisemann08a,Schwarz09] featuring state-of-the-art chapters, and as the four authors met at various conferences, the plan to transform these chapters into a book started to take shape. As a first step, we wrote extended notes for a course that was held at SIGGRAPH Asia 2009 [Eisemann09] and Eurographics 2010 [Eisemann10]. While the course was relatively exhaustive, we realized that the topic is much broader than what could be covered in a course. Further, recent years brought related developments, such as volumetric shadows, that have not yet been covered in an overview. It turned out that our initial plan to explain, analyze, and discuss all important shadowing techniques was more than ambitious. It was a project that, in the end, took us roughly more than two years to finish.

Writing such a detailed overview was an exhausting challenge, but we hope you agree that it was worth it. This book covers many different algorithms, addresses more than 300 publications, and, hopefully, closes the void that previously existed. We hope you will enjoy the book and that it will enlighten your way to more realistic and convincing imagery.

Acknowledgements

Writing a book obviously involves the authors, but there are many people behind the scenes that contributed enormously to making this book what it is today. As you might notice, many all-new illustrations can be found throughout this book. Many of them illustrate algorithms in action, which were made possible by the kind help of various people who supported us with their input, images, and photos:

Erik Sintorn, Brandon Lloyd, Jing Huang, Zhao Dong, Louis Bavoil, Cyril Crassin, Tobias Ritschel, Robert Herzog, Matthias Holländer, Julia Lövenich, and Betuca Buril. In particular, we would like to thank Erik Sintorn for the cover image of this book. Further, our gratitude goes to Martin Stingl for writing the software that was used to create the comparison images and plots in Chapter 4, and Louis Bavoil for providing us with code that helped us in producing other illustrations in this document.

To ensure the quality of the descriptions, all chapters were proofread by many people. They verified the description and analysis of each of the many described algorithms, the math, the analysis—even the new ideas and algorithms that are presented in this book for the first time. Consequently, this proofreading took quite a while and we would like to express our deepest gratitude for the effort of the following reviewers: Erik Sintorn, Oliver Klehm, Emmanuel Turquin, Martin Eisemann, Louis Bavoil, Hedlena Bezerra, Bert Buchholz, Brandon Lloyd, Aaron Lefohn, and Andrew Lauritzen.

This publication would have never seen the light without Alice Peters and her advice and patience. We cannot express enough gratitude for her help and understanding, as well as the support of all the people at A K Peters. We would also like to thank our colleagues, the people at Telecom ParisTech (Tamy Boubekeur, Isabelle Bloch, Yves Grenier, . . .), TU Vienna (Werner Purgathofer, Daniel Scherzer, . . .), and Chalmers University (Ola Olsson, Markus Billeter, . . .) for their kind help.

The models in this book are from various sources. Without the help of the following people and groups, most images would look much less exciting: Marko Dabrovic (Sibenik model), Martin Newell (Utah Teapot), Stanford 3D Scanning Repository, INRIA, De Espona, and Aim@Shape.

Finally, we would like to thank all our friends, partners, and families, for their understanding and support. Thank you very much.

CHAPTER 1
Introduction

An old saying tells us that there is *no light without shadow*, and although it is originally a metaphor, it is perfectly true: without light, everything is dark ... and definitely not very exciting; but as soon as there is a light source, there are also cast shadows.

On the one hand, shadows are important for the understanding of scenes. We better comprehend spatial relationships between objects and better succeed in localizing them in space. Further, we can deduce shape information, not only of the shadow-casting elements but also of the receiver, by interpreting shadow deformations.

Shadows are also an artistic means. Many movies exploit shadows to illustrate the presence of some person or object without revealing its actual appearance (just think of the hundreds of Dracula movies out there). Figure 1.1 shows an example where shadows are used in this manner. While we cannot directly see the camels, their shadows complete our understanding of the scene.

Consequently, shadows are naturally a crucial element of image synthesis—and remain a particular challenge for real-time graphics: while conceptually relatively simple to compute, naive methods are usually extremely costly. Only via alternative scene representations and GPU-adapted algorithms can one achieve the performance that is needed to match today's needs. Hence, the topic has spurred many scientific publications in recent years, and the field of shadow algorithms today shows a variety never seen before. Despite this wealth of publications, currently, no single algorithm would prove convincing and satisfying in every given scenario, and it is unlikely that the situation will change in the near future.

While the existence of many algorithms might seem confusing and redundant at first, it is actually a big advantage! Many algorithms satisfy particular constraints and might offer some advantages over its competitors. In fact, there is an appropriate shadow algorithm for most application scenarios, but finding one's way

Figure 1.1. Even objects outside the view can project visible shadows that can help us to establish a more complete understanding of the scene (courtesy of Betuca Buril).

through the jungle of possibilities is difficult without advice. This book discusses more than 200 shadow papers in a consistent way and gives direct advice on which algorithms to choose, ignore, or combine. The most important methods are described in detail, and pseudocode will help you in realizing your own implementations and support your quest for an appropriate trade-off between quality and performance.

This book can serve as a course for beginners with some computer graphics knowledge and coding experience who want to rise to the level of a shadow expert. It can also be used as a reference book for experts and real-time graphics programmers who might want to jump directly to the parts they are interested in.

If you were ever curious about shadows, or you were impressed by modern games and wanted to get an insight in one of their most striking effects, this book is for you. Even if you have little experience and 200 papers sounds overwhelming, there is no reason to be worried. We start at the very beginning and guide you on this journey one step at a time, starting off almost naively by asking the most basic question: what is a shadow?

Figure 1.2. A very large light source (yellow square) leads to soft shadows. All points on the floor are actually lit to some degree.

1.1　Definition

What is a shadow? This is a good question, and because of the fuzziness of the term, even dictionaries have trouble giving an accurate definition. WordNet [Princeton University09] states: "Shade within clear boundaries" or "An unilluminated area." By looking at Figure 1.2, one realizes rapidly that this definition is not accurate enough. The same holds for other definitions that try to capture the common notion that a shadow is often attributed to a certain object; for instance, Merriam-Webster [Merriam-Webster09] states:

> The dark figure cast upon a surface by a body intercepting the rays from a source of light.

A better definition is given in the American Heritage Dictionary of the English Language [Pickett00]:

> An area that is not or is only partially irradiated or illuminated because of the interception of radiation by an opaque object between the area and the source of radiation.

Figure 1.3. What we define as *shadow* depends upon the scale at which we look at objects. In the real world, the definition is thus very ambiguous; in a virtual world, described by a mathematically accurate framework, precise definitions are possible and meaningful. The left image shows a close-up of a plant, revealing a fine and shadow-casting surface structure (courtesy of Prof. U. Hartmann, Nanostructure Research and Nanotechnology, Saarland University). The right image illustrates a distant view for which the fine structure becomes invisible, making the shadows disappear.

This definition brings us closer, and coincides more readily with a proposition from the graphics domain [Hasenfratz03]:

> Shadow [is] the region of space for which at least one point of the light source is occluded.

This definition implicitly makes two important assumptions. First, only direct illumination is considered, direct illumination being the illumination coming directly from a light source. Light bouncing off surfaces is ignored. Second, occluders are assumed to be opaque, which is not necessarily always the case in the real world.

But even in this restricted scenario of opaque objects and direct illumination, a shadow definition for the "real world" is not as simple as the above descriptions lead us to believe. Take a look at Figure 1.3 (left): do we see shadows in this picture? Without exactly knowing what is depicted, most people would say "yes." However, this picture shows a microscopic zoom of a leaf just like the one in Figure 1.3 (right). If one presents solely this latter picture, most people would tend to argue that there is no visible shadow. The underlying principle is that what we see and how we interpret it depends highly on the scale at which we look at things. The impact of these small-scale variations can be enormous. A CD-ROM is a good example of this: if you look at its back, you see a rainbow of colors caused by the fine surface structure that is used to store data. Much of a surface's reflection behavior is influenced by microscale light blocking. Hence, there is actually a fine line between shading, which is the variation of brightness across the surface based on its material and shape, and shadows that are cast from a different location in space.

In our artificial world, small-scale geometric variations are usually omitted because, in practice, we cannot afford to work at the scales necessary to capture these effects. Usually, we tend to represent objects coarsely but rely on specialized shading functions that encode fine-scale material properties on the surface that otherwise would be lost. Further, the fact that these functions live on the surface hint at another very common approximation: we rely on boundary representations (at least in the case of triangular meshes). Boundary representations are somewhat similar to ceramic figures, since you usually cannot look beneath the surface and, hence, there is no way to tell that they are hollow. Nonetheless, it is not uncommon that effects take place underneath the surface that make the object appear differently; for example, marble and wax show a certain glow because the light is scattered in its interior. To address these phenomena, a great deal of research focuses on simulating these interactions approximately on the surface. In Appendix C, we present a quick overview of some of the most common shading models, some of which even account for the visibility of small-scale details explicitly.

This distinction between shading and shadows leaves us with an interesting situation. In the real world, shadows might have all kinds of ambiguities. By contrast, in our artificial universe, details are limited, and shadows are described independently of scale and purely in terms of visibility. A definition such as the one given by Hasenfratz et al. [Hasenfratz03] is mostly sufficient—at least as long as only opaque objects and direct lighting are considered. Completely general real-time algorithms, going beyond opaque objects and direct-lighting restrictions, remain a hefty challenge, likely to keep computer graphics experts busy for the foreseeable future.

In order to handle all cases of shadows, we propose a different, mathematically sound shadow definition, which will apply for all algorithms presented in this book. The experienced reader might want to skip this part and solely take a look at Figure 1.5 to be familiar with the most important terms, as well as Equations (1.4) and (1.6), which will be referred to hereafter.

1.1.1   Terminology

In this section, we will introduce the terminology that will be used throughout this book. In order to facilitate understanding, we will avoid a complex mathematical definition and assume that our scene corresponds to a triangle mesh with per-face normals.[1] Then, the *scene geometry*, or simply *geometry*, S is a set of *scene points* that form the triangles. Each scene point $\mathbf{p}$ has a corresponding normal $\mathbf{n_p}$ defined by the underlying triangle.

A light source $\mathcal{L}$ is a set of points $\mathbf{l}$ forming the light surface. We will refer to these points as *light (source) samples*. The light source emits energy into the

---

[1]Readers familiar with the concepts of manifolds will realize that these definitions easily extend to such a case.

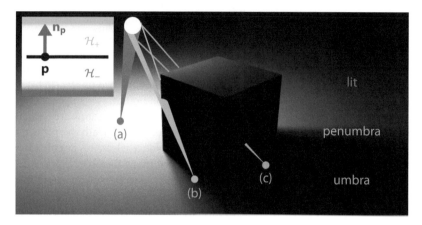

Figure 1.4. A point is either (a) lit or (b, c) shadowed. In the latter case, we further distinguish between (b) penumbra and (c) umbra, depending on whether the light source is only partially or completely hidden.

scene, and throughout this book, we will assume that light travels along straight lines (even though in some situations this is not a valid approximation, e.g., in the case of atmospheric diffraction or near black holes). Consequently, to find out whether light can travel from one point to another, we need to consider whether the connection between the two points is not obstructed.

To this end, we define that **p** *sees* **q**, where **p** and **q** are two points in three-dimensional space, if and only if the segment connecting the two points does not intersect the scene other than at its extremities. Mathematically, this can be equivalently expressed by imposing that no intersection occurs between the scene geometry S and the open segment $(\mathbf{p}, \mathbf{q}) := \{\mathbf{r} \mid \mathbf{r} := \mathbf{p} + \alpha(\mathbf{q} - \mathbf{p}), 0 < \alpha < 1\}$.[2]

Building on this definition, the point **p** lies in *shadow* if and only if there exists a light sample **l** such that **p** does not see **l**. This can be equivalently stated as $\overline{\mathcal{V}}_{\mathcal{L}}(\mathbf{p}) \neq \varnothing$, where

$$\overline{\mathcal{V}}_{\mathcal{L}}(\mathbf{p}) = \{\mathbf{l} \in \mathcal{L} \mid \mathbf{p} \text{ does not see } \mathbf{l}\} \tag{1.1}$$

denotes the set of all light samples that are not seen by **p**. If $\overline{\mathcal{V}}_{\mathcal{L}}(\mathbf{p}) = \mathcal{L}$, meaning that the whole light source is blocked by the scene geometry, **p** is said to be in the *umbra*. If only some light samples are not seen (i.e., $\mathcal{L} \neq \overline{\mathcal{V}}_{\mathcal{L}}(\mathbf{p}) \neq \varnothing$), **p** is in the *penumbra*. Finally, if **p** is not in shadow (i.e., $\overline{\mathcal{V}}_{\mathcal{L}}(\mathbf{p}) = \varnothing$), it is said to be *lit*. The different shadow cases are illustrated in Figure 1.4.

In practice, a scene is rarely a true collection of points. Rather, these points constitute objects, like triangles, or even bunnies. In this sense, we will refer to an object that can intersect segments from **p** to the light as an *occluder* (or, equiv-

---

[2]This says that the segment $(\mathbf{p}, \mathbf{q})$ consists of all points **r** that are located between **p** and **q**.

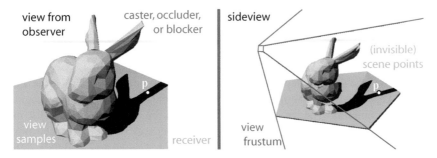

Figure 1.5. A view sample **p** is the three-dimensional location corresponding to a pixel **p** in the rendered view. Occluders/blockers/shadow casters are all elements that obstruct the light from **p**.

alently, as a *blocker* or *shadow caster*) for **p**. Objects containing such points in shadow (i.e., objects onto which a shadow is cast) are called *receivers*. There are situations where receivers and blockers are distinct, or where each receiver is only shadowed by a subset of occluders. Notably, some algorithms do not allow self-shadowing (blocker and receiver are the same object).

In practice, we will mostly be interested in computing the shadow for a special set of receivers, notably the view samples. A *view sample* is the three-dimensional point that corresponds to a given pixel of an image. This notion is interesting because, when we produce an image for a given view, a correctly shadowed rendition of the scene only needs to compute a correct color for each pixel, not for all points in the scene.

Figure 1.5 illustrates most of the here-defined terms and can be used as a reference for the remainder of this book.

1.1.2 The Rendering Equation

So far, we have clarified where we can find shadows. Now, we will discuss their actual influence on the appearance of a scene. For this, we need to understand how light interacts with the surfaces of a scene. Further, we will get to know the corresponding energetic quantities that allow us to mathematically describe the physical behavior. While the interactions can be very complex in a physical environment, perhaps involving quantum mechanics on a microscale and specialized relativity theory on a larger scale, in most practical scenarios of computer graphics, these effects can be neglected. Even Maxwell's equations only play a role in particular cases of computer graphics. The most prominent and usually visible effects can be described with a much simpler equation.

Before analyzing the physical model, we will first introduce the central notion of light energy: *radiance L*.[3] It is defined as radiant flux (light energy per unit time;

---

[3] In this book, we will not consider wavelength dependence, as it is less relevant for shadows.

measured in Watt) per unit solid angle and per unit projected area. The *solid angle* subtended by an object at a point **p** is the size of this object projected on the unit sphere around the point **p**; in other words, it is a measure of how large an object appears from **p**. Intuitively this makes sense because the farther a light is away, the smaller it will appear and, similarly, the less energy arrives at the location. Anyone who ever walked around with a candle in the dark should recognize this phenomenon. The second observation is that the definition involves *per unit projected area*. Physically, it is impossible to have energy be emitted from a single point; instead, all (real-world) light sources have some actual area, and the emitted energy is defined in terms of this area.

The main principle is that the outgoing radiance L_o leaving a given scene point **p** in a certain direction ω is the result of an interaction between the incoming radiance L_i (which is the light that arrives on the surface) and the surface properties f_r (that define how light is reflected, depending on the material). This process is described by one of the fundamental equations in computer graphics, the so-called *rendering equation*, introduced by Kajiya [Kajiya86] and Immel et al. [Immel86]:[4]

$$L_o(\mathbf{p}, \omega) = L_e(\mathbf{p}, \omega) + \int_{\Omega_+} f_r(\mathbf{p}, \omega, \hat{\omega})\, L_i(\mathbf{p}, \hat{\omega})\, \cos(\mathbf{n_p}, \hat{\omega})\, d\hat{\omega}, \qquad (1.2)$$

where $\mathbf{n_p}$ is the surface normal at **p** and Ω_+ denotes the hemisphere above the surface at **p**. The equation puts the following functions into a relation:

- L_o describes the outgoing radiance as a function of position **p** and direction ω. Simply put, it quantifies the light (direct and indirect) leaving a point in a given direction. This term is the one we are interested in for producing an image (see infobox on page 9).

- L_e yields the emitted radiance. Put simply, this is the light produced at a given point for a given direction. The term is nonzero for light sources.

- L_i is the incoming radiance. In principle, this incoming radiance can itself depend on the outgoing radiance L_o at a different scene point. This situation is taken into account in the case of global illumination, where bounced light is considered; for example, a red surface next to a white wall might reflect some of its red color onto the wall, leading to so-called color bleeding.

- f_r is a bidirectional reflectance distribution function (BRDF). It describes how much of the incoming light from direction $\hat{\omega}$ is reflected in direction ω at a given point **p**. Note that this function can be very complex, but might also just be a constant. (More information on this topic can be found in Appendix C).

---

[4]Kajiya introduced the equation in a different formulation, but for our explanation this simpler form is more appropriate.

> ### Radiance Captured by a Camera
>
> At this point you might wonder, after all these definitions, how to actually produce an image even if we had the outgoing radiance $L_o(\mathbf{p}, \omega)$ at disposition. After all, L might be defined in each scene point but is still given per unit area. To understand how this relates to pixel values, let's quickly remember how a pinhole camera works, which is the standard camera used in most real-time applications. There are more complex models, but these are out of the scope of this work. For a real-world pinhole camera, light falls through a pinhole before reaching a receptor. The receptor integrates the incoming light and transforms it into a pixel color. The receptors themselves have a certain size, which is exactly how the area quotient disappears in L. Furthermore, light can only reach a sensor if it passes through the camera's pinhole. Hence, we need to evaluate $L_o(\mathbf{p}, \omega)$ with a direction ω such that the line through $\mathbf{p}$ in direction ω passes through the camera's pinhole (in DirectX and OpenGL, this corresponds to the camera center). When precisely evaluating the incoming light on a receptor for a given pixel, one would need to take the angular variation for different points on the receptor into account. In practice, this is usually neglected and only a single point is evaluated.

The rendering equation is physically based and describes the equilibrium of energy in a scene. While it is a good model of illumination transport, solving the equation analytically is difficult (except for a few uninteresting cases). Photorealistic rendering aims at finding efficient ways to approximate and populate this equation. The equation inherently depends upon itself because the outgoing light at some point might end up being the incoming light for another point. This dependency makes the computation particularly difficult.

Surface-Based Formulation

Employing the notation $\mathbf{p} \to \mathbf{q} := \frac{\mathbf{q}-\mathbf{p}}{\|\mathbf{q}-\mathbf{p}\|}$, the following relationship holds:

$$L_i(\mathbf{p}, \mathbf{p} \to \mathbf{q}) = L_o(\mathbf{q}, \mathbf{q} \to \mathbf{p})$$

for a point $\mathbf{p}$ that sees $\mathbf{q}$. Along this segment, the energy exchange will not be hindered by scene geometry. Consequently, the outgoing illumination from one side is exactly the incoming illumination on the other side and vice versa.

The integration over the directions as denoted in Equation (1.2) can be reinterpreted. It corresponds to an integration over a sphere centered at $\mathbf{p}$ onto which all the surrounding geometry is projected as seen from $\mathbf{p}$. We can hence perform a change of variables and equivalently integrate over the surfaces of the scene S instead of the directions on a hemisphere, leading to

$$L_o(\mathbf{p}, \omega) = L_e(\mathbf{p}, \omega) + \int_S f_r(\mathbf{p}, \omega, \mathbf{p} \to \mathbf{q}) \, L_o(\mathbf{q}, \mathbf{q} \to \mathbf{p}) \, G(\mathbf{p}, \mathbf{q}) \, V(\mathbf{p}, \mathbf{q}) \, d\mathbf{q}, \quad (1.3)$$

where

$$G(\mathbf{p}, \mathbf{q}) = \frac{\cos(\mathbf{n}_p, \mathbf{p} \to \mathbf{q}) \cos(\mathbf{n}_q, \mathbf{q} \to \mathbf{p})}{\|\mathbf{p} - \mathbf{q}\|^2},$$

and V encodes a binary visibility function; it is one if $\mathbf{p}$ sees $\mathbf{q}$ and zero otherwise.

1.1.3   Simplifications for Shadow Computations

For our purpose of shadow computation, we can simplify the equation. The term L_e is not of high importance for our discussion because there is no interdependence with the scene. We can simply omit it and add its contribution in the end—in practice, this could mean that the light source is simply drawn on top of the final image. We are only interested in direct illumination that removes the equation's dependency on itself. Consequently, for all points $\mathbf{q}$ in the scene, $L_o(\mathbf{q}, \mathbf{q} \to \mathbf{p})$ is zero, except for those locations $\mathbf{q}$ that lie on a light source. Also, the additivity of the integral allows us to treat several lights sequentially by summing up their contributions.

We thus assume that there is only one light source in the scene, thereby obtaining the *direct-lighting equation* (with shadows):

$$L_o(\mathbf{p}, \omega) = \int_{\mathcal{L}} f_r(\mathbf{p}, \omega, \mathbf{p} \to \mathbf{l}) \, L_e(\mathbf{l}, \mathbf{l} \to \mathbf{p}) \, G(\mathbf{p}, \mathbf{l}) \, V(\mathbf{p}, \mathbf{l}) \, d\mathbf{l}. \tag{1.4}$$

In practice, this equation is typically simplified further, and often, visually similar results can be obtained with these simplifications, while the cost of computing them is significantly lower. A common approach builds on the observation that if the distance of the light to the receiver is relatively large (with respect to the light's solid angle) and the light's shape is simple, then the geometric term G varies little. This situation and the assumption that the BRDF f_r is mainly diffuse together allow for the approximation of separating the integral, which means that we can split the integral over the product of the two functions G and L_e into a product of integrals:

$$L_o(\mathbf{p}, \omega) = \underbrace{\int_{\mathcal{L}} f_r(\mathbf{p}, \omega, \mathbf{p} \to \mathbf{l}) \, G(\mathbf{p}, \mathbf{l}) \, d\mathbf{l}}_{\text{Shading}} \cdot \underbrace{\frac{1}{|\mathcal{L}|} \int_{\mathcal{L}} L_e(\mathbf{l}, \mathbf{l} \to \mathbf{p}) \, V(\mathbf{p}, \mathbf{l}) \, d\mathbf{l}}_{\text{Shadow}}. \tag{1.5}$$

Basically, the simplification results in a decoupling of shading and shadows.

Furthermore, we typically assume that the light source has homogeneous *directional* radiation over its surface, causing L_e to simplify to a function of position $L_c(\mathbf{l})$ only. If the light source is uniformly colored, it further reduces to a constant $\bar{L}_c$. Because a constant does not vary, we can take it out of the integral. These uniformity assumptions on position and direction are very common and ultimately result in the equation

$$L_o(\mathbf{p}, \omega) = \text{directIllum}(\mathbf{p}, \omega, \mathcal{L}, \bar{L}_c) \cdot V_{\mathcal{L}}(\mathbf{p}),$$

Analytical Solutions

If all surfaces in the scene are Lambertian (perfectly diffuse), the BRDF 2ρ becomes independent of directions, that is, $f_r(\mathbf{p}, \omega, \hat{\omega}) = \rho(\mathbf{p})/\pi$, and can be moved out of the integral. Interestingly, for the remaining integral $\int_{\mathcal{L}} G \, d\mathbf{l}$, accurate analytic solutions exist for the relatively general case where $\mathcal{L}$ is a polygon—even if we integrate further over all $\mathbf{l}$ within another polygonal region [Schröder93]. This latter possibility can be useful if subpixel information is evaluated to achieve a very high image quality and is usually employed in offline contexts or global illumination computations. Although it is an important theoretical contribution that remained unsolved until 1993 (despite many early attempts, such as Lambert's in 1790), the exact formula is often considered too complex for practical applications. For complex BRDFs or visibility configurations, we are generally left with sampling as the only option (e.g., via so-called Monte Carlo techniques).

---

where the *visibility integral*

$$V_{\mathcal{L}}(\mathbf{p}) = \frac{1}{|\mathcal{L}|} \int_{\mathcal{L}} V(\mathbf{p}, \mathbf{l}) \, d\mathbf{l} \qquad (1.6)$$

modulates the shading

$$\text{directIllum}(\mathbf{p}, \omega, \mathcal{L}, \bar{L}_c) = \bar{L}_c \int_{\mathcal{L}} f_r(\mathbf{p}, \omega, \mathbf{p} \to \mathbf{l}) \, G(\mathbf{p}, \mathbf{l}) \, d\mathbf{l},$$

which boils down to computing the (unshadowed) direct illumination. In practice, instead of integrating over the whole light source, the shading computation typically only considers a single light sample $\mathbf{l}' \in \mathcal{L}$ for performance reasons, that is,

$$\text{directIllum}(\mathbf{p}, \omega, \mathcal{L}, \bar{L}_c) \approx \text{directIllum}(\mathbf{p}, \omega, \mathbf{l}', \bar{L}_c).$$

Usually, for real-time applications, determining the integral in Equation (1.6) is what is meant when talking about *soft-shadow computation*, and most solutions aim at calculating it. In general, Equation (1.6) is not physically correct and the approximation can be quite different compared to a reference solution based on Equation (1.4). Only the amount of visibility is evaluated and not which part is blocked. Precisely, the term $G(\mathbf{p}, \mathbf{l})$ makes the influence of the light source on the point $\mathbf{p}$ nonuniform and it falls off with distance and orientation. This variation is no longer captured when separating the integrals. Estimating the actual difference between the nonseparated and separated version can be complex though [Soler98a]. Nonetheless, results are often convincing.

A further simplification that is encountered in many real-time applications is choosing a point light as light source, making the light $\mathcal{L}$ consist exclusively of one point $\mathbf{l}'$. This simplifies the computation of the visibility integral from Equation (1.6) to $V(\mathbf{p}, \mathbf{l}')$. Since the visibility function V is binary, as $\mathbf{p}$ either sees $\mathbf{l}'$ or does not, the resulting shadow comprises only an umbra and is hence called *hard shadow*. By contrast, shadows cast by a light source with some spatial extent are referred to as *soft shadows*, since they typically feature a soft transition from lit to shadowed regions. While assuming a point light source offers significant performance gains, it usually also notably reduces the visual quality. This is because, in reality, basically no point lights exist, and even the sun subtends a solid angle large enough to result in penumbra regions—which just don't occur with point lights.

1.2   Importance of Shadows

Why should we care about shadows? One obvious reason is that for photorealistic rendering, one tries to produce images that are indistinguishable from real photographs. This necessarily includes computing shadows and, in particular, accurate and physically based shadows. But even when dropping the hard constraint of photorealism, computing reasonable shadows is important to provide clues concerning the spatial relationship of objects in the scene or the shape of a receiver and to even reveal information hidden from the current point of view.

Several experiments underline the importance of shadows. For instance, Kersten et al. [Kersten96] investigated the influence of shadows on perceived motion. In their many experiments, they also displayed a sphere above a plane, not unlike Figure 1.6 (left). Just as you can see in this image, the position of the shadow influences the perceived position. If the shadow moves up in the image, the trajectory will further influence how we will perceive the sphere itself, and we will have the impression that the sphere moves to the back of the box towards the ground. This effect is strong enough that our visual system even prefers to assume that the sphere grows when moving to the back, rather than rejecting the shadow information. As Miller [Miller07] points out, it is almost paradoxical *that seeing some parts of what we see less well than others can help us to understand the whole of what we see better.* But these cues are surprisingly strong and, interestingly, Kersten et al. [Kersten96] found that more natural shadows with a soft boundary can lead to even stronger cues than shadows with a crisp border.

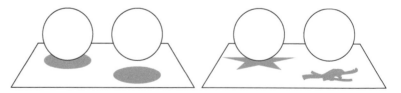

Figure 1.6. Shadows have an important influence on the interpretation of spatial relationships in a scene (left). Nevertheless, even coarse approximations can achieve the same effect (right).

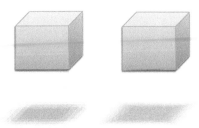

Figure 1.7. Superpositions of shadows can look much less appealing and less smooth than the same amount of copies placed in a concentric fashion.

Perceptual results are often cited to stress the importance of shadows, and they seem to illustrate this point well. But it is arguable whether the conclusion is that we should aim at realistic shadow computations. Gooch et al. [Gooch99] found that regular concentric shapes can deliver shadows that are preferred by several subjects over other, potentially more precise approximations. An extreme example is shown in Figure 1.7, which illustrates how strongly perceptual effects can influence our judgement of quality.

Even very approximate shadows can often provide sufficient information to interpret the spatial relationships. Take a look at Figure 1.6 (right). We understand the scene just as before, but the shadows are far from realistic. Other experiments [Ni04] illustrated that it actually suffices to add dark indications underneath the object. An observer automatically establishes the connection and accepts the shadow. In fact, this allowed for the use of simple disc-shaped shadows underneath characters in many older video games.

Similar principles allowed the utilization of shadows to convey messages. A decade ago, one of these shadow deformations became very popular in the form of the famous advertisement for the Star Wars movie *Episode 1: The Phantom Menace*. Here, the young Skywalker casts a shadow that has the actual shape of his later alter ego Darth Vader. Such shadow deformations actually have a long history in art. They are often used to depict premonitions or even death [Miller07] and have recently also found their way into the toolbox of automatic non-photorealistic rendering techniques [DeCoro07].

Interestingly, it can also happen that we draw conclusions about casters. Especially when shadows are detailed, we often make unconscious assumptions concerning the blocker's shape that can be surprisingly wrong (Figure 1.8). Some artists exploit this fact, such as Shigeo Fukuda in the installation *Dirty White Trash (with Gulls)*. Here, the shadow resembles two human beings, while the scene actually consists of the trash produced by the artists during a period of six months. Our conclusions can be drastically wrong. While it is usually very difficult to build objects that cast a specific shadow, for virtual objects, the construction is relatively

Figure 1.8. Shadows might give a false impression of the actual object's shape, an effect that has been exploited by several artists but is usually difficult to achieve. This virtual object was constructed in an automatic fashion [Mitra09], whose authors kindly provided us with the illustration.

simple. Only little user interaction was needed to produce the output in Figure 1.8 when using the algorithm by Mitra and Pauly [Mitra09] that optimizes the object's shape according to a set of target images.

Such results hint at the fact that it is not necessary to create accurate shadows to explain a scene. But the question is, how far we can simplify while maintaining spatial information, and ultimately also realism? Unfortunately, this is very difficult to decide, even for artists. Cavanagh [Cavanagh05] mentions several perceptual problems when approximating shadows and other physical phenomena. Despite their importance, we are very bad in estimating the *correctness* of a shadow. Hence, it seems tempting to try to benefit from the limited perceptual capabilities of the human visual system, but this proves very difficult. For dynamic scenes, an acceptably approximated configuration might change into an obvious visual deficiency. In particular, the illusion often breaks when shadows start to overlap or move in proximity to each other. As a direction for future research, however, this is a promising field. This also concerns the degree to which approximations can be applied to shadows.

It is actually hard to *fake* shadows, especially if lights and objects are dynamic. One should be careful because incorrect shadows decrease the realism of an image dramatically, which is problematic if a sufficiently realistic rendering is needed, for instance, for architectural design. While an architect may be capable of imagining the light interactions in a building, a potential customer will usually lack the necessary experience. Illumination previews help to bridge this gap and often enable even novices to better understand design choices.

For a faithful rendition of light interaction, also indirect, meaning bounced, light that is reflected from the surrounding usually needs to be taken into account. Shadows play an important role in this simulation and are often the first step of a real-time global illumination algorithm. Recent work on global (including reflected light) dynamic relighting underlines the importance of decoupling direct from indirect lighting. Due to its typically smooth variation, indirect lighting can often be coarsely computed. In contrast, direct light consists of relatively high emitted energy, usually resulting in often detailed and precise (high-frequency) content; hence, fewer approximations are possible than for indirect lighting. Consequently, compromises for direct illumination are often visible, and achieving a realistic composite of direct and indirect lighting necessitates an accurate direct-lighting pass. The cost of this pass should not be underestimated, even outside of a real-time context, such as for movie productions, direct lighting is often costly because the light sources need very accurate sampling.

When performance is crucial (e.g., for a realistic game), we only need to evoke the notion of realism. Nonetheless, inconsistencies have to be avoided because they can destroy the immersion in this virtual world. Furthermore, in some situations, accurate shadows might even be part of the game play, such as a player who casts a shadow around a corner, revealing her/his position, identity, or even equipment. Furthermore, shadows can facilitate understanding distances; for example, in a jump-and-run game, platform positions can be better estimated and the height of elements can be better understood.

We should provide *sufficient* realism, not necessarily exactitude. The keywords in this context are *plausible* and *convincing*. Unfortunately, it is not easy to achieve this goal. Ultimately, only Equation (1.4) seems to be foolproof, but Equation (1.6) is sufficient in a large number of cases. Any further approximation is likely to fail in some common configurations. This is a major dilemma: we should compute approximate solutions, but in practice, only physically based shadows seem to be convincing in all situations. Fortunately, it is not always necessary to have a solution that works for all cases. This book will help you decide when to apply which technique in order to achieve the best effect. But before coming to solutions, we will first illustrate some of the main failure cases that make shadows such a challenging topic.

1.3   Difficulty of Computing Shadows

It is difficult to compute shadows. This fact can be particularly well illustrated when looking at soft shadows, so let's go back to Equation (1.6). One major challenge of computing soft shadows according to this formula is that occluders can usually not be considered independently. Even if an accurate blocking contribution for each particular object can be computed, it is generally not possible to derive a good

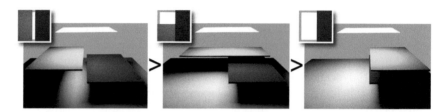

Figure 1.9. Different occluder-fusion scenarios for a view sample in the center of the scene with decreasing occlusion from left to right. On the left, both blockers occupy separate parts of the hemisphere. In the middle, they partially overlap. The example on the right depicts one blocker being entirely hidden by the other. (Inlays show the light source as seen from the center view sample.)

estimate of the entire visibility integral. It is true that these values can be used to deliver upper and lower bounds for the exact visibility integral, but not more.

Let $\{\mathcal{B}_i\}$ be the set of blockers for a receiver point $\mathbf{p}$, and let us further assume that for each blocker $\mathcal{B}_i$, we are given the result V_i of computing Equation (1.6) with all blockers except $\mathcal{B}_i$ removed from the scene. Then the following inequality holds:

$$1 - \sum_i (1 - V_i) \leq V_{\mathcal{L}}(\mathbf{p}) \leq \min_i V_i. \tag{1.7}$$

Figure 1.9 shows an illustration of different cases. The upper bound is produced if, as seen from the receiver point $\mathbf{p}$, all blockers are superimposed, the lower bound if all their projections are disjoint. This problem of combining different blocker contributions is referred to as *occluder fusion*, and we will investigate it in more detail in Section 6.2.3. To underline the importance of correct occluder fusion, Figure 1.10 shows an extreme case for a very simple scene where shadows can become very unrealistic if blocking contributions are not combined properly.

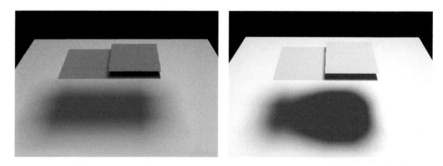

Figure 1.10. Even for simple scenes (left), classical approximations can cause noticeable artifacts (right). As can be seen, the umbra is overestimated.

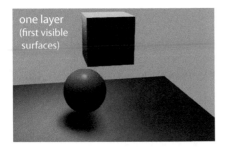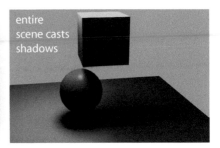

Figure 1.11. Only using the first visible surface from the light's center might not be enough for convincing shadows (left). On the right is an accurate shadow solution.

The intricate relationship between shadows and visibility introduces further implications. To determine which objects are potential shadow casters, it is not enough to check whether the object is visible from a single light sample. This important observation is illustrated in Figure 1.11. The image on the right correctly involves all triangles that should participate in the shadow computation, but on the left, only those triangles visible from the light source's center participate in the shadow computation. (The visibility determination itself is carried out with highest accuracy.) One can see significant problems: the shadow on the sphere is lost and, especially, half of the shadow below the sphere seems to be missing. Although this part of the scene is not visible from the light source's center, it has an important impact on the appearance of the shadow. In consequence, artifacts and even temporal incoherence can arise.

1.3.1 Isn't There Anything Simple about Shadow Computations?

It is surprising how much attention is needed when evaluating Equation (1.6) because a valid approximation simplifies the equation drastically. When sampling the light, we obtain

$$\frac{1}{|\mathcal{L}|} \int_{\mathcal{L}} V(\mathbf{p}, \mathbf{l}) \, d\mathbf{l} \approx \frac{1}{n} \sum_{i=0}^{n-1} V(\mathbf{p}, \mathbf{l}_i),$$

where $\mathbf{l}_i \in \mathcal{L}$ are uniformly placed light source samples. In this equation, $V(\mathbf{p}, \mathbf{l}_i)$ basically encodes whether a point light source placed at $\mathbf{l}_i$ illuminates the point $\mathbf{p}$ in the scene. In other words, we can compute shadows by approximating the light source with many point lights. Adopting such a sampling scheme, even the more general Equation (1.4) can be well approximated. We will discuss this approach in more detail in Section 6.2.4.

Note that this also offers a direct link between hard shadows produced by point light sources and soft shadows: shrinking an area light to a point leads to hard shadows, and sampling an area light with point light sources results in soft shadows.

Figure 1.12. This scene shows one example of the importance of soft shadows in obtaining a convincing and realistic-looking scene. On the left is the result using a single hard-shadow sample, whereas the right shows the outcome of a soft-shadow computation.

Figure 1.12 shows the difference between hard and soft shadows. In this case, the hard shadow results in an unrealistic image. Even though a large amount of light is impinging in the room, the fruit basket casts a shadow that is overly dark and large. In reality, a small object would not block the light of the entire window. This is a situation where even a novice realizes that something is not quite right. This can be particularly disturbing in an animation because even small objects can block visibility of a point light, bathing the entire scene in darkness. The soft-shadow image, on the other hand, does not exhibit these artifacts. Shadows near contact points stay sharp and the scene receives a realistic amount of direct light. Depending on the context, hard shadows can prove useful, though: very distant and tiny light sources can be well approximated with a point-light assumption.

Unfortunately, as we will see in the next chapter, even hard shadows for a single light remain a computationally involved issue, and for convincing soft shadows, often a high amount of samples is needed; 256–1,024 samples are not uncommon for standard settings, and large area lights might necessitate even more. When adopting an according brute-force computation (see Section 6.3), the geometry of the scene needs to be processed for each light sample. For 1,000 samples, the cost of such a computation will thus be roughly 1,000 times higher than for a single point light, and this cost scales linearly with the number of light samples.

Therefore, even if the sampling of the light source seems to be simple and robust, it is generally also (very) slow. Note that such a sampling strategy is the usual approach in ray-tracing solutions, which have become increasingly popular and, hence, are briefly covered in Section 10.4. Nonetheless, at the time of writing, their performance is clearly lower than solutions that exploit alternative scene representations and GPU-adapted algorithms, which will be the focus of this book.

1.4   Overview

This book will investigate various aspects of shadow computations. We will first introduce the most basic approaches in Chapter 2: the very commonly used shadow mapping [Williams78] and shadow volumes [Crow77]. Both are fundamental to the understanding of the more advanced approaches in the following chapters. Interestingly, these algorithms will already exploit most of the GPU features that we will build upon in this book. Readers that are less familiar with GPU programming can follow Appendix A in parallel with this first technical chapter to learn about the most important elements of GPU programming.

Building upon the previously introduced solutions, we then address general hard-shadow techniques in Chapters 3 and 4. Here, we still focus on a single point light. In this context, we will see a mathematical analysis of the limitations of the shadow-map technique. Its usage can lead to stair-stepping artifacts that can be reduced by applying proper solutions. The goal is to reduce the scale of these deficiencies such that they are no longer perceivable in the current rendering. We will see that this solution relates to computing more accurate results at the locations of the view samples, and we will present several alternative and efficient approaches that aim in this direction.

The reason for the stair-stepping artifact of shadow maps is that the computations take place in image space. Here, the original scene representation is discretized. Consequently, one way to avoid artifacts is to perform a proper shadow reconstruction based on signal theory. In other words, we will investigate, in Chapter 5, various ways to reconstruct the shadow signal from a shadow-map result. This chapter presents those algorithms that are currently of highest relevance in practice because they deliver a good trade-off between cost and benefit.

We will then address the topic of computing soft shadows in two separate chapters. These shadows result from area lights and exhibit a much more natural behavior because sharp contact shadows and soft-shadow boundaries for distant casters are both handled. Chapter 6 gives a general introduction and deals with solutions that, like shadow maps, approximate the scene with an image-based representation. These techniques are often more efficient than the geometric approaches covered in Chapter 7, though Chapter 7's approaches can be more accurate.

The book then continues with more advanced topics in the realm of shadow computations. Chapter 8 addresses shadows cast by semitransparent objects. Then, Chapter 9 discusses solutions for shadows in the presence of participating media, like fog. Here, shadows lead to visible shafts, a phenomenon that is also often referred to as *God rays*.

Further advanced topics are investigated in Chapter 10, where we give an overview of various techniques that are of practical interest. We explain in detail how to address the precise evaluation of the incoming radiance, as well as colored (or textured) light sources. While this first part can be seen as an extension of the previous chapters, the latter sections introduce modern topics that seem very promising for the future. In particular, we address voxel-based shadow techniques. Voxels are currently of high interest, not only for medical applications but also soon-to-appear game engines that exploit this representation. In this context of future techniques, we also present approaches from the realm of ray tracing, an alternative to the standard GPU pipeline. We further discuss environmental lighting and pre-computed radiance transfer, as both have found applications in recent games.

The book concludes in Chapter 11 with a discussion and recipes to decide which algorithm is the best suited for particular scenarios.

1.5   General Information for the Reader

In this book, the following conventions are used for denoting mathematical entities:

- Points and vectors are represented by bold, lowercase letters, like $\mathbf{p}$ and $\mathbf{l}$. Their components are denoted by adding according subscripts, such as $\mathbf{p}_x$ for the x-component of $\mathbf{p}$. If the entity is considered to be within a certain space, it is annotated by a corresponding superscript; for instance, $\mathbf{p}^{\text{L}}$ indicates the use of the light-space coordinate system.

- Matrices are denoted by bold, uppercase letters, like $\mathbf{M}$.

- Scalar quantities are represented by italic letters, such as V and z.

- Sets and objects (which can be interpreted as an (infinite) set of points) are labeled with uppercase script letters, like $\mathcal{L}$ for a light source.

For an overview of the symbols used in this book, please refer to Appendix F.

To help the reader in putting the covered algorithms into practice and working code, relevant commands, snippets of real code, and pseudocode are given throughout the book. In order to keep the presentation consistent and concise, we always use OpenGL (2.x and 3.x/4.x in the compatibility profile) to this end. Users of Direct3D and newer OpenGL versions' core functionality can find the according equivalents in Appendix B.

CHAPTER 2
Basic Shadow Techniques

Over the last years, many contributions have been made in the field of shadows, and many have found their way into computer games. But at the time of this book's writing, even though we have come a long way, accurate soft shadows cannot be obtained in sufficient quality in real time, and we are only on the verge of achieving pixel-accurate hard shadows for geometrically complex scenes at acceptable speed.

Both areas still leave room for improvement, especially as a scene with a single point light is not a very common scenario. In modern movie productions, hundreds of lights are placed by hand to create a wanted illumination. In this chapter, we analyze standard techniques to compute shadows based on point lights, where each point light gives rise to a so-called hard shadow. The name stems from the fact that such a shadow is binary in nature; either a point is lit or it lies in shadow, creating a sharp, or hard, boundary. A hard shadow can only be created by an infinitesimally small light source, which in practice never appears in real life. Nevertheless, in computer graphics, they give useful results and serve as an approximation for very distant light sources. Typically, they also represent the basis for more evolved methods.

In the following, we will start by presenting probably the most simple algorithm for hard shadows: projection shadows (Section 2.1). Then, we give an overview of the two most common and also more general techniques used for hard shadow computation on graphics hardware, namely, shadow mapping (Section 2.2) and shadow volumes (Section 2.3). We will see that these latter two algorithms are relatively well adapted to current hardware and are at the basis of many algorithms available today. Shadow mapping is particularly interesting because it only requires a little information about the actual scene geometry and solely relies on an image that encodes the distance to the light source (plane). Nevertheless, there are shortcomings and, over the years, much research has focused on improving the algorithms. Besides explaining the main principles in detail, we will hence also take

History

The very first algorithm in computer graphics that was capable of producing shadows was created by Appel [Appel68]. It used ray casting to compute hard shadows. The medium for drawing was a digital plotter. Plus ('+') signs of different sizes were used to simulate different gray levels of shading. The geometry was visualized using line drawing. The shadow borders could also be outlined.

The first *scan-line* (i.e., rasterization)-based approach was presented two years later by Bouknight and Kelley [Bouknight70] and was targeted for CRT (cathode ray tube) display hardware with 256 levels of intensity. It combined two scanning operations—one from the eye and one from the light source—to determine if the point of a screen-space pixel was shadowed by a polygon. In other words, the polygons were rasterized both from the eye and the light source. While outdated concerning the details, this method is conceptually quite similar to the two methods *shadow textures* and *shadow mapping* presented in Section 2.1.2 and Section 2.2.

More generally, three-dimensional computer graphics saw its birth in 1963 [Johnson63], with wireframe rendering and no hidden-line removal. In the following years, most efforts were targeted at hidden line removal [Appel67] and surface shading [Wylie67] with one point light source. In 1971, Gouraud shading was devised [Gouraud71].

In 1966, the first listing of unsolved problems in computer graphics was presented [Sutherland66], which has been updated many times since [Newell77, Heckbert87, Blinn98, Foley00]. For shadows, Newell and Blinn list creation of nonsharp boundaries as the main problem [Newell77]. It is interesting to note that they mention that such shadows are created not only from area light sources but also by the diffraction of light at the boundaries of shadowing objects (in other words, from the fact that light slightly bends around corners). Extensive progress has been made on the former topic, but the latter has barely been touched over the years. In 1987, with Paul Heckbert's listing of ten remaining important unsolved problems, the question was formulated as to how to efficiently compute shadows without using ray tracing [Heckbert87]. The evolution in this area is the main topic of this book.

Surveys of shadow algorithms have regularly been presented through the decades that the algorithms have developed and matured [Crow77, Woo90, Hasenfratz03].

a closer look at such enhancements. Due to their volume, more advanced topics relating to shadow mapping are covered later in Chapters 3, 4, and 5.

2.1 Projection Shadows

Projected shadows are very simple but suffer from several shortcomings, which nowadays render them a somewhat outdated method for most real-time applications. However, they still have their use cases when artistic freedom of modifying the shape, color, and texture of the shadows is more important than physical accuracy.

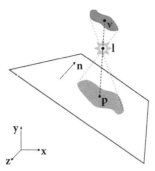

Figure 2.1. If the light source is located between the plane and any part of the shadow caster, the projection erroneously gives rise to so-called *anti-shadows*.

2.1.1   Planar Projected Shadows

Planar projected shadows are based on the perhaps most simple idea for creating hard shadows on a planar ground. We have seen that a point is in shadow if one of its segments towards the light source intersects the geometry. Because the light is a point, all segments meet at the same location. In other words, there is a one-to-one mapping between the segments and the points on the ground. Hence, if we would *push down* the geometry along those segments on the ground, it would end up covering exactly those points on the ground that lie in shadow. This pushing down of the shadow-caster polygons is actually nothing else but a projection from the light source onto the planar receiver. As for standard rasterization, such projections can be described in the form of a matrix expression. Using such a custom projection matrix, one can then simply draw the triangles as dark objects on the planar surface [Blinn88]. The complete derivation of the projection matrix is described on page 24. To project the caster geometry with this matrix, apply it to each caster vertex in the vertex shader before applying the camera matrix.

One problem of planar projected shadows appears when the light source is located between the ground plane and any point of the shadow caster (see Figure 2.1). In such situations, the caster would not be able to cast a shadow on the ground, but the projection matrix still leads to a point on the receiver plane. It is easy to test for a single vertex if such a situation occurs (its w value is negative). To ensure correct behavior for a triangle with at least one positive and one negative w value for its vertices, w could be interpolated and tested per fragment.

Because the projection delivers a point on the ground plane, another observation is important. The ground plane and shadow projection will coincide at the same depth location in space. This leads to trouble because z-buffering usually only keeps the pixel that is nearest to the observer, and imprecisions will basically lead to a random choice between a ground plane or shadow pixel. The corresponding artifact is called *z-fighting*.

Projection Matrix for Planar Shadows

We will here derive the transformation matrix $\mathbf{M}$ for projecting an object down to a planar surface, with a plane defined by the equation

$$\mathbf{n} \cdot \mathbf{x} + d = 0, \tag{2.1}$$

from a point-light position $\mathbf{l}$ [Blinn88, Akenine-Möller08]. That is, we want to find the matrix $\mathbf{M}$ such that $\mathbf{v}' = \mathbf{M}\mathbf{v}$, where $\mathbf{v}$ is a vertex of the object and $\mathbf{v}'$ its projection. Projecting a vertex $\mathbf{v}$ onto the plane is similar to computing the intersection point between the plane and a ray

$$\mathbf{r}(t) = \mathbf{l} + t\mathbf{d} \qquad \text{with} \qquad \mathbf{d} = \mathbf{v} - \mathbf{l} \tag{2.2}$$

from the light-source position $\mathbf{l}$ through the vertex $\mathbf{v}$ (see Figure 2.2). This intersection is easily derived by substituting $\mathbf{x}$ in Equation (2.1) with Equation (2.2) and solving for t:

$$\mathbf{n} \cdot (\mathbf{l} + t\mathbf{d}) + d = 0 \qquad \Rightarrow \qquad \hat{t} = -\frac{\mathbf{n} \cdot \mathbf{l} + d}{\mathbf{n} \cdot \mathbf{d}}.$$

The intersection point is then

$$
\begin{aligned}
\mathbf{v}' = \mathbf{r}(\hat{t}) &= \mathbf{l} - \frac{\mathbf{n} \cdot \mathbf{l} + d}{\mathbf{n} \cdot (\mathbf{v} - \mathbf{l})}(\mathbf{v} - \mathbf{l}) \\
&= \frac{(\mathbf{n} \cdot (\mathbf{v} - \mathbf{l}))\,\mathbf{l} - (\mathbf{n} \cdot \mathbf{l} + d)(\mathbf{v} - \mathbf{l})}{\mathbf{n} \cdot (\mathbf{v} - \mathbf{l})} \\
&= \frac{(\mathbf{n} \cdot \mathbf{l} + d)\,\mathbf{v} - (\mathbf{n} \cdot \mathbf{v} + d)\,\mathbf{l}}{\mathbf{n} \cdot \mathbf{l} - \mathbf{n} \cdot \mathbf{v}},
\end{aligned}
$$

where the final step is obtained by removing the terms that cancel out and also negating the denominator. In order to write this expression in matrix form, we utilize the fact that the division can be achieved by making use of homogeneous coordinates. The idea is to put the needed denominator in the w-component of $\mathbf{v}'$, which is then defined as

$$
\begin{aligned}
\mathbf{v}'_x &= (\mathbf{n} \cdot \mathbf{l} + d)\,\mathbf{v}_x - (\mathbf{n}_x\mathbf{v}_x + \mathbf{n}_y\mathbf{v}_y + \mathbf{n}_z\mathbf{v}_z + d)\,\mathbf{l}_x, \\
\mathbf{v}'_y &= (\mathbf{n} \cdot \mathbf{l} + d)\,\mathbf{v}_y - (\mathbf{n}_x\mathbf{v}_x + \mathbf{n}_y\mathbf{v}_y + \mathbf{n}_z\mathbf{v}_z + d)\,\mathbf{l}_y, \\
\mathbf{v}'_z &= (\mathbf{n} \cdot \mathbf{l} + d)\,\mathbf{v}_z - (\mathbf{n}_x\mathbf{v}_x + \mathbf{n}_y\mathbf{v}_y + \mathbf{n}_z\mathbf{v}_z + d)\,\mathbf{l}_z, \\
\mathbf{v}'_w &= \mathbf{n} \cdot \mathbf{l} \qquad\;\; - (\mathbf{n}_x\mathbf{v}_x + \mathbf{n}_y\mathbf{v}_y + \mathbf{n}_z\mathbf{v}_z),
\end{aligned}
$$

since for homogeneous coordinates $(x, y, z, w) \equiv (x/w, y/w, z/w, 1)$. Therefore, $\mathbf{v}'$ represents exactly the position of the intersection with the ray. It is easy to identify that the resulting matrix is

$$
\mathbf{M} = \begin{pmatrix}
\mathbf{n} \cdot \mathbf{l} + d - \mathbf{n}_x\mathbf{l}_x & -\mathbf{n}_y\mathbf{l}_x & -\mathbf{n}_z\mathbf{l}_x & -d\mathbf{l}_x \\
-\mathbf{n}_x\mathbf{l}_y & \mathbf{n} \cdot \mathbf{l} + d - \mathbf{n}_y\mathbf{l}_y & -\mathbf{n}_z\mathbf{l}_y & -d\mathbf{l}_y \\
-\mathbf{n}_x\mathbf{l}_z & -\mathbf{n}_y\mathbf{l}_z & \mathbf{n} \cdot \mathbf{l} + d - \mathbf{n}_z\mathbf{l}_z & -d\mathbf{l}_z \\
-\mathbf{n}_x & -\mathbf{n}_y & -\mathbf{n}_z & \mathbf{n} \cdot \mathbf{l}
\end{pmatrix}. \tag{2.3}
$$

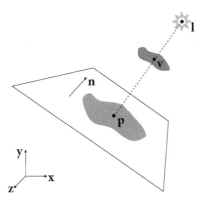

Figure 2.2. Planar projected shadows produce shadows on planar receivers by projecting the polygons of the shadow caster onto the plane and drawing it with a dark color. Here, **v** is a vertex of a polygon of the occluding object, and **p** is the vertex after the projection.

In the case of projected shadows, z-fighting can be solved easily by first drawing the ground plane, then disabling culling and the depth test when projecting the shadows (thereby enforcing them being drawn), and, finally, rendering the rest of the scene with standard settings and activated depth buffering. The situation becomes more complex when shadows are not supposed to be completely black (details can be found in the box below).

Blending Projected Shadows onto Planar Receivers

Simply relying on alpha blending while drawing the projected shadow casters is not enough because the number of overlapping triangles in the shadow casters might vary, leading to a nonuniformly colored shadow. The easiest way to solve this problem is to use the stencil buffer [Kilgard99]. It is initially cleared to zero. Then the ground is rendered into the stencil buffer, setting the stencil to one for all covered pixels. Next, deactivate the depth test, and set the stencil operations as follows for OpenGL: `glStencil-Func(GL_EQUAL, 1, 0xffff)` and `glStencilOp(GL_KEEP, GL_INCR, GL_INCR)`. The effect is that when the first shadow pixel is drawn on the planar receiver, the color is output and the stencil is incremented. The second time, the same pixel no longer has a stencil value of one; therefore, the stencil function fails and the pixel is ignored. Consequently, exactly one shadow pixel is output for each pixel that should receive shadows. During the drawing, the blending should be activated, that is, `glBlendFunc(GL_SRC_ALPHA, GL_ONE_MINUS_SRC_ALPHA)`, to combine the color of the ground plane with the incoming shadow attenuation. The initialization to one using the ground plane ensures that shadows are not drawn outside of its boundaries, in case the ground is limited in size.

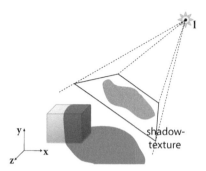

Figure 2.3. Shadow textures. A shadow image is used as a projective texture to cast shadows onto receivers.

2.1.2   Shadow Textures

It is possible to extend projection shadows to also work on curved surfaces by using the planar shadow image as a projective texture onto receivers. Imagine a projector at the light source that casts an image of the shadow onto the receiver. This method is called the *shadow-texture* method [Akenine-Möller08], although different combinations of the words occasionally have been used, including *texture-based shadows*. In the game community, the technique has also been known as the shadow-map method or *projective shadow mapping* [Nagy00, Akenine-Möller08]. However, this name could easily be confused with the more common terminology where *shadow mapping* refers to the more general technique described in Section 2.2.

To describe the method, let's assume a very simple scenario where we have a scene that consists of a shadow receiver and a point light **l**, as well as a distinct set of occluders, or blockers, that are placed in between the two (see Figure 2.3). Let us now place a camera at the light source in the direction of the receiver (the exact setup will be described hereafter). From there, we render a binary image of the scene that is initially cleared to white and in which we draw all shadow casters in black. This image will allow us to query whether a point lies in shadow.

Following the definition in Section 1.1 (see also Equation (1.1)), a point **p** is in shadow if the open segment between **p** and **l** intersects the scene. To test whether this segment intersects the scene, we use a simple observation: just like the segments projected to points with the previously seen projection matrix (see page 24), each segment projects to a single point for the camera at the light source that was used to produce the binary image.

Consequently, a single texture lookup allows us to test for shadows: if the pixel containing the segment was filled while drawing the occluders, the point has to lie in shadow; otherwise, it is lit. Such a lookup can be performed directly using projective texture mapping while rendering the receiver—resulting in the so-called shadow-texture method.

Here is an overview of the shadow-texture algorithm:

1. Render blockers into the shadow texture.
2. Render shadow receivers with the shadow texture enabled.

Next, we will explain how to set up the camera used by step 1. This is followed by an explanation of how to compute the shadow texture coordinates in step 2.

The Camera

We will now outline the details of the camera used for projecting the shadow casters onto the shadow texture. A camera matrix can be defined as $M_c = M_p M_v$, where M_p is a parallel or perspective projection matrix and M_v is a matrix transforming a vertex from world space into camera space. This transform is a simple matter of a change of frame and consists of a translation, to place the origin at the camera position, and a rotation. The space in which the origin is located in the light center and the view direction is aligned with the normal of the shadow projection plane, is called *light view space* or just *light space* for short.[1] Note that the view direction is along the negative z-axis of the view space for a right-handed coordinate system, which is what we use.

Figure 2.4 illustrates the *light view matrix* M_v^L that transforms a vertex into light space. In OpenGL, perhaps the most simple way to set up M_v^L is to use the `gluLookAt()` function. A common configuration is to have the shadow project straight down onto the plane $y = 0$, which then gives the following light view

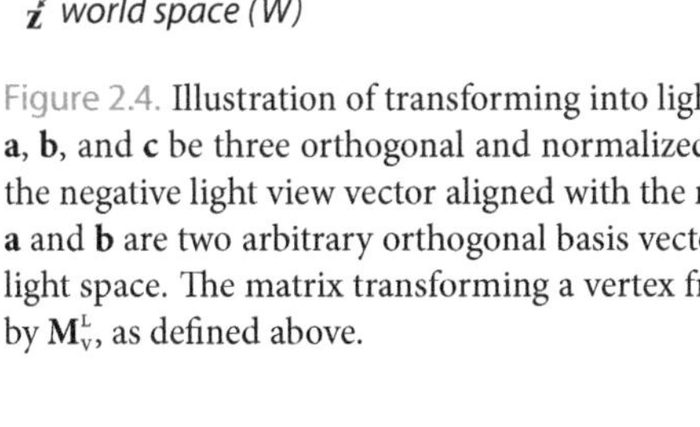

$$\iff M_v^L = \begin{pmatrix} a_x & a_y & a_z & -(a \cdot l) \\ b_x & b_y & b_z & -(b \cdot l) \\ c_x & c_y & c_z & -(c \cdot l) \\ 0 & 0 & 0 & 1 \end{pmatrix}$$

Figure 2.4. Illustration of transforming into light space. Let l be the light position. Also, let a, b, and c be three orthogonal and normalized vectors defined in world space, where c is the negative light view vector aligned with the normal of the shadow projection plane, and a and b are two arbitrary orthogonal basis vectors. This describes the frame of our desired light space. The matrix transforming a vertex from world space to light space is now given by M_v^L, as defined above.

---

[1]As an analogy to *eye space*, where the origin is located in the eye position instead and uses the eye's view and up direction.

matrix if $\mathbf{a} = -\mathbf{z}$, $\mathbf{b} = -\mathbf{x}$ and $\mathbf{c} = \mathbf{y}$:

$$\mathbf{M}_v^L = \begin{pmatrix} 0 & 0 & -1 & \mathbf{l}_z \\ -1 & 0 & 0 & \mathbf{l}_x \\ 0 & 1 & 0 & -\mathbf{l}_y \\ 0 & 0 & 0 & 1 \end{pmatrix},$$

where $\mathbf{l}$ is the light position.

We also need to construct a proper *light projection matrix* $\mathbf{M}_p^L$. This matrix projects the geometry, either using a parallel (orthogonal) projection or a perspective projection, and thereby provides the transformation into *light clip space*. A parallel projection can be used for directional light (i.e., when light rays are parallel and come from a light source infinitely far away). This is a common approximation for sunlight. Such a matrix simply scales the x, y-coordinates with a uniform factor to end up in $[-1, 1]$ and sets all z-values to a desired projection depth or depth interval. The details for that type of matrix are provided on page 30.

For a point light, we instead need a perspective projection. To derive such a matrix, we can utilize the matrix $\mathbf{M}$ in Equation (2.3) on page 24. This matrix projects objects onto any given plane $\mathbf{n} \cdot \mathbf{x} + d = 0$. The normal $\mathbf{n}$ of our projection plane is $(0, 0, 1)$ in light space, and d is our desired distance between the light position and the projection plane. In addition, $\mathbf{l}$ in Equation (2.3) is the light position, which is $(0, 0, 0)$ in light space. Thus, the projection matrix simplifies to

$$\begin{pmatrix} d & 0 & 0 & 0 \\ 0 & d & 0 & 0 \\ 0 & 0 & d & 0 \\ 0 & 0 & -1 & 0 \end{pmatrix}.$$

However, in practice, we also want to limit the coordinate range of our projected x, y, z-values to $[-1, 1]$, since the graphics hardware clips geometry outside the unit cube. Thus, choosing $d = 1$ is a reasonable option, which projects to the plane $z = -1$. To limit the x, y-coordinate range, we add scaling of the x, y-components to the matrix. If a horizontal field of view of *fovx* degrees is desired, the scaling factor of x becomes $s_x = \cot(fovx/2)$. Analogously, the scaling factor of y is $s_y = \cot(fovy/2)$, where *fovy* is the vertical field of view. It is, however, common to express *fovx* in terms of the aspect ratio $\alpha = w/h$ instead, where w and h are the image width and height. Thus, $s_x = s_y/\alpha$. Furthermore, since we chose the projection distance $d = 1$, this means that $\cot(fovx/2) = w$ and $\cot(fovy/2) = h$, which simplifies (s_x, s_y) to $s_x = w$ and $s_y = h$. This gives us the expression for the light projection matrix as

$$\mathbf{M}_p^L = \begin{pmatrix} \frac{1}{\alpha}\cot\frac{fovy}{2} & 0 & 0 & 0 \\ 0 & \cot\frac{fovy}{2} & 0 & 0 \\ 0 & 0 & 1 & 0 \\ 0 & 0 & -1 & 0 \end{pmatrix} = \begin{pmatrix} w & 0 & 0 & 0 \\ 0 & h & 0 & 0 \\ 0 & 0 & 1 & 0 \\ 0 & 0 & -1 & 0 \end{pmatrix}.$$

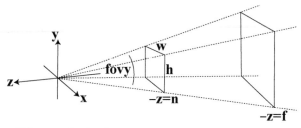

Figure 2.5. Specifying a projection frustum.

General camera. The planar projection above collapses all z-values to $z = -1$. It is common to want to keep relative z-information in order to resolve visibility when using a z-buffer. This is the case for a standard camera when rendering from the eye, and also when rendering images from the light in the shadow-map–based techniques described later on in this book. We can also use it for shadow textures, since z-values do not matter for this technique. To keep relative z-information, it is necessary to set $\mathbf{M}_p^L(2, 3)$ (i.e., the element of the third row, fourth column) to nonzero. The rationale is that after applying the projection transform to a point $\mathbf{v}$, we will get a new point $\mathbf{v}' = (\mathbf{v}'_x, \mathbf{v}'_y, \mathbf{v}'_z, \mathbf{v}'_w)$. The homogenization will divide all components by $\mathbf{v}'_w$, which currently is set to $-\mathbf{v}_z$ by the matrix. One can think of this division as a way to obtain the foreshortening effect in x and y with increased depth to give the illusion of three-dimensional space when the image is visualized in two dimensions. To avoid the z-component being the same constant value $\mathbf{v}'_z = -1$ for all pixels, we set $\mathbf{M}_p^L(2, 3) = c$, so that $\mathbf{v}'_z = \mathbf{v}_z + c$, which keeps relative z-information after the division with $\mathbf{v}'_w = -\mathbf{v}_z$.

Typically, the user wants to set light-space near and far planes of the view frustum by specifying their distances n and f from the origin (see Figure 2.5). Note that these values are positive $(0 < n < f)$, while the light view direction is the negative z-axis. All geometry will be clipped against the six frustum planes (near, far, left, right, top, bottom) by the hardware unit-cube clipping, before being sent to rasterization. In order to distribute the z-values in the range $z \in [n, f]$ over the unit cube range $(x, y, z) \in [-1, 1]$, we should set $\mathbf{M}_p^L(2, 2) = -(f + n)/(f - n)$ and $\mathbf{M}_p^L(2, 3) = -2fn/(f - n)$. This maps $z = -n$ to -1 and $z = -f$ to $+1$. The projection matrix becomes

$$\mathbf{M}_p^L = \begin{pmatrix} \frac{1}{\alpha} \cot \frac{fovy}{2} & 0 & 0 & 0 \\ 0 & \cot \frac{fovy}{2} & 0 & 0 \\ 0 & 0 & -\frac{f+n}{f-n} & -\frac{2fn}{f-n} \\ 0 & 0 & -1 & 0 \end{pmatrix}.$$

In OpenGL, $\mathbf{M}_p^L$ can be set up with the gluPerspective() function. Note that for DirectX, the matrix is slightly different (see Appendix B.1.3 for details).

To summarize, our desired camera matrix is now given by $\mathbf{M}_c^L = \mathbf{M}_p^L \mathbf{M}_v^L$.

Shadow Texture and Directional Light

For directional light, the light source does not have a specific position. Instead, all light rays enter from a user-set direction $\mathbf{d}$. OpenGL defines this light direction as the normalized vector *to* the light. Therefore, $\mathbf{c} = \mathbf{d}$ in the expression of $\mathbf{M}_v^L$ in Figure 2.4, and $\mathbf{l}$ is a position along the vector $\mathbf{d}$ from the center and outside of the region of interest. Assume that $\mathbf{p}_c$ is the center position for a bounding sphere of the part of our scene for which we want to render a shadow texture, and assume that r is the sphere radius. Then, we can, for example, simply set $\mathbf{l} = \mathbf{p}_c + 1.5\, r\, \mathbf{d}$.

If w and h are the light-space width and height of the region of interest for which to create the shadow texture, and n and f are the near- and far-plane distances, then the light projection matrix becomes (using OpenGL standard)

$$\mathbf{M}_p^L = \begin{pmatrix} \frac{2}{w} & 0 & 0 & 0 \\ 0 & \frac{2}{h} & 0 & 0 \\ 0 & 0 & -\frac{2}{f-n} & -\frac{f+n}{f-n} \\ 0 & 0 & 0 & 1 \end{pmatrix}.$$

Texture Coordinates

In the vertex shader when rendering the shadow receivers, the texture coordinates into the shadow texture should be computed as $\mathbf{v}' = \left(\mathbf{M}_p^L \mathbf{M}_v^L\right) \mathbf{v}$, where $\mathbf{v}$ is the incoming vertex and $\mathbf{M}_p^L$ and $\mathbf{M}_v^L$ are the same light view and projection matrices used when creating the shadow texture. The x, y-texture coordinates then also need to be shifted from $[-1, 1]^2$ to the more conventional texture space $[0, 1]^2$. This is either done in the shader by taking $\mathbf{v}_{xy}^s = (\mathbf{v}_{xy}' + 1)/2$ or by baking this shift into the complete transform $\mathbf{v}^s = \left(\mathbf{M}_t \mathbf{M}_p^L \mathbf{M}_v^L\right) \mathbf{v}$, where $\mathbf{M}_t$ looks as follows:

$$\mathbf{M}_t = \begin{pmatrix} 0.5 & 0 & 0 & 0.5 \\ 0 & 0.5 & 0 & 0.5 \\ 0 & 0 & 0.5 & 0.5 \\ 0 & 0 & 0 & 1 \end{pmatrix}.$$

Note that we denote the shadow-texture coordinates for a point $\mathbf{p}$ as $\mathbf{p}^s$.

Texture coordinates that fall outside $[0, 1]$ represent unshadowed regions. This could be checked for as a special case in the fragment shader. If shaders are not available, another alternative is to use a texture border of white color (i.e., no shadow), which can be specified with the `glTexParameterfv(..., GL_TEXTURE_BORDER_COLOR, ...)` command. Clamping of the texture coordinates to the border should then be enabled, which is achieved by calling `glTexParameteri(..., GL_TEXTURE_WRAP_{S,T}, GL_CLAMP_TO_BORDER)`. A third option, mostly outdated but avoiding the need of a texture border, is to ensure that the shadow texture has at least a one-pixel wide margin of no shadow and then enable clamping of the texture coordinates to inside the image region, which is done with the `glTex Parameteri(..., GL_TEXTURE_WRAP_{S,T}, GL_CLAMP_TO_EDGE)` command. More details are presented by Nagy, with accompanying source code [Nagy00].

2.1.3   Discussion

A drawback of the shadow-texture algorithm is that blockers and receivers need to be separated, requiring a shadow texture per blocker and resulting in an inability to handle self-shadowing.

Similar to the anti-shadows (see Figure 2.1), the receivers should not lie behind the light source. Otherwise, the shadow texture might erroneously be applied here. As before, this situation can be dealt with by testing the w-coordinate for its sign.

Shadow textures have some interesting aspects. Soft shadows could easily be faked by filtering the shadow mask. In the offline community, artists like the ability to modify the shadow texture by shape, color, or intensity. Such texture masks are called light-attenuation masks, cookie textures,[2] or gobo maps.[3]

2.2   Shadow Mapping

The shadow-texture method described in the previous section is a simplified version of today's most famous solution to computing shadows in real-time applications—namely shadow mapping [Williams78]. This method no longer needs to separate occluders from receivers and is thereby also capable of managing self-shadowing, as we will see. The principle is to render an image of the scene from the position of the light source. Every point that appears in such an image is necessarily lit, while regions not visible are in shadow. To determine whether a certain three-dimensional position is in shadow then becomes a matter of checking whether it is visible in the image from the light source or not.

Although theoretically very simple, the fact that the scene is sampled, in terms of a discrete image resolution, leads to the requirement of a tolerance threshold when doing the position comparisons, which causes concerns. It is interesting to note that in the 1970s, before the domination of the z-buffer algorithm for hidden surface removal, similar shadow techniques existed without any such drawback [Weiler77, Atherton78]. The caveat with those techniques is that the hidden-surface removal is done by geometrical polygon clipping instead, which can be very slow. Here follows the shadow-mapping algorithm in detail.

---

[2]"Cookie" is the informal term for "cucaloris," which means an opaque card with cutouts, used to cast patterns of shadows [Barzel97].

[3]Gobo refers to "GOes Before Optics" and is typically a metal or glass object, inside or very close to the light source, that creates shadow or light patterns.

2.2.1 Basic Algorithm

Shadow mapping builds upon the observation that the light *sees* all lit surfaces of the scene. Every hidden (unseen) element lies in shadow. To determine the visible surfaces as seen from the light, shadow mapping starts by creating an image from the light's position. In this image, the so-called *shadow depth map* or simply shadow map, each pixel holds the depth (i.e., the distance from the light) of the first visible surface. Graphics hardware supports the creation of such depth maps at very little cost because the same mechanism is used to resolve visibility during standard rendering. The second step of the algorithm performs a rendering of the scene from the actual viewpoint. For each rasterized fragment (which we will call view sample), its position $\mathbf{p}$ is transformed into light clip space, yielding $\mathbf{p}^{\text{LC}} = (\mathbf{p}_x^{\text{LC}}, \mathbf{p}_y^{\text{LC}}, \mathbf{p}_z^{\text{LC}})$. Note that $(\mathbf{p}_x^{\text{LC}}, \mathbf{p}_y^{\text{LC}})$ is the position in the depth map to where the fragment would project when seen from the light, and $\mathbf{p}_z^{\text{LC}}$ is the distance of the fragment to the light source. Hence, to determine whether the fragment is visible from the light, it is sufficient to compare its depth value $\mathbf{p}_z^{\text{LC}}$ to the value stored in the shadow map at position $(\mathbf{p}_x^{\text{LC}}, \mathbf{p}_y^{\text{LC}})$. If $\mathbf{p}_z^{\text{LC}}$ is larger than the stored value, the fragment is necessarily hidden by some other surface nearer to the light source and consequently lies in shadow. Otherwise, it is lit. This process is illustrated in Figure 2.6.

There are two details to note. First, in practice, the depth map is accessed not directly with the light-clip-space position $\mathbf{p}^{\text{LC}}$, but with the according shadow (map)-texture coordinates $\mathbf{p}^{\text{s}}$, which can be derived as discussed at the end of Section 2.1.2. Second, the depth $\mathbf{p}_z^{\text{LC}}$ is measured along the light view direction, which is the negative z-axis of the light space in our definition (which assumes a right-handed coordinate system). More generally, we will refer to both this depth value and $-\mathbf{p}_z^{\text{L}}$ as light-space depth in the following, denoting it as $\mathbf{p}_{\tilde{z}}^{\text{L}}$.

The technique is particularly interesting as it is usable with almost any arbitrary input, as long as depth values can be produced. Further, the fact that both steps involve standard rasterization gives it a huge potential for acceleration on graphics cards. In fact, OpenGL provides extensions to perform the algorithm without shader intervention (today, most people would just use shaders, which is more convenient). Currently, shadow mapping and variants are the most popular techniques for creating shadows in games. Nevertheless, several problems are inherent to this method. The most important difficulties are the treatment of omnidirectional light sources (Section 2.2.2), imprecisions due to the depth test (Section 2.2.3), and aliasing artifacts arising from the pixel representation of the depth maps. We will analyze these problems more closely in the following.

2.2.2 Omnidirectional Shadow Maps

The fact that the shadow map is produced via rendering makes it necessary to specify a light frustum, which in turn implies that the technique is mostly aiming at spot

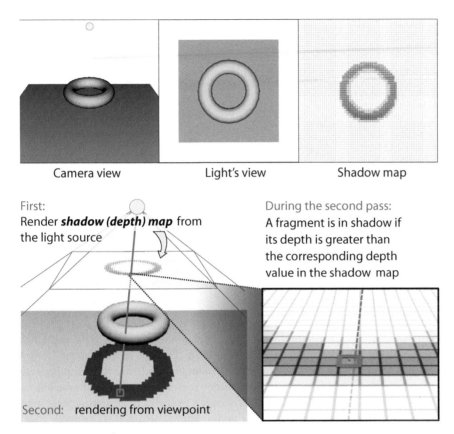

Camera view   Light's view   Shadow map

First:
Render **shadow (depth) map** from
the light source

During the second pass:
A fragment is in shadow if
its depth is greater than
the corresponding depth
value in the shadow map

Second: rendering from viewpoint

Figure 2.6. Illustration of the shadow-map algorithm. The camera view, light's view, and corresponding shadow map (top). A depth map (shadow map) is created from the light (bottom). To determine whether the point of a screen-space pixel is in shadow, its x, y, z–coordinate is warped into this map. If the point is farther from the light source (higher depth) than the stored value in the map, then the point is in shadow.

lights. The typical way to handle omnidirectional sources is to create, for example, six light frustums centered around the light source (one for each side of a cube) that together cover the entire sphere of directions. This solution is currently standard. Wan et al. [Wan07] noticed that a so-called six-face spherical map provides better utilization of resolution than cube maps do. A six-face sphere can be thought of as a cube that is inflated to a spherical shape such that each side is a dome instead of flat.

Nevertheless, using six light frustums means that the scene's geometry needs to be processed several times. Geometry shaders can perform this projection on a cube map in a single pass, but the fact that geometry is duplicated for each cube face

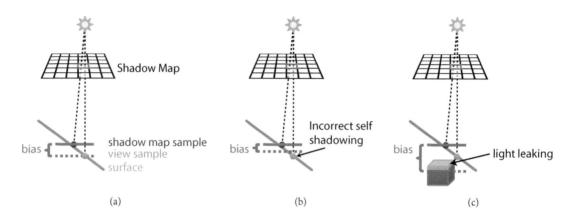

Figure 2.7. Depth bias. (a) The view sample has higher depth than the shadow-map sample, but should not be regarded as being in shadow. Therefore, a bias is added. (b) A too small bias leads to incorrect surface self-shadowing, called z-fighting (see also Figure 2.8(a)). (c) A too large bias can cause light to leak onto objects that should be in shadow (see also Figure 2.8(b)).

introduces a significant penalty. Instead of a cube, Brabec et al. [Brabec02b] point out that a parabolic mapping [Heidrich98] enables the extraction of the entire field of view with only two renderings. Furthermore, lookups in these maps are very cheap. The fact that the domain is not rectangular and that the sampling ratio might vary by a factor of four are two minor reasons why this technique has not yet received more attention. The main reason is probably that creating these maps is difficult. Lines need to be transformed to curves, which is incompatible with the standard rasterization pipeline. The solution by Brabec et al. [Brabec02b] is to transform only vertices in a vertex shader to the correct position and assume that the scene is tessellated finely enough to provide the correct solution. Recently, Gascuel et al. [Gascuel08] proposed to compute the deformed and curved elements on graphics hardware, but the algorithm remains costly. It has been pointed out that since a tetrahedron is the polyhedron with the smallest number of faces that encloses a point, this can be more advantageous than using cube maps [Fortes00, Takashi06, Liao07, Liao10]. Nevertheless, using cube maps is the norm today, so we will not discuss the other alternatives in more detail.

2.2.3   Depth Bias

To test whether a point is farther away than the reference in the shadow map requires some tolerance threshold for the comparison (see Figure 2.7(a)). Otherwise, the discrete sampling due to the limited shadow-map resolution, and also numerical issues, can lead to incorrect self-shadowing, which (as also mentioned in Section 2.1.1) is referred to as z-fighting or surface acne (see Figure 2.8(a)). This

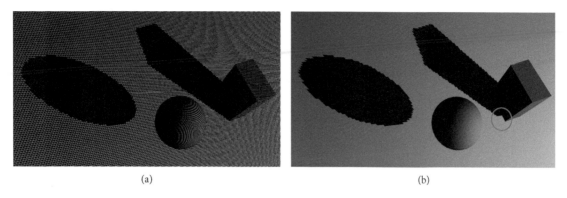

Figure 2.8. (a) Z-fighting due to a too small bias. (b) A too high bias often leads to light leaking. This is most visible at contact shadows (right, at the cube's lower corner).

results in visible shadow sparkles on lit surfaces and can be explained as follows. If the shadow map had infinite resolution, then the shadow testing would be a matter of checking if the point is represented in the shadow map (i.e., visible from the light and therefore not in shadow). However, with the discrete shadow-map resolution, sample points from the eye are compared to an image consisting of pixels. Each pixel's value is defined solely by the world sample corresponding to the pixel's center. Hence, when querying a view sample, it will rarely project to the location that was actually sampled in the shadow map. Consequently, one can only compare values of nearby points. This can lead to problems when the view sample is farther from the source (has a higher depth from the light) than the corresponding value in the shadow map (see Figure 2.7(b)) because unwanted shadows can occur. For example, imagine a tilted receiver plane. Within each shadow-map pixel, the depth values of the world samples vary, and some lie below and others above the corresponding pixel-center depth. The ones below will be declared shadowed despite them actually being visible. In order to address this issue, a threshold can be introduced in the form of a *depth bias* that offsets the light samples slightly farther from the light source (see Figure 2.9).

Defining the depth bias is more problematic than it might seem at first. The greater the surface's slope, as seen from the light source (i.e., the more edge-on), the more the depth values change between adjacent shadow-map samples, which means that a higher bias is needed to avoid the surface incorrectly shadowing itself. On the other hand, a too high bias will lead to light leaking at contact shadows (see Figure 2.8(b)), making the shadows disconnected from the shadow caster. This is called *Peter Panning* or the *Peter Pan* problem, referring to the famous character by James Matthew Barrie that got detached from his shadow.

The standard approach supported by graphics hardware is to rely on biasing with two parameters instead of just one: a constant offset and an offset that depends

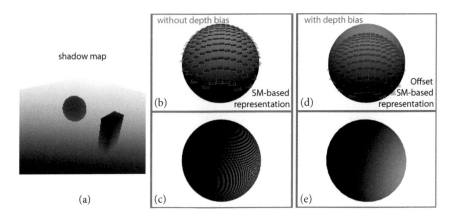

Figure 2.9. (a) The shadow map (SM) is a discretized representation of the scene. (b) Each SM pixel can be considered to be a geometric quad that is situated in the scene at its according depth. This also explains the often jig-jaggy shadow appearance. Furthermore, this can create self-shadowing everywhere where the quads extend beyond the object's geometry. (c) The problems resulting from these imprecisions are referred to as z-fighting and lead to so-called surface acne. (d) Offsetting the depth values in the depth map lifts many of the depth ambiguities, and here removes the incorrect self-shadowing (e).

on the slope of the triangle as seen from the light [Lengyel00, Schüler05, Schüler06]. Applying the biasing is done already during the rendering of the shadow map by using the `glPolygonOffset()` command available in OpenGL. Unfortunately, the parameters need to be hand adjusted. There are no perfect choices for all situations. Typically problematic cases are triangles inside concavities and near silhouette edges as seen from the light.

2.2.4   Decreasing the Need for a Bias

A straightforward solution to increasing depth precision is to better fit the near and far plane of the light's frustum to the scene. This can be based on a scene bounding box, but more recent and advanced solutions will be presented in Chapter 4 that also address aliasing.

Another direction is to work on the depth values themselves. A typical projection matrix is set up so that the z-buffer becomes nonlinear in its distribution of depth values. This makes sense for hidden-surface removal because it puts more precision on nearby elements but is not necessarily a good choice for shadow mapping. A region far from the light can actually be very close to the observer and, thus, have limited precision where most precision is needed. Brabec et al. [Brabec02a] show how a linearized z-buffer can avoid such problems (an idea introduced by Heidrich [Heidrich99a]). Consequently, depth precision is more evenly balanced, and it can nowadays be achieved very easily in the vertex shader as follows.

First, the incoming vertex $\mathbf{v}$ is multiplied by the light view matrix, so that $\mathbf{v}' = \mathbf{M}_v^L \mathbf{v}$. Next, $\mathbf{v}'$ is multiplied by the light projection matrix, such that $\mathbf{v}'' = \mathbf{M}_p^L \mathbf{v}'$. Then, the z-value of $\mathbf{v}''$ is replaced by $\mathbf{v}_z'' = -((\mathbf{v}_z' + n)/(f - n))\mathbf{v}_w''$, where n and f are the light frustum's near and far plane distances. Finally, $\mathbf{v}''$ is the vertex position that we output by the vertex shader.

Using a combination of shadow textures (introduced in Section 2.1.2) and shadow mapping has also been proposed as a way to lower the biasing problems of shadow mapping [Oh07]. Since it is based on separating shadow casters and receivers, which prohibits self-shadowing, we will here instead focus on more general methods.

Polygon IDs

A classic suggestion to remove any depth-precision issues is to use indices for each polygon instead of depth samples [Hourcade85]. The idea is that this eliminates the need for a bias because instead of testing depth, one compares only indices. If the index stored in the shadow map agrees with the view sample's, it is considered to be visible from the light. However, along borders between adjacent triangles, problems still remain since a triangle could be incorrectly shadowed by neighboring triangles. Furthermore, today, this technique is difficult to use because many triangles have subpixel size, but only one index can be stored per pixel. Also, if alternative representations are used (e.g., height fields) or triangles are subdivided (e.g., using the tesselation unit), the attribution of indices is difficult.

Hybrid visibility determinations could be imagined that use these indices to then initialize a search on the original mesh, but this becomes prohibitively slow. Most of these problems disappear if indices are used per object, instead of per polygon [Dietrich01, Forsyth07]. Then, however, self-shadowing is no longer possible.

Second-Depth Shadow Mapping

Wang and Molnar [Wang94] suggest using only the second layer of surfaces visible from the light source, which in its basic version only works for *watertight*[4] (solid) objects with some thickness larger than any z-buffer imprecision. In practice, this is achieved by rendering the back-facing instead of the front-facing polygons into the shadow map. The rationale is that z-fighting is not a problem for back-facing geometry, since back-facing surfaces can never receive light from the source and will, hence, always be in shadow. Consequently, such surfaces are always drawn in black—the same color that is used for shadows. Put differently, z-fighting is mainly a problem for surfaces represented in the shadow map, since incorrect self-shadowing can occur if a nonsuitable bias is used. By storing only back-facing geometry in the shadow map, for which incorrect self-shadowing does not lead to

---

[4]Watertight is also sometimes referred to as manifold or closed. The definition we use here is that each triangle edge has one and only one neighboring triangle, which means that the model separates an interior from an exterior region in space.

any visual difference, most of the biasing problems are circumvented. Silhouette regions (convex and concave) are still problematic, as well as where objects are in contact, penetrate, or self-intersect, resulting in light or shadow bleeding. These problems can be reduced by reintroducing the bias again. The algorithm is popular in the gaming industry, since watertight objects can be guaranteed at modeling time by the artist and the method significantly reduces the biasing problems by pushing it to fewer regions.

Most bias problems arise from insufficient scene knowledge. Basically, a single shadow map does not provide enough data to address all problems. Hence, it can be beneficial to rely on more than a single shadow map. In the following, we will examine these solutions.

Midpoint Shadow Maps

Woo [Woo92] proposed the use of *midpoint shadow maps* that extract two layers of depth instead of just one. The shadow map can then be set to the average distance. This means that the first layer will not be shadowed, while the second will be shadowed. The *virtual occluder* that is produced by averaging the values lies in between the two surfaces (hence the name midpoint shadow maps). The method requires two passes to extract the first and second layers (see Figure 2.10). However, on modern GPUs it is possible to improve upon this for watertight scenes by redirecting front- and back-facing triangles to different render targets. Outputting the depth values with minimum-blending can be used for both targets to simulate two depth buffers.

The advantage with respect to second-layer depth maps is that the method is potentially compatible with non-watertight scenes. However, the main limitations are similar to those for second-depth shadow mapping. In the left-most figure in Figure 2.10, midpoint shadow maps fail when a rasterized pixel from the second or higher depth layer is closer to the light than the stored discrete-sampled midpoint value in the shadow-map texel. Note that in this image, the problem only applies for the third depth layer as the second depth layer here is back facing and, therefore, automatically in shadow by the shading.

In the right-most illustration in Figure 2.10, we can clearly see that for rasterized pixels belonging to the first depth layer, incorrect self-shadowing can still appear when their depth value is higher than the midpoint value stored in the shadow-map texel. However, this technique is ameliorating the biasing problem by pushing its need to only the few pixels along silhouette edges. A small bias could also be added to further limit the problem along silhouettes, but the problem does not completely disappear.

Dual Depth Layers

One problem of midpoint shadow maps is that the difference between the first and second depth layer can be very large, leading to an overestimation of the needed

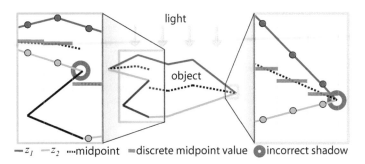

Figure 2.10. Midpoint shadow maps. The blue line indicates the depth layer closest to the light, while the green indicates the second depth layer. The black dotted line illustrates the midpoints between the first and second depth layer. The magenta shows the used midpoint values, due to discretization from the limited shadow-map resolution. Midpoint shadow maps use the average of the two closest layers (blue and green) as shadow-map depth. This still results in problematic situations due to the discretization. The left zoom shows incorrect light-leaking (red circle) because parts of the surface (black) are closer to the light than the midpoint value in the shadow map (magenta). The right zoom illustrates incorrect self-shadowing because parts that are supposed to be lit (blue) are behind the midpoint value in the shadow map.

depth bias. Weiskopf and Ertl [Weiskopf03] point out two failure cases of the midpoint shadow map (see Figure 2.10), where a carefully adjusted bias sometimes can help. Their solution is to combine midpoint shadow maps with a standard depth bias and to choose the minimum of a fixed distance threshold and the depth average. In this way, the offset will never exceed a predefined bias. In addition, they also discuss the possibility of back-face culling for watertight objects because back faces are black due to shading.

Shadow-Map Reconstruction

The biasing problem can also be reduced by trying to find a better estimation of the actual depth of the occluding triangle. To do so, Dai et al. [Dai08] propose to store the actual triangle information (i.e., the three vertices) of the nearest triangle with each shadow-map sample. Thus, the depth value in the shadow map can be very accurately reconstructed, and the bias only needs to account for quantization differences. However, for this technique to work, all shadow-caster triangles need to be present in the shadow map, and a relatively expensive consistency check with neighboring samples has to be carried out. Arvo and Hirvikorpi [Arvo05], on the other hand, store shadow maps as scan lines and can interpolate depth values more accurately than the regular representation in standard shadow maps. However, these compressed shadow maps cannot be generated interactively.

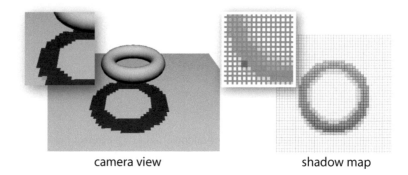

camera view   shadow map

Figure 2.11. Illustration of shadow aliasing due to limited shadow-map resolution, with the camera view (left) and the corresponding shadow map (right). All screen-space points lying in the orange region are tested for shadows against the same shadow-map pixel (in red), which causes the jagged shadow edges in the camera view.

2.2.5   Aliasing

Another drawback of working with an image-based scene representation is that the shadow map has limited resolution. This results in aliasing artifacts, which means that a cast shadow will reflect the discretization of the image in the form of pixels. Consequently, the shadow boundaries contain visible stair-stepping artifacts (see Figure 2.11). The reason is that several view samples on a receiver might project into the same shadow-map texel. Hence, they all receive a similar shadow response. As soon as the view samples project to the next adjacent texel, the shadow response might change drastically. To limit this problem, many modern games use shadow-map resolutions that far exceed the window size; $4,096^2$ to $8,192^2$ are typical choices. The probability of two view samples falling into the same shadow-map texel is thereby reduced, but not removed.

Attempts exist to use a shadow map per object that adapts its resolution [Buntin07]. On the one hand, such solutions are often difficult to use in practice as they imply specialized scene structures, separated rendering passes, and a strict object notion. On the other hand, this approach is particularly useful to provide a high-quality shadow for particular elements of the scene (e.g., the boss of a video game level).

Aliasing is the major source of artifacts for shadow-mapping techniques and has received much attention in these last years. Due to its importance for the visual quality of a rendering, we will provide a detailed analysis and description in Chapter 3.

2.2.6   Implementing Standard Shadow Mapping in Practice

We present here the code for standard shadow maps at quite a detailed level, since a major part of the characteristics and important tricks to think about lie here. The code is for OpenGL.

First, a shadow-map texture is created:

```
glGenTextures(1, &shadowMapTexture);
glBindTexture(GL_TEXTURE_2D, shadowMapTexture);
glTexImage2D(GL_TEXTURE_2D, 0, GL_DEPTH_COMPONENT32,
    shadowMapResolution, shadowMapResolution, 0,
    GL_DEPTH_COMPONENT, GL_FLOAT, 0);
glTexParameteri(GL_TEXTURE_2D, GL_TEXTURE_MIN_FILTER, GL_LINEAR);
glTexParameteri(GL_TEXTURE_2D, GL_TEXTURE_MAG_FILTER, GL_LINEAR);
glTexParameteri(GL_TEXTURE_2D, GL_TEXTURE_WRAP_S, GL_CLAMP_TO_BORDER);
glTexParameteri(GL_TEXTURE_2D, GL_TEXTURE_WRAP_T, GL_CLAMP_TO_BORDER);
glTexParameteri(GL_TEXTURE_2D, GL_TEXTURE_COMPARE_MODE,
    GL_COMPARE_REF_TO_TEXTURE);
glTexParameteri(GL_TEXTURE_2D,GL_TEXTURE_COMPARE_FUNC,GL_LEQUAL);
float ones[] = { 1.0f, 1.0f, 1.0f, 1.0f };
glTexParameterfv(GL_TEXTURE_2D, GL_TEXTURE_BORDER_COLOR, &ones);
```

Note that we set the border color to 1.0, which corresponds to the maximum depth, and use the wrap mode of GL_CLAMP_TO_BORDER. This ensures that tests that fall outside the view of the light return the far depth and will thus not be shadowed. This also works for a spotlight when we want everything outside the cone angle to be black, since the angle test automatically handles this case.

Subsequently, a framebuffer object is created, and the shadow-map texture is attached as depth buffer, such that we can render to the shadow map:

```
glGenFramebuffers(1, &shadowMapFBO);
glBindFramebuffer(GL_FRAMEBUFFER, shadowMapFBO);
glFramebufferTexture2D(GL_FRAMEBUFFER, GL_DEPTH_ATTACHMENT,
    GL_TEXTURE_2D, shadowMapTexture, 0);
```

This preparatory work needs to be done only once at program start-up. The created objects can then be used each frame for shadow mapping, where a shadow map is rendered as follows:

```
Activate FBO shadowMapFBO
glPolygonOffset(2.5f, 10.0f);
glEnable(GL_POLYGON_OFFSET_FILL);
Render scene from light
glDisable(GL_POLYGON_OFFSET_FILL);
Deactivate FBO shadowMapFBO
```

It is then applied when rendering the scene from the eye. To this end, the vertex shader has to derive the shadow-map texture coordinates for each scene vertex:

```
uniform mat4 lightMatrix;
out vec4 shadowMapCoord;
void main() {
  gl_Position = gl_ModelViewProjectionMatrix * gl_Vertex;
  shadowMapCoord = lightMatrix * gl_Vertex;
}
```

The uniform `lightMatrix` has to be set in the calling program:

```
float4x4 offsetMatrix = {
  0.5f, 0.0f, 0.0f, 0.5f,
  0.0f, 0.5f, 0.0f, 0.5f,
  0.0f, 0.0f, 0.5f, 0.5f,
  0.0f, 0.0f, 0.0f, 1.0f };
Set uniform lightMatrix to offsetMatrix * lightProjectionMatrix *
    lightModelViewMatrix
Render scene from eye
```

Note the offset matrix `offsetMatrix` that is multiplied by the light matrix. This is to transform the shadow-map texture coordinates from range $[-1, 1]$ to range $[0, 1]$ without having to add any extra lines of code for this in the shaders.

Finally, the shadow-map texture coordinates are used in the fragment shader to query the shadow map:

```
in vec4 shadowMapCoord;
uniform sampler2DShadow shadowMapTex;
void main() {
  vec3 color = ...;
  float visibility = textureProj(shadowMapTex, shadowMapCoord);
  gl_FragColor = vec4(color * visibility, 1.0);
}
```

2.2.7   Shadow Mapping for Large Scenes

When shadowing large scenes, the overhead for shadow mapping can become significant. Even if the main rendering algorithm uses a visibility algorithm to reduce the geometry to be sent to the graphics hardware, in scenes with a large extent, a shadow map might cover a huge area and might require the rendering of the whole scene. Therefore, it is useful to create the shadow map only where the resulting shadows will be visible to the observer.

Fitting

One simple method to reduce the overhead of shadow mapping is to *focus* the shadow map on the view frustum. This is also called *fitting*. In large outdoor scenes, fitting is also required to make the best possible use of the available shadow-map resolution, in order not to waste shadow-map pixels on areas that are not even in the view frustum. Therefore, fitting will be described in more detail in Chapter 4.

However, in applications with large view frusta, fitting may not be enough to reduce shadow-map rendering overhead. In the context of shadow-volume rendering, Lloyd et al. [Lloyd04] already proposed to cull shadow casters based on whether they influence any shadow receivers (see Section 2.4.7).

Shadow-Caster Culling

Bittner et al. [Bittner11] generalize this approach to shadow mapping and show several ways to accurately cull shadow casters and thus reduce shadow-map creation overhead. The main idea of this approach is to use occlusion culling to create an accurate *mask* in light space that contains the information where potential shadow receivers are. The algorithm has four steps:

1. Determine *potential shadow receivers* (PSRs).

2. Create a mask of shadow receivers.

3. Render shadow casters using the mask for culling.

4. Compute shading.

(1) The potential shadow receivers are determined by rendering the scene from the camera viewpoint using an online occlusion-culling algorithm like CHC++ [Mattausch08]. Occlusion culling returns a list of objects (PSRs) that are visible in the camera view. (2) The potential shadow receivers are rendered into the *stencil buffer* attached to the shadow map. For this step, bounding volumes for the objects or the actual geometry can be used. The former is faster but less accurate. (3) The shadow casters are rendered into the shadow map again using an occlusion-culling algorithm. The culling is set up so that a fragment is rejected if it fails the depth test or if it is not included in the receiver mask created in the previous step. Thus, only shadow casters that influence visible shadow receivers are rendered.

The advantage of using an occlusion-culling algorithm for steps (1) and (3) is that in both steps, the rendering cost is proportional only to the visible part of the scene. In step (3), occlusion culling will cull invisible casters (i.e., shadow casters that are themselves completely in shadow) and casters that do not cast shadows on a visible part of the scene and, thus, do not influence the final image.

One problem in creating the receiver mask is that the accuracy of the mask depends on the notion of what a "visible object" actually is. Consider a ground plane spanning the whole scene, for example—as an object, the ground plane is always visible, causing the mask to be completely filled, however, only small parts of the ground plane may be visible at any one time. To create a mask that is as tight as possible in step (2), Bittner et al. therefore propose a so-called *fragment mask* that uses an additional check before setting a pixel in the mask. The idea is to reverse the roles of light and camera views, and test each shadow-receiver fragment against the depth buffer of the camera view for visibility. If the fragment is hidden in the camera view, then the mask remains untouched. This allows creating a mask that contains exactly those pixels where a shadow receiver is actually visible.

Note that shadow-caster culling is used in very similar ways to shadow-volume rendering (see Section 2.4.7). The main difference is that those methods use a shadow map, which is created without using acceleration by culling shadow casters, whereas for shadow mapping, the creation of the shadow map itself needs to be accelerated.

Light Culling

Another problem that might occur in large scenes is a high number of shadow-casting light sources, even though only a few lights actually have an effect on the objects in the current view frustum. If in a many-lights scene, most lights have a bounded extent, then it is possible to improve performance by *light culling*. For this, the extent of the light's influence needs to be given by some geometric shape, for example, a sphere (for point lights).

A simple optimization is then to apply view-frustum culling to the light extent and only use lights that intersect the view frustum. This can save both the shadow-mapping pass, as well as the fragment computations for shading a pixel using that light.

Often, the effect of a light is not visible due to occlusion. This could be tested using the following algorithm: first, render the back faces of the light extent, with a depth-comparison function of "greater than or equal," and mark pixels in the stencil buffer that pass this depth test. Then, render the front faces of the light extent, with a depth-comparison function of "less than or equal" and with stencil testing enabled, so that only pixels marked in the first step are considered. If this second pass is rendered using an occlusion query, the GPU returns the number of pixels that are both visible *and* inside the light extent. If this number is lower than a predefined threshold, the light can be culled.

2.3   Shadow Volumes

We have seen so far a shadow solution that was based on an image representation of the scene. While conceptually simple, we also realized that many problems are introduced by the fact that the scene is approximated in image space. Here, we focus on a different basic algorithm that works directly in object space. Instead of transforming the scene into a set of pixels, shadows can be described by attaching new geometric elements to the scene—so-called *shadow volumes* [Crow77]. Being accurately constructed from geometry, this algorithm does not share the downsides of the previously seen shadow mapping and delivers accurate hard shadows, but it also often results in increased computation cost.

Shadow volumes have a long history in the relatively young science of computer graphics. The algorithm has matured gradually for over three decades, since its birth in 1977. Crow [Crow77] introduced the concept of creating volumes of shadow for scenes described by polygons, which also gave rise to the name *volumetric shadows*. This term is, however, nowadays more commonly reserved for the type of shadow algorithms that create shadows in participating media, such as fog, clouds, or smoke (Chapter 9).

The best way to understand the shadow-volume algorithm is to think of the basic concept as creating "volumes of shadow in space" (hence the name shadow volumes) for each scene triangle that potentially casts a shadow on the scene.

For a single triangle, the shadow-volume region is defined by the triangle itself and three quads that extend to infinity (see Figure 2.12). Each quad is defined by two edge vertices and by an extrusion of these two vertices to infinity along the line from the light source through the vertex. Although it may sound impossible to project these points to infinity, we will show that homogeneous coordinates do the trick again (Section 2.3.2). The resulting four vertices define a quad. Each triangle defines three quads that together with the triangle itself form the triangle's shadow volume. Because the triangle adds a *cap* to the volume, it is usually referred to as the *near cap*. With this definition, a point then lies in shadow if it is located within one or more of these volumes.

While shadow volumes seem conceptually as simple as shadow maps, an efficient implementation is far from trivial. We will discuss hereafter various ways that will lead to an optimized computation.

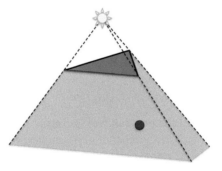

Figure 2.12. A point inside a triangle's shadow volume.

2.3.1 Naive Shadow-Volume Algorithm

To understand the complexity of a naive shadow-volume algorithm, just imagine how one would test whether a view sample lies in shadow. One solution could be to first render the entire scene without shadows to produce view samples. Next, for each triangle T, one could render a screen-filling quad with a special fragment shader. Each drawn pixel first reads its underlying view sample and tests it for containment in the shadow volume of the given triangle T. If it lies inside, a black pixel is output, otherwise the result is discarded, thereby keeping the original pixel of the rendered scene. Such a naive solution sounds extremely costly from a modern hardware perspective, since each triangle affects a computation on all pixels. Interestingly, however, Fuchs et al. [Fuchs85] showed in 1985 that the existing specialized graphics hardware of the time—the Pixel-Planes machine—allowed a very efficient execution of the above algorithm. Pixel-Plane machines had the unique property that the rasterization time for a triangle was independent of the triangle's covered screen area [Everitt02]. Consequently, a screen-filling quad was as cheap as drawing any small triangle in the scene. Therefore, testing all screen pixels for their containment in the shadow frustum (one plane for each of the three frustum sides and the triangle itself) proved extremely cheap.

Unfortunately, the higher the resolution, the more costly such specialized hardware becomes and, nowadays, with our full-HD image content, a hardware acceleration such as the Pixel-Plane machine becomes unfeasible and better solutions are needed.

Precomputed Solutions

Instead of constructing shadow volumes on the fly, it is also possible to employ precomputation. Some early shadow-volume approaches clipped the scene geometry by planes along the shadow volumes to divide the objects in lit and shadowed parts. The final scene representation often involved complex structures like a BSP tree (or even two [Chin89]). Although a moving object could be rather efficiently removed and reinserted [Chrysanthou95], light-position changes were almost infeasible for real-time usage. For static sources, this can sometimes still make sense for modern approaches if the static scene representation is already organized in such a tree structure, as is often the case to support efficient visibility queries.

2.3.2 Shadow-Volume Construction

Previously, we mentioned the possibility of testing all view samples against each shadow volume. To reduce the number of view samples, one simple improvement is to construct the actual shadow volume and render it into the current view. Only the covered view samples can potentially lie inside the shadow volume and, thus, need to perform the tests against the planes. While this solution reduces the cost on modern hardware, it is still infeasible in practice to test each pixel against all shadow-volume planes of all shadow-casting triangles whose shadow volume covers the pixel. It will just be too much rasterization of shadow-volume polygons to run in high frame rates, unless the scenes are fairly small. In Section 2.4.6, we will see how to construct the shadow volumes from only the silhouette edges instead of from each triangle. Nonetheless, the actual shadow-volume geometry on a per-triangle basis proves useful in the more advanced algorithms, which is why it is worth analyzing their construction here.

To robustly extrude shadow volumes to infinity, one can make use of homogeneous coordinates. Given a vertex in homogeneous coordinates, $\mathbf{p} := (\mathbf{p}_x, \mathbf{p}_y, \mathbf{p}_z, 1)$, we need to move this point to infinity along the line from the positional point light source $\mathbf{l} := (\mathbf{l}_x, \mathbf{l}_y, \mathbf{l}_z, 1)$. Using homogeneous coordinates, any point on a line between these two points is given by $\alpha \mathbf{l} + \beta \mathbf{p}$, with $\alpha, \beta \in \mathbb{R}$ (see infobox on page 48). Consequently, the particular point $\mathbf{p} - \mathbf{l} = (\mathbf{p}_x - \mathbf{l}_x, \mathbf{p}_y - \mathbf{l}_y, \mathbf{p}_z - \mathbf{l}_z, 0)$ (for $\alpha = -\beta = -1$) lies on the line that corresponds to the direction into which the vertex should be extruded. Interestingly, this point also lies at infinity because its w-coordinate equals zero. Consequently, to produce the extruded shadow-volume quad for an edge defined by two vertices $\mathbf{v}_1, \mathbf{v}_2$, we only need to output the vertices $\mathbf{v}_1, \mathbf{v}_2, \mathbf{v}_1 - \mathbf{l}$, and $\mathbf{v}_2 - \mathbf{l}$. For clarity reasons, it is worth pointing out that the w-component is thus equal to one for the first two vertices and zero for the two latter vertices that are extruded to infinity.

For a directional light $(\mathbf{l}_x, \mathbf{l}_y, \mathbf{l}_z, 0)$, the process is even simpler because the two vertices at infinity are actually located at the same position (the quad becomes a triangle); the light itself describes the direction into which the vertices should be extruded. These extruded vertices simply become $(-\mathbf{l}_x, -\mathbf{l}_y, -\mathbf{l}_z, 0)$, following OpenGL's convention where the light direction is the normalized vector to the light. All points are transformed as expected by the projection matrices because the pipeline does not differentiate between points at infinity and others. It is conceived for general homogeneous points.

The shadow-volume quads should be oriented in such a way that their plane equations have the interior of the shadow volume on the inside and the exterior on the outside. To create a quad with the correct orientation, we first need to check on which side of the triangle plane the light source is located. Without loss of generality, we can create the plane equation using the right-hand rule and test the side of the light source by calculating $((\mathbf{v}_2 - \mathbf{v}_1) \times (\mathbf{v}_3 - \mathbf{v}_1)) \cdot (\mathbf{l} - \mathbf{v}_1) \geq 0$. If this result is positive, the correct vertex order for the three shadow-volume quads of the triangle becomes $(\mathbf{v}_2, \mathbf{v}_1, \mathbf{v}_1 - \mathbf{l}, \mathbf{v}_2 - \mathbf{l})$, $(\mathbf{v}_3, \mathbf{v}_2, \mathbf{v}_2 - \mathbf{l}, \mathbf{v}_3 - \mathbf{l})$, and $(\mathbf{v}_1, \mathbf{v}_3, \mathbf{v}_3 - \mathbf{l}, \mathbf{v}_1 - \mathbf{l})$. The quad vertices are here given in counterclockwise order, when looking at the quads on their front/outer side.[5] If the result of the test is negative, then the vertex order should instead be reversed internally for each quad.

---

[5]Direct3D often uses a left-handed system, and for that, the vertex order should be inverted. See also Appendix B.1.1.

Homogeneous Lines

At first glance, it might look surprising that two real numbers are used to describe a line, but this is only a consequence of the fact that any homogeneous coordinate is defined up to a nonzero scalar. In order to gain confidence in this notation, let's look at a point on the line defined by $\mathbf{p}, \mathbf{l}$:

$$\alpha\mathbf{l} + \beta\mathbf{p} = (\alpha\mathbf{l}_x, \alpha\mathbf{l}_y, \alpha\mathbf{l}_z, \alpha) + (\beta\mathbf{p}_x, \beta\mathbf{p}_y, \beta\mathbf{p}_z, \beta)$$
$$= (\alpha\mathbf{l}_x + \beta\mathbf{p}_x, \alpha\mathbf{l}_y + \beta\mathbf{p}_y, \alpha\mathbf{l}_z + \beta\mathbf{p}_z, \alpha + \beta).$$

In affine space, the coordinate $w = 1$. Hence,

$$\left(\frac{\alpha\mathbf{l}_x + \beta\mathbf{p}_x}{\alpha + \beta}, \frac{\alpha\mathbf{l}_y + \beta\mathbf{p}_y}{\alpha + \beta}, \frac{\alpha\mathbf{l}_z + \beta\mathbf{p}_z}{\alpha + \beta}, 1 \right)$$

$$= \left(\frac{\alpha}{\alpha + \beta}\mathbf{l}_x + \frac{\beta}{\alpha + \beta}\mathbf{p}_x, \frac{\alpha}{\alpha + \beta}\mathbf{l}_y + \frac{\beta}{\alpha + \beta}\mathbf{p}_y, \frac{\alpha}{\alpha + \beta}\mathbf{l}_z + \frac{\beta}{\alpha + \beta}\mathbf{p}_z, 1 \right).$$

One observation is that $\frac{\alpha}{\alpha+\beta} + \frac{\beta}{\alpha+\beta} = 1$. Consequently, renaming $\tau := \frac{\beta}{\alpha+\beta}$, we obtain

$$((1-\tau)\mathbf{l}_x + \tau\mathbf{p}_x, (1-\tau)\mathbf{l}_y + \tau\mathbf{p}_y, (1-\tau)\mathbf{l}_z + \tau\mathbf{p}_z, 1) = \mathbf{l} + \tau(\mathbf{p} - \mathbf{l}).$$

The last equation is typically used for lines in affine space, but it does not describe all points on the line for homogeneous coordinates. How come? We divided by $\alpha + \beta$ to define τ, so implicitly, we assumed that this sum is not zero. The latter happens for $\alpha = -\beta$, leading to $\beta\mathbf{p} - \beta\mathbf{l} = \beta(\mathbf{p}_x - \mathbf{l}_x, \mathbf{p}_y - \mathbf{l}_y, \mathbf{p}_z - \mathbf{l}_z, 0)$, which corresponds to the point at infinity that reflects the direction of the line.

Interestingly, although the two points $\mathbf{p} - \mathbf{l}$ and $\mathbf{l} - \mathbf{p}$ are the same from a homogeneous-coordinate view (remember that homogeneous coordinates are defined up to a scalar), they are not treated the same way by the graphics pipeline. The reason is that the GPU first performs a clipping against the view frustum before performing the actual division by w. Therefore, the above choice leads to differing results. Fortunately, it is simple to understand the clipping behavior. A point with a zero w-coordinate should be considered a direction. Defining a vertex with such a direction will extrude connected edges exactly along this vector. Here, we do not need to know more about the pipeline, but more details on the clipping stage can be found in the OpenGL Programming Guide [Shreiner09]. It also details why the choice of clipping before dividing is crucial to ensure that geometry behind the camera is always ignored.

2.4   Stencil Shadow Volumes

It was not until 1991, with Heidmann's *stencil shadows* [Heidmann91] that shadow volumes became feasible for real-time dynamic scenes. One major benefit was that no real geometric computations (intersections or containment tests) were used any longer, but instead, were mapped on the existing z- and stencil-buffer operations.

2.4.1   Assumptions

We will, for the moment, assume that the eye is located in light and not in shadow. Later, we will show how to lift this constraint (see Section 2.4.4).

Heidmann's core idea is related to the Jordan theorem [Jordan87] extended to three dimensions. It states that for any closed shape, the set of points in space is divided into two sets: those that define ray origins for which each ray has an even number of intersections with the shape and those with an odd number of intersections, where tangency is counted as two intersections. In simple words, closed shapes, such as shadow volumes, always define an interior and exterior, and we can test containment by shooting an arbitrary ray along which we count the number of intersections with shadow volumes. If this number is odd, the origin of the ray lies in shadow; otherwise, it is lit. For the moment, to simplify explanations, we will assume that the scene geometry itself satisfies the Jordan condition, meaning that it is watertight (see footnote on page 37). It exactly separates the space into an interior and exterior region. For example, a single triangle would not satisfy this condition, whereas a cube does. We lift this constraint in Section 2.4.6.

2.4.2   Overview

Heidmann decides to test the number of intersections along the rays from the eye to each view sample. On the way, he counts how many times a ray enters versus exits a shadow volume. More precisely, he increases/decreases the counter every time the ray enters/exits a shadow volume. Based on our assumption that the eye is located outside the shadow, the final count indicates the number of shadow volumes containing the view sample (Figure 2.13). In particular, a count different from zero implies that the view sample is located in shadow.

Instead of actually testing rays explicitly against the shadow volumes, Heidmann proposes a more GPU-friendly computation. His observation is that a ray enters a shadow volume always through a front-facing polygon, while leaving it through a back-facing polygon. As each ray is defined by a pixel in the image, he concluded that one could implicitly test whether a ray enters a shadow volume by simply drawing its front faces. All pixels covered by the drawn quad will effectively enter the volume. Rendering all back-facing quads equally determines pixels whose associated rays would leave the corresponding volume. In order to realize the counters, Heidmann proposes to rely on the stencil buffer. The counting can then be performed with the stencil buffer by rendering all shadow-volume quads and incrementing/decrementing the stencil values for front- and back-facing polygons, respectively, since it represents entering/exiting shadow volumes. The previously described shadow-volume construction (Section 2.3.2) ensures the correct orientation of each quad, but no near cap is needed. Finally, in order to only treat those shadow volumes that lie between the camera and the view sample, standard z-culling is used, where the depth buffer contains the shadow receiving scene,

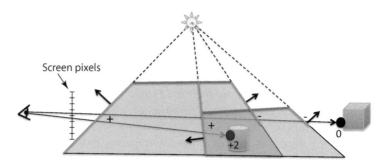

Figure 2.13. The figure illustrates the shadow volumes from two triangles. For a point outside the shadow (see upper ray), the difference in the number of intersected front- and back-facing triangles is zero. For points in shadow, the difference is positive. The lower ray intersects two front-facing quads, but no back-facing quad, meaning that the lower point is located inside two shadow volumes. The difference directly corresponds to the number of shadow volumes that the corresponding point is located within, and we are mainly interested in whether this count is zero or more. Notice that the rendering of the back-facing quads is depth culled behind the cylinder, providing the proper stencil count for the lower point.

and any updates to the z-buffer are disabled when rasterizing the quads (see pseudocode on page 51). In this way, the stencil buffer will contain the correct counter per pixel after having rendered all quads.

In the following, we will give a detailed description to present all subtleties of the technique.

2.4.3   Stencil Counting Implementation—Z-Pass

In the first step, the scene is rendered from the viewpoint to create the z-buffer. Typically, the ambient-lighting contribution is computed into the color buffer at the same step. Secondly, one deactivates the depth write (glDepthMask(GL_FALSE)), while keeping the depth test enabled. Now, all front-facing shadow-volume quads are rendered to the stencil buffer and increment the stencil values (glStencilFunc(GL_ALWAYS, 0, 0xffff), glStencilOp(GL_KEEP, GL_KEEP, GL_INCR)), meaning that the stencil is incremented only when a shadow-volume fragment passes the depth test. This step is followed by rendering the back-facing quads and decrementing the stencil values for the rasterized pixels (glStencilFunc(GL_ALWAYS, 0, 0xffff), glStencilOp(GL_KEEP, GL_KEEP, GL_DECR)). Rendering quads of the correct facing only can be controlled by glEnable(GL_CULL_FACE) and glCullFace(GL_FRONT/GL_BACK). In the final pass, the scene is rendered again, adding the specular- and diffuse-lighting contribution into the color buffer, while using the stencil buffer as a mask to discard any pixels in shadow (glStencilFunc(GL_EQUAL, 0, 0xffff), glStencilOp(GL_KEEP, GL_KEEP, GL_DECR)).

Specialized Extensions

Heidmann's stencil shadow volumes dramatically improved the usability and performance of the shadow-volume technique and received strong support by hardware vendors who even added an extension to increment and decrement the stencil buffer depending on a triangle's orientation (glStencilOpSeparate()). Thereby, separate stencil operations can be set for front- and back-facing polygons, making it possible to render the shadow-volume quads with incrementation/decrementation in a single render pass. Furthermore, with the introduction of multiple render targets, it is standard to render the ambient and specular + diffuse contribution into two separate buffers in one pass and then combine them when the stencil has been computed.

Stencil Shadow Volumes (Z-Pass)

First pass: Render the scene with ambient lighting to one buffer and specular + diffuse to a second buffer.

Second pass: Turn off z-buffer and color writing (i.e., draw to stencil buffer only, with enabled depth test). Render shadow-volume quads to stencil buffer with increment/decrement of stencil counter for front/back-facing quads, respectively.

Third pass: Output ambient buffer with the addition of the second buffer for pixels where stencil counter = 0.

Stencil Precision

A stencil buffer of only 8 bits will overflow when the depth complexity of quads is more than 256. To avoid such behavior, the increment/decrement operations are preferably set to a wraparound mode (GL_INCR_WRAP and GL_DECR_WRAP that replace GL_INCR and GL_DECR, respectively). This mode avoids overflow/underflow problems by wrapping around values that exceed the upper/lower limit to the lower/upper limit (e.g., 255 + 1 becomes 0). Nevertheless, the 8-bit standard stencil buffer can quickly become too limited for a complex scene (e.g., 256 superposing shadow volumes basically cancel out). Stencil buffers of more than 8 bits are still rarely supported in hardware, but today, using render to texture with additive blending and a shader that outputs ±1 depending on the facing can be used to simulate the same counters. In practice, a 16-bit buffer is more than enough.

Summary and Outlook

The presented stencil updates are often referred to as the *z-pass* algorithm because the modifications to the buffer are all triggered by fragments that *pass* the depth test. It is much more efficient than the previously described naive implementation, but several basic improvements remain possible that we will present in the remainder of this chapter.

Furthermore, we will address the previous restrictions. First, we will no longer have to assume that the camera is outside all shadows but can be located at an arbitrary position in the scene (Section 2.4.4). Second, our scene will no longer have to be watertight (Section 2.4.6). In this context, we will also explain one of the most crucial accelerations, which is to not construct a shadow volume per triangle, but, instead, to restrict oneself to a certain subset of edges, the so-called silhouettes.

2.4.4   Z-Fail

Eye Location Problem

If the eye happens to be located inside one or more shadow volumes, then the stencil counts will be wrong (see Figure 2.14). The stencil buffer will be offset by the number of shadow volumes that the eye lies within. One solution is to readjust the stencil buffer by computing the number of shadow volumes it is contained in (e.g., with geometrical tests of the eye against the shadow volumes on the CPU). This could be complex and inflict a burden on the CPU. It would be preferable to run the whole algorithm on the GPU. In addition, a more complex problem is that the near plane of the viewing frustum might intersect one or more shadow-volume planes, in which case, different portions of the screen would require different offsets (see Section 2.4.5). One possibility is to close the resulting shadow-volume holes geometrically by adding capping planes on the near plane [Diefenbach96, Batagelo99, Bestimt99, Dietrich99, Kilgard00, Kilgard01]. Unfortunately, such approaches are generally not robust [Everitt02, Akenine-Möller08]. Instead, an alternative is to change the way we perform the stencil counting, which results in the so-called *z-fail algorithm*. It was first invented and patented by Bilodeau and Songy [Bilodeau99] in October 1998 and briefly hinted upon at GDC [Dietrich99]. In 2000, Carmack independently discovered the method at id Software and used it in DOOM 3 [Carmack00]. Since Carmack announced the technique to a broader audience, the algorithm is often referred to as *Carmack's reverse*.

Main Principle

As implied by the Jordan theorem (see Section 2.4), to test the containment of a view sample in the shadow volumes, one can shoot a ray to any arbitrary reference point for which we know the number of shadow volumes in which it is contained (i.e., this point does not necessarily have to be the eye). One good choice is to select a reference point that is always in light. One such point is the position of the light source itself, but shooting rays in this direction is only efficiently achievable with current GPUs if we render the scene from the light source, which basically

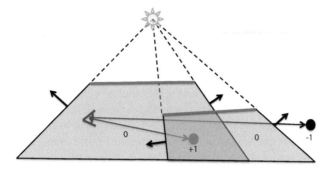

Figure 2.14. Eye location problem for the z-pass algorithm. Stencil counts will be offset by the number of shadow volumes that the eye is located within.

transforms the method into the shadow-map algorithm, with the same pros and cons, including aliasing and biasing problems.

However, if we restrict the shadow volumes to a finite extent (see Figure 2.15) (e.g., restricting it to the bounding box of the geometry), all shadow tests inside the scene would still work, but it is easy to find a point outside all shadow volumes: a point at infinity. It is possible to use a reference point at infinity (i.e., infinitely far away) for each pixel by simply reversing the depth test when rasterizing the shadow-volume geometry.

By convention, the increment/decrement for front-/back-facing polygons are also reversed, with the effect that the counting is done for virtual rays from each view sample to infinity along the line through the eye (see Figure 2.15). Not switching the "inc" for "dec" and vice versa would only mean that negative stencil values

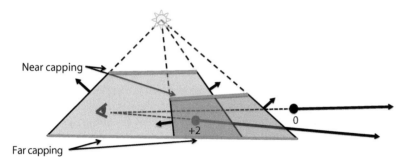

Figure 2.15. The z-fail algorithm. Counting is done from the point along the ray to infinity instead, by simply inverting the z-test and stencil inc/dec. The shadow volumes need to be closed by near and far capping to ensure that the reference points at infinity are always in light (i.e., outside any shadow volume).

represent shadows instead. This method is called *z-fail*, since the stencil buffer is updated when the depth test fails. In practice, this is achieved by setting the depth test to GL_GREATER instead of the standard GL_LESS.

One important catch is that the Jordan Theorem is only valid for closed shadow volumes. A simple truncation to the scene extent would lead to holes in the shadow volumes that need to be filled. Closing the shadow volumes means that we have to render a near cap—the front-facing triangles themselves—and a far cap usually based on the back-facing triangles. The construction will be detailed next, where we will also show that we can avoid truncating to a scene extent and instead produce closed volumes *at* infinity that still lead to a correct behavior with respect to the z-fail algorithm. This solution will solve many robustness issues.

Robust Z-Fail Far Capping

When rendering the shadow volumes, the polygons will be clipped by the near and far planes of the view frustum. The near-plane clipping cannot affect the rendering of the z-fail algorithm in any harmful way, since the stencil buffer is only updated for quads that are farther away from the eye than the scene geometry in the depth buffer. Thus, only clipping at the far plane causes concern. In order to fix this problem in a simple and convenient way, Everitt and Kilgard [Everitt02] suggest using an ad-hoc depth-clamping rasterization feature that was added in graphics hardware by NVIDIA and, now, has become standard. The easiest and most efficient solution is to just turn on this GL_ARB_depth_clamp extension, which bounds *z*-values to the interval of $[0, 1]$. This disables clipping at the near/far planes and causes geometry behind the far plane to be rasterized on the far plane itself (i.e., with depth values set to the *far* value) (and analogously geometry in between the eye and the near plane will be rasterized on the near plane). For a solution that does not rely on clamping, see page 56.

2.4.5   Alternatives to Z-Pass and Z-Fail

Z-pass often performs faster than z-fail, partly due to not needing to rasterize any caps and also for its general tendency to cull more quad fragments. It is not unusual that the z-pass method is up to twice as fast as z-fail. It therefore makes sense to use z-pass whenever possible, and only use the z-fail algorithm when the eye is inside a shadow volume or when the near plane of the view frustum risks intersecting a shadow volume (see Section 2.4.4). Hornus et al. [Hornus05] solved this problem with a theoretically elegant approach, called ZP+. This solution automatically handles the eye-inside-shadow-volume problem, computing the correct stencil offsets per pixel for a following standard z-pass rendering.

The idea of ZP+ is to project the scene from the light onto the camera's near plane and thus initialize the stencil buffer from the view with the correct values to

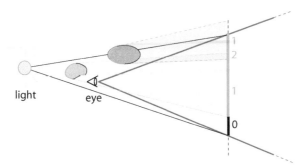

Figure 2.16. ZP+. The idea of the algorithm is to solve the problem with the z-pass method of having to initiate the stencil buffer with the number of shadow volumes that the eye is located within. This is done by rendering the near-capping triangles from the light's position, with the far plane identical to the near plane from the eye's position. This initiates the stencil buffer, which can then be used when continuing with the standard z-pass from the eye's position. This approach works unrestrictedly of the light and eye position (e.g., much more differently than shown here), except for when the light source happens to lie in or very close to the near plane, preventing the creation of a robust projection matrix.

allow the application of z-pass (see Figure 2.16). The rasterization from the light source counts the number of geometrical layers (i.e., shadow-volume near-capping layers) per pixel, from the light up to the camera's near plane, by incrementing the stencil buffer for each generated fragment. The algorithm is cheap and theoretically simple, but numerical precision might lead to cracks for a few single pixels, and the correction of these cracks is rather awkward, involving a specialized vertex shader. This vertex shader must identify four special cases concerning the polygon/near-plane intersection, which makes the code complex. The cause of the numerical problems comes from the polygon clipping against the two different unit cubes. The polygons will be clipped differently, when rasterizing from the light source (to initiate the stencil buffer per pixel) and from the camera (for the standard z-pass step). Clipping produces new primitives whose vertices cover the triangle part to be rendered, but the produced vertices can be different for the two cases. Therefore, the generated fragments during the two render passes may be slightly inconsistent, leading to inconsistent stencil values. The specialized vertex shader manually assures that the clipping results will be identical for the two different projections.

When setting the camera at the light position and rendering the near-capping triangles, it is important that no triangle intersects the near plane of the currently used light frustum. Fragments that are culled against that near plane obstruct the correct initiation of the stencil buffer. Hornus et al. proposed the introduction of a hardware depth clamping only at the near plane and not at the far plane. At the time, hardware clamping was only possible for both the near and far planes,

---

Robust Z-Fail Far Capping without Depth Clamping

If the depth-clamping extension is not supported, and also for historical reasons, we will here provide an alternate solution, which works for perspective, but not orthographic, projections.

The idea is to set the far plane at infinity. This is done in such a way that the shadow volumes, which are still extruded to infinity and closed, never will risk being clipped by the far plane. To set the far plane at infinity, avoiding floating-point precision problems, the projection matrix used when rendering the shadow volumes needs to be tweaked [Blinn93, Everitt02].

The standard projection matrix for OpenGL is constructed as follows (see also matrix B.1 on page 315):

$$\mathbf{M}_{\mathrm{P}} = \begin{pmatrix} \frac{1}{\alpha} \cot \frac{fovy}{2} & 0 & 0 & 0 \\ 0 & \cot \frac{fovy}{2} & 0 & 0 \\ 0 & 0 & \frac{n+f}{n-f} & \frac{2nf}{n-f} \\ 0 & 0 & -1 & 0 \end{pmatrix},$$

where α is the aspect ratio, $fovy$ is the vertical field of view, and n and f are the near- and far-plane positions. If f is infinity, the third row becomes

$$\begin{pmatrix} 0 & 0 & -1 & -2n \end{pmatrix}.$$

For clarity, here is the full OpenGL projection matrix with the far plane at infinity:

$$\mathbf{M}_{\mathrm{P}} = \begin{pmatrix} \frac{1}{\alpha} \cot \frac{fovy}{2} & 0 & 0 & 0 \\ 0 & \cot \frac{fovy}{2} & 0 & 0 \\ 0 & 0 & -1 & -2n \\ 0 & 0 & -1 & 0 \end{pmatrix}.$$

Surprisingly, the numerical loss of precision for the z-buffer range when moving the original far plane, f_o, to infinity normally turns out to be small. The amount of numerical range lost is just $\frac{n}{f_o}$, which for normal values of n corresponds to a negligible effect on precision [Akenine-Möller08, Kwoon03].

---

with the GL_ARB_depth_clamp extension. Clamping at the light frustum's far plane (located at the eye's near plane) would destroy the stencil counting of shadow volumes up to the eye's near plane. Since 2010, such a new extension exists (GL_AMD_depth_clamp_separate) that enables us to choose the plane on which the clamping is performed (here, glEnable(GL_DEPTH_CLAMP_NEAR_AMD)).

Another potential problem occurs when the light source happens to be in, or sufficiently close to, the camera's near plane, preventing the construction of a robust projection matrix from the light onto the plane. Nevertheless, this latter situation is very rare and does not impose much of a practical problem.

++ZP Approach

In this book, we present a different approach that is much simpler and often robust enough in practice. As mentioned above, the stencil buffer must be initiated with the number of shadow volumes that the eye is located within for the z-pass to work properly. In addition, the near plane of the view frustum may intersect shadow-volume polygons, leading to different initialization values per pixel. The latter can be solved by enabling near-plane clamping. Therefore, the only remaining task is to count how many shadow volumes the eye is located within. We notice that testing the eye can be done rather efficiently on the GPU. The idea is to set up a new orthographic camera from the light's position to the eye position. This camera has a 1×1 pixel-sized viewport. Now, render the scene, incrementing the stencil buffer for each rasterized fragment, delivering the exact number of shadow volumes that the eye is located within.

Why is this method not 100% robust? The reason is that the counting by the rasterization of the two steps (from the light source to the eye and the z-pass) must be done exactly the same—without being affected by different clipping or different 32-bit float rounding issues when multiplying polygon vertices with the model-view-projection matrix. This is not the case, since the model-view-projection matrices differ, resulting in both different geometrical clipping of the polygons and different matrix rounding errors. In other words, the counting is done for scene geometry that will be slightly different between the pass that counts to the light source and the z-pass. Nevertheless, visible errors are rarely detected in practice.

Reasonably Robust Z-Pass Algorithm

Count shadow volumes containing the eye:

1. Set up orthographic camera between light position and eye position, with the near and far planes coinciding with these positions, respectively. Use a viewport with a size of 1×1 pixel.

2. Initialize the 1×1 stencil buffer to zero and render the scene, with the stencil function set to increment.

3. Read back the stencil value, v, to the CPU.

Render the shadow-volume quads:

4. Restore the camera and viewport. Initiate the stencil buffer with v (`glClearStencil(v)`), then `glClear(GL_STENCIL_BUFFER_BIT)`.

5. Enable depth clamping by `glEnable(GL_DEPTH_CLAMP)`, or preferably `glEnable(GL_DEPTH_CLAMP_NEAR_AMD)` if available.

6. Render shadow volumes using standard z-pass.

Figure 2.17. An interior edge makes two quads that cancel out (left). Finding the silhouette edges gets rid of many useless shadow-volume quads (right).

2.4.6   Silhouette-Based Shadow Volumes for General Models

For a watertight model, one realizes that adjacent shadow-casting triangles lead to an "inner" boundary for which the generation of shadow-volume quads can be omitted (see Figure 2.17) because these two quads basically cancel out. Any ray piercing the quad would leave the current shadow volume and directly end up in the adjacent shadow volume. Thus, while moving along the ray, the count of the number of shadow volumes that contain the current position does not change. Consequently, such triangles should be merged and the quad omitted. In fact, this observation was already pointed out by Crow [Crow77]. Ultimately, only the model's silhouette edges, as seen from the light, need to be extruded, where *silhouette edges* of a watertight model are those edges that are adjacent to a front- and back-facing triangle with respect to the light source. The near cap of the shadow volume is formed by the front-facing triangles (with a triangle normal oriented towards the light). The silhouette edges are typically found by searching for shared edges between one triangle that is front facing and one triangle that is back facing the light source.

Historical Implementations

The shadow-volume algorithm used in DOOM 3 is described by van Waveren [vanWaveren05], including Streaming SIMD Extensions (SSE) optimizations for the Pentium 4. When vertex shaders appeared in graphics hardware, it was rapidly shown how to use these to accelerate both the silhouette-edge detection and the shadow-volume generation [Brennan02, Brabec03]. Microsoft also provides example code as part of the Direct3D SDK.[6] The drawback of using the vertex shader is that it cannot create new vertices. Thus, degenerate quads are inserted between each mesh edge, which are extruded in runtime by the vertex shader only for silhouette edges. Nowadays, it is easier to use the geometry shader [Stich07].

Manifold Models

However, creating shadow-volume quads only from the silhouette edges has a caveat for nonclosed objects, which has led to the common misconception that ob-

---

[6]See ShadowVolume Sample at http://msdn.microsoft.com/en-us/library/ee418792.aspx.

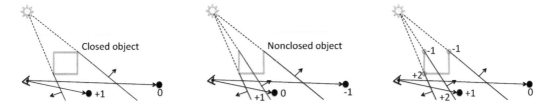

Figure 2.18. Z-pass for a closed object (left). Stencil counts fail for a nonclosed object (middle). Bergeron notes that for nonclosed objects, silhouette edges with two adjacent triangles should create shadow quads that inc/dec the count by two, while quads for open silhouette edges inc/dec by one (right).

jects need to be watertight for the shadow-volume algorithm to work properly. The middle image in Figure 2.18 illustrates what happens when shadow-volume quads are created from the contours of a nonwatertight object. One main difficulty are boundary edges (i.e., edges only belonging to one triangle). For an isolated triangle to cast a shadow, its boundary edges need to define shadow volumes. Nonetheless, just adding shadow volumes to boundary edges is not a general solution because the stencil counting might become incorrect.

A first step in the right direction was made by Bergeron [Bergeron86] that deals with manifold meshes (meshes that contain only edges with one or two adjacent triangles). He noticed that objects should actually have two quads per silhouette edge that is shared by two triangles, and only one quad if the edge is a boundary (i.e., only belongs to one triangle). In other words, silhouette edges with two adjacent triangles should increment/decrement the stencil buffer by a value of two, while open edges should use a value of one (see Figure 2.18, right). To circumvent the fact that the stencil buffer only allows modifications by ± 1, additive blending to an offscreen buffer could be used [McGuire07], instead of rendering the quads twice.

General Models

As a matter of fact, Bergeron's solution proves to be just a special case of a more general observation, noted by Aldridge and Woods [Aldridge04]. Reformulating their observation enables the description of a simpler and more efficient solution. In particular, that and most previous methods rely on determining light front- and back-facing triangles for the silhouette extraction. The facing is by definition based on the triangles' winding order.[7] This means that the triangles' winding orders require some consistency. However, for a general polygon soup, the concept of facing and consistent winding does not necessarily exist and imposes a superfluous restriction.

---

[7]The two triangles $(\mathbf{v}_1, \mathbf{v}_2, \mathbf{v}_3)$ and $(\mathbf{v}_1, \mathbf{v}_3, \mathbf{v}_2)$ are identical but with different winding order.

A naive solution would call the shadow method twice—once for front-facing and once for back-facing geometry. Nevertheless, it would lower efficiency. Kim et al. [Kim08] presented the first solution that avoids this and any concept of facing or consistent winding, by the addition of a minor modification. We will here present that idea slightly differently and in more detail, but it follows the work by Kim et al. closely.

The idea is to not focus on triangles to determine shadow volumes but to concentrate on the edges in the scene. These edges do not need to be unique in order to make the algorithm work, but if they are, it maximizes performance; that is, an edge $(\mathbf{v}_0, \mathbf{v}_1)$ with three adjacent triangles could appear in the list twice (e.g., as one instance with an identified connectivity for two of the triangles, and the other instance with a single connectivity for the third triangle). This will still generate the same shadows, but by possibly drawing more quads than necessary.

For each scene edge (with an arbitrary number of connected triangles), the idea is to generate a shadow-volume quad that increments/decrements by k, where k is the number of noncanceling quads that would be generated if one quad was created per triangle that is adjacent to this edge. If all quads cancel out, we do not output a shadow-volume quad for the edge.

Before going into the details, let's illustrate how Bergeron's suggestion can be rediscovered via this description. At a boundary edge, we have $k = 1$ because there is only one triangle, and the two definitions coincide. For a nonsilhouette edge, both triangles define adjacent shadow volumes that cancel out, leading to $k = 0$, which means that no shadow volume is constructed, which reflects Bergeron's suggestion again. Finally, for a real silhouette with adjacent front- and back-facing triangles, the shadow quad does not cancel out because both shadow volumes overlap. Hence, $k = 2$, which shows that also the last case coincides.

The question is how to formalize the notion of *canceling out* for more general configurations where many triangles meet at the same edge. To explain this further, let's first take a step back and revisit the case for two shadow-casting triangles. While moving along a shadow-volume counting ray (from the eye for z-pass or from infinity for z-fail), as mentioned, we maintain a counter that indicates the number of shadow volumes the ray is contained in. Now, two triangles cancel each other out if the ray's counter, when passing through the shadow-volume quad, does not change. In the same way, for many triangles, we will be interested only in the change of the counter when passing through the edge's shadow-volume quad. This change is exactly the number k mentioned above. If $k = 0$, the shadow-volume quad is unnecessary and can be ignored.

Principle. The main structure of the algorithm follows.

1. Create a list of all edges with their adjacent triangles. Each edge in the list also stores its adjacent triangles.

2. To render the shadow-volume quads, loop through the edge list and for each edge

   - compute the number, k, of noncanceling quads—for each adjacent triangle, modify k depending on whether a quad from that triangle edge would inc or dec;

   - output a shadow-volume quad that incs/decs by k; no quad is output if $k = 0$.

Creating the triangle-connectivity list for each edge is similar to most previous silhouette-edge extraction approaches, but the list does not need to assume any edge direction and can have more than two connected triangles. That is, edges with the same vertices are considered identical, no matter the vertex order.

Implementation. The edge list is preferably generated in a preprocessing step, where each edge stores two vertices (indices or coordinates).

For reasons of compactness and also for avoiding random memory accesses with pointers,[8] the adjacent-triangle information is preferably stored as the triangle's plane equation and one boolean indicating if the triangle edge's vertex order is the same as the vertex order of the edge in the list. For every edge belonging to the triangle, the exact same plane equation must be used for robustness (and the assembler instructions should be identical for each computation per edge when using the plane equation, to avoid internal rounding differences). Otherwise, there is a risk that the computations will result in inconsistency for the triangle facing between the three edges. As long as this consistency is guaranteed, the algorithm will robustly cope with both limited precision and degenerate triangles.

If the geometry shader is fed the list of edges, one by one, it can easily handle both the computation of k and the generation of a quad when the value ends up nonzero. In the fragment shader, determine eye-facing order for the shadow-volume quad (e.g., by using the boolean `gl_FrontFacing` in OpenGL), in order to decide whether to inc or dec with the signed k. The quad should be generated with a vertex order corresponding to the right-hand rule (i.e., the same rule that we used for computing the plane equations of all triangles). That is, the quad's vertices should be in the order $(\mathbf{v}_1, \mathbf{v}_0, \mathbf{v}_2, \mathbf{v}_3)$, where $\mathbf{v}_2$ is the extrusion of vertex $\mathbf{v}_0$ and $\mathbf{v}_3$ the extrusion of $\mathbf{v}_1$. Since the geometry shader can only output triangle strips and not quads, we have to output $(\mathbf{v}_0, \mathbf{v}_2, \mathbf{v}_1, \mathbf{v}_3)$ in reality.

The reason the quad orientation becomes correct is because an explicit vertex order $\mathbf{v}_0, \mathbf{v}_1$ is stored per edge in the edge list. Furthermore, for each triangle, we then check how quads from the triangle's edges (which have a well-defined orientation) would affect the number of noncanceling quads k for quads generated

---

[8]This is particularly important on certain game consoles and, for example, when batching jobs on the SPUs of the PS3 with their 256-KB storage.

from the corresponding list edges. As just mentioned, these latter quads are always created with an orientation corresponding to a fixed vertex order. Therefore, no ambiguity exists.

Without loss of generality, we compute the plane equations $\mathbf{n}_{tri} \cdot \mathbf{x} + d_{tri} = 0$ for each triangle using the right-hand rule; that is,

$$\mathbf{n}_{tri} = (\mathbf{v}_1 - \mathbf{v}_0) \times (\mathbf{v}_2 - \mathbf{v}_0),$$
$$d_{tri} = -(\mathbf{v}_0 \cdot \mathbf{n}_{tri}).$$

Here is an example of the data structure for an edge:

```
struct Edge {
    v₀, v₁;
    // data for adjacent triangles:
    list of {(n_tri, d_tri), bool reversed_vertex_order},
        where reversed_vertex_order is true if the triangle edge's
        vertex order is (v₁, v₀) and false if it is (v₀, v₁).
}
```

In practice, it is rare that edges have more than two adjacent triangles, so for efficiency, such edges could be stored in a separate list. Thus, the main edge list can have a constant size, storing up to two triangles.

For every frame during the rendering, process the edge list as follows:

```
for each edge in list
    k = 0
    for each adjacent triangle
        1. Compute quad direction for the triangle's edge
        2. Update the counter k accordingly
    if k ≠ 0, output quad that incs/decs with signed k
```

More explicitly, this corresponds to the following simple code:

```
for each edge e
    k = 0
    for each adjacent triangle tri
        // Compute triangle facing with respect to the light source.
        s = sign(n_tri · light_position_xyz + d_tri) // sign of one 4-component dot product
        // This sign is dependent on the vertex order of the triangle used when
        // computing the triangle's plane equation (n_tri, d_tri). A light front-facing triangle
        // generates a quad with vertex order, i.e., orientation, consistent with the
        // triangle's vertex order. If the sign is negative, the vertex order should be reversed
        // for the triangle's generated quad, which is identical to inverting the inc/dec
        // term for the quad.
        // In addition, the term should be inverted if the triangle edge's vertex order
        // (when computing the plane equation) is opposite of edge e's vertex order.
        if (reversed_vertex_order)
            s = −s  // edge e's vertex order is opposite of the triangle edge's vertex order
        k += s
    if k ≠ 0, generate quad from edge and send the k-value to the fragment shader
```

Here is the fragment shader when rendering the shadow-volume quads:

if not gl_FrontFacing, then $k = -k$
output k

For the z-fail algorithm (see Section 2.4.4), we also need to create the near- and far-capping polygons. Then, for general nonclosed geometry, all triangles need to be used as both near caps and far caps, since the theory states that each triangle should give rise to a closed shadow volume. However, for watertight shadow casters, it is enough to use the front-facing triangles as near caps and the back-facing triangles as far caps, with an inc/dec factor of two instead.

For deformable objects (e.g., skinned characters), it can be convenient to store the information for edge-adjacent triangles as a vertex index per edge connectivity, instead of as the plane equation. This is more compact, even though extra information needs to be stored on which order to use the vertices when computing the plane equation. Again, the plane equation must be computed exactly the same way for each of the triangle's three edges, for full robustness. The situation we want to avoid is that the sign of the plane equation becomes different for the triangle's three edges, which otherwise could happen if the triangle is degenerate (a thin line) or is edge-on to the light source.

2.4.7   Advanced Improvements

We have seen how to produce robust and accurate hard shadows based on shadow volumes, but, unfortunately, the current approaches fall short when scenes are detailed and contain many polygons. The two bottlenecks are geometry processing to create the shadow volumes and also the fill rate because shadow volumes produce many pixels on the screen that update the stencil buffer. For this reason, shadow volumes were particularly popular at the time of the release of DOOM 3. For the first time, pixel shaders offered the possibility to simulate geometry details in form of normal maps, thereby enabling the use of very simple geometry that was, in turn, well suited for shadow-volume shadows. Nonetheless, today, typical game scenes are relatively complex, and, with tessellation becoming increasingly popular, shadow volumes are difficult to apply directly. In this section, we will briefly visit a couple of techniques that have been proposed to improve the speed of the stencil updates. For complex scenes, these strategies lead to a significant improvement. An overview is also given by Steiner [Steiner06].

Shadow Volumes and Level of Detail

The geometric overhead of shadow algorithms can generally be reduced by simplifying the geometry. Clark [Clark76] proposed to adapt shadow quality based on covered screen area. Still today, it is interesting to approximate the geometry that is used to cast shadows. For instance, the Spider-Man 3 game by Activision uses levels of detail (LODs) containing different amounts of geometry. Here, shadows were rendered using a coarser resolution than the geometric complexity of the original objects, thereby lowering the rendering cost of the shadow volumes. For shadow volumes from lower LODs, such a change of the shadow-casting geometry can produce shadows on the original geometry with visible artifacts.

In watertight scenes, there is a simple solution to avoid such unwanted shadows for different LODs. The idea is to not produce shadow volumes from the triangles that are front facing the light source but to rely solely on back-facing triangles as near capping. Thereby, the shadow volumes are no longer complete, but the missing part of the shadow volume lies inside the object itself. Hence, it can be useful to simply reverse the way light front- and back-facing triangles are extended for the near- and far-capping triangles of the shadow volumes [Zioma03]. It is less sensitive because the capping triangles do not need to correspond exactly to the original occluder geometry. The reason is that they no longer enclose the entire object but are only attached to the back faces. Hence, it becomes possible to rely on a different level of detail for the shadow-volume computation. This reversing trick is not fully robust but works well in many cases. One important observation is that the shading for triangles that are back facing the light source needs to produce the same color, regardless of whether the point that is shaded is inside or outside a shadow volume. Otherwise, shadow artifacts could occur on back faces. Using LODs has also been proposed by Govindaraju et al. [Govindaraju03]. In general, it is difficult to avoid artifacts in such cases, and the topic remains an area of future work.

Reducing the Geometric Overhead by Caster Culling

It is also useful to cull shadow casters completely according to whether they can influence the final rendering that will appear on the screen. Such an idea was also already presented in 1976 by Clark [Clark76], before the birth of the shadow-volume algorithm. Clark hierarchically culls shadow casters that themselves lie in shadow and restricts computations to visible parts of the scene. Instead, we will concentrate on useful methods particularly targeted for shadow volumes.

A significant cost comes from overlapping shadow volumes. Preferably, one would like to only draw the outer shadow-volume geometry and skip the parts of the volumes that are in shadow, since those are superfluous. Geometrically clipping the volumes against each other [Batagelo99, Vlachos02] is, however, not a viable option in real time. Instead, McCool [McCool00] examines extracting the shadow silhouette edges from a shadow map and constructs the shadow-volume quads from these. This means that only a parity bit instead of a sum is needed in the stencil buffer (we are either in a shadow volume or not). The disadvantages are that the shadow-volume quads are numerous, and it remains unclear how to better approximate the shape. Creating a volume per pixel leads basically to a shadow-map equivalent and the potential advantage of geometric shadow boundaries vanishes.

Lloyd et al.'s CC Shadow Volumes [Lloyd04] provide a more modern solution to reduce rendering costs by shadow-caster culling, based on the earlier work for geometric shadow generation by Govindaraju et al. [Govindaraju03]. They remove those casters that are located completely in shadow or whose shadows are not visible to the eye. Furthermore, shadows that do not influence visible shadow receivers are culled as well. The tests are usually based on a shadow depth map from the light's view. In addition, the shadow receivers are rendered (still from the light's view) to the stencil buffer and set the stencil value whenever their depth test fails. The stencil buffer then reflects those pixels of the shadow map where shadowed regions of the scene may occur. In other words, if the stencil buffer is not set, any shadow volume created above those pixels wastes resources, as it will never shadow any receiver.

The so-created depth and stencil maps (*depth/stencil map* hereafter) can then be used to cull casters. In order to test whether a shadow caster can be ignored, one can use occlusion queries that allow us to count the number of pixels that are drawn on the screen during rendering. We deactivate depth writing, and for each caster, we render its bounding box from the viewpoint of the light into the shadow map while relying on the depth and stencil test (where the stencil test fails for set values). The use of a bounding box is a conservative choice that avoids having to treat the entire geometry of the caster. Via the occlusion-query counting mechanism, we can recover the number of pixels that passed the test. If this pixel count turns out to be zero, the shadow caster is either itself in shadow (the depth test fails) or does not influence any visible shadow receiver (the stencil test fails). In this case, the caster's shadow volumes can safely be ignored.

A more recent approach [Stich07], used by Mental Images, exploits a scene organization in the form of a bounding-volume hierarchy to reduce the shadow-volume cost. Building such a scene hierarchy can typically be done rapidly even for dynamic scenes. Organizing data in such a way is useful in general, as large sets of objects (nodes in the tree) can potentially be culled quickly before descending to each individual object. Instead of culling shadow casters in light space, the algorithm simply performs an occlusion query in eye space. This is done by rendering the shadow volume of an axis-aligned bounding box of a potential shadow-casting node in the tree. If this shadow volume is not visible, it means that any shadow cast by an object inside the node cannot be visible. Thus, the rendering of shadow volumes for any of the objects in the node and its subtree can safely be skipped.

View-sample–based caster culling.   The idea of using the stencil buffer to test for shadowed receivers can be further extended. Instead of using the stencil buffer to test for the presence of shadow receivers, one can try to actually use only casters that have an impact on the view samples—after all, these are the only locations in space for which we need to compute a shadow.

One simple optimization during the depth/stencil-mask creation is to set the stencil mask only when the corresponding pixels also fall into the view frustum.

The easiest solution to perform this operation is to first render the scene from the light once to produce the depth values and then render the scene again from the light to initiate the stencil values. During the second render pass, one only draws pixels that fail the depth test and compute their projection in the view frustum via the vertex shader. This position is then passed to the fragment shader in the form of texture coordinates. Here, looking at the texture coordinates allows us (like for shadow mapping, the x, y-coordinates need to lie inside $[-1, 1]^2$) to determine whether the pixel actually projects inside the frustum. If not, it is simply culled.

To push this idea further, Décoret proposed the litmap approach [Décoret05]. Here, the algorithm first applies a rendering from the viewpoint to recover a depth buffer D_v. While rendering casters into the depth/stencil mask, each fragment is tested for containment in the view frustum but also against D_v to eliminate all pixels that are hidden from the current view. Intuitively, this enables us to limit all geometry that is rendered into the depth/stencil mask, to also be visible from the eye. Consequently, if we now query casters against this new mask, only those that affect the current view are kept. This optimization leads to a substantial reduction in geometric complexity.

Max culling. A final improvement, which is slightly more involved, is to keep the maximum depth value for each pixel in the depth/stencil mask. In this case, we can test if a caster is even farther away from the light than the visible scene, which implies that the caster cannot project a shadow on the visible scene. Imagine, for example, a game where the player is on one floor of a building and the tested casters are on the floor below. Without storing the maximum depth value, one would not be able to detect that the caster is on the floor below.

Instead of rendering the actual casters or their several-pixels-spanning bounding boxes, Décoret [Décoret05] points out that simple point queries suffice when relying on a so-called N-buffer constructed from the depth map. For each given caster bounding box $\mathcal{B}$, this structure allows him to determine the maximum depth value (and potentially also stencil value) of an axis-aligned bounding quad that contains the projection of $\mathcal{B}$ into the depth/stencil map with a single texture look-up. The so-derived maximum depth is a conservative value that, if the caster's bounding box is farther away, can be used to safely cull the caster geometry. The construction and functioning of N-buffers is described precisely in Appendix D.

Improving Fill Rate

A relatively straightforward solution to reduce fill rate is to downsample the screen buffer, for example, by a factor of two in both the x- and y-directions. The shadow volumes are then computed there, and finally the bufffer is upsampled again [Röttger02]. Röttger et al. show that lowering the resolution to one-fourth provides a roughly four-times speedup. Nonetheless, the resulting shadows can exhibit artifacts for detailed scenes, and one of the major benefits of shadow volumes, the accuracy, is reduced. Instead, there are solutions to reduce the fill rate without compromising quality.

Light attenuation. One interesting case is to improve fill rate when there is a light falloff. As we have seen in Chapter 1, the further the light is from the impact point, the more energy is lost. In this chapter, we have so far assumed that the falloff is negligible. In practice, it can make sense to limit the distance that light is emitted in the scene. Often, a quadratic falloff is used (e.g., $1/d^2$, where d is the distance to the light). Such distance attenuation can easily be added to the fragment shader when performing the final shadow-volume pass exploiting the stencil-buffer counters. The important observation is that the energy of the source can become very weak, even weak enough that we can ultimately clamp away its contribution; that is, if its influence on the view samples falls below the smallest displayable gray difference, all farther pixels would appear black anyway.

To exploit this situation, one can make use of the scissor test, which in OpenGL is controlled by the glScissor(x, y, w, h) command [Lengyel02, McGuire03]. This operation restricts all pixel outputs to a window positioned at pixel (x, y) with size $w \times h$. It is therefore possible to restrict the shadow-volume rendering to a small area on the screen. To apply this feature for shadow volumes, we first compute a bounding sphere around the light that contains all points in space that, if unshaded, still receive a noticeable light energy. Next, we can project this sphere in the current view and bound it by a rectangle that is used for the scissor test. Consequently, updates during the shadow-volume stencil pass will only be applied to the restricted set of pixels.

One observation is that this optimization only considers restrictions in the image plane of the view. The fact that depth is excluded can lead to stencil computations in view samples that are contained in the scissor window but actually not in the three-dimensional bounding sphere around the light. To remedy this situation, another extension was proposed [Everitt03, McGuire04a] that adds depth bounds along the z-direction of the camera. In this way, many view samples not contained in the bounding sphere can be ignored because their depth is outside the range defined by the depth bounds. This is controlled by glDepthBounds(zMin, zMax) of the GL_EXT_depth_bounds_test extension.

In general, attenuated sources can facilitate computations in the case of shadow maps, as well as shadow volumes. Casters that are too distant from the light can simply be ignored and the proposed LOD strategies merge nicely with such setups as well.

Clamping. For lights without falloff, other solutions need to be applied. In addition to using culling (see above), Lloyd et al.'s CC Shadow Volumes [Lloyd04] also use clamping of the shadow volumes to avoid unnecessary rasterization. The idea is to cut each shadow volume along its extrusion into parts, as shown in Figure 2.19. All parts of the volume that do not englobe scene geometry can be eliminated and do not need to be rasterized. The key is to reduce the fill rate by drawing only

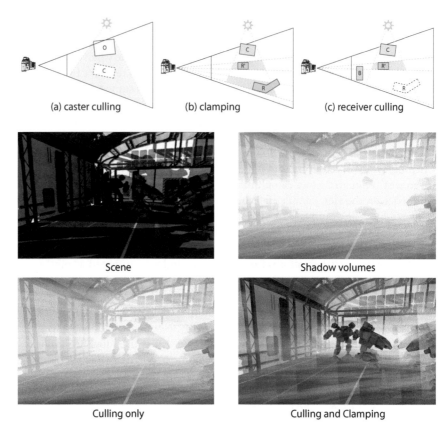

Figure 2.19. Top: The principle of shadow volume culling and clamping. (a) Shadow caster C is fully in the shadow of O so its shadow volume can be culled. (b) The shadow volume for C needs only to extend through regions containing shadow receivers. (c) If a shadow receiver R is not visible from the viewpoint, the shadow volume for C does not need to be rendered around it. Bottom: Images showing the overdraw from standard shadow volumes versus shadow volumes with culling and clamping (courtesy of Lloyd et al. [Lloyd04]).

parts of the shadow volume. Care has to be taken that these parts are still consistent with the shadow-volume algorithm, meaning that for a given eye ray, it either pierces no shadow volume or it passes through two of its quads, thereby leaving the main method intact. This creates a natural trade-off between geometric complexity (many shadow-volume parts) and fill rate (avoidance of rasterizing in empty space). Lloyd et al. present two different clamping methods that could be used in combination.

The first proposition is called continuous shadow clamping, where shadow volumes are clamped using axis-aligned bounding boxes (AABBs) around the shadow

receivers to achieve clamped shadow volumes only around the regions of interest. This is done as follows. For each shadow caster, the list of potential shadow
receivers are found by testing all receivers' AABBs against the caster's AABB for
overlap in light-projection space. The depth range (min and max z from the light
source) of the identified potential receivers is used to clamp that caster's shadow
volume to this z-min and z-max extrusion-range only. Thus, rasterization for a
large part of the shadow volume that does not cover any receiver in eye space could
potentially be avoided.

The second suggestion is called discrete shadow clamping and clamps the
shadow volumes to intervals defined by slicing planes that divide the rendered image into bands. Shadow-volume parts are then defined according to these bands
(Figure 2.19(b)). The bands in image space are usually oriented such that they are
as orthogonal to the projected light direction as possible. Each band boundary
represents a slicing plane in three dimensions that passes through the viewpoint
(simply imagine that a line in image space is extended in depth).

According to this setup, the scene is rendered multiple times from the light,
every time using two slicing planes, hence, representing a band in the view against
which geometry is clipped. The rationale behind it is that potential receivers are
only rendered if they fall within the two delimiting planes. The resulting query
image Q is binary and contains black pixels where no receiver is present and white
pixels where a receiver fell in the range between the two planes.

We test casters against this representation in order to decide whether the corresponding shadow-volume part can be eliminated. Whenever no receiver can be
found, it is possible to ignore the shadow-volume part, thereby reducing the fill
rate. To this extent, we need to test whether the caster covers any receiver pixel.
Consequently, we can render the caster in the light's view and discard all its fragments that do not lie above the lower slicing plane, as well as those that do not

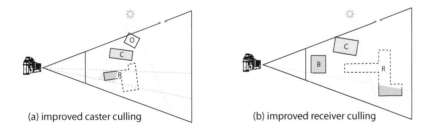

(a) improved caster culling   (b) improved receiver culling

Figure 2.20. Cases that benefit from pixel-accurate culling. (a) Instead of just culling the
shadow volume of C around the whole receiver R, the shadow volume can be clamped even
tighter, since a part of R (the one dashed) is actually shadowed by another caster O. (b) A
receiver R that is visible by the observer but cannot actually receive shadows, which also can
be accounted for with pixel-accurate culling.

cover any white pixel in Q. If no fragments are output (tested with an occlusion query together with, for instance, a stencil test for allowing rendering only to white pixels in Q), the shadow-volume part can be clamped.

This clamping was improved upon by Eisemann and Décoret [Eisemann06a]. Instead of rasterizing the entire scene multiple times, once for each slice, they use a single-pass voxelization technique to derive the layers (presented in Chapter 8.2.2). Further, they voxelize the geometry visible from the viewpoint again, in the same way as for the previously explained caster culling (see Figure 2.20).

Split shadow volumes. An interesting observation is that one should actually aim at a general reduction of the number of stencil updates, which motivated split shadow volumes [Laine05a]. The algorithm is based on the fact that from one object to the next, one can toggle between z-fail and z-pass if we assure that the stencil buffer is modified in a coherent way. For z-fail, only shadow-volume fragments that fall behind view samples will lead to a stencil update, whereas for z-pass it is the other way around. Therefore, the choice of z-fail and z-pass is based on which one is likely to be the fastest (see Figure 2.21). In addition, the per-object toggle can be decided on a per-pixel basis. It is an attractive idea, but in practice, since we still lack hardware support, it is currently not efficient.

We will now explain the idea of the algorithm. Let's for the moment assume one single shadow volume. The stencil operations are set such that if one side of the shadow volume lies in front and the other behind the view sample $\mathbf{p}$, both methods (z-fail and z-pass) will result in a stencil buffer containing the value one. In other words, z-pass should increment the stencil for the visible front-facing quads and z-fail should increment for invisible back-facing quads. If the shadow volume lies entirely in front or entirely behind $\mathbf{p}$, both (z-fail and z-pass) lead to a value of zero in the stencil buffer.

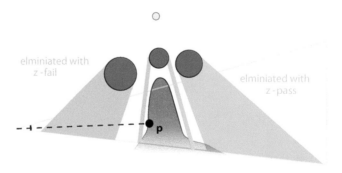

Figure 2.21. Split shadow volume: the idea is to select z-pass or z-fail on a per-pixel basis, depending on which method is likely the most efficient, that is, culls the most shadow-volume fragments during the rasterization.

Using early z-culling, it is possible to reduce unnecessary stencil updates. The observation is that for z-fail, the stencil buffer is modified solely by fragments that lie behind $\mathbf{p}$, whereas for z-pass, the stencil buffer is modified only if fragments are in front of $\mathbf{p}$. Therefore, the better choice of the two options is the one that is more likely to not perform any update for a given object, which means that z-fail should be chosen if it is more likely that the entire volume lies in front of $\mathbf{p}$. In the opposite case, z-pass should be used.

To select an appropriate strategy, an additional value z_{split} is computed per pixel and object. Laine defines two ways to do this, but basically, they just aim at drawing a quad that approximately splits the shadow volume. This quad defines a barrier that toggles between the two methods. Based on the depth of z_{split} and the depth of $\mathbf{p}$, a per-pixel choice is made. If $\mathbf{p}$ is closer than z_{split}, the volume is likely to be behind $\mathbf{p}$, and thus, z-pass is chosen (eliminating all fragments behind $\mathbf{p}$). In the opposite case, z-fail is used.

Of course, one would not gain much if z_{split} was rasterized at full view resolution because then each object would draw one supplementary quad, leading to an again increased fill rate. But because the z_{split} values have no influence on the correctness of the result, only on performance, it is possible to render them in a much lower resolution buffer—optimally one whose resolution matches the highest level in the hierarchical z-buffer [Greene93] to ensure the best early culling behavior.

Hybrid of shadow maps and shadow volumes. It is interesting to see that depth maps (which are similar to shadow maps) can be used to accelerate shadow volumes. Nonetheless, they all made explicit use of the shadow-volume geometry to reduce the fill rate. In this last example, we will present an algorithm to reduce the fill rate by implicitly detecting shadow discontinuities in the image that are only locally corrected by shadow volumes in the form of an image-based solution.

Chan and Durand [Chan04] suggested having two shadow passes. They first apply a shadow-mapping algorithm. Here, all shadows can exhibit zigzaggy boundaries, but they use the shadow map to mark and detect shadow boundaries. These correspond to discontinuities of the shadow test. In other words, for a given view sample, we not only compare the depth to its corresponding texel in the shadow map but also to the surrounding depth values. If the depth tests do not all agree, the pixel is considered to lie on a shadow boundary. Only those marked pixels will be updated during the following shadow-volume pass. They set the depth buffer such that it blocks all fragments outside the marked region and then apply the shadow-volume algorithm. Because graphics hardware typically employs a hierarchical z-test, the hardware quickly discards large areas of fragments, thereby rendering the shadow-volume algorithm much more efficient.

A variant of this solution has been presented by Aila and Akenine-Möller [Aila04a] who compute intersections of the shadow volumes with 8×8 pixel tiles and mark boundary tiles. Each tile that is not on a boundary lies entirely in the volume, and they can restrict the shadow computations to a single pixel per tile. On the contrary, for boundary tiles, all per-pixel computations are performed. The solution is accurate. The algorithm, however, requires hardware modifications in order to be efficient. If these additions could be included, the main drawbacks of shadow volumes would be gone (i.e., the high fill rate demand). Without the hardware modification, the algorithm is generally considered too costly, and thus, it has not been much exploited.

2.5   Transparency

An aspect that we have overlooked so far is shadows from transparent objects, including situations when using texture masks with no/full transparency or semitransparent textures. The shadow maps automatically handle alpha-textured geometry where the alpha is either zero or one, as long as fragments with alpha equal to zero are simply discarded from rendering into the shadow map. In order to handle multiple layers of semitransparent textures, a solution with layered shadow maps could be explored.

For shadow volumes, Hasselgren and Akenine-Möller [Hasselgren07] have presented a solution that handles semitransparent textures (and thereby also texture masks). However, it requires an extra render pass where the shadow volumes need to be rendered one by one per semitransparent triangle. This could be very costly and prohibit real-time performance if there are many thousands of such semitransparent triangles in the current scene. On the other hand, there are several common situations where there are only a few semitransparent textured polygons in the scene, such as a textured glass window of a church, making this method work great.

Kim et al. [Kim08] note that if individual objects in the scene have constant color and transparency, then shadows from these objects can be rendered with the shadow volume algorithm by modifying the stencil incrementation/decrementation from plus/minus one to multiplication/division by the transparency of the object, respectively. For reasons of numerical precision, this is preferably implemented by incrementing/decrementing a floating-point buffer by $\log(1-\alpha)$, where α is the object's opacity, and then by using the exponential of the resulting buffer. Nevertheless, if there are transparent shadow receivers in the scene, then it might be necessary to check more than one shadow-receiving point per screen pixel. This is not doable with a standard framebuffer that can only store one depth value per pixel. Self-shadowing for the transparent objects thus can be problematic.

More information about transparency can be found in Chapter 8.

2.6   Summary

When choosing a shadow algorithm and trying to decide whether shadow maps or shadow volumes is the better choice, there are the following general characteristics to consider. Shadow maps are generally faster. The cost is roughly the same as the cost involved in rendering the image for the viewpoint. Shadow maps can also generate shadows from any rasterizable geometry, in contrast to shadow volumes, where the shadow-casting geometry should be polygonal in order to be able to extract silhouette edges. The downsides of shadow maps are the biasing issues, under-sampling artifacts in the form of jagged shadow edges, and the limitation to a single frustum, so that omnidirectional lights typically require six shadow maps. Shadow volumes, on the other hand, produce perfectly sharp shadows but are considered slow. They require three render passes, but more severely, the elongated quads of the shadow volumes cause a high fill rate. In addition, extracting silhouette edges has for a long time been considered expensive, although that should no longer apply for the GPU-accelerated versions.

CHAPTER 3
Shadow-Map Aliasing

Even though shadow algorithms have been around for almost as long as computer graphics itself, robust and efficient hard-shadow generation is still not a solved problem. While geometry-based algorithms produce pixel-perfect results, they suffer from robustness problems with different viewer–light configurations and are often slow due to the enormous overdraw involved in rasterizing shadow volumes.

Shadow-map algorithms, on the other hand, are very fast as their complexity is similar to standard scene rendering, but they suffer from aliasing artifacts since the sampling of the shadow map and the sampling of the image pixels projected into the shadow map usually do not match up. In this chapter, we will analyze aliasing in more detail. We first show the different components of aliasing in a signal-reconstruction framework (Section 3.1) and then go into more detail on the principal aliasing components, *initial sampling error* (Section 3.2) and *resampling error* (Section 3.3).

3.1   Shadow Mapping as Signal Reconstruction

It is instructive to view shadow mapping as a signal reconstruction process similar to texture mapping, but with a texture that is also sampled from the scene.[1]

---

[1] A good introduction to signal reconstruction in the context of computer graphics can be found in Wolberg's book [Wolberg94] or, more extensively, in Glassner's basic textbook [Glassner94]. One of the best treatises on resampling for texture mapping in particular is still Heckbert's Master's thesis [Heckbert89].

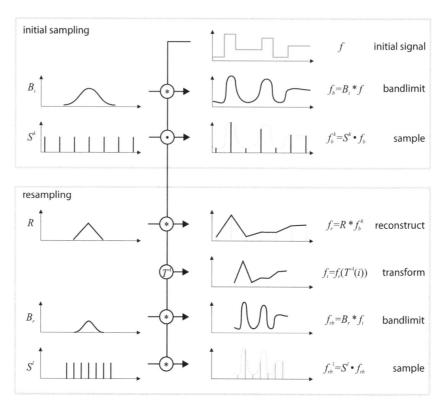

Figure 3.1. A continuous input signal is initially sampled (top) and then resampled (bottom) for a particular output resolution after a transformation.

Signal-Reconstruction Pipeline

The signal-reconstruction pipeline starts with an original (continuous) signal $f(s)$. Here, for easier illustration, $f(s)$ is a function in one parameter, for example, a one-dimensional image. The goal is to first store this signal in a discrete (sampled) form and then to allow resampling the signal at different output resolutions. This pipeline has the following steps (see also Figure 3.1):

1. *Initial sampling.* This consists of two steps, which in practice are usually combined:

   (a) *Bandlimit* the original signal to remove frequencies higher than half the sampling frequency in order to avoid aliasing, using an initial band-limiting filter B_i: $f_b = B_i \star f$, where $\star$ is the convolution operator.

   (b) *Initially sample* the signal f_b, for example, by taking a picture with a digital camera or by rendering a snapshot of a scene. Note that in the former case, B_i is basically integrated in the optics and response function of the camera chip, while in the latter case, B_i is usually approximated by multisampling. Sampling multiplies the continuous signal with an impulse train S^k with frequency ω_k, so this step gives samples $f_b^k = S^k \cdot f_b(s)$.

2. *Resampling.* Here the sampled signal (texture, image) is resampled for a particular output resolution, also accounting for a transformation of the signal.

    (a) *Reconstruct* (or interpolate) the signal from its sampled representation to give $f_r(s)$ using a reconstruction filter R. In texture mapping, this is usually done with *bilinear filtering.*

    (b) *Transform* the signal into the output domain: $f_t(i) = f_r(T^{-1}(i))$. The transformation is one reason for changes in sampling frequency.

    (c) *Bandlimit* the reconstructed, transformed signal with a bandlimiting filter B_r so that frequencies higher than the output resolution are removed. The number of initial samples that need to be integrated can be found by back-transforming the filter footprint, which is often two to three image pixels wide in practice, into the original signal domain. Therefore, both the output sample spacing as well as the transformation applied at the image pixel strongly influence the filter width. Since the back-transformed filter footprint can become very large, especially under perspective transformations, the bandlimiting step is usually precomputed using *mipmapping.* This step gives $f_{r_b}(i) = B_r \star f_t$.

    (d) *Resample* the reconstructed signal at the final pixel positions: $f_{r_b}^l = S^l \cdot f_{r_b}$.

Note that in practice, reconstruction and bandlimit filters do not re-create a full continuous signal but are only evaluated for the final desired sampling positions.

What Is a Good Initial Sampling Rate?

While this pipeline assumes a given initial sampling rate ω_k, for shadow mapping (and for any image-based rendering technique) ω_k can be adapted. Therefore, the question arises what is the optimal choice for ω_k in step 1(b). For this, we consider our output sampling rate ω_l, which determines the maximum frequency that can be represented in screen space. We know that the ideal screen-space shadow signal $f(T^{-1}(i))$ has infinite frequencies, so this signal has a frequency content that certainly surpasses ω_l. We thus view the shadow map as a sampling of this signal that should at least accurately reconstruct frequencies up to ω_l. In shadow-map space, this transforms to $\omega_k = (dT^{-1}/di)\omega_l$. This means that to represent the maximum

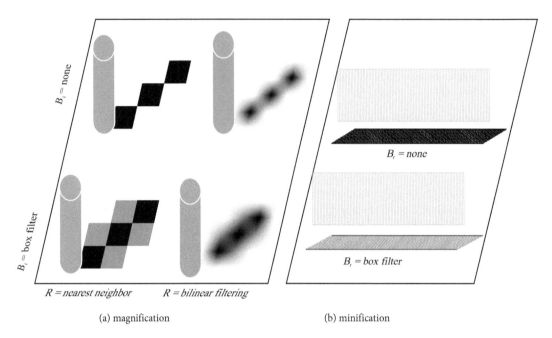

(a) magnification   (b) minification

Figure 3.2. Examples of combinations of different sampling errors. (a) The left part shows shadows from a strongly magnified shadow map, which makes the pixel structure apparent. Strong reconstruction error appears for nearest-neighbor reconstruction compared to bilinear filtering. Initial sample aliasing (absence of B_i) cannot be avoided for standard shadow mapping; remedies will be discussed in later chapters, and results using a box filter for B_i are shown in this image. (b) The right part shows the shadow of a high-frequency fence. Omitting the bandlimiting step when resampling the strongly minified shadow map leads to resampling aliasing, while even a simple box filter alleviates the situation.

detail allowed by the screen resolution, the shadow-map sampling rate ω_k should correspond to the screen sampling rate ω_l, multiplied by a scale factor given by the transformation between the two spaces.

Errors and Typical Remedies in Signal Reconstruction

Errors can occur at several stages in the signal-processing pipeline. They can be attributed to insufficient *sampling* (step 1(b)), missing or insufficient *bandlimiting* (steps 1(a) and 2(c)), and insufficient *reconstruction* (step 2(a)). Errors in band-limiting lead to so-called *aliasing*, which occurs when higher frequencies "alias" as lower frequencies due to a sampling process. Errors in reconstruction lead to a pixelated appearance, especially under magnification. Let us discuss the different errors in more detail (see also Figure 3.2):

1. Initial sampling errors

   (a) *Initial sample aliasing.* In general, geometric structures projected to an image plane have unlimited frequencies and therefore require a band-limiting filter to avoid aliasing. The major aliasing artifact from the initial sampling phase are staircase artifacts. In texture mapping, the original texture could be generated from a photograph (which includes a bandlimiting filter already in the digital camera) or from a camera rendering with supersampling. Shadow mapping, on the other hand, samples depth values, which cannot be filtered in this stage.

   (b) *Undersampling.* This is by far the most plaguing problem for shadow mapping. We call undersampling the problem where the initial sampling frequency is lower than the final screen sampling frequency (i.e., after resampling). This means that details in the original signal (like thin structures) can be lost completely. Most importantly, undersampling magnifies initial sampling aliasing, so that the pixel structure of the shadow map will be visible as oversized staircase artifacts in the final image. On the other hand, if initial sample aliasing has been removed using a bandlimiting filter, undersampling will lead to overly blurry edges.

2. Resampling errors

   (a) *Reconstruction error.* This is typically due to an inappropriate reconstruction filter like nearest-neighbor sampling. Reconstruction error is visible either as pixel-flickering artifacts under motion or by showing obvious texel outlines under magnification. This error is typically reduced by employing bilinear filtering in graphics hardware, which again is not trivially possible in the case of shadow mapping. However, even proper reconstruction can make up for neither missing detail from the initial sampling phase nor initial sampling aliasing. In particular, the latter will be visible as blurred staircases, even for an ideal reconstruction filter.

   (b) *Resampling aliasing.* This happens when, after projection onto receiver geometry and to the viewer camera, the frequency of the shadow-map samples (and of the represented signal!) is higher than the pixel frequency in the output image. This occurs, for example, when a high-frequency structure like a fence has been captured with sufficient accuracy in a shadow map, but the resulting shadow is in a distant area of the screen. The same problem occurs for standard texture mapping in the minification case and is usually solved using a bandlimiting filter precomputed in a mipmap pyramid. Again, it is not possible to apply such a filter to a standard shadow map because the shadow-map comparison function depends on the fragment depth value, which cannot be incorporated in the filter.

Shadow Mapping and Signal Reconstruction

In shadow mapping, we deal with functions in two parameters, that is, $f(\mathbf{t})$ for texture coordinates $\mathbf{t} = (s, t)$. Furthermore, the shadow signal depends on another parameter, the reference depth $\tilde{z}$: $f(\mathbf{t}, \tilde{z}) = s(z(\mathbf{t}), \tilde{z})$, where the shadow-comparison function s returns zero if a view sample is in shadow and one otherwise. Maybe the easiest way to think about shadow mapping as a signal-reconstruction process is to consider the function $f_0(\mathbf{t}) = s(z(\mathbf{t}), \tilde{z}_0)$ for some fixed reference depth $\tilde{z}_0$ (i.e., the shadow projected to some fixed plane parallel to the shadow map).

There are two main differences between standard signal processing, like texture mapping, and shadow mapping: First, shadow mapping allows more control over the initial sampling phase. Second, the shadow signal cannot be filtered before evaluation because it depends on the depth value where it is evaluated.

Regarding the first point, it should be noted that changing the initial sampling influences all types of error, and thus, most publications on shadow mapping take this approach. In Section 3.2, we will therefore discuss initial sampling error in more detail. In Chapter 4, we will discuss several ways to influence the initial sampling phase to obtain a better sampling.

The second point has an impact on resampling because neither reconstruction nor bandlimiting can be done using standard texture-mapping methods. The reasons for this will be elaborated in Section 3.3, while several methods to overcome the problem are the topic of Chapter 5.

Another error that needs to be taken into account in all shadow-map approaches is temporal aliasing, which will be especially apparent for nonoptimal reconstruction if undersampling occurs. This manifests itself in flickering artifacts if the rasterization of the shadow map changes each frame.

View-Sample Mapping

The signal-reconstruction pipeline is valid for most shadow-mapping algorithms. However, some algorithms find the exact sampling locations in light space and do not perform any resampling (Section 4.5). These methods are, therefore, unaffected by resampling errors and undersampling. They are, however, still prone to initial sample aliasing as the infinitely high frequencies of a shadow transition lead to staircase artifacts and missed shadow detail. Therefore, even view-sample mapping methods require a bandlimiting step. Since the shadow boundaries are not available when only individual samples are evaluated, exact bandlimiting (i.e., prefiltering) is not possible, but supersampling can be achieved.

It should be noted that in this section and in Chapter 4, we use the term *aliasing* analogously to undersampling and ignore the required initial bandlimiting filter, as this is most consistent with the prominent shadow literature. However, as discussed in the previous section, one should keep in mind that even an image with no undersampling at all will show aliasing at the pixel level if no initial bandlimiting filter is used, since the edges in the shadow map exhibit infinitely high frequencies. Conversely, an initial bandlimiting filter could remove aliasing completely even if strong undersampling occurs, resulting in a very blurred (but not aliased) image.

3.2 Initial Sampling Error—Undersampling

In this section, we will deal with the issue of undersampling, that is, when the initial sampling frequency of the shadow-map samples—when projected to the screen— is lower than the screen-space sampling frequency.

3.2.1 Definition of Sampling Error

At the root of most algorithms to reduce shadow-map sampling errors is an analysis of the distribution of sampling errors in a scene.

Coordinate Systems

We assume the shadow map is given in (s, t) coordinates in the range $[0, 1] \times [0, 1]$. Furthermore, we parametrize pixels in the camera image as $\mathbf{p} = (i, j)$, likewise in the range $[0, 1] \times [0, 1]$. The shadow map has a resolution of $r_s \times r_t$ texels, and the viewport has a resolution of $r_i \times r_j$ pixels. A lookup into the shadow map is an evaluation of a mapping

$$\begin{pmatrix} s \\ t \end{pmatrix} = \mathbf{T}^{-1}(i, j, z) = \begin{pmatrix} s(i, j, z) \\ t(i, j, z) \end{pmatrix}, \tag{3.1}$$

where z is the eye-space z-coordinate of the geometry visible in a pixel (see Figure 3.3). Furthermore, to simplify notation, we use a left-handed coordinate system for this section and Chapter 4 (i.e., the viewer looks down the *positive z-axis*). Thus, the orthogonal eye-space distance of a point to the viewpoint corresponds to its eye-space z-value.

Exact Sampling Error Using the Jacobian

The sampling error is characterized by the Jacobian of the reverse mapping. The Jacobian matrix is made up of the partial derivatives of a given mapping and is thus the linear approximation of the mapping. Its column vectors can also be interpreted as the tangent vectors of the mapping, so in this case, the column vectors

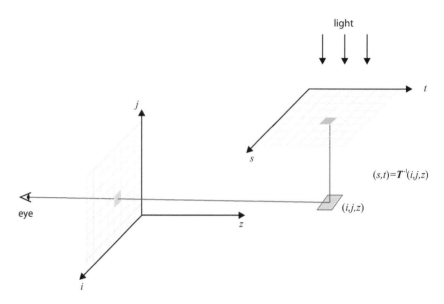

Figure 3.3. Coordinates used in the sampling-error analysis. Note that T need not be a linear transform but can incorporate any (invertible) reparametrization of the shadow map.

define the extents of a shadow-map texel projected to screen space. In order to take the actual shadow-map and screen resolutions into account, the entries are also scaled with the respective resolutions:

$$\begin{pmatrix} i \\ j \end{pmatrix} = \begin{pmatrix} \frac{r_i \partial i}{r_s \partial s} & \frac{r_i \partial i}{r_t \partial t} \\ \frac{r_j \partial j}{r_s \partial s} & \frac{r_j \partial j}{r_t \partial t} \end{pmatrix} \begin{pmatrix} s \\ t \end{pmatrix}. \tag{3.2}$$

Note that the entries of the matrix also depend on z. While it is hard to make general observations about sampling error using this exact formulation, it is actually very convenient for analyzing a particular frame in a practical application. The partial derivatives are readily available in the fragment shader using the dFdx and dFdy instructions, defined as

$$dFdx = \begin{pmatrix} \frac{\partial s}{r_i \partial i} \\ \frac{\partial t}{r_i \partial i} \end{pmatrix}, \quad dFdy = \begin{pmatrix} \frac{\partial s}{r_j \partial j} \\ \frac{\partial t}{r_j \partial j} \end{pmatrix}, \tag{3.3}$$

and can be used to visualize sampling error through color coding.

In a full three-dimensional setting, to get a scalar value for the sampling error, a suitable norm has to be chosen to evaluate the Jacobian. Similar to mipmapping, the length of the longer of the two column vectors could be used, which would ensure that no side of the projected texel footprint is longer than a pixel.

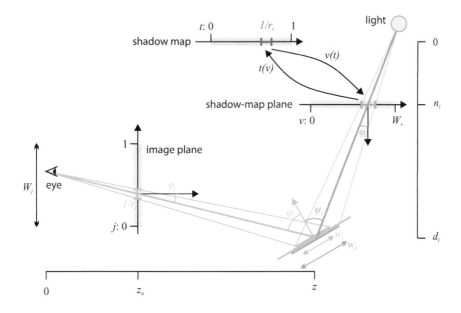

Figure 3.4. The terms used in the geometric interpretation of undersampling.

3.2.2   Geometric Interpretation

While the exact error formulation using the Jacobian is convenient for individual pixels, our goal is to analyze undersampling over the whole view frustum. Later, this analysis will be used to find better parametrizations that reduce undersampling.

To understand aliasing geometrically, it is helpful to think about the beams created by shadow-map texels and image pixels. In the following, we will assume that the shadow-map t-direction is aligned with the view-space z-direction, and s is aligned with x. We thus ignore the off-diagonal elements of the Jacobian and, in the following, concentrate on the error in the two shadow-map axes, which we call m_t and m_s:

$$m_t = \frac{r_j \partial j}{r_t \partial t}, \quad m_s = \frac{r_i \partial i}{r_s \partial s}.$$

(3.4)

The partial derivatives scaled by the respective resolutions describe the ratio of pixel and texel sizes. This ratio can also be expressed by the ratio of the beam widths of an eye beam and a light beam projected on a particular surface element (Figure 3.4 shows how the terms used in the following equations fit together). Let us start by constructing the eye beam in j-direction, with width w_j:

$$w_j = \frac{W_j}{r_j} \frac{z}{z_n} \frac{\cos \varphi_j}{\cos \psi_j}. \tag{3.5}$$

The variable W_j is the height of the viewport in world space, so that W_j/r_j represents the size of a pixel in world space; z is the eye-space z-coordinate (in a left-handed coordinate system); φ_j is the angle between the view direction and the direction of the pixel at location j. This corrects for pixel beams getting thinner (when measured orthogonally to the beam direction) towards the border of the view frustum. Finally, ψ_j is the angle between the beam direction and the surface normal. Note that this term is the only term that depends on the orientation of the surface element. Similarly, we measure the width w_i of the eye beam in i-direction:

$$w_i = \frac{W_i}{r_i} \frac{z}{z_n}. \tag{3.6}$$

This analysis is somewhat simplified because we assume in Figure 3.4 that the j-direction and t-axis lie in the same plane (the plane defined by the "paper" in Figure 3.4), so that standard trigonometry applies. The i-direction and shadow-map s-axis, on the other hand, do not lie in the same plane but are parallel (they both point orthogonally away from the plane defined by the paper). We therefore measure the error on a surface element at the intersection of two planes: one defined by the viewpoint and the horizontal pixel edge, and one defined by the light position and the texel edge in s-direction. This slightly simplified assumption basically eliminates the terms that depend on the orientation of the surface element for m_s. For symmetric view frusta, we observe that $W_j/z_n = 2\tan\theta$, with 2θ being the view frustum field-of-view angle, and $W_i/z_n = 2a\tan\theta$, with a being the aspect ratio of the viewport.

Light beams are constructed somewhat similarly, but in this case, we need to take into account the shadow-map parametrization. We do this by introducing an intermediate coordinate system (u, v) on the shadow-map plane in world space in the range $[0, W_u] \times [0, W_v]$. A parametrization maps from this coordinate system into the shadow-map coordinates (s, t). Thus,

$$w_t = \frac{1}{r_t} \frac{dv}{dt} \frac{d_l}{n_l} \frac{\cos \varphi_t}{\cos \psi_t}, \tag{3.7}$$

$$w_s = \frac{1}{r_s} \frac{du}{ds} \frac{d_l}{n_l}. \tag{3.8}$$

Here, d_l and n_l are the distances of the surface to the light and to the near plane of the light, respectively, similar to the term $\frac{z}{z_n}$ in Equation (3.5). The angle terms are defined analogously to the eye beam. The dependence of the beam on the light projection as well as any possible reparametrization is encoded in the differentials $\frac{dv}{dt}$ and $\frac{du}{ds}$, which transform from texel space to world space. In summary, aliasing error can be written as

$$m_t = \frac{w_t}{w_j} = \frac{r_j}{r_t} \frac{dv}{dt} \frac{d_l}{n_l} \frac{\cos \varphi_t}{\cos \psi_t} \frac{\cos \psi_j}{\cos \varphi_j} \frac{z_n}{W_j} \frac{1}{z}, \tag{3.9}$$

$$m_s = \frac{w_s}{w_i} = \frac{r_i}{r_s} \frac{du}{ds} \frac{d_l}{n_l} \frac{z_n}{W_i} \frac{1}{z}. \tag{3.10}$$

Equation (3.9) is the most general geometric formulation of shadow-mapping sampling error (i.e., undersampling). It does not assume an overhead or directional light and takes into account the variation of error over the view frustum (φ_t, φ_j). This formulation mostly follows Lloyd's analysis [Lloyd08, Lloyd07a], with the exception that we parametrize (u, v) in world space instead of $[0, 1]$.

3.2.3   Aliasing Components

As first noted by Stamminger and Drettakis [Stamminger02], sampling error can be split into a component that depends on the orientation of the surface element, called *projection aliasing*, and the remaining error that is mostly due to the perspective foreshortening of the camera, thus called *perspective aliasing*.

Projection aliasing is a local phenomenon that is greatest for surfaces almost parallel to the light direction and is described by the term $\cos \psi_j / \cos \psi_t$. Reducing this kind of error requires higher sampling densities in such areas. Only approaches that adapt the sampling density locally based on a scene analysis can achieve this (Sections 4.4 to 4.7).

Perspective aliasing, on the other hand, is caused by the perspective projection of the viewer. If the perspective-foreshortening effect occurs along one of the axes of the shadow map, it can be influenced by the *parametrization of the shadow map*, $(s(v), t(u))$. We therefore study mainly perspective aliasing and define this as aliasing error with the projection-aliasing term (i.e., the cos term) canceled out:

$$\tilde{m}_t = m_t \frac{\cos \psi_t}{\cos \psi_j}, \tag{3.11}$$

$$\tilde{m}_s = m_s. \tag{3.12}$$

If a different parametrization is chosen, this will lead to a different sampling density distribution along the shadow map.

Perspective Error of Standard Shadow Mapping

The standard uniform parametrization has du/ds and dv/dt constant, and therefore m_t, m_s are large when $1/z$ is large (Equation (3.9)). This happens close to

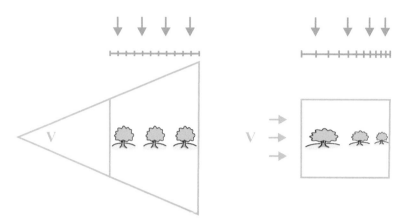

Figure 3.5. The uniform distribution of a shadow map in world space (left) degrades near the observer due to perspective foreshortening. This effect is visible in post-perspective space (right). Much fewer samples are spent on nearby elements.

the near plane, which leads to very visible errors (compare Figure 3.5). In order to reduce perspective aliasing, there are several approaches to distribute more shadow-map samples near the viewer, either by using a different parametrization or by splitting the shadow map into smaller parts (Sections 4.2 and 4.3).

3.2.4   Storage Factor

In order to remove perspective aliasing, one has to choose a shadow-map resolution so that the maximum perspective error over the whole view frustum is below one. For a particular view frustum V, the maximum error along each shadow-map axis is

$$M_t = \max_{\mathbf{p} \in V}(\tilde{m}_t(\mathbf{p})), \tag{3.13}$$

$$M_s = \max_{\mathbf{p} \in V}(\tilde{m}_s(\mathbf{p})). \tag{3.14}$$

One way to characterize the error in one scalar, and independently of the actual shadow-map and image resolutions, is the so-called storage factor S, which is computed as

$$S = \frac{r_t}{r_j} M_t \frac{r_s}{r_i} M_s. \tag{3.15}$$

The storage factor describes the factor by which the shadow-map resolution (in terms of total number of texels) has to be higher than the screen resolution in order to avoid aliasing in both directions separately. Note that the storage factor assumes that shadow-map resolutions are chosen independently in the s and t directions to make $M_t = M_s = 1$, so a particular storage factor might require a rectangular shadow map, which can pose problems in practice. We will calculate the storage factor for some reparametrizations in Sections 4.2.2 and 4.2.4.

3.3   Resampling Error

Reconstruction Error

Reconstruction error can be reduced by using a better reconstruction filter. In the case of shadow mapping, percentage-closer filtering (PCF) [Reeves87] (Chapter 5) is the equivalent to bilinear or higher-order reconstruction for texture mapping. Basically, PCF treats shadows as a projected texture by first evaluating the shadow function and then applying the filter kernel. Better reconstruction can also be achieved by changing the reconstruction algorithm itself (see Section 4.6).

Resampling Aliasing

Resampling aliasing is usually avoided in image processing by bandlimiting the reconstructed signal before resampling it. For texture mapping, this is done efficiently by precomputing filtered versions of the signal (mipmaps). However, for shadow mapping, this is not possible. To see why, let us analyze the shadow-mapping function in more detail. The shadow-mapping function f for a fragment that projects to shadow-map coordinates $\mathbf{t} = (s, t)$ and has a depth $\tilde{z}$ in shadow-map space is the result of the evaluation of a depth comparison with the depth value $z(\mathbf{t})$ sampled from the shadow map:

$$f(\mathbf{t}, \tilde{z}) = s(z(\mathbf{t}), \tilde{z}) = H(z(\mathbf{t}) - \tilde{z}), \tag{3.16}$$

where the shadow comparison function s is implemented using the so-called "Heaviside" step function:

$$H(x) = \begin{cases} 1 & x \geq 0, \\ 0 & x < 0. \end{cases} \tag{3.17}$$

Any linear filter on the shadow signal would look like the following:

$$f_{\text{filter}}(\mathbf{t}, \tilde{z}) = \sum_{\mathbf{t}_i \in \mathcal{K}} H(z(\mathbf{t}_i) - \tilde{z}) k(\mathbf{t}_i - \mathbf{t}), \tag{3.18}$$

where $\tilde{z}$ is the fragment depth in light space, and $\mathcal{K}$ is the set of filter samples. The problem here is that this expression cannot be precomputed because it depends on the fragment depth $\tilde{z}$.

For shadow mapping, one option is to evaluate PCF with large filter kernels; however, this is slow already for moderate filter sizes and does not scale to larger kernels. Recent research has proposed clever ways to reformulate the shadow function f so that it is separable in $\mathbf{t}$ and $\tilde{z}$:

$$f(\mathbf{t}, \tilde{z}) = f_1(\mathbf{t}) f_2(\tilde{z}), \qquad (3.19)$$

so that precomputed filtering can be applied to f_1, both for initial sampling and for resampling (see Chapter 5).

Another class of approaches drops the signal-theoretic view altogether and treats filtering of the shadow map as a statistical problem: the question is what is the probability that a given depth value $\tilde{z}$ is in front of a set of values stored in the shadow map:

$$Pr(\tilde{z} \leq z(\mathbf{t})), \qquad (3.20)$$

where $\mathbf{t}$ is a random variable that represents the samples that lie in the desired filter kernel. This probability is then used as a grayscale value to represent the shadow test result.

CHAPTER 4
Shadow-Map Sampling

In this chapter, we will concentrate on sampling error introduced in the initial sampling phase (i.e., undersampling) and present several methods to improve sampling. One of the simplest methods is to *fit* the frustum of the light source to the view frustum (Section 4.1). This is also a requirement for the more advanced methods, for example, *warping* the shadow map to achieve a better parametrization (Section 4.2) or *partitioning* the shadow map *globally* (Section 4.3) or *locally* (Section 4.4) in order to spend more shadow-map samples where they are needed.

Even higher quality can be achieved by calculating shadows for the exact view-sample locations visible in the final image (Section 4.5). Alternatively, the reconstruction algorithm can be improved to provide smoother edges (Section 4.6). Finally, temporal aliasing as well as sampling accuracy can be improved by temporal reprojection of shadow-map samples (Section 4.7).

4.1   Fitting

One of the most straightforward ways in which the shadow-map sampling rate can be improved is to make sure that no shadow-map space is wasted. Especially in outdoor scenes, if a single shadow map is used for the whole scene, then only a small part of the shadow map will actually be relevant for the view frustum. Thus, fitting or focusing techniques, introduced by Brabec et al. [Brabec02a], fit the shadow-map frustum to encompass the view frustum.

In order to produce correct results, we need to include all objects in the shadow map that potentially cast a shadow on objects (receivers) in the view frustum. Therefore, the first step is to find potential shadow receivers (PSRs).

Finding Potential Shadow Receivers

We want to exclude receivers outside the viewing cone of the light source, outside the view frustum, and outside the scene bounding box (especially for large view frusta), as these objects can never receive a shadow that is visible in the final image. The volume of PSRs is thus given by the intersection of light frustum $\mathbf{L}$, view frustum $\mathbf{V}$, and scene bounding box $\mathbf{S}$:

$$\mathbf{PSR} = \mathbf{L} \cap \mathbf{V} \cap \mathbf{S}.$$

Focusing on PSRs in Shadow-Map Space

The focusing extent on the shadow map can be easily calculated from $\mathbf{PSR}$ when working directly in (post-perspective) shadow-map space. One computes the bounding rectangle $(x_{\min}, y_{\min}), (x_{\max}, y_{\max})$ of the vertices of $\mathbf{PSR}$ projected onto the shadow map. It is applied through a scale/translate matrix $\mathbf{F}$ (in a way, an "inverse" viewport matrix) that maps this bounding rectangle to the range $[-1, 1]$ in each coordinate:

$$\mathbf{F} = \begin{pmatrix} s_x & 0 & 0 & o_x \\ 0 & s_y & 0 & o_y \\ 0 & 0 & 1 & 0 \\ 0 & 0 & 0 & 1 \end{pmatrix}, \tag{4.1}$$

where $s_x = 2/(x_{\max} - x_{\min})$, $o_x = -(s_x(x_{\max} + x_{\min}))/2$ are the scale and offset values for x; the values for y are analogous. The matrix $\mathbf{F}$ is then simply multiplied with the view-projection matrix of the light source to obtain the final shadow matrix. Since we work in post-perspective light space, we automatically include all potential shadow casters. The reason is that in post-perspective space, all light rays are parallel to the z-axis, which is not modified by the fitting matrix $\mathbf{F}$. Thus, if an object blocks a light ray to a shadow receiver in the focused region, it is itself part of the focused region in the x, y-plane.

Note that for standard shadow mapping, a fixed orientation of the shadow map is usually assumed. However, most algorithms to improve sampling error (in particular, those in Sections 4.2 and 4.3) require the shadow-map up vector to be aligned with the view vector, so that the view-frustum near plane is found at the bottom of the shadow map and the far plane at the top.

Finding Potential Shadow Casters

In order to make best use of the available shadow-map depth resolution, it is also advisable to calculate a suitable near-plane distance for the light view, for which we need to identify the nearest potential shadow casters (PSCs). This can be done by calculating the convex hull of $\mathbf{PSR}$ and the light position $\mathbf{l}$ (for directional lights, this position is at infinity), clipped by the scene bounding box:

$$\mathbf{PSC} = (\mathbf{PSR} + \mathbf{l}) \cap \mathbf{S}. \tag{4.2}$$

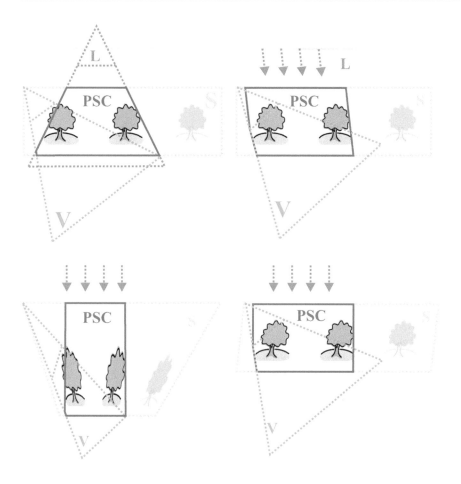

Figure 4.1. Intersection body **PSC** used for focusing (top); point light (left) and directional light (right). Below are the corresponding bodies in light clip space.

Since we are dealing with convex bodies, the intersection of two bodies is easily implemented by clipping all polygons of one body by all the planes defined by the polygons of the other body, inserting a new polygon for each hole created by a clipping plane. The convex hull can be implemented by removing all light-facing polygons from the body and connecting the open edges with the light position using new polygons [Wimmer06] (see Figure 4.1).

Note, however, that this part can be completely omitted if depth clamping (e.g., GL_ARB_depth_clamp) is available. The observation is that the actual depth value of shadow casters that do not themselves receive visible shadows is irrelevant as long as it is nearer than all objects in **PSR**. Therefore, when depth clamping is enabled, the light-frustum near and far planes can tightly enclose **PSR**, and the depth of invisible shadow casters will be clamped to the light-frustum near plane. This increases the accuracy of depth values in the shadow map.

Using Visibility Information

The focus region can be further reduced using visibility information. Brabec et al. [Brabec02a] originally proposed to find **PSR** through a separate render pass from the light source. The result of that render pass was read back and analyzed on the CPU to find the extents of geometry visible from the light source, which gives more accurate information than using the scene bounding box alone. Due to the added complexity of the analysis step, this approach was not widely adopted.

It is much more promising to use visibility information from the camera view. This can be done by first rendering a camera depth-only pass with an on-line occlusion-culling algorithm like coherent hierarchical culling (CHC) [Mattausch08] before creating the shadow map. Then, the far-plane distance can be reduced to just cover the furthest visible object, reducing **PSR** in the calculations above. To get an even tighter fit, the bounding box of all visible objects can be used to reduce **PSR**, as proposed by Bittner et al. [Bittner11].

Lauritzen et al. [Lauritzen11] go one step further and analyze the distribution of actually visible z-values in the camera view in order to restrict the view-frustum extents that go into the calculation of **PSR**. This can be done by creating a min/max-mipmap pyramid of the depth buffer and reading back the minimum and maximum depth values, which allows constructing a fitting body that perfectly adapts to the visible samples in the z-direction. On today's hardware, this can be feasible but it was actually already described in this way for the original perspective shadow-map approach [Stamminger02]. However, it is possible to further improve the result by including the x-values in the min/max pyramid. In this way, the body can also be adapted in width. This is most useful for the z-partitioning approaches discussed in Section 4.3.1.

Simplified Fitting

In many cases, one can avoid actual clipping operations to find **PSR**. The term $\mathbf{V} \cap \mathbf{S}$ in the fitting equation (Equation (4.2)) can be approximated by an adapted view frustum $\mathbf{V}'$ where the near and far planes have been adapted to the scene extents or to the extent of the visible objects as discussed above. The remaining term $\mathbf{V}' \cap \mathbf{L}$ can also be calculated easily by transforming $\mathbf{V}'$ into light space, clipping by the near clipping plane of the light and projecting the clipped body onto the shadow map. The focus region is then given by the bounding rectangle (clamped to the light frustum) of the projected vertices. However, an accurate determination of the focused light-frustum near-plane distance still requires a convex hull and clipping operation as described above.

Temporal Aliasing

In general, fitting leads to temporal aliasing or so-called shadow swimming because the rasterization of the shadow map changes each frame. For example, when nearing the borders of the scene, shadow quality can be very high when looking towards the outside, while degrading dramatically when looking inside. Still, such changes depend smoothly on the viewer's orientation and position. However, when adding occlusion information, strong temporal discontinuities can occur: consider a city where distant skyscrapers are sometimes hidden by nearby buildings and sometimes visible.

Temporal aliasing can be somewhat reduced by trying to keep texel boundaries at fixed locations in light space. This was first proposed by Valient [Valient08] for translations, while scaling was basically disallowed. Later, Zhang et al. [Zhang09] introduced an approximate solution that allowed quantizing the scale of the shadow map as well. Both these techniques work only in the case of a fixed world-space shadow-map orientation. For sampling-error reduction techniques that require alignment of the shadow-map orientation with the view vector, like warping for example (see Section 4.2), the following is not applicable.

Maintaining light-space texel boundaries works by quantizing the values of the fitting matrix $\mathbf{F}$: the offset value o (o_x or o_y) should be quantized to texel increments assuming r is half the shadow-map resolution:

$$o' = \frac{\text{ceil}(or)}{r}.\tag{4.3}$$

The quantization of the scale value should ensure a reasonable number of scaling steps for the focus region, for example, by snapping the scale value to the nearest value $1/f$, with f being an integer in a certain range.

4.2   Warping

The error analysis of shadow mapping, in particular perspective error, shows that higher sampling densities are required near the viewpoint and lower sampling densities far from the viewpoint (Section 3.2.3). Fortunately, it is possible to reduce perspective aliasing in some cases by warping. Warping means changing the shadow-map parametrization, that is, the function that maps from (u, v)-coordinates on the world-space shadow-map plane to (s, t)-coordinates in the actual shadow-map texture. This was first discovered by Stamminger and Drettakis [Stamminger02] and used in perspective shadow maps (PSM).

Perspective parametrizations can be achieved using graphics hardware and have thus attracted a lot of interest [Wimmer04, Martin04, Chong03, Chong04]. In Section 4.2.1, we thus show a practical implementation of such a parametrization. An important research problem has become how to optimally choose the parameters of perspective parametrizations. We show a solution for this problem in Section 4.2.2. In Section 4.2.4, we will look for an optimal (not necessarily perspective) parametrization and find that perspective error can be eliminated by a *logarithmic* parametrization in the *t*-axis and a *perspective* parametrization in the *s*-axis of the shadow map. Unfortunately, this optimal parametrization is not feasible for a practical hardware implementation. Finally, in Section 4.2.5, we discuss alternative optimality criteria geared towards optimizing error on certain planes in the view frustum.

Initially, warping was applied to a single shadow map; however, it has been later combined with partitioning algorithms to further improve sampling rates (Section 4.3.3).

4.2.1 Warping—Practice

As a representative of warping algorithms, we discuss light space perspective shadow maps (LiSPSM) introduced by Wimmer et al. [Wimmer04], which is mostly equivalent to trapezoidal shadow maps (TSM) introduced independently by Martin et al. [Martin04]. In an insightful work, Lloyd et al. [Lloyd06b] proved that for overhead lights, all perspective warping algorithms (PSM, LiSPSM, TSM) actually lead to the same *overall* error (storage factor, Section 3.2.4) when considering both *s* and *t* shadow-map directions, but among these algorithms, LiSPSM gives the most even distribution of error among the directions and is therefore advantageous.

The main idea of perspective shadow mapping is to apply a perspective transformation to the scene before rendering it into the shadow map. Thus, the distribution of shadow-map samples is changed so that more samples lie near the center of projection and less samples near the far plane of the projection (see Figure 4.2 for an illustration). The near-plane distance of the perspective transformation determines the *strength* of the warp (i.e., how strong the perspective distortion will be).

Algorithm

The only change that has to be applied to standard shadow mapping in order to enable LiSPSM (or similar global warping algorithms) is to replace the shadow transformation $\mathbf{S}$, which transforms from model space to shadow-map space, with a new warped transformation $\mathbf{S_w}$. This new transformation is then used for both creating the shadow map and applying the shadow map during rendering.

Therefore, we only need to describe how to calculate $\mathbf{S_w}$. Let us first fix the notation for different spaces: a vertex is transformed via the model matrix $\mathbf{M}$ to world space, then via the light view matrix $\mathbf{M_v^L}$ to (pre-perspective) light space, and via the light projection matrix $\mathbf{M_p^L}$ to (post-perspective) light space. In standard shadow mapping, a scale and bias fitting matrix $\mathbf{F}$ is used to focus the shadow

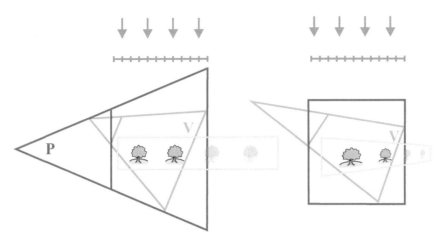

Figure 4.2. An example configuration of LiSPSM with view frustum V and the frustum defining the perspective transform P. Left: directional light, a view frustum V, and the perspective transformation P. Right: after the warp, objects near the viewer appear bigger in the shadow map and therefore receive more samples.

map, giving a total transformation of $\mathbf{S} = \mathbf{FM}_p^L\mathbf{M}_v^L\mathbf{M}$. Recall that $\mathbf{F}$ is calculated by transforming a fitting body $\mathbf{PSR}$ using $\mathbf{M}_p^L\mathbf{M}_v^L$ and calculating its bounds in (post-perspective) light space.

To arrive at $\mathbf{S}_w$ for perspective shadow mapping, fitting is still the last step, but before that, a warping matrix $\mathbf{W}_p\mathbf{W}_v$ is inserted. Furthermore, the shadow map needs to be rotated using a matrix $\mathbf{L}_r$ so that the shadow-map t-axis is aligned with the viewer z-direction in order for the warp to be most effective. Also, the strength of the perspective warp needs to be determined. The total warping shadow transformation is

$$\mathbf{S}_w = \mathbf{FW}_p\mathbf{W}_v\mathbf{L}_r\mathbf{M}_p^L\mathbf{M}_v^L\mathbf{M}. \tag{4.4}$$

The algorithm to find $\mathbf{S}_w$ is as follows:

1. Calculate fitting body $\mathbf{PSR}$ (Section 4.1).

2. Calculate shadow-map orientation, giving a rotation matrix $\mathbf{L}_r$ (see below).

3. Find near and far planes of warping frustum using $\mathbf{PSR}$ transformed by $\mathbf{L}_r\mathbf{M}_p^L\mathbf{M}_v^L$.

4. Calculate parameter n that determines warping strength (Section 4.2.2).

5. Set up perspective warping view and projection matrix $\mathbf{W}_v$ and $\mathbf{W}_p$ using info from steps 3 and 4 (see below).

6. Transform **PSR** into warped light space using $\mathbf{W_p W_v L_r M_p^L M_v^L}$.

7. Fit projection to **PSR**, giving a scale and bias fitting matrix **F**.

The matrix $\mathbf{S_w}$ can be used directly instead of **S** as the model-view-projection matrix for the shadow rendering pass. For the main rendering pass, like for standard shadow mapping (Section 2.2.6), we use an additional scale/bias matrix to transform from the resulting coordinates in the range $[-1, 1]$ to coordinates in texture space in the range $[0, 1]$.

Determining the Shadow-Map Orientation $\mathbf{L_r}$

In order for the perspective warp to be effective, the warping direction needs to be along the view frustum z-axis. This is most easily achieved by rotating the shadow map so that the t-axis is aligned with the z-axis. This also makes better use of the space in the shadow map.

Normally, the warping direction $\mathbf{v_p}$ can simply be chosen as the world-space view direction $\mathbf{v}$ projected onto the shadow map ($\mathbf{v_p} = \mathbf{M_v^t v}, \mathbf{v_p}.z = 0$). For point lights, however, the view direction cannot be simply projected onto the shadow map since the result depends on where the view vector originates. Therefore, we take the line segment from the eye point to a point sufficiently far away from the eye point along the view vector. We clip this line segment by the near plane of the light frustum. Finally, we project the endpoints of the resulting segment onto the shadow map and calculate the view vector from these endpoints. A suitable rotation matrix $\mathbf{L_r}$ is then constructed using a standard look-at matrix in light space using $\mathbf{v_p}$ as the view direction and the light-space z-direction (i.e., $(0, 0, 1)$) as the up vector.

In any case, the length of the projected view vector can become too small. In this case, the light comes from behind or front, in which case we need to turn off perspective shadow mapping and fall back to uniform shadow mapping.

Setting up the LiSPSM Warping Matrix $\mathbf{W_p W_v}$

Given the correct shadow-map orientation, we need to find the near and far planes of the LiSPSM matrix, as well as a center of projection **p**. The near and far planes are given by the bounding rectangle of **PSR** projected on the shadow map. The center of projection is located a distance n away from the near plane and a distance f from the far plane. For now, we assume that n is given; later, we will discuss how to calculate this value, which will allow influencing the warping strength. The distance f is calculated as n plus the distance between the near and far planes.

The only remaining degrees of freedom are the x- and z-coordinates of **p**. These two values basically define how "skewed" the warp is in x- and z-directions, where z only influences the quantization of the depth values in the shadow map. A convenient choice are the coordinates implied by the center of **PSR** in projected light space.

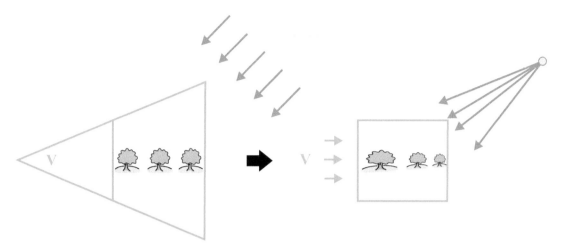

Figure 4.3. PSM problems. In the post-perspective space of the camera, a directional light can become a point light.

A perspective matrix can then be created using a translation of the center of projection to the origin for $\mathbf{W}_v$ and the equivalent of `glFrustum(-1,1,-1,1,n,f)` (along the t-axis) for $\mathbf{W}_p$. Note that it is not necessary to exactly determine the frustum x- and y-boundaries, as they do not influence the warping effect. Instead, we focus the frustum after carrying out the warp using the method discussed in Section 4.1 by transforming the fitting body **PSR** into warped space using $\mathbf{W}_p\mathbf{W}_v\mathbf{L}_r\mathbf{M}_p^L\mathbf{M}_v^L$.

LiSPSM versus TSM versus PSM

Perspective shadow mapping methods differ in the way the perspective transformation is set up. In the original PSM, this transform was chosen to be equivalent to the viewer projection. However, this changes the direction of the light or even the type of the light (from directional to point, or vice versa; see Figure 4.3) and requires adjustments to include all potential shadow casters (see Figure 4.4). Most importantly, PSM distributes the error in a nonoptimal way (see Section 4.2.2).

In LiSPSM, the perspective transformation is always aligned to the axis of the light frustum, and therefore, lights do not change direction or type. In order to deal with point lights, the projection of the point light is applied first, converting the point light to a directional light, and LiSPSM is done in the post-perspective space of the light. Applying the light perspective has a similar effect on the scene as the transformation depicted in Figure 3.5, when interpreting the viewpoint as a light source.

The setup of the warp for TSM, on the other hand, although described differently, leads to the same transformation as LiSPSM.

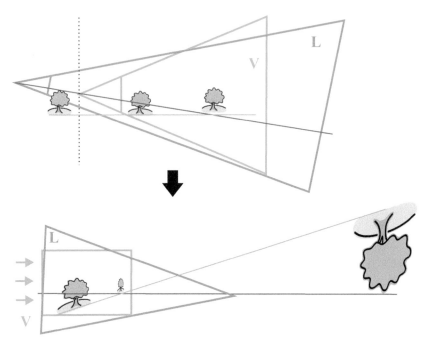

Figure 4.4. PSM problems. Shadow casters behind the camera would get "wrapped around" at infinity and require moving the camera backward to include them.

4.2.2 Calculating the Optimal Parameter for Warping

The most important factor influencing the shadow quality in perspective shadow mapping is the choice of the warp parameter n (i.e., the near-plane distance of the warping frustum). While this can be set manually or empirically (as is done in TSM), it would be better to find an optimal parameter automatically. The main idea is to find a parameter n that minimizes the maximum errors M_t and M_s (Section 3.2.4). While an analysis of the error over the whole view frustum is very tedious, it is actually possible to find a closed-form solution under some restrictions. In particular, one can analyze the error $\tilde{m}_t$ along specific lines through the view frustum and choose n in such a way that the maximum error along that line becomes minimal. We will show a choice of line that gives a good approximation for overhead lights and will gracefully transition to uniform shadow mapping for lights where warping does not bring any benefit (e.g., directly behind). Note that analyzing error along only one certain line can miss the actual point of maximum error in the rest of the view frustum.

In the following, we will first discuss the necessary coordinate transformations for individual lines, then derive an optimal parameter, show some simpli-

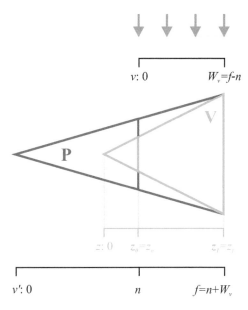

Figure 4.5. Warping frustum for overhead directional light.

fications for directional lights, and introduce optimizations that allow focusing shadow quality on a subset of the view frustum.

Error along Certain Lines

In order to analyze error along a line through the view frustum, all variables in $\tilde{m}_t$ or $\tilde{m}_s$ need to be expressed in terms of a suitable parameter along that line. For example, u, v can be expressed in terms of z. We will consider only lines that are parallel to the shadow-map plane and have constant $u = W_u/2$, where W_u is the world-space width of the shadow-map plane. We also assume that the t-direction of the shadow map is aligned with the z-axis of the viewer (this can be achieved using fitting; see Section 4.1). Thus, for the special case of an overhead directional light, this line goes through the center of the view frustum, and $v = z - z_n$ and $u = x$ (see Figure 4.5).

For a more general configuration, the view frustum may be tilted around the x-axis. For this configuration, we look at the z- and v-coordinates where the line intersects the warping frustum (i.e., at $v = 0$ and $v = W_v$). Note that these points lie on the near plane and the far plane of the warping frustum. Note also that for stronger tilt angles, the near plane of the warping frustum will not touch the near plane of the view frustum, but the far plane. Let us call the corresponding z-coordinates z_0 and z_1 (see Figure 4.6).

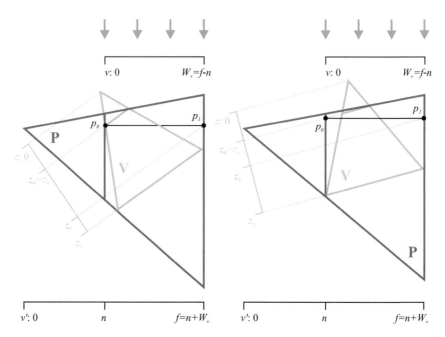

Figure 4.6. Configuration of a directional light with a tilted view frustum. The variables z_0 and z_1 are the view-space z-values along a line parallel to the shadow-map plane. The near plane of the warping frustum P may touch the view frustum V at its near plane (left) or far plane (right), depending on the tilt angle. Due to focusing, $z_0 \neq z_n$ may occur (not shown in image).

Then z can be transformed to v using

$$v = \frac{z - z_0}{z_1 - z_0} W_v.$$

(4.5)

Note that the x- and u-coordinates are not affected by a tilt, so we will only analyze $\tilde{m}_t$ for now.

Furthermore, we will analyze error in terms of warping frustum coordinates (i.e., after transforming (u, v) by $\mathbf{W}_v \mathbf{M}_p^L$). We call these coordinates (u', v') and note that they can be calculated using a simple scale and translate (note that we assume we already know the parameter n for the moment—this does not matter, as it will fall out later on):

$$(u', v') = \left(\left(u \frac{2 W_{u'}}{W_u} \right) - W_{u'}, v \frac{W_{v'}}{W_v} + n \right).$$

(4.6)

Thus, for directional lights, $W_{u'} = W_u$ and $W_{v'} = f - n$, and therefore $v' = n + v$. For spot lights, the frustum after the light perspective transformation is

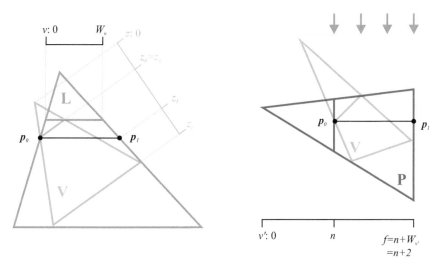

Figure 4.7. Configuration of a spotlight with a tilted view frustum, in world space (left) and after the perspective transformation of the spotlight (right).

normalized, so $W_{u'} = W_{v'} = (f - n) = 2$, and therefore $v' = n + \frac{2v}{W_v}$. See Figure 4.6 for directional-light configurations, and Figure 4.7 for a spotlight configuration.

Finding z_0 and z_1

For tilted view frusta, we need to find eye-space z-values that correspond to the intersection of the line under consideration with the warping-frustum near and far planes. We first construct $\mathbf{p}_0$ so that the projection of $\mathbf{p}_0$ back into the view frustum has the nearest z-coordinate present in **PSR**. The coordinate $\mathbf{p}_0$ can be found by choosing a vertex of **PSR** with the smallest z-coordinate, constructing a plane parallel to the frustum near plane through that point and intersecting that plane with the light frustum and a plane with $u = W_u/2$. The coordinate $\mathbf{p}_1$ is constructed from the orthographic projection of $\mathbf{p}_0$ onto the warping-frustum far plane (see Figure 4.6). The coordinates z_0 and z_1 are then the z-coordinates of $\mathbf{p}_0$ and $\mathbf{p}_1$ back-projected into the view frustum (see Figure 4.7 for a spotlight configuration). Note that using this construction, we have uniquely determined the line we are going to use for our analysis. There may be other lines that give better results, but we will not investigate this further.

Derivation of Optimal Warping Parameter for General Case

First of all, perspective shadow mapping uses a perspective reparametrization of the shadow map, which, following the definition of a perspective projection in

OpenGL (see definition of the `gluPerspective()` function) can be expressed as

$$s(u', v') = \frac{u'}{2v' \tan \theta'} + \frac{1}{2}, \tag{4.7}$$

$$t(v') = \frac{f + n}{2(f - n)} + \frac{fn}{v'(f - n)} + \frac{1}{2}, \tag{4.8}$$

where θ' is half the field-of-view angle of the perspective frustum in the x-direction. From this, we can calculate

$$\frac{ds}{du'} = \frac{1}{v'} \frac{1}{2 \tan \theta'}, \tag{4.9}$$

$$\frac{dt}{dv'} = -\frac{1}{v'^2} \frac{fn}{f - n}. \tag{4.10}$$

Plugging this into Equations (3.9) and (3.10) to calculate the error yields

$$\tilde{m}_t = \frac{r_j}{r_t} \frac{d_l}{n_l} \frac{\cos \varphi_t}{\cos \varphi_j} \frac{z_n}{W_j} \frac{v'^2}{z} \frac{W_v}{W_{v'}} \frac{f - n}{fn}, \tag{4.11}$$

$$\tilde{m}_s = \frac{r_i}{r_s} \frac{d_l}{n_l} \frac{z_n}{W_i} \frac{v'}{z} \frac{W_u}{W_{u'}} 2 \tan \theta', \tag{4.12}$$

using

$$\frac{du}{ds} = \frac{du}{du'} \frac{du'}{ds} = \frac{W_u}{W_{u'}} \frac{1}{2} \frac{du'}{ds}, \tag{4.13}$$

$$\frac{dv}{dt} = \frac{dv}{dv'} \frac{dv'}{dt} = \frac{W_v}{W_{v'}} \frac{dv'}{dt}. \tag{4.14}$$

In order to find the optimal error along the t-direction, we analyze the error along a line parallel to the shadow-map plane, as described before. We want to deal with the general case of a tilted view frustum; therefore, we substitute z using Equation (4.5), to obtain an expression that depends only on v. Then we calculate $d\tilde{m}_t/dz$ and find that there is a local minimum in $[0, W_v]$. Therefore, the maximum error in this range is minimized if $\tilde{m}_t(0) = \tilde{m}_t(W_v)$. This corresponds to (omitting all the constant terms as they cancel out)

$$\frac{n^2}{z_0} = \frac{f^2}{z_1}. \tag{4.15}$$

After some symbolic manipulation and solving a quadratic equation for n, this results in a solution for the optimal parameter n_{opt}:

$$n_{opt} = \frac{f - n}{z_1 - z_0} \left(z_0 + \sqrt{z_0 z_1} \right). \tag{4.16}$$

Note that this optimal parameter is independent of all the constants in $\tilde{m}_t$. Furthermore, one has to understand what this parameter means. It basically equalizes the perspective error $\tilde{m}_t$ along the t-axis between the near and far planes of the warping frustum. For tilted frusta, the mechanism of calculating z_1 leads to a reduced view-space z-range available for warping, which is the expected behavior, since the shadow-map t-direction does not perfectly represent the view-space z-direction that is responsible for perspective aliasing anymore. This way of calculating n_{opt} is only an approximation, since we still only analyze error along one single line through the view frustum, and we ignore the angle-dependent terms φ_j and φ_t that might have a stronger influence for more tilted view frusta.

Simplified Optimal Parameter for Directional Lights

For directional lights, some simplifications apply. In particular, the depth range depends on the tilt angle γ between view direction and light direction, so that $z_0 = z_n$ and $z_1 = z_n + (f - n)\sin\gamma$. Thus,

$$n_{\text{opt}} = \frac{1}{\sin\gamma}\left(z_n + \sqrt{z_n(z_n + (f - n)\sin\gamma)}\right), \qquad (4.17)$$

which is the formula derived in the original LiSPSM paper [Wimmer04]. For overhead lights (i.e., $\gamma = \pi/2$), we obtain the simplest formulation from that paper:

$$n_{\text{opt}} = z_n + \sqrt{z_n z_f}. \qquad (4.18)$$

The interpretation of the dependence on γ is that as the viewer is tilted towards the light or away from it, the usable depth range decreases, as discussed before. Thus, n has to be increased, so that it reaches infinity when the viewer looks exactly into the light or away from it. In this case, perspective warping cannot bring any improvements; therefore, no warping should be applied. In practice, it is preferable to use the general formulation with z_0, z_1, as this can account for view frusta clipped due to fitting.

However, Lloyd [Lloyd07a] showed that the falloff implied by the $\sin\gamma$ term is not fast enough once the angle passes the point where one of the view-frustum planes becomes parallel to the shadow-map normal. He proposes a different falloff function that avoids this problem, but it is a bit too involved to reproduce here, so we refer the reader to Sections 5.1.2.1 and 5.2.1 of Lloyd's thesis [Lloyd07a] for the exact equations. Another falloff function based on different simplifications has been proposed by Zhang et al. [Zhang06b].

Pseudo-Frusta Optimizations

Many applications tend to use a generous far plane and a very tight near plane to avoid near-plane clipping. This creates a tension with shadow mapping since perspective error increases as a function of z_f/z_n (see below).

Pseudo near plane.   An interesting solution is to use a different view-frustum near-plane distance, a so-called pseudo near plane, for the computation of n_{opt}. The rationale is that the nearest depth range does not often show shadows, but a lot of precision is wasted on this range using the optimal warping parameter. If a pseudo near plane is used, shadow quality will be optimized for the range between pseudo near plane and far plane, but shadows will still appear on objects that are closer, though with lower quality.

A pseudo near plane can be implemented easily by adding an offset δ_n to the value z_n in the square root (but only if this makes it larger than z_0):

$$n_{opt} = \frac{f - n}{z_1 - z_0} \left(z_0 + \sqrt{\max(z_n + \delta_n, z_0) z_1} \right).$$

If δ_n becomes too large, Lloyd shows that the maximum does not occur in the depth range anymore, and the optimal value should rather be calculated as (for details see [Lloyd07a], Section 5.1.9)

$$n_{opt} = \frac{\delta_n}{2 - 3\frac{\delta_n}{z_f - z_n}}.$$

Pseudo far plane.   Similar to a pseudo near plane, a pseudo far plane can be desirable. Especially for large frusta, the optimal parameter will become closer to uniform shadow mapping in order to keep quality in the distance high. However, usually it is preferable to have high quality nearby, and thus an adapted z_f can be used in the calculation that specifies up to which point the shadow quality should be good.

Final Formula

The final formula for n_{opt} is

$$n_{opt} = \frac{f - n}{z_1 - z_0} \left(z_0 + \sqrt{\max(z_n + \delta_n, z_0) \min(z_f - \delta_f, z_1)} \right),$$

where n and f are near- and far-plane positions in light space, z_0 is the first available z-coordinate of the intersection body, and z_1 is the corresponding z-coordinate at the warping frustum space far plane, which for directional lights with simple intersection bodies boils down to $z_1 = z_0 + (f - n) \sin \gamma$.

Exact Derivations for General Configurations

In the previous sections, we investigated parameter choices for n based on simplifying assumptions. Let us now consider the feasibility of an exact solution for general configurations. For an exact solution, we first need to be able to calculate the maximum perspective error over the whole view frustum. Lloyd [Lloyd07a] has shown that the maximum perspective error along a light ray occurs on a *view-frustum face* or, more precisely, at a face of the intersection body **PSR**. Therefore, it is sufficient to consider the error on the faces of **PSR**.

An algorithm to compute an ideal parameter n would have to minimize the perspective error over all faces of the body **PSR**. This is not trivial, since the shape of **PSR** can lead to multiple local minima for any particular parameter n. A possible algorithm to find an exact solution would, therefore, be to sample the parameter space of n and choose the value that leads to minimum error. The error for any particular n can be calculated by comparing error at view-frustum vertices and possible local minima of error at view-frustum faces and edges. However, such an approach is not only tedious, it is also not guaranteed to lead to better image quality because the error might be distributed in a completely different way on the view samples that are actually visible.

These considerations show that LiSPSM does not necessarily provide minimum error over the whole view frustum, but only for a representative ray in the center of the view frustum. While in the case of an overhead light, the resulting error distribution for LiSPSM is still very good, it is difficult to predict the behavior for more general cases, like a tilted view frustum or a more complex body **PSR**.

4.2.3   Storage Factor for Perspective Warping for Overhead Directional Light

In this section, we will derive the perspective error for perspective warping for the simple case of an overhead directional light. Following Lloyd et al. [Lloyd06b], we show that in this case the overall perspective error is constant for a range of warping parameters starting with n_{opt}.

For directional lights, some simplifications apply; in particular, $\frac{d_l}{n_l}$ goes to one as both terms approach infinity,

$$\frac{z_n}{W_j} = \frac{az_n}{W_i} = \frac{1}{2\tan\theta}, \quad \text{and} \quad \frac{W_v}{W_{v'}} = \frac{W_u}{W_{u'}} = 1.$$

We also decide to ignore the view-frustum angles φ_t, φ_s and φ_j, φ_i.

The restriction to an overhead light allows us to set $v = z - z_n$ and $\tan\theta' = (z_f/f)a\tan\theta$. By plugging this into Equation (4.11), we obtain

$$\tilde{m}_t(z, n) = \frac{r_j}{r_t}\frac{1}{2\tan\theta}\frac{(n + z - z_n)^2}{z}\frac{f - n}{fn}, \quad (4.19)$$

$$\tilde{m}_s(z, n) = \frac{r_i}{r_s}\frac{1}{2a\tan\theta}\frac{n + z - z_n}{z}2\tan\theta'. \quad (4.20)$$

It can be shown that the maximum of $\tilde{m}_s$ always occurs on the near plane, while the maximum of $\tilde{m}_t(z, n)$ occurs on the near plane for $n > n_{opt}$ and on the far plane otherwise, thus the maximum errors along t and s in dependence of the warping parameter n are

$$M_t(n) = \frac{r_j}{r_t} \frac{z_f - z_n}{2 \tan \theta} \begin{cases} \frac{f}{n z_f} & n \leq n_{opt}, \\ \frac{n}{f z_n} & n > n_{opt}, \end{cases} \tag{4.21}$$

$$M_s(n) = \frac{r_i}{r_s} \frac{n z_f}{z_n f}. \tag{4.22}$$

An interesting result is that the combined error S, which measures the required factor between shadow-map and screen resolutions for reconstruction free from perspective aliasing, is constant for $n \leq n_{opt}$:

$$S = \frac{r_t}{r_j} M_t(n) \frac{r_s}{r_i} M_s(n) = \frac{z_f/z_n - 1}{2 \tan \theta} \begin{cases} 1 & n \leq n_{opt}, \\ \frac{n^2 z_f}{f^2 z_n} & n > n_{opt}. \end{cases} \tag{4.23}$$

However, to obtain such an alias-free reconstruction, the shadow map needs to be rectangular, as it needs to allocate the resolution to the s- and t-axes in a way that $M_t = M_s = 1$. This may lead to strongly rectangular shadow maps depending on the choice of n. If we look at the ratio between the two errors for $n = n_{opt}$,

$$R = \frac{r_t}{r_j} M_t(n_{opt}) \bigg/ \frac{r_s}{r_i} M_s(n_{opt}) = \frac{(1 - z_n/z_f)}{2 \tan \theta}, \tag{4.24}$$

we can see that the optimal parameter leads to an even distribution of error between the shadow-map axes; that is, for an alias-free reconstruction, the shadow map can be almost square for all but very short view frusta, while if we decrease n, we need more and more resolution for the t-axis. In practice, this means that if square shadow maps are used, n_{opt} is a good choice for the warping parameter. Note that for square shadow maps and $R \neq 1$, error could theoretically be further improved by adapting n so that R becomes one.

This behavior can also be seen in Figure 4.8, which compares the aliasing error along the shadow-map t- and s-axes for uniform shadow maps, perspective shadow maps with warping parameter as in the original PSM paper, and the optimal warping parameter.

A side result of Equation (4.23) is that the storage factor for uniform shadow mapping is

$$S = \frac{z_f}{z_n} \frac{z_f/z_n - 1}{2 \tan \theta}, \tag{4.25}$$

so a uniform shadow map requires a factor of z_f/z_n more texels, which is quite significant for common view frusta.

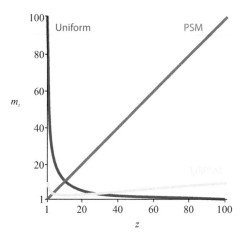

Figure 4.8. Perspective aliasing errors plotted against z-coordinate for different shadow mapping techniques for an overhead directional light.

4.2.4 Optimal Parametrization for Overhead Directional Light

Finally, we investigate the question of what would be an optimal parametrization if we consider more general warping functions, beyond perspective transformations. An *optimal parametrization* would make $\tilde{m}_t$ and $\tilde{m}_s$ constant at one over the whole available depth range. We will analyze this case only for an overhead directional light, along a line in the center of the view frustum; similar to the previous section, some simplifications apply: n_l/d_l converges to one, $\cos \varphi_t$ will be constant, and since the light is overhead, $u = x$ and $v = z - z_\mathrm{n}$.

Pluggin this into Equation (3.9) results in

$$\tilde{m}_t(z) = \frac{r_j}{r_t} \frac{dz}{dt} \frac{1}{2 \tan \theta} \frac{1}{z} = C_t \frac{dz}{dt} \frac{1}{z} = 1, \qquad (4.26)$$

$$\tilde{m}_s(x, z) = \frac{r_i}{r_s} \frac{dx}{ds} \frac{1}{2a \tan \theta} \frac{1}{z} = C_s \frac{dx}{ds} \frac{1}{z} = 1, \qquad (4.27)$$

with constant terms represented as C_t and C_s. These are ordinary differential equations of first order, which are easy to solve by integration:

$$t(z) = \int \frac{dt}{dz} dz = \int \frac{C_t}{z} dz = C_t \ln(z) + C_0, \qquad (4.28)$$

$$s(x, z) = \int \frac{ds}{dx} dx = \int \frac{C_s}{z} dx = C_s \frac{x}{z} + C_1. \qquad (4.29)$$

Taking into account the boundary conditions,

$$t(z_\mathrm{n}) = 0, \quad t(z_\mathrm{f}) = 1, \quad s(0, z_\mathrm{n}) = 1/2, \quad s(z_\mathrm{f} a \tan \theta, z_\mathrm{f}) = 1, \qquad (4.30)$$

leads to

$$t(z) \quad = \quad \frac{\ln z/z_n}{\ln z_f/z_n}, \tag{4.31}$$

$$s(x, z) \quad = \quad \frac{x}{z} \frac{1}{2a \tan \theta} + \frac{1}{2}. \tag{4.32}$$

This means that applying a perspective transform before rendering the shadow map will lead to an optimal error in the s-direction, at least in this particular configuration. This observation is the basis for perspective shadow mapping, as discussed in the previous sections. Unfortunately, the error in t-direction cannot be optimized so easily. The formulation above shows that the scene needs to be transformed with a logarithmic function in the z-direction, which is nonlinear and, thus, cannot be implemented efficiently in existing hardware.

Furthermore, it is interesting to study the actual error achieved by the optimal parametrizations by plugging Equation (4.32) into the definition of $\tilde{m}_t(z)$ and $\tilde{m}_s(x, z)$:

$$\tilde{m}_t \quad = \quad \frac{r_j}{r_t} \frac{\ln z_f/z_n}{2 \tan \theta}, \tag{4.33}$$

$$\tilde{m}_s \quad = \quad \frac{r_i}{r_s}. \tag{4.34}$$

This means that a perspective parametrization of the shadow map can achieve sampling free from perspective aliasing in the s-direction if the shadow map has the same resolution as the screen. For the t-direction, however, even the optimal logarithmic parametrization requires a factor of

$$S = \frac{\ln z_f/z_n}{2 \tan \theta} \tag{4.35}$$

higher resolution than the screen, which is also the storage factor for the combined parametrization.

Logarithmic Perspective Shadow Maps

In more recent work, Lloyd et al. [Lloyd08] have revisited the logarithmic mapping and combined it with a perspective warp, leading to logarithmic perspective shadow maps (LogPSM). In a very involved mathematical treatise, they derive warping functions that approach the optimal constant error very closely, based on the exact sampling-error formulation. They also consider fully general three-dimensional configurations. Unfortunately, such a parametrization is not practical for implementation on current hardware. Lloyd et al. [Lloyd07b, Lloyd06a] propose simple modifications to the current rasterization pipeline to make logarithmic rasterization feasible, but we do not expect this to be available until rasterization becomes fully programmable.

The logarithm could be applied in a vertex program. However, pixel positions and all input parameters for pixel programs are interpolated hyperbolically. This makes graphics hardware amenable to perspective mappings, but not logarithmic ones. As a proof of concept, logarithmic rasterization can be evaluated exactly in the fragment shader by rendering quads that are guaranteed to bound the final primitive and discarding fragments that fall outside the primitive. However, this is too slow for practical implementation.

4.2.5 Plane Optimal Perspective Warping

The approaches discussed so far consider perspective error in the whole view frustum. The original motivation for perspective shadow mapping, however, came from the observation that perspective warping leads to a constant error when the shadow is projected to a particular plane in the scene [Stamminger02]. It is important to note that in this case, constant error stems from a *combination* of perspective and projective errors, not from perspective error alone. As we already saw, constant perspective error (along the t-axis) can only be achieved by logarithmic warping. Figure 4.9 illustrates the difference between these two views. The figure shows small edges that all project to the same height on the image plane. To get constant error, one needs to introduce a warp that makes the projections of these edges to the shadow map exactly equal. The element that is translated along the z-axis has a constant projective error term, and thus, only considers perspective aliasing. Therefore, the projection of these elements to the shadow map corresponds to the logarithmic spacing. The element that is translated along the plane, however, has a varying projective error (in particular, the term $\cos \psi_j$ varies along the plane). Therefore, making the projections of these elements constant in the shadow-map plane will lead to an ideal error distribution along that particular plane, but not along the whole view frustum. This corresponds to the perspective shadow-map spacing. As can be seen, the spacing of the shadow-map projections becomes very large for distant edges.

However, optimizing the error on a number of particular planes may still be useful, for example, with scenes that have a small number of dominant planes (ground plane, etc.). Chong and Gortler [Chong04] generalized the observation shown in Figure 4.9. They observed that perspective warping can also be achieved by an affine transformation of the shadow-map plane. So instead of deriving parameters of an additional perspective transform in the shadow-map matrix, they observed that the resulting transform is still a projective transform and optimize for the parameters of that combined transform directly. In this way, the projection can be optimized by solving a small linear system, delivering constant error along a specified plane in the scene. If there is more than one dominant plane in the scene, one shadow map is created for each plane, and during rendering, the

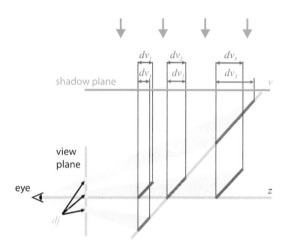

Figure 4.9. Difference between perspective and logarithmic error optimization. All elements project to the same image-space length dj but to different shadow-plane lengths dv_i. Logarithmic error optimization leads to constant error for an element translated in the z-direction. Perspective error optimization leads to constant error for an element translated along a given plane. The variation in dv_i is much stronger in this case, which is not desirable.

fragment shader decides which of the shadow maps to use. The problem with that approach is that the dominant planes have to be specified beforehand. The authors later [Chong07] presented an optimization approach that reads back a low-resolution framebuffer and uses a numerical optimization scheme to find the parameters of the shadow-map projection based on the actual content of the scene. For dynamic scenes, this obviously leads to temporal aliasing. Furthermore, it is likely that the information gained by a read back of the scene can be even better utilized by an approach that also reduces projective error, as presented in Section 4.4. A similar, but more heuristic, approach was discussed by Forsyth [Forsyth06].

4.3 Global Partitioning

While warping works very well in some configurations, especially if the light is overhead, there are other configurations where no benefit can be reaped, for example, if the light is directly behind the viewer. In this case, one global perspective warp will not change the sampling densities along the z-axis of the viewer, and therefore, warping must degenerate to uniform shadow mapping to avoid increasing error. A much better alternative is to use more than one shadow map. There are two main ways to do that: z-partitioning, where different shadow maps are created for different z-ranges of the view frustum, and frustum-face partitioning, where one shadow map is created for each view-frustum face.

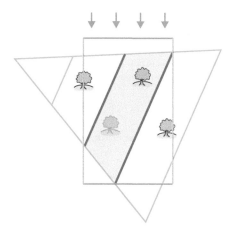

Figure 4.10. PSSM: the shadow map for the middle of three partitions of the view frustum (side view).

4.3.1   Z-Partitioning

The most prominent approach and one of the most practical algorithms to improve initial sampling for shadow mapping is to subdivide the view frustum along the z-axis and calculate a separate equal-sized shadow map for each sub-frustum. This approach goes by the names of cascaded shadow maps (CSM) [Engel06], parallel split shadow maps (PSSM) [Zhang06a], or z-partitioning [Lloyd06b]. The original idea of using multiple shadow maps for a distant light source was already discovered much earlier by Tadamura et al. [Tadamura99, Tadamura01]. They describe the special case of the sun as a light source, also including considerations for the penumbra caused by the sun. Figure 4.10 shows an example of a PSSM where the view frustum is split into three partitions, and the shadow map for the middle partition map is shown. Using this approach, the sampling density decreases for each successive partition because the same number of shadow-map samples cover a larger and larger area, also depending on the split positions.

In the most naive implementation, a PSSM scheme with n partitions requires n shadow rendering passes. Zhang et al. [Zhang07a] describe different methods to reduce the number of rendering passes, for example, by using the geometry shader to replicate each triangle into each of the required shadow maps during the shadow rendering pass. On the other hand, they also show a multipass method that does not require shaders and runs on older hardware.

In contrast to global warping schemes, the effect of z-partitioning is not limited to the directions implied by the axes of the shadow map, but even works for cases where the axes of the shadow map are orthogonal to the view direction (i.e., when the light is directly behind the viewer). This is the main advantage of z-partitioning

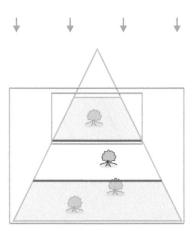

Figure 4.11. The nearest shadow map covers a smaller area than the farthest shadow map and therefore leads to higher resolution.

over warping approaches and the reason why z-partitioning is much more robust in general configurations. Figure 4.11 shows the nearest and farthest partition in a situation with the light directly behind the viewer. The shadow map for the nearest partition covers a much smaller area, and therefore, the perceived resolution is higher, just as is the case for the viewer projection.

Algorithm

For z-partitioning, the view frustum is split into n partitions according to one of the split-placement rules discussed later on. To create the shadow maps, for each partition i, we calculate the set of potential shadow receivers $\mathbf{PSR}_i$ (Section 4.1) and render a shadow map focused on it.

During the main rendering pass, in the fragment shader, the z-coordinate of the fragment is compared to the split boundaries, and the appropriate shadow map is sampled accordingly.

Placing the Splits

The most important question in this method is where to position the split planes (see Figure 4.12).

Logarithmic splits. One way is to go back to the derivation of the shadow-map resampling error. Each shadow-map partition could be interpreted as a big texel of a global shadow map, so that z-partitioning becomes a discretization of an arbitrary warping function. We have shown before that the optimal warping function is

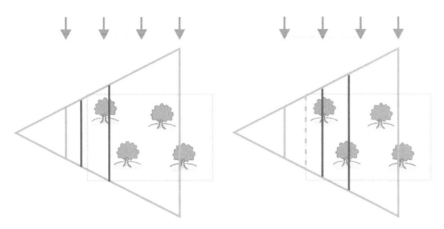

Figure 4.12. Logarithmic splits without (left) and with (right) a pseudo near plane (dashed line). Not using a pseudo near plane wastes a complete partition in this example.

logarithmic; therefore, the split positions C_i should be determined by

$$C_i^{\log} = z_\mathrm{n} \left(\frac{z_\mathrm{f}}{z_\mathrm{n}} \right)^{\frac{i}{m}},$$

(4.36)

where m is the number of partitions [Lloyd06b]. This can be seen easily by solving Equation (4.31) for z. Replacing z by C_i and t by i/m then gives Equation (4.36). A variant of logarithmic splits was already used by Tadamura et al. in their original work concerning plural sunlight depth buffers [Tadamura99, Tadamura01].

Practical splits. Zhang et al. [Zhang06a] note that the optimal partition scheme is not practical because it allocates most resolution close to the near plane, which is often not populated with objects. They therefore propose computing the split positions as a weighted average between the logarithmic scheme and a simple equidistant split-plane distribution:

$$C_i^{\mathrm{pract}} = \alpha C_i^{\log} + (1 - \alpha) \left(z_\mathrm{n} + \frac{i}{m(z_\mathrm{n} - z_\mathrm{f})} \right).$$

(4.37)

Pseudo near plane. An alternative solution to improving the logarithmic split scheme that better respects the theoretical properties of shadow-map aliasing is to use a pseudo near plane, just as in warping [Lloyd07a, Section 5.1.8]. This can be achieved simply by replacing z_n by an adapted value z_n' in Equation (4.36) for $C_i, i > 0$, with C_0 remaining fixed at z_n.

Sample distribution splits. As mentioned in Section 4.1, Lauritzen et al. [Lauritzen11] propose analyzing the actual distribution of the depth values in the view frustum. A min/max mipmap pyramid allows extracting accurate near and far planes for the view frustum, so that the logarithmic splitting scheme can be applied without wasting resolution on invisible parts of the scene. The bounds for each split region can be further improved by creating a separate pyramid for each split that takes into account only the relevant z-values for the split and also generates bounds in the x-direction. Especially for farther regions, this can significantly reduce the size of the fitting body and thus improve shadow-map resolution. Lauritzen et al. also describe advanced solutions that create a depth histogram on the GPU using DirectX 11 compute shaders and compute the split positions using k-means clustering. Even if the required operations are available in hardware, the added cost has to be compared against adaptive subdivision approaches (Section 4.4), which might provide even better quality.

Other Considerations

Zhang et al. [Zhang09] discuss a number of practical issues related to z-partitioning regarding flickering artifacts, shadow-map storage strategies, split selection, computation of texture coordinates, and filtering across splits. An interesting observation is that, in some cases, a point belonging to one partition could actually be shadowed using a shadow map generated for a different partition. This happens when the light is almost parallel to the view direction. In this case, the shadow maps for the partitions nearer the viewpoint will provide better resolution.

There are various strategies for how to *store* the shadow maps: in separate textures, which requires more samplers to evaluate but is also compatible with older hardware; in a texture array, which only runs on DirectX 10.1-class or later hardware, or in a texture atlas, which might limit the maximum texture resolution but is the most practical solution otherwise. For example, the texture atlas for four splits would consist of four equally sized shadow maps arranged in a 2×2 pattern.

There are also various strategies for how to *sample* the shadow map: in multiple passes, which works on all hardware, or using a comparison in the fragment shader to determine the split for each fragment, which is faster. Zhang et al. [Zhang07a] discuss various implementation strategies, including a method that uses the geometry shader to generate all shadow maps in a single pass.

Special care needs to be taken when *filtering* across splits (Chapter 5). If only the neighboring texel is accessed by the graphics hardware upon a shadow-map lookup, a one-texel border is sufficient to avoid artifacts. Precomputed filtering methods (Section 5.3), however, calculate derivatives by comparing texture coordinates from neighboring pixels, which might index different partitions and would, therefore, be meaningless. To avoid this, the required derivatives can be calculated analytically by properly scaling derivatives calculated for standard shadow mapping for the respective split [Zhang09]. In any case, the transition from one split to the next usually remains visible. This effect can be slightly reduced by combining z-partitioning with warping (Section 4.3.3).

4.3.2 Frustum-Face Partitioning

An alternative global partitioning scheme is to use a separate shadow map for either each front face or each back face of the view frustum as projected onto the shadow-map plane and use warping for each shadow map separately. This can also be interpreted as putting a cube map around the post-perspective view frustum and applying a shadow map to each cube face [Kozlov04]. Each frustum face can be further split to increase quality.

This scheme is especially important because it can be shown that it is optimal for LogPSM (i.e., the combination of logarithmic and perspective shadow mapping introduced by Lloyd et al. [Lloyd08]). However, we will not elaborate this scheme here because Lloyd et al. [Lloyd06b] also showed that for practical situations, such as a large far plane to near plane ratio and a low number of shadow

Figure 4.13. Examples of z-partitioning with one to three partitions (left to right). The shadow map used for each fragment is color coded: camera view (top row), close-up of shadowed region (middle row), and outside view showing the view frustum, the partitions, and the intersection bodies (bottom row). Inlays show the depth maps.

maps, z-partitioning (optionally combined with warping) is superior to frustum-face partitioning with perspective warping.

4.3.3   Combining Warping and Global Partitioning

Z-partitioning can be combined with warping by rendering each partition using perspective warping. This increases quality, especially for situations where warping works well (overhead lights). Indeed, the combination of the two methods is straightforward as each sub-frustum can be handed off to the warping algorithm in a completely independent way. Another advantage is that transition artifacts can be reduced, as error in the t-direction matches up more closely at split boundaries if warping is used for each partition.

One special case of such a combination is to use one uniform shadow map and one perspective shadow map and calculate a plane equation that separates areas where the one or the other provides better quality [Mikkelsen07]. This will improve error, especially in the farther region, compared to warping alone, but

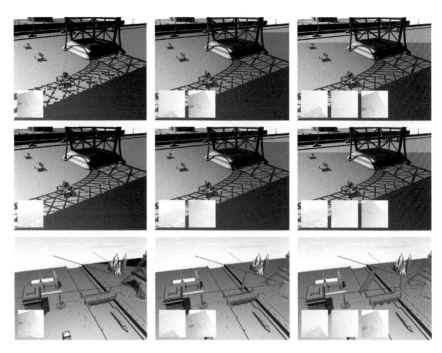

Figure 4.14. Examples of z-partitioning with and without warping for one to three partitions (left to right). The shadow map used for each fragment is color coded: camera view, uniform (top row); camera view, warping (middle row); and outside view showing the view frustum, the partitions, and the intersection bodies (bottom row). Inlays show the depth maps.

the maximum error (assuming the same overall number of samples in the shadow maps) actually increases, so this method has to be applied carefully.

Figure 4.13 shows the effect of z-partitioning. The split distances are chosen according to Zhang's practical split scheme. Figure 4.14 shows the effect of z-partitioning versus warping and the combination of the two. Warping alone has a similar effect as z-partitioning and can further improve the quality of z-partitioning if used in combination. Figure 4.15 shows a case that is not amenable to warping due to a nearly overhead light, while z-partitioning still improves quality. All examples use a directional light source.

Further examples of different combinations of warping and z-partitioning can be found in Figures 4.16, 4.17, and 4.18. These figures show the observer image, the light views, a visualization of the view frustum and its partitions, and the plots of $\tilde{m}_t$ and $\tilde{m}_s$. Note that $\tilde{m}_t$ and $\tilde{m}_s$ do not depend on the actual geometry, so surfaces visible in the images might exhibit different error than predicted by the shown curves. The views also show the texel grid of the shadow map projected

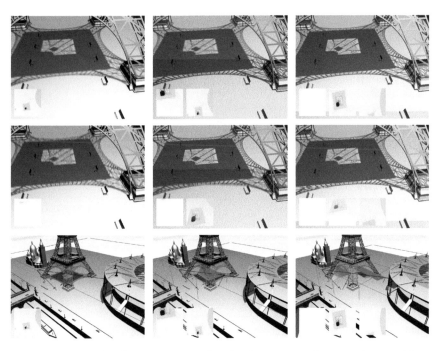

Figure 4.15. Examples of z-partitioning with and without warping for one to three partitions (left to right), here showing an example that is not amenable to warping. Using hardware PCF, the quality differences become more obvious: camera view, uniform (top row); camera view, warping (middle row); and outside view showing the view frustum, the partitions, and the intersection bodies (bottom row). Inlays show the depth maps.

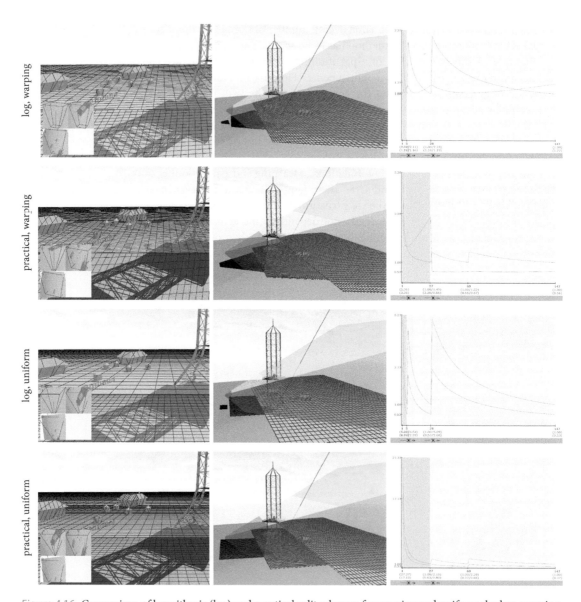

Figure 4.16. Comparison of logarithmic (log) and practical split schemes for warping and uniform shadow mapping. The partitions are marked with different colors (left), and the shadow map texel grid as well as the light views are overlayed (middle). The error graph (right) shows $\tilde{m}_t$ (blue, "x-dir") and $\tilde{m}_s$ (orange, "y-dir").

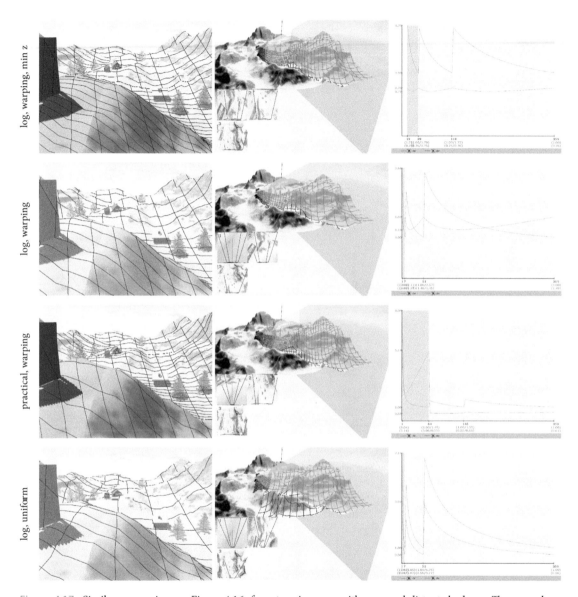

Figure 4.17. Similar comparison as Figure 4.16, for a terrain scene with near and distant shadows. The rows show logarithmic (log) versus practical split scheme, warping versus uniform shadow mapping, and the use of a near plane adjusted to the minimum read-back z-value (min z).

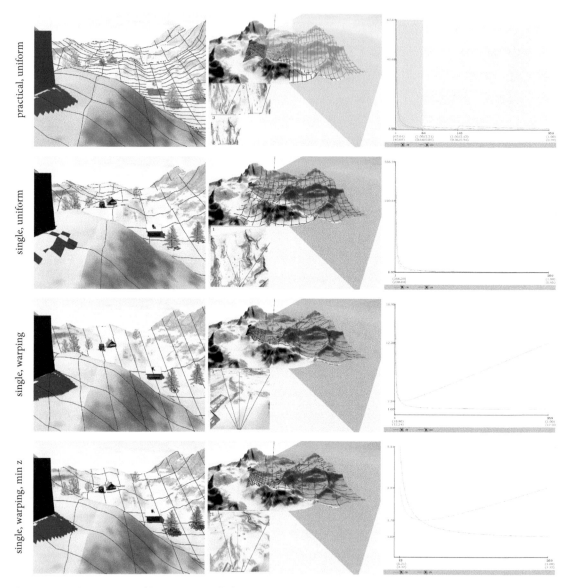

Figure 4.18. Continuation of Figure 4.18, including comparisons with a single shadow map (single).

onto the terrain. Figure 4.16 compares the logarithmic split scheme with Zhang's practical split scheme (parameter 0.5), both for uniform shadow mapping and for warping with $n = n_{opt}$. It can be seen that for the logarithmic split scheme and warping (first row), the error $\tilde{m}_t$ (blue plot) matches up at the split boundaries, leading to the lowest maximum error among the shown examples. The error $\tilde{m}_s$ (orange plot) has a peak at the beginning of each partition and then falls off. In the observer view, this fact is demonstrated by the texel grid visualization. While the (screen-space) height of the texels does not change significantly at split boundaries, the width of the texels almost doubles.

Figures 4.17 and 4.18 show a terrain scene with detailed shadows both near and far from the observer. A common problem with the logarithmic split scheme is that the first partition is often not used because it is very short (see Figure 4.17, second row). While Zhang's practical split scheme alleviates this (third row), a similarly good distribution of split boundaries with even better maximum error can be achieved by determining the minimum z-value in the scene through a read back of the z-buffer and adjusting the near plane accordingly. Using this method, the near-plane distance can be pushed from one (second/third row) to 13 (first row). We also show uniform shadow mapping with the two split schemes (Figure 4.17, fourth row, logarithmic split scheme; Figure 4.18, first row, practical split scheme). Figure 4.18 shows shadow mapping without z-partitioning for reference: uniform shadow mapping (second row), warping with $n = n_{opt}$ (third row), and warping with the near plane distance pushed to the minimum z-value of the scene (fourth row). The software that was used to create these visualizations is available for download at the book's webpage.

4.3.4   Partitioning—Error Analysis

We will base some general observations on a simplified error analysis. Figure 4.19 [Lloyd06b] shows the overall error (here called storage factor), which takes into account error in both shadow-map directions, of different schemes for different numbers of shadow maps for overhead lights (ideal for warping) and a light behind (no warping possible). It is interesting to see that for a moderate number of shadow maps, z-partitioning combined with warping provides the best results for overhead lights, and is equivalent to z-partitioning for light behind.

Adding warping to z-partitioning has another advantage: since warping with the optimal parameter n_{opt} equalizes error $\tilde{m}_t$ for near and far planes, the error of two adjacent partitions at a boundary will be the same, at least if the logarithmic split scheme is used. This is because for n_{opt}, the maximum error of a partition is proportional to the ratio of far plane to near plane (i.e., C_{i+1}/C_i), and for the logarithmic splitting scheme, this ratio is constant. This reduces visible transition artifacts in the t-direction. For the s-direction, warping also reduces transition artifacts, but they remain noticeable. Only a perspective warp with $n = z_n$, as in

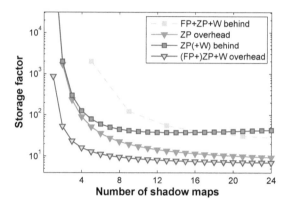

Figure 4.19. Total error of different schemes for varying shadow-map numbers. FP is frustum-face partitioning, ZP is z-partitioning, W is warping (courtesy of Brandon Lloyd).

PSM, would remove transitions in $\tilde{m}_s$. Also, warping leads to the largest quality difference between different light directions, which may not be desirable.

More exactly, using the results from Section 4.2.2, the error of combined warping and partitioning can be characterized by the storage factor, which for k partitions is simply k times the storage factor for an individual partition if the logarithmic split scheme is used. So for uniform shadow mapping, using Equation (4.25):

$$S_k^{\text{uniform}} = k(z_f/z_n)^{1/k} \frac{(z_f/z_n)^{1/k} - 1}{2a\tan\theta}. \tag{4.38}$$

For warping with $n \le n_{\text{opt}}$, the $(z_f/z_n)^{1/k}$ factor goes away (Equation (4.23)), so

$$S_k^{\text{warping}} = k\frac{(z_f/z_n)^{1/k} - 1}{2a\tan\theta}. \tag{4.39}$$

As k increases, it can be shown, via expansion of

$$(z_f/z_n)^{1/k} = \exp^{1/k\ln z_f/z_n}$$

$$= 1 + \frac{1}{k}\ln\frac{z_f}{z_n} + \frac{\left(\frac{1}{k}\ln\frac{z_f}{z_n}\right)^2}{2!} + \dots,$$

that this expression converges to the optimal parametrization (Equation (4.35)):

$$S^{\text{logarithmic}} = \frac{\ln z_f/z_n}{2a\tan\theta}. \tag{4.40}$$

This is another significant advantage of z-partitioning over warping alone: z-partitioning gives a better approximation to the optimal parametrizations because the splits can be chosen optimally. Each partition could be seen as a (huge) texel in a very low-resolution logarithmic shadow map.

4.4 Adaptive Partitioning

The advantage of global partitioning algorithms is that they are very fast. On the other hand, they completely ignore surface orientation and can therefore not improve undersampling due to surfaces that are viewed almost edge-on by the light source (projection aliasing).

In this section, we show a number of algorithms that try to allocate samples in a better way by analyzing the scene before creating the shadow map. This inevitably incurs some overhead due to the analysis step (which often necessitates a read back) but leads to much better results in general cases. Furthermore, to make best use of the shadow-map resolution, even global partitioning algorithms rely on a scene-analysis step to discover the depth distribution of samples in view space, for example, to obtain tight near and far planes. Thus, it is only a small step towards using the gathered information for a more thorough analysis. Given the constantly growing power of GPUs, it is becoming feasible to carry out the scene analysis pass directly on the GPU, so that read backs can be kept to a minimum.

Prominent examples are queried virtual shadow maps (QVSM) [Giegl07b], adaptive shadow maps (ASM) [Lefohn05], fitted virtual shadow maps (FVSM) [Giegl07a], resolution matched shadow maps (RMSM) [Lefohn07], and tiled shadow maps (TiledSM) [Arvo04a].

All of these approaches rely on a hierarchical data structure (usually a quadtree) to refine the shadow map. They differ mainly in the termination criteria and the measures that are required to determine this termination criterion.

4.4.1 Iterative Hierarchy Refinement

One approach to adaptive partitioning is to start with a shadow map (e.g., 2,048 × 2,048) for the whole scene and iteratively split the shadow map into sub-tiles with the same resolution. For each sub-tile, a new shadow map is created. This process is repeated recursively until a termination criterion is met.

Queried Virtual Shadow Maps

QVSM, introduced by Giegl and Wimmer [Giegl07b], are maybe the simplest adaptive partitioning scheme to implement because they do not require a read back to compute the termination criterion and do not require implementing hierarchical data structures on the GPU. The idea is very simple: after each refinement step, check whether the shadow generated by the refined shadow maps differs from the shadow generated using the lower-resolution shadow map.

Figure 4.20. Standard $4,096^2$ shadow map with perspective warping, rendering at 64 FPS (left). QVSM with a maximum refinement level of 32×32 and $1,024^2$ tiles, rendering at 32 FPS (right).

For this, the shadow generated by each tile is written to a so-called shadow texture (in screen space), and the number of changed pixels is counted. If a certain threshold is exceeded, refinement continues. The way to make this fast is to do all calculations on the GPU by using the occlusion query mechanism to count the number of changed pixels. This works by instructing the fragment shader to emit a fragment only if the result differs from the shadow texture generated in the previous pass.

QVSM require quite a high number of scene-rendering passes, one for each refinement attempt. In order to avoid re-rendering the scene multiple times, Giegl and Wimmer propose to first render the scene into a linear depth buffer from the camera viewpoint, so that each rendering pass just uses this buffer to calculate shadows. In a deferred shading system, the G-buffer can be used. The authors also describe heuristics that allow skipping refinement levels in certain situations.

Figure 4.20 shows a comparison of a large standard shadow map with QVSM.

Adaptive Shadow Maps

While QVSM use a heuristic based on the resulting shadow texture as a termination criterion, Fernando et al. [Fernando01] propose using a scene analysis to determine the required shadow resolution. This analysis is based both on the projected size of a texel in the shadow map and on the observation that higher shadow resolution is only required for shadow edges. Therefore, for each iteration, an edge-detection step is run on the new shadow-map tile, and only those samples mapping to shadow edges are considered for node refinement.

In particular, the mipmap mechanism is used to estimate the size of the foot-print of a texel in the shadow map and, thus, the required resolution level. For each node, the number of silhouette texels with insufficient resolution are counted, and refinement is terminated if this number is lower than a threshold.

GPU implementation. While the original ASM were based on a read back of the complete camera view (containing the calculated mipmap levels for each sample), a GPU-based version was also proposed [Lefohn05]. This version uses a GPU quadtree, which basically corresponds to a mipmapped page table stored in GPU memory. Each page-table entry stores whether the corresponding shadow tile has been generated. After each refinement step, the algorithm iterates over all view samples containing edges; looks them up in the page-table texture at the correct mipmap level; and if the corresponding tile is missing, a refinement request is generated. GPU-based stream compaction [Billeter09] is used to condense these refinement requests into a compact list containing only unique tiles that need to be refined. Note that in comparison to QVSM, each iteration step can generate several refinement requests in different locations of the shadow map.

However, ASM in general suffer from significant problems. First, the varying number of iterations required to converge each frame makes performance unpredictable. Second, iterative refinement starting from a coarse depth image poses severe problems in accuracy: if an edge does not exist in the coarse depth image, refinement will never find it unless by luck (e.g., if the missing edge gets refined because it ends up on the same page as a detected edge). Third, it is not suited for dynamic scenes, since the whole hierarchy has to be iteratively regenerated if the light or an object moves.

4.4.2   Direct Hierarchy Evaluation

Iterative refinement has proven expensive due to its iterative nature: both approaches require repeated evaluations of shadow maps, and ASM, in addition, require an edge-detection pass in each iteration that is not guaranteed to robustly find edges that might appear in more detailed levels. Therefore, both ASM and QVSM have been evolved into algorithms that generate the hierarchy directly, without intermediate refinement. RMSM [Lefohn07] are an evolution of ASM that also drop the edge-detection pass. Giegl and Wimmer [Giegl07a] introduced FVSM, which improve upon QVSM.

The main idea of both algorithms is to determine the required resolution for each view sample directly, without intermediate rendering passes. The main idea of direct hierarchy evaluation is to create information about the required shadow-map resolution for each view sample during the camera-rendering pass and create a hierarchy to match these requirements. The main challenge is to convert the information generated in the camera pass into a hierarchy because this requires a projection of this information into the shadow map, which is a scatter operation that is not directly supported by the standard graphics pipeline. The direct hierarchy evaluation that is the basis for both RMSM and FVSM works as follows:

1. *Camera pass.* In a camera-rendering pass, create for each view sample both the shadow-map lookup coordinates and resolution-requirements information $(s, t, r, \mathbf{l})$ (with (s, t) the shadow-map coordinates, r the light-space depth value, and $\mathbf{l}$ a resolution information, for example, a mipmap level).

2. *Determine shadow maps to create.* Iterate over the view samples and convert them to a hierarchy of required shadow-map tiles.

3. *Create and apply shadow maps.* Render the required shadow-map tiles and shadow the scene with them.

In both RMSM and FVSM, the required resolution for each view sample is determined using the texture gradients $\frac{dF}{dx} = \left(\frac{du}{dx}, \frac{dv}{dx} \right), \frac{dF}{dy} = \left(\frac{du}{dy}, \frac{dv}{dy} \right)$. These gradi-

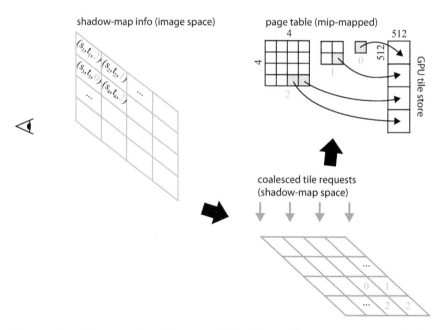

Figure 4.21. Shadow mapping using a page table. A first rendering pass generates a buffer containing texture coordinates and mipmap levels. This buffer is converted into a set of tile requests. The requested tiles are rendered to a GPU tile store, and the page table is updated to mark the available tiles. The page table is a small mipmapped texture that stores a GPU tile ID if the respective tile resides in memory (for RMSM) or the number of samples that request this tile (for FVSM). Here, for a page table size of 4 × 4 and a tile size of 512 × 512, a shadow map resolution of 2,048 × 2,048 can be obtained.

ents bound the projection of a pixel into the shadow map. For example, if $\frac{du}{dx} = 0.001$, then the resolution of the shadow map should be at least 1,000 texels in u-direction to handle the image's x-direction (for that view sample). The two algorithms use different metrics to calculate the desired resolution from the texture gradients.

Both algorithms create a hierarchical data structure in shadow-map space to coalesce the shadow map requests from the previous step. This data structure basically corresponds to a mipmapped *page table* known from virtual texturing, that is, it contains one entry for each possible shadow-map tile. For example, for a 32 K × 32 K "virtual" shadow-map resolution and 1 K × 1 K shadow-map tiles, the page table has a resolution of 32 × 32, one entry for each tile (see Figure 4.21). The page table is mipmapped so that, for example, 16 × 16, 8 × 8, etc., versions exist, which corresponds to a quadtree hierarchy. For example, the 2 × 2 version of the page table corresponds to a 2 K × 2 K shadow map resolution. The information stored in the page table is different for the two algorithms.

FVSM and RMSM differ in the specifics of how each individual step is implemented. In particular, FVSM uses the CPU to carry out step 2, while RMSM uses parallel processing primitives on the GPU for that step.

Fitted Virtual Shadow Maps

Camera pass. FVSM calculate the gradients in step 1 by finite differencing on a linear eye-space depth buffer created in a previous step. The required resolutions are derived from the axis-aligned bounding box of the gradients in shadow-map space.

Determine shadow maps to create. FVSM determine the required shadow maps by creating a mipmapped page table in four steps (the page table stores the minimum required resolution for the corresponding tile in both x- and y-directions): (1) Read back the buffer generated in the previous step to the CPU. (2) Project all view samples, along with the resolution information, directly into the full-resolution page table (e.g., 32 × 32) and compare it with the resolution stored in the corresponding page-table entry. Each page-table entry keeps track of the highest requested resolution among any sample projected to it. Requested resolutions are maintained separately for the x- and y-axes, derived from the dimensions of the axis-aligned bounding boxes of the pixel footprints. (3) Create a max mipmap from the page table. (4) Traverse the hierarchy (i.e., page-table mipmap chain) top-down (from low to high resolution), and terminate when the requested resolution stored in a page-table entry matches the tile resolution corresponding to that entry. The traversal uses binary or quadtree splitting, depending on whether only one or both shadow-map axes require refinement. This can lead to rectangular shadow maps, which better adapt to the required resolutions.

As an example, consider the situation where the recursive traversal processes a page-table entry in the 8×8 page table. If the entry contains a required resolution value larger than 8,096 in both the u- and v-directions, then a quadtree split is done and the four child nodes in the 16×16 page table are traversed. If the required resolution value is lower than 8,096 in both directions, then a 1 K $\times$ 1 K shadow-map tile for the entry is created, rendered, and used to shadow the scene (see below). If only the u-direction requires a resolution larger than 8,096, then only the u-direction is split. Note that in this case, subsequent recursive evaluations need to consider rectangular subregions of the page table. Only if all splits are quadtree splits will each region correspond to exactly one page-table entry.

FVSM uses a lower-resolution camera pass, so that read back and CPU analysis of the camera view do not become a bottleneck. While this may lead to a few pixels that do not obtain the required shadow-map resolution, these pixels typically correspond to areas of inhomogeneous shadows, where artifacts are not readily apparent.

As a further optimization, the authors propose using a simple histogram per page-table entry to count the number of texels that require a specific resolution (for example, using three bins). Thus, resolutions that are only requested by a low number of view samples can be discarded.

Create and apply shadow maps.   In FVSM, shadow maps are created *and applied* already during the recursive traversal of the mipmap chain. Since only leaf nodes in the hierarchy are used as actual shadow-map tiles, these tiles constitute a partition of the total shadow map, and each view sample is shadowed using exactly one of them. Like for QVSM, it is necessary to solve the problem that the scene has to be rendered multiple times using different shadow-map tiles. Again, the solution is to first render the scene into a temporary depth buffer. For each render pass applying a requested shadow-map tile to the scene, the view samples to be shadowed are not created by rendering, but by reconstruction from this eye-space depth buffer. View samples that project outside the current tile are discarded. The results of the different render passes are accumulated in an eye-space shadow texture. For shadow-map tile rendering, tight view-frustum culling should be used to avoid multiple rerenderings of the same objects. Note that because each tile is immediately used for shadowing, only one shadow-map buffer is required to shadow the whole scene. In a final pass, the shadow texture is used to calculate the shading of the framebuffer.

Resolution-Matched Shadow Maps

Camera pass.   RMSM calculate the required texture gradients directly in the fragment shader. The required shadow-map resolution is estimated using the area of the projected pixel, $A = |\frac{dF}{dx} \times \frac{dF}{dy}|$, which gives a more accurate result for anisotropic pixel footprints than taking the longer diagonal, as in standard mipmapping. The resulting mipmap level is then $\log_2(\sqrt{A})$.

Determine shadow maps to create. RMSM determine the required shadow maps directly on the GPU. While FVSM can afford recursive traversals of the page table on the CPU, for RMSM, the page table is maintained in a very similar manner to virtual texturing [Chajdas10]. The main conceptual difference to FVSM here is that lower-resolution nodes are also created if requested by a view sample, while FVSM only creates tiles with the highest requested resolution in the hierarchy. This simplifies the tile-determination step, since each view sample can be converted directly into a tile request, and no hierarchical dependencies between view samples exist. The drawback is that more tiles are created than necessary, since tiles for interior nodes of the hierarchy have to be created.

More specifically, the following steps have to be carried out: (1) Each view sample is converted to a tile request. A tile request (or tile ID) consists of the mipmap level and the integer coordinates of the page-table entry the view sample projects to. (2) All tiles for which a tile request has been issued are determined and transferred to the CPU. This step requires sorting of tile requests by tile ID and compaction of the resulting buffer to eliminate all duplicates. Both of these tasks can be carried out efficiently on a GPU using parallel sort and scan primitives, which, for example, allow stream compaction in $O(n)$ time [Billeter09].

As an optimization, the authors propose to eliminate tile requests from homogeneous areas, that is, for view samples whose (e.g., left and bottom) neighbors request the same tile. Followed by a stream-compaction step eliminating such unnecessary tile requests, the performance of the subsequent sort can be greatly improved.

Create and apply shadow maps. After all unique tile requests have been transferred to the CPU, all tiles are created by standard shadow-map rendering. Similar to FVSM, tight view-frustum culling should be employed to avoid duplicate renderings. In contrast to FVSM, RMSM requires enough free graphics memory to store all requested tiles. The address of each tile in graphics memory is then stored in the page table and transferred to GPU memory. Finally, the scene is rendered again using shadow mapping. Similar to virtual texturing, each shadow-map lookup first accesses the page table to determine the relevant tile.

Tiled Shadow Maps

An early attempt at the idea of adaptive shadow-map subdivision was presented by Arvo [Arvo04a]. Instead of a hierarchical subdivision of the shadow-map texture space into a hierarchy of equal-sized shadow-map tiles, Arvo subdivides a given shadow map consisting of a fixed number of tiles using a binary cut algorithm that recursively shifts the tile boundaries. The subdivision borders are placed so that more "important" regions are assigned larger partitions.

The importance is calculated in a separate rendering pass, creating a low-resolution shadow map. The importance value for a region is the sum of the importance values for the individual shadow-map samples contained in that region. The importance value for a shadow-map sample takes into account depth discontinuities in the shadow map: for discontinuity pixels, it is the magnitude of that discontinuity and, for other pixels, the distance of that pixel from the viewer.

While this algorithm shares some ideas with the subdivision approaches presented earlier in this section, it is of a more heuristic nature. In particular, all the other algorithms directly treat view samples and their projections into the shadow map, whereas this algorithm only looks at light samples, which precludes an accurate heuristic.

4.4.3   Comparison

While FVSM and RMSM differ in a number of aspects, the components of both algorithms could easily be mixed. For example, RMSM uses a more straightforward way to determine texture gradients in the shader, which could also be used in FVSM. On the other hand, the memory requirements in RMSM could be reduced by rendering and applying shadow maps iteratively, just as in FVSM. Since each view sample requests exactly one shadow-map tile, each rendering pass would loop over all view samples (by rendering a full-screen quad) and shadow only those that correspond to the current shadow tile. Rectangular tiles, on the other hand, would be more difficult to accommodate in RMSM. Similar to FVSM, it would be possible to start with a low-resolution eye view in order to reduce the number of view samples that have to be transformed into page requests. While this is not as critical as in FVSM, where read back and CPU treatment of view samples is a bottleneck, it could still improve performance. With DirectX 11-class hardware, it should be possible to implement both algorithms fully on the GPU, with the only traffic to the CPU being the information of which shadow pages to render.

Furthermore, it is interesting to compare the choice of allowing shadow tiles to be generated for intermediate nodes or not. For FVSM, the tiles constitute a partition of the shadow map, and no intermediate nodes are required. On the other hand, some of the nodes might actually not even be required, for example, if shadow detail is only visible in one of the sub-tiles of a tile. In that case, it is more efficient to just generate the tile and one of its sub-tiles. Note that even in RMSM, intermediate nodes are only generated if view samples actually request them—if all view samples request high-resolution tiles, the lower-resolution tiles are never generated.

Comparing RMSM and ASM, both approaches use a page-table texture and carry out all important steps on the GPU using GPU sort and stream compaction. But while ASM only accesses the current hierarchical shadow-map structure and then determines whether refinement is necessary, RMSM creates the complete hierarchy in one pass.

Note that all adaptive subdivision algorithms share aspects with view-sample mapping (see Section 4.5), which also maps view samples to shadow-map space, but drops the idea of a shadow-map quadtree completely and instead decides to just shadow the transformed view samples directly. Another observation is that the calculation of the required shadow-map resolution is very similar to the calculation of the required tiles in a virtual-texturing solution. Basically, the shadow map can be interpreted as a large virtual texture [Chajdas10] whose tiles are generated on demand depending on the current view. Thus, adaptive shadow-map subdivision should integrate easily into an existing virtual-texturing system, as has become popular in modern game engines. Actually, RMSM *is* a GPU-based implementation of virtual texturing, such as that discussed by Chajdas et al. [Chajdas10]. The main difference is that requested tiles are not streamed from disk but generated by shadow rendering.

4.5 View-Sample Mapping

The aliasing artifacts in hard shadow mapping stem from the fact that the shadow-map query locations do not correspond to the shadow-map sample locations. Ideally, one would like to create shadow-map samples exactly in those positions that will be queried later on. Difficult as that may seem, it is actually possible and has been proposed independently by Aila and Laine [Aila04b] under the name of *alias-free shadow maps* and Johnson [Johnson05] under the name of *irregular z-buffers*.

The algorithm proceeds by rendering an initial eye-space pass to obtain the desired sample locations, similar to adaptive shadow-map subdivision methods. These sample locations are then used as pixel locations for the subsequent shadow-map generation pass. The challenge is that these new sample locations do not lie on a regular grid anymore. Therefore, view-sample–accurate shadow algorithms have to solve the problem of irregular rasterization. While Johnson [Johnson05] proposes hardware modifications to implement dynamically managed linked lists to maintain a so-called irregular z-buffer, Sintorn et al. [Sintorn08b] manage to implement irregular rasterization on current GPUs using the NVIDIA CUDA framework. Another hardware implementation [Arvo07] is based on depth peeling, requiring one render pass per depth layer, and is therefore slower.

The basic idea of irregular rasterization algorithms is similar. After the eye-space pass, the generated view samples are projected into light space and stored in a light-space buffer. Each pixel of this buffer contains a list of view samples that fell into this pixel. Some lists will be empty, while some lists will contain several samples. These view samples are then tested for shadows by rasterizing the shadow-casting triangles (typically all triangles in the scene) from the light's viewpoint. Note that this rasterization has to be *conservative*, i.e., it has to include all pixels that are intersected by a triangle. This can be achieved by extending each triangle by a half-pixel size. For each covered rasterized fragment, the fragment shader tests all view samples in the corresponding per-fragment lists of the light-space buffer.

If a view sample is in shadow, this is indicated by flagging it. Finally, a screen-space quad is rendered in eye space, where each fragment does a shadow query by testing its corresponding list entry for the shadow flag. The method is suited to be combined with reparametrization methods.

4.5.1 Hardware Implementation

An efficient hardware implementation of irregular rasterization faces two problems: first, the projection of view samples into light space is a data-scattering operation that cannot be easily implemented using the standard graphics pipeline. Second, when rasterizing shadow casters, multiple view samples have to be repeatedly updated per shadow-map texel. Since rasterization can only output to the render targets associated with one pixel, the number of view samples per pixel is limited by the number of bits available in the render targets associated with the light buffer.

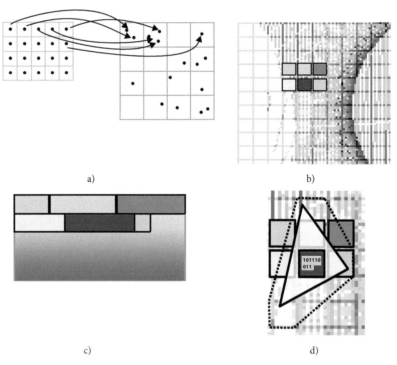

Figure 4.22. (a) In a hardware implementation of view-sample mapping, the view samples are first projected from screen space into the light view. (b) The image shows some shadow-map texels on a concrete object. (c) The view samples for each texel are stored compactly in a buffer created using CUDA. (d) Visibility information for each view sample is stored in bitmasks that are generated by rasterizing the occluding geometry into the light view.

In Sintorn et al.'s implementation, the first problem is solved using the efficient scattering capabilities available through CUDA. The projection of view samples happens in two passes (see Figure 4.22): in the first pass, only the number of samples falling onto each shadow-map texel are counted, as well as the local index of each new view sample in a pixel. At this stage, the projected samples are not yet stored. Using a running-sum scan, the sample counts are then converted to offsets into a global memory buffer. In the second pass, the view samples are projected again and stored at the appropriate offset (taking into account their local index) in the global buffer. Through this data-scattering operation, the size of the global view-sample buffer is given by the number of samples. Note that recent GPUs allow scattering in the standard graphics pipeline through the append buffer functionality (DirectX 11).

The second problem is solved by representing the shadowed/lit flag of each view sample using only one bit. The rasterization of shadow casters is carried out using the standard graphics pipeline into a framebuffer that contains, in each pixel, a bitmask of shadow flags for all view samples that project into that pixel. When rasterizing a shadow caster, the fragment shader first calculates the shadow status of each view sample with respect to the shadow caster and updates the framebuffer with that information using a logical OR blending operation. On newer GPUs, at least 128 bits can be written per output render target. Using multiple render targets (currently eight are possible) allows us to store and treat up to 1,024 view samples per shadow-map texel. The algorithm uses multipass rendering if more bits are needed. The final rendering is quick because each view sample knows its corresponding bitmask entry through its local index and simply fetches the appropriate value. Note that the second problem could alternatively be solved by implementing the rasterization in CUDA as well and using scattering to update the shadow flags.

4.5.2   Transparency

Irregular rasterization approaches allow the use of transparent shadow casters. Each view sample stores, in addition to its shadow flag, a transparency value, which is initialized to fully transparent. Whenever a semitransparent shadow caster is rasterized and lies in front of a view sample, the transparency of that view sample is multiplied with the transparency of the caster. Colored transparency requires a full RGB transparency value to be stored with each view sample. However, only a few bits can be used for transparency in a hardware implementation, so only a few levels of transparency are possible.

4.5.3   Supersampling

While view-sample mapping techniques eliminate initial sampling (under-sampling) and resampling artifacts, they are still prone to initial sample aliasing, like any other part of the rendering pipeline that discretizes hard-edged geometric primitives. A common remedy against initial sample aliasing is multisampling, where multiple samples per pixel (so-called subpixels) are evaluated to determine the coverage of a geometric primitive, but the fragment shader for that pixel is only computed once. Since view-sample mapping is computed in the shader, this shader needs to be evaluated for each subsample as well, which corresponds to the more expensive supersampling.

Pan et al. [Pan09] have come up with a method to evaluate just the shadow term for multiple subpixels at a cost that is practically independent of the number of subpixels. The remaining shading computations are carried out at pixel level. Their first observation is that subpixel sampling is only required for pixels that contain shadow boundaries. Therefore, in a first step, a silhouette-mask map is created that marks all shadow-map texels that contain a (visible) shadow edge. Their second observation, and the main idea of the approach, is that the evaluation of multiple subpixels can be carried out efficiently using *visibility masks* [Eisemann07], which allow a shadow-casting triangle to instantly mark several subpixels as occluded or nonoccluded with respect to that triangle.

Eisemann et al. [Eisemann07] show that the intersection of a half-plane with a number of regular samples can be precomputed, storing bitmasks in a table that contain one coverage bit per sample. When transforming a shadow-caster triangle into pixel space, the coverage of the subpixels can be determined by combining the bitmasks of the half-planes given by the three triangle edges using bitwise AND. Thus, evaluating multiple subpixels is a constant-time operation, and only the cost for combining the subpixels depends on the number of samples.

To determine the actual pixels and caster triangles that should interact in that way, Pan et al. represent each pixel by a rectangular facet and rasterize that facet into the shadow map to determine which texels might influence that pixel. This corresponds to the view-sample projection step in the original view-sample mapping technique, but instead of projecting only the pixel center, the whole pixel rectangle is projected. If a pixel only covers non-silhouette texels, it will be evaluated using standard view-sample mapping. Then, shadow casters are rasterized into the shadow map, projected to each pixel stored in that texel, and subpixel tests using visibility masks are carried out. The visibility-mask test complements the simple proximity test in standard view-sample mapping by determining which of the subpixels are actually affected by the shadow caster.

4.6   Shadow-Map Reconstruction

All methods discussed so far have assumed that shadow maps are sampled at certain positions, and reconstruction accesses these samples. In this section, we will introduce methods that focus not on the sampling but on the reconstruction. The main observation is that a more accurate reconstruction of shadow edges, by storing, for example, information about silhouettes in the shadow map, can improve shadow quality.

4.6.1   Forward Shadow Mapping

Zhang et al.'s forward shadow mapping [Zhang98] splats the texels seen from the light to the view. This inverses the usual test, which would look up depth values in the shadow map, and instead looks up depth values from the eye view to test whether they match. If they do, it is actually illumination and not shadows that will be splat into the eye view. The splat can have a smooth degrading kernel that leads to softer transitions between the samples. Currently, the practical relevance of this method is rather low, but it is an interesting idea to build upon, and in fact, splatting of illumination has become a common solution for recent methods in the context of global illumination [Lehtinen08].

4.6.2   Silhouette Shadow Maps

A method that reconstructs piecewise linear shadow boundaries was presented by Sen et al. [Sen03]. The method is relatively simple and could be implemented on current graphics hardware. The idea is to store additional information about silhouettes in a so-called *silhouette map*. If an object's silhouette edge intersects a texel of the silhouette map, an (arbitrary) point of that silhouette is stored in that texel. Texels that intersect no silhouettes are marked empty. The stored silhouette points allow reconstructing the silhouette edges using the neighboring texels.

To determine the shadow status of a view sample, it is projected into the silhouette map. Then, five samples are looked up in the silhouette map: the center and its four neighbors. Virtual edges connecting the stored silhouette points are added between these positions, creating four quadrants. For each quadrant, an evaluation

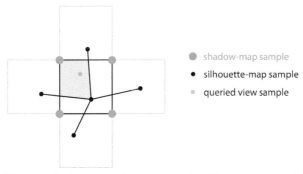

     ⬤ shadow-map sample

     ● silhouette-map sample

     ○ queried view sample

Figure 4.23. Silhouette shadow maps: the area around a silhouette map texel is partitioned into four quadrants by connecting to the neighboring samples. The shadow status of the queried view sample depends on the shadow-map sample that is located in the respective quadrant.

of the shadow map decides whether that quadrant is considered shadowed or lit. For this to work, the shadow map needs to be shifted by a half-pixel in each coordinate with respect to the silhouette map (see Figure 4.23), so that the depth samples fall within the quadrants. Finally, the algorithm determines which of the quadrants the view sample lies in and returns the shadow status of the corresponding quadrant as result.

Major limitations are that each pixel only stores one silhouette point. In areas where two silhouettes project close to each other, noticeable artifacts can appear. Furthermore, the curvature of silhouettes is limited by the piecewise linear approximation and, thus, by the resolution of the shadow map. The creation of this map involves a silhouette-determination step, which can be done on the geometry shader on today's hardware, and the rasterization of silhouette edges to create the representative silhouette points in the silhouette map. This rasterization is rather costly because each edge needs to be rendered as a quad to make sure all adjacent pixels are touched.

Silhouette shadow maps can be interpreted as a deformation of the regular shadow-map grid according to the silhouette-map entries. This idea has also been used later to preserve sharp edges for texture magnification [Sen04].

4.6.3   Alternative Shadow-Map Storage

Dai et al. [Dai08] go one step further and propose storing the complete actual triangle information (via the three vertex positions) in each shadow-map texel. To find the silhouette, or rather the triangle that actually occludes the view sample, the triangles in neighboring texels have to be taken into account using consistency checks. The method fails, however, if not all occluding triangles are hit by a shadow-map sample.

Arvo and Hirvikorpi [Arvo05] leave the concept of traditional shadow maps altogether and use a data structure that stores only scan lines. This leads to a compression for scenes with homogeneous depth values because only startpoints and endpoints of scan lines need to be stored. This allows higher shadow-map resolution, but no interactive algorithm for the generation of such compressed shadow maps has been presented.

4.7   Temporal Reprojection

Finally, one way to increase the sampling rate is by reusing samples from previous frames through reprojection [Scherzer07]. The main idea is to jitter the shadow-map viewport differently in each frame and to combine the results over several frames, leading to a much higher effective resolution.

This method requires an additional buffer, called the history buffer, to store the current accumulated shadowing result (in view space). In the current frame, the result of the shadow-map lookup is combined with the result from the previous frame, which can be looked up in the history buffer using reprojection. If a depth discontinuity between the new and the reprojected sample is detected, then the old result is not used since it is probably due to a disocclusion. The result is again stored in the history buffer.

Reprojection requires some application support, as the complete transformation matrices for both the current and the previous frame need to be passed to the vertex shader. The transformation matrix for the previous frame gives the texture coordinates for the lookup in the history buffer.

In order to make shadow quality converge to a pixel-perfect result, the weights between the current and the previous frame result have to be chosen carefully. In particular, Scherzer and Wimmer have proposed determining the weight according to the *confidence* of the shadow lookup:

$$\mathrm{conf}_{x,y} = 1 - \max\left(\left|x - \mathrm{center}_x\right|, \left|y - \mathrm{center}_y\right|\right) \cdot 2,$$

where $\mathrm{conf}_{x,y}$ is the confidence for a fragment projected to (x, y) in the shadow map and $(\mathrm{center}_x, \mathrm{center}_y)$ is the corresponding shadow-map texel center.

The confidence is higher if the lookup falls near the center of a shadow-map texel, since only near the center of shadow-map texels is it likely that the sample actually represents the scene geometry.

Note that reprojection-based approaches take a few frames to converge after quick motions. Also, they cannot deal well with moving objects or moving light sources.

4.8 Cookbook

We want to give some practical hints as to which algorithms to use in what situations. In general, we can observe that achieving higher quality goes hand in hand with obtaining more information about the scene. While global partitioning algorithms require only bounding volumes, adaptive partitioning algorithms already look at information gained from a rendering of the scene, while view-sample mapping analyzes each individual pixel in view space to obtain perfect results.

If the requirement is that only a single shadow map should be used (i.e., the algorithm should run at the same speed as standard shadow mapping), then LiSPSM, with the modification by Lloyd et al., is the best algorithm. This algorithm will achieve excellent quality in many configurations, especially in outdoor scenarios with roughly overhead lighting; however, it can easily degrade to the quality of (focused) uniform shadow mapping. With the modification by Lloyd et al., it will never degrade below the quality of uniform shadow mapping. LiSPSM is relatively easy to integrate in a rendering engine, but it does require some care when implementing focusing, shadow-map rotation, and the relevant z-range. These are geometric calculations that will influence the robustness of the approach.

If more than one shadow map is allowed (i.e., some performance loss can be accepted), the best-known tradeoff between efficiency and quality is achieved by z-partitioning (CSM, PSSM). The distribution of multiple shadow maps mimics a very rough approximation of the optimal logarithmic shadow-map parametrization. Furthermore, each shadow map can adapt optimally to one part of the view frustum, thus improving the quality in each spatial dimension, independent of the orientation of the view frustum. It is possible to combine z-partitioning with warping; however, temporal aliasing is increased by this approach, and the gain is not very high. If warping is not used, the flickering artifacts due to focusing can be reduced by snapping to texel boundaries. Z-partitioning requires some application support because multiple shadow maps have to be rendered. On the other hand, fewer geometric operations than in warping are required, making it simpler to implement.

One major advantage of the aforementioned algorithms is that they are scene-independent, and thus do not require interaction (e.g., read back) with the scene. On the other hand, this is also a strong limitation. It can be observed that a very simple scene analysis providing minimum and maximum depth values already greatly increases the quality and robustness of both warping and partitioning algorithms. Given the speed and flexibility of today's GPUs, the scene-analysis pass can be carried out completely on the GPU (e.g., by creating a min/max mipmap pyramid), and only a few values have to be read back from the bus. The complexity of today's deferred-rendering pipelines with several full-screen passes makes it easy to hide the latency of read backs.

Furthermore, warping and z-partitioning deal with perspective aliasing only, while local aliasing effects due to different surface orientations, causing projection aliasing, cannot be improved. Given the fact that these approaches work best with a scene analysis, it is a rather small step towards fully adaptive partitioning algorithms that handle both perspective and projective aliasing. Of particular interest are subdivision approaches with direct hierarchy evaluation (RMSM, FVSM). In particular, RMSM is virtually identical to current virtual-texturing approaches, and for engines that already support virtual texturing, it is straightforward to include RMSM as well. The only limitation could be the time required for the high number of shadow rendering passes when compared to global approaches. It stands to reason that soon, even irregular sampling approaches, which really result in a pixel-accurate solution, will become feasible.

All of the covered approaches, in particular, the more accurate ones, are useful for a small number of light sources that cover a large part of the scene. If many light sources are required, light-culling techniques become important, and a fallback to standard shadow mapping may be necessary. For example, standard shadow mapping could be used for local light sources that have a limited region of influence, while a more accurate sampling method is used for sunlight shadows.

CHAPTER 5
Filtered Hard Shadows

We have seen in Chapter 3 that image-based hard shadows are prone to aliasing. Recall that errors due to the discrete shadow-map sampling can be categorized into initial sampling errors (which happen when creating the shadow map) and resampling errors (which happen when rendering using the shadow map). Chapter 4 showed several approaches to reduce initial sampling error (i.e., undersampling) by adapting the shadow-map resolution in various manners.

In this chapter, we will discuss several filtering methods for shadow mapping, which are mainly useful for reducing resampling error. Furthermore, filtering is also often used to make undersampling artifacts less pronounced by smoothing or *blurring* the shadow boundaries. In fact, simple upscaling techniques for low-resolution images also rely on filters to remove the quad appearance induced by the pixels of the input image. At second glance, this becomes even more interesting because it results in shadow boundaries that resemble to some extent the appearance of physically based soft shadows at a much lower computational effort. However, none of the following methods in this chapter give physically meaningful soft shadows—their main purpose is to address the aliasing problem efficiently.

In practice, most of the techniques presented in this chapter, as well as their extensions, which we will discuss in Section 6.5.3, are standard solutions in game contexts and are of high practical value. The simplicity of the implementation, the relatively good performance, the simple tradeoff between performance and quality, and the reasonable outcome (at least for most configurations) make them usually a good choice.

The interested reader is also referred to the talk by Bavoil at GDC08 [Bavoil08a]. This talk summarizes many of the practical implementation aspects and serves as a good overview for the techniques that will be presented in this chapter.

We will first discuss why filtering shadow maps needs special attention (Section 5.1), then show the applications of filtering (Section 5.2), namely blurring, proper filtering and reconstruction, and faking soft shadows. Section 5.3 will deal with the important topic of accelerating the evaluation of larger filter kernels using precomputation.

5.1 Filters and Shadow Maps

In this chapter, we call filtering any approach that takes into account several shadow-map samples in order to calculate a final shadow result value for a specific view sample. In principle, filtering can be used for several purposes: reducing resampling error (for reconstruction and bandlimiting the signal), smoothing shadow boundaries to hide undersampling artifacts, and faking a soft-shadow appearance. However, while filtering shadows is useful, the nature of the shadow test makes filtering significantly less straightforward than for other signals, like standard textures. In the following, we will first show why simply filtering the depth map does not work and then present a reference solution, percentage-closer filtering.

5.1.1 Filtering Notation

Let us first recall some important notation from Section 3.3, where the depth function was defined as $z(\mathbf{t})$ in dependence of the shadow-map coordinates $\mathbf{t} = (s, t)$. Standard shadow mapping evaluates the shadow comparison function s: $f(\mathbf{t}, \tilde{z}) = s(z(\mathbf{t}), \tilde{z})$ for a *reference depth* value $\tilde{z}$ (i.e., the light-space depth of a view sample), returning zero if the view sample is in shadow and one otherwise. The standard shadow comparison function is the Heaviside step function: $s(z, \tilde{z}) = H(z - \tilde{z})$.

Filtering aims to average a set of samples from a *filter kernel* $\mathcal{K}$ (also called window). Note that while our filtering notation is defined in shadow-map space, at this moment, we do not yet specify in which space the filter samples themselves are determined, since this depends on the application case (see Section 5.2). Finally, the samples are averaged using a *kernel function* k, which takes the distance of the reference sample to the current sample from the kernel as a parameter.

5.1.2 Fail: Blurring Shadow Maps

A first intuition could lead one to perform filtering by blurring the depth values stored in the shadow map and then performing a standard shadow test. This would correspond to averaging the depth signal using some filter kernel k and shadow testing the result:

$$f_{\text{filter}}^{\text{blur}}(\mathbf{t}, \tilde{z}) = H\left(\sum_{\mathbf{t}_i \in \mathcal{K}} k(\mathbf{t}_i - \mathbf{t}) z(\mathbf{t}_i) - \tilde{z} \right). \tag{5.1}$$

Unfortunately, such a blur does not make much sense. The depth values would be averaged, but the resulting shadows would still show the same aliasing artifacts because for each view sample, the shadow test still leads to a binary outcome. Furthermore, averaging depth values across discontinuities would lead to nonintuitive results.

To extend this idea, one might be tempted to replace not only the shadow map by a blurred version but also the binary shadow test function H with some smoother, continuous variant H_c. This solution has been used by Luft and Deussen [Luft06]. With some parameter tweaking, those shadows can be visually pleasing for simple configurations but can be very far from any physical reference. Furthermore, nearby superposing objects, as seen from the light, might lead to light bleeding. On the other hand, the method by Luft and Deussen was proposed in the context of non-photorealistic rendering in order to *abstract* shadows and give a visually smoother result. For this latter purpose, such an algorithm is well suited, but it can hardly fool the observer into taking the shadows for real.

5.1.3 Defining a Reference: Percentage-Closer Filtering

A more plausible outcome can be achieved by realizing that the goal is to filter the *shadow signal f*, not the *depth signal z*. This approach is called *percentage-closer filtering* (PCF) [Reeves87]. Formally, it is as simple as changing the order of depth testing and filtering:

$$f_{\text{filter}}^{\text{pcf}}(\mathbf{t}, \tilde{z}) = \sum_{\mathbf{t}_i \in \mathcal{K}} k(\mathbf{t}_i - \mathbf{t}) H(z(\mathbf{t}_i) - \tilde{z}). \tag{5.2}$$

The simplicity and relatively satisfying quality of this approach makes it particularly interesting. Figure 5.1 shows some of the results obtained with this technique. The entire algorithm is summarized in Figure 5.2. However, the cheapness of the method needs to be put into perspective. Even though at first glance, Equation (5.2) might resemble a convolution of the shadow map, which could be precomputed, it is not: the depth test needs to be performed *before* the filtering. This

Shadow Mapping

Percentage-Closer Filtering

Figure 5.1. PCF suffers less from shadow-map aliasing (left) and results in reasonable shadows for smaller light sizes (middle). For larger sources, some inconsistencies can occur (right, shadow under left foot).

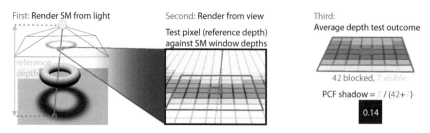

Figure 5.2. Overview of the PCF algorithm.

test implies a large performance penalty because the complete filter kernel needs to be evaluated for every shadow lookup. For a small window (3 × 3), it might not seem problematic, but for larger windows, the cost grows rapidly, and we will see in Section 5.3 several ways to accelerate this computation.

5.1.4   PCF Implementation

Regular Nearest-Neighbor Sampling

There are several ways to implement PCF. The simplest version and the one implied by many simple explanations is to sample the shadow results from a kernel $\mathcal{K}$ using a regular grid of $n \times n$ sample values around the texel **t** and a constant kernel function k (i.e., equal weights or a box filter). Each shadow result returns either zero or one, so only $n^2 + 1$ "shades" of shadow are possible (for example, $0, 0.25, 0.5, 0.75, 1$ for a 2×2 filter kernel). This leads to obvious banding artifacts.

Bilinear Sampling

Better results can be achieved using a tent-shaped kernel function k, which corresponds to bilinear filtering in standard texture mapping for a kernel $\mathcal{K}$ containing the 2×2 neighborhood of a sample location **t**. The bilinear filter weights are $(du\,dv, du(1 - dv), (1 - du)dv, (1 - du)(1 - dv))$, where $du = |u - \mathrm{clamp}(u)|$, and (u, v) are the texel coordinates of a sample. Bilinear filtered PCF has even been integrated in graphics hardware and is automatically enabled for shadow-map queries if the appropriate bilinear filtering mode is used (in DirectX 10, the filter mode has to be `COMPARISON_MIN_MAG_LINEAR_MIP_POINT`). Higher-order filters could also be implemented using appropriate kernel functions, for example, bicubic filtering. In particular, Sigg and Hadwiger [Sigg06] showed how to exploit hardware bilinear lookups (e.g., bilinear PCF) to implement third-order filtering at low cost. Bilinear lookups can also be used to remove the obvious quantization of larger regular sampling patterns by evaluating each sample using a bilinear PCF lookup.

Poisson Disk Sampling

Another popular sampling set $\mathcal{K}$ is a set of samples taken from a Poisson disk distribution (see the overview of Lagae and Dutré for a comparison of methods to generate such a set [Lagae08]). Poisson disk sampling makes very good use of the samples, so less samples are needed for equal quality than with a regular sample set. Also, since the sample set is irregular, banding artifacts are basically treated against noise, which is visually less objectionable. The actual sample locations are usually precomputed and stored in a lookup table in a texture or in uniform storage.

The shadow-map lookups required for the individual samples can be done using nearest neighbor or bilinear sampling, with the latter giving smoother results. In order to avoid banding, the sample set can also be rotated for each pixel. This could be implemented by storing a random rotation in an $m \times m$ texture that is sampled using the pixel coordinates, so that the same sampling pattern is only repeated every m pixels [Isidoro06].

Interleaved Sampling

The burden of evaluating larger filter kernels can be distributed among different pixels by using interleaved sampling [Keller01]. For this, the sample set is split into $k \times k$ random subsets. Each pixel uses only one of these subsets, determined by the tiling of a $k \times k$ pattern onto the screen. An approximation to the original sampling pattern is recovered by applying an average filter on the resulting shadow values with a $k \times k$ kernel. In order to avoid averaging over different unrelated surfaces, a cross-bilateral filter [Paris06] sensitive to depth discontinuities should be used.

Adaptive Sampling

One approach that attempts to overcome the performance hit for large filter kernel sizes in PCF was presented by Uralsky [Uralsky05]. The solution performs well if efficient branching is possible on the GPU and the scene is not too complex. In a first step, only a small set of samples is used. If the shadow result is not unanimous, only then are more samples evaluated. This leads to a strong speed-up, and samples are added mostly in the penumbra region, where they are needed.

Similar to Poisson disk sampling, Uralsky uses different sample sets for different pixels to trade banding artifacts against noise. The original sampling pattern is generated by warping a set of samples that are jittered on a regular grid to a disk and jittering again for each pixel. Alternatively, rotated Poisson disk sampling could be used. In order to ensure a continuous result, the sample set in the first iteration should be representative of the samples in the filter window. This means again that a larger window implies more initial samples, which reduces the overall effectiveness of the approach for larger filter windows.

PCF Self-Shadowing

For larger PCF filter kernels, the assumption of a constant reference depth value $\tilde{z}$ might not hold anymore. Especially if the receiver plane is tilted with respect to the shadow-map plane, one part of the receiver will be strongly self-shadowed (see Section 2.2.3, and Figure 5.3, right). A remedy proposed by Isidoro [Isidoro06] is to use an individual $\tilde{z}$ for each sample lookup by reconstructing the receiver plane from the partial derivatives of the texture coordinates in a pixel. However, in contrast to many cases where screen-space derivatives are applicable, in this case, we need the derivatives of depth with respect to texture coordinates. These can be calculated by applying the chain rule and using the inverse transpose of the Jacobian of the texture coordinates with respect to screen space to transform screen-space derivatives to texture-space derivatives:

$$\begin{pmatrix} \frac{\partial \tilde{z}}{\partial u} \\ \frac{\partial \tilde{z}}{\partial v} \end{pmatrix} = \begin{pmatrix} \frac{\partial u}{\partial x} & \frac{\partial u}{\partial y} \\ \frac{\partial v}{\partial x} & \frac{\partial v}{\partial y} \end{pmatrix}^{-T} \begin{pmatrix} \frac{\partial \tilde{z}}{\partial x} \\ \frac{\partial \tilde{z}}{\partial y} \end{pmatrix}. \tag{5.3}$$

Note that planar approximations fail in areas of high curvature. Similar approaches were proposed to reduce the need for depth bias by Schüler [Schüler05] and by Lauritzen [Lauritzen07] in the context of variance shadow maps. Burley [Burley06] proposes a simpler method in the context of percentage-closer soft shadows (see Section 6.5.3).

5.2   Applications of Filtering

There are several ways in which filtering, in particular PCF, can be used. They differ mainly in the choice of samples $\mathcal{K}$ and the filter kernel k.

5.2.1   Smoothing or Blurring Shadows

The simplest application of filtering is to smooth or blur the shadows coming from shadow mapping. For this, the filter kernel $\mathcal{K}$ contains a set of samples that are symmetrically arranged in shadow-map space around the projected view sample.

One common example are regular filters, for example, a kernel taking into account 3×3 or 5×5 samples around the current sample in the shadow map. Another popular arrangement is to distribute a fixed number of samples in a Poisson disk fashion, so that samples have roughly the same mutual distance from each other. Such sampling patterns are usually precomputed (as offsets to **t** texture coordinates) and stored in a lookup texture.

Using simple blurring, undersampling artifacts can be hidden but not removed. For best quality, the filter kernel function k is usually chosen as a Gaussian.

5.2.2   Reducing Resampling Error: Reconstruction versus Bandlimiting Filter

Reconstruction

The most basic and important use of PCF is to reduce resampling error by providing proper *reconstruction filtering*. Recall that the first step in resampling is to reconstruct the continuous shadow signal f from its sampled representation. Similar to bilinear filtering in texture mapping, looking up a value in the shadow map will usually not fall exactly in the center of a texel. Therefore, we need to reconstruct the shadow-map value at the desired sampling location by interpolating from the neighboring texel location. But in contrast to texture mapping, we do not have a sampled representation of the shadow signal itself available, only a depth map, from which we need to recover shadow values using the reference depth value as described above. Hardware bilinear PCF reconstruction as described above achieves this with quality equivalent to standard bilinearly filtered texture mapping.

Bandlimiting

The second source of errors in resampling is oversampling due to minification in the transformation T between shadow-map space and screen space, for example, when viewing shadows from a distance. This needs to be avoided using a bandlimiting filter, which removes high frequencies before resampling. Bandlimiting can be implemented using PCF by calculating the approximate footprint of the back projection of a pixel into the shadow map using similar calculations as for the mipmap LOD factor. The radius of this footprint then defines the radius of the filter kernel set $\mathcal{K}$ in shadow-map space. Samples within this kernel size can be generated using any of the methods already described for blurring (Section 5.2.1). Likewise, the kernel function should incorporate a falloff away from the sample evaluation point **t**. Ideally, the kernel function should be a sinc function, but since this function has problematic properties in practice, a Gaussian kernel is usually used.

Unfortunately, using PCF for bandlimiting is not feasible in practice. Since the filter kernel size can vary arbitrarily, a single shadow-map lookup could lead to the evaluation of a huge number of samples, especially in distant regions where many shadow-map samples project to a single pixel in screen space. In Section 5.3, we will therefore discuss methods how to precompute the bandlimiting filter similar to mipmapping for texture filtering.

5.2.3   Filtering versus Soft Shadows

When using PCF to blur shadows, one observes that a larger filter kernel window leads to smoother shadows, a smaller one to hard shadows. This can be used to emulate the look of physically based soft shadows.

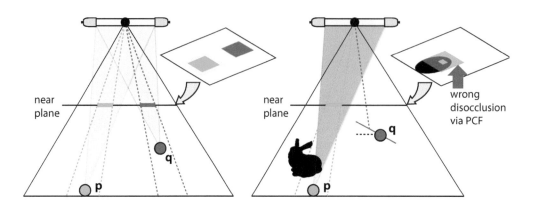

Figure 5.3. Why PCF does not compute soft shadows. Averaging is done over the shadow map instead of over the scene (left). Example of wrong disocclusion and error due to constant fragment depth assumption (right).

In practice, if the window remains of reasonable size, the shadows still look convincing because the overall look of the hard shadows is not altered too much, giving the impression of a very small, but not point, source. The eye-pleasing look that results from the blur has even been used in various movie productions, the first being the Pixar movie *Luxo*. From today's point of view, one can see that the resulting umbra is too large and the penumbra too small when compared to the shadows from a real large lightbulb. Nonetheless, no aliasing is visible, leading to appealing and cheap shadows, which was the main goal.

It has to be underlined again that the resulting shadows are not physically based. We saw in Section 1.3 that we should integrate rays over the light source. PCF, however, tests for each point of the scene depth samples from a constant window around the projection into the shadow map (Figure 5.3, left, dashed border). This is a coarse approximation. First, these windows should have different sizes depending on the distance to the light (Figure 5.3, left, **p**, **q**); second, the tested rays should leave from the impact point towards different locations on the light (Figure 5.3, left, transparent areas). Except for the shadow-map texels that contain the point itself, none of the shadow-map texels corresponds to a ray that originates at the impact point. Instead, each texel corresponds to a ray through the light itself. Consequently, the shadow estimate is often approximate. Umbrae are introduced where a physically based shadow would still be partially lit, or a point is considered to be in the penumbra, although it already lies in the umbra (Figure 5.3, right, **p**).

However, in Chapter 6, we will introduce a method called percentage-closer soft shadows (PCSS), which uses PCF with a varying filter kernel size to more accurately simulate soft shadows.

5.3   Precomputing Larger Filter Kernels

As already discussed above, an important drawback of PCF is that larger filter window sizes require evaluating more samples. This quickly becomes prohibitive, especially for bandlimiting filters. In this section, we will describe the theory and application of approaches that precompute parts of the filter to solve this problem.

5.3.1   Precomputed Filter Theory—Linear Signal Processing versus Statistics

Precomputing filters on shadow maps as is common for texture mapping is impossible because the result relies on the reference depth. But if we cannot apply filtering to the shadow test function directly, we can still try to reformulate the shadow test function so that precomputed filtering becomes possible.

Fixing Filtering for Linear Signal Theory

Let us look again at Equation (3.18), respectively Equation (5.2):

$$f_{\text{filter}}(\mathbf{t}, \tilde{z}) = \sum_{\mathbf{t}_i \in \mathcal{K}} H(z(\mathbf{t}_i) - \tilde{z}) k(\mathbf{t}_i - \mathbf{t}) = \sum_{\mathbf{t}_i \in \mathcal{K}} s(z(\mathbf{t}_i), \tilde{z}) k(\mathbf{t}_i - \mathbf{t}), \qquad (5.4)$$

with shadow comparison function $s(z, \tilde{z}) = H(z - \tilde{z})$. A standard approach to speeding this up is to precompute the convolution for different filter kernel radii, so that at runtime, a lookup into an appropriate texture is sufficient. This is called mipmapping. For shadow mapping, however, the expensive convolution cannot be precomputed because the result depends on the value of $\tilde{z}$, which changes for every visible fragment. Nor is it possible to draw the convolution into the function evaluation because the function $s(z, \tilde{z})$ is not linear in its first argument (as we

---

Prefiltering versus Precomputation

Before we proceed, we need to clarify some often mistaken terminology. In shadow mapping and texturing literature, the term *prefiltering* is often used for approaches that precompute filter values. However, prefiltering in signal theory is just a different term for a bandlimiting filter (see Chapter 3). It is called prefiltering because the signal is bandlimited *before* it is sampled. This is in contrast to *postfiltering*, which in computer graphics is equivalent to supersampling: the signal is first sampled at a higher resolution and then filtered to obtain an approximation to a bandlimited version of the signal. Postfiltering shifts the problem of aliasing to higher frequencies but cannot avoid aliasing, whereas proper prefiltering can do so.

In this chapter, however, we discuss the *precomputation* of filter kernels, regardless of whether they are used for prefiltering (i.e., bandlimiting) or blurring.

already found in Section 5.1.2):

$$\sum_i \alpha_i s(z_i, \tilde{z}) \neq s\left(\sum_i \alpha_i z_i, \tilde{z}\right). \tag{5.5}$$

This is due to the use of the step function H. The main idea is now to decompose the shadow comparison function in a way that it becomes "simultaneously" linear in factors that are separate from $\tilde{z}$:

$$s(z, \tilde{z}) = s(B_1(z), B_2(z), ..., \tilde{z}), \tag{5.6}$$

so that

$$\sum_i \alpha_i s(B_1(z_i), B_2(z_i), ..., \tilde{z}) = s\left(\sum_i \alpha_i B_1(z_i), \sum_i \alpha_i B_2(z_i), ..., \tilde{z}\right). \tag{5.7}$$

This is especially the case if s can be written as a (usually infinite) expansion of additive basis function B_i:

$$s(z, \tilde{z}) = \sum_k a_k(\tilde{z}) B_k(z). \tag{5.8}$$

This means that the convolutions of the basis functions, $B_k^{\text{conv}} = \sum_i \alpha_i B_k(z_i)$, can be precomputed and stored in memory. In our case, the summation comes from taking into account neighboring shadow-map samples, so

$$B_k^{\text{conv}}(z) = \sum_{\mathbf{t}_i \in \mathcal{K}} k(\mathbf{t}_i - \mathbf{t}) B_k(z(\mathbf{t}_i)). \tag{5.9}$$

At runtime, for evaluating the shadow test for a certain filter radius, we need to look up the values B_k^{conv} in the appropriate precomputed map, calculate $a_k(\tilde{z})$, and multiply and sum up the results.

This idea was first introduced as convolution shadow mapping (CSM) [Annen07], using a Fourier series as expansion, and will be discussed in more detail in Section 5.3.4.[1] Later, a simpler expansion into one exponential function was discovered (exponential shadow maps (ESM); see Section 5.3.5).

Ditching Linear Signal Processing in Favor of Statistics

Another fundamentally different approach to solving the problem of precomputing filter kernels is to completely abandon linear signal theory and not try to evaluate specific filter kernels through convolution. Instead, the idea is to turn to statistics and try to answer the basic question, "What is the probability that my view sample is in shadow with respect to a given set of depth samples?"

---

[1]The abbreviation CSM is also used for cascaded shadow maps, see Section 4.3.

The depth samples would be given by the same filter kernel set $\mathcal{K}$ as in linear approaches, so depending on whether bandlimiting or soft shadows are desired, the set of samples would adapt. But then, the depth of the samples would be interpreted as realizations of a random variable D, and we would calculate

$$f(\mathbf{t}, \tilde{z}) = Pr(\tilde{z} \leq D). \tag{5.10}$$

This probability would be used as a scalar value to determine shadow intensity. This works by using the samples $z(\mathbf{t}_i), \mathbf{t}_i \in \mathcal{K}$ to estimate a number of parameters, $p_1, p_2, \ldots$, of the probability distribution of the random variable D as a function of those parameters and then use the knowledge about the distribution to calculate the probability given above.

Precomputed filtering using statistics works in the way that the parameters that are estimated from the distribution are precomputed for all required filter kernel sizes, similar to the basis functions B_k in linear filtering. For example, variance shadow mapping [Donnelly06], the most prominent example of a statistical filtering method, estimates an upper bound to the desired probability from the mean and variance of the kernel samples. So, only the first and second moments, depth and squared depth (from which the variance can be recovered) need to be precomputed and stored in a mipmap pyramid. Precomputation is more efficient if the parameters for larger filter sizes can be derived from the parameters for the smaller filter sizes. Fortunately, this is true for many statistical estimators, like the first and second moments.

The major difference to linear filtering is that statistical estimators need not be linear in the sense of Equation (5.5), and have the potential to provide better estimations than linear filtering. Also note that the samples from $\mathcal{K}$ can still be weighted using the kernel function k, for example, to implement Gaussian filters. This basically changes the measure of the distribution.

In another method based on statistics, Gumbau et al. [Gumbau11] use the shadow map samples to estimate the cumulative distribution function (CDF) of the depth distribution. The CDF is approximated using a power function that increases smoothly between the minimum and maximum depth values.

5.3.2   Variance Shadow Maps

Variance shadow maps (VSM), which were introduced by Donnelly and Lauritzen [Donnelly06], are a beautiful example of a simple mathematical formula that leads to a powerful algorithm. VSM are the first example of using statistics to facilitate precomputation of shadow-map filtering. Figure 5.4 shows some results obtained with the method.

Instead of sampling each entry in the shadow map, Donnelly and Lauritzen observed that simple statistics can be used to estimate the depth-sample repartition inside the filter window. They rely on the mean μ and variance σ of the depth samples.

Figure 5.4. Variance shadow maps result in shadows that resemble PCF (left). The algorithm achieves much higher frame rates by approximating the computation. This may lead to slight light leaks (middle left); these can be addressed with simple solutions (middle right), but this affects the shadow smoothness. Especially for larger light sources (right, five times larger), the performance gain is tremendous.

Fortunately, mean and variance can be obtained efficiently from a *linearized* depth map. Although one might assume that depth values are typically nonlinear, in this chapter, we will always consider linearized depth values.

To find the mean μ and variance σ of the depth samples, one only needs to apply a simple box filter of the size of the filter window ($\mathcal{K}$) to the depth and a squared-depth map.[2] The resulting textures then hold what is called the first (M_1) and second moment (M_2). The simple relationships $\mu = M_1$ and $\sigma = M_2 - M_1^2$ allow us to derive the mean and variance inside the PCF window, and we avoid the usual high cost of evaluating all samples during the shadow computation.

Once this depth-distribution information is available, the outcome of the shadow tests in the filter window can be estimated. In order to avoid any further assumptions on the distribution, the Chebyshev inequality is used, which provides a bound for the outcome independent of the actual distribution. Precisely, given a shadow-map depth-value distribution with mean μ and variance σ, the probability $Pr(\tilde{z} \leq z)$ that a random depth value z drawn from this distribution is greater or equal to a given depth value $\tilde{z}$ has an upper bound of

$$p(\tilde{z}) = \frac{\sigma^2}{\sigma^2 + (\tilde{z} - \mu)^2} \geq Pr(\tilde{z} \leq z). \tag{5.11}$$

This means that, at most, a percentage $p(\tilde{z})$ of the shadow-map region contained in the filter region is not closer to the light than a receiver point **p** with light-space depth $\tilde{z} = \mathbf{p}_{\tilde{z}}^{l}$ and, hence, cannot occlude it. Note that the Chebyshev inequality is valid only for $\tilde{z} > \mu$. Hence, the value of p is set to one if $\tilde{z} \leq \mu$. This is a continuous extension of this function. The key is that this simple, rational function

---

[2]Fast box-filter approximations can be applied and need significantly less lookups (e.g., using summed area tables [Hensley05]; see box on page 329). Such an extension was proposed by Lauritzen [Lauritzen07].

Figure 5.5. Variance shadow maps estimate the depth-sample repartition inside the filter kernel window solely based on the variance and mean. Such an approximation leads to light bleeding. The light is coming from above, the shadow casters in the depth map are indicated in red, and the gray levels illustrate what the shadow value would be if a receiver were located at the corresponding position in space.

depends solely on the reference distance $\tilde{z}$ and the mean/variance (μ, σ) of the depth distributions in a given filter window.

Figure 5.5 illustrates what the computed shadow would look like for view samples placed at arbitrary locations in the scene. The gray levels indicate the blackness of the cast-shadow approximation. Because the Chebyshev inequality is a bound, the correct shadow could be darker, but never brighter, than this estimate. Unfortunately, if the variance is high (*one occluder on top of another*), light leaks can occur, and the error might become very pronounced, making shadowed areas appear lit. This is somewhat coherent with the missing information from the depth map (*does the lower occluder have a hole where the upper is hiding it?*), but shows a clear limitation of the distribution estimate. Nonetheless, in the special case of a parallel planar receiver and planar occluder, one should point out that the bound is actually exact and becomes an equality.

The results generated with variance shadow maps are similar to percentage-closer filtering with large kernels. Performance-wise, the method is groundbreaking in comparison to standard PCF and of very high practical value. The memory overhead is small. Typically, only one 2-channel 32-bit texture is used to represent the moments. The major disadvantages are the resulting light leaks, for which we will discuss remedies in the following. In order to avoid self-shadowing, the variance has to be clamped to a user-defined minimum value.

Self-Shadowing in VSM

As discussed in Section 5.1.4, self-shadowing can appear for larger filter kernels. In the context of VSM, Lauritzen [Lauritzen07] proposed an elegant solution in the spirit of the approach by Isidoro et al. [Isidoro06]. Instead of considering the depth distribution to be constant over the entire shadow-map texel, a local linear approximation is computed in the form of a plane equation. Inside a texel, the surface is thus represented as

$$f(u, v) := z + u \operatorname{ddx}(z) + v \operatorname{ddy}(z), \qquad (5.12)$$

where z is the depth value encountered during rendering into this VSM texel and ddx and ddy are derivative operators applied to this quantity. The first moment is given by $M_1 = z$; the second moment can be written as

$$M_2 = z^2 + E(u^2) \operatorname{ddx}(z)^2 + E(v^2) \operatorname{ddy}(z)^2 \qquad (5.13)$$

because $E(u) = E(v) = E(uv) = 0$. Representing the pixel as a Gaussian distribution with half a pixel variance implies $E(u^2) = E(v^2) = \frac{1}{4}$, and consequently,

$$M_2 = z^2 + \frac{1}{4} \left(\operatorname{ddx}(z)^2 + \operatorname{ddy}(z)^2 \right). \qquad (5.14)$$

5.3.3   Layered Variance Shadow Maps

Initially, Lauritzen [Lauritzen07] presented very simple solutions to deal with light leaks. One possibility is to map all values smaller than some threshold ε directly to black, hence removing subtle leaks. In order to maintain continuous shadow-boundary variations, all shadow values bigger than ε need to be remapped to the range $[0, 1]$, for example, using a `smoothstep` function. Even though light leaking is reduced, such a tampering also makes shadows look darker and shrinks the smooth boundary regions. Another possibility is to clamp the variance to some maximum value, but this also affects the quality of the penumbra regions.

Layered variance shadow maps (LVSM) [Lauritzen08] aim at solving the light-leaking issue in a more elegant fashion. The observation is that strongly differing depth samples result in a large variance value, which in turn makes Equation (5.11) very unreliable. It would be much better if the depth samples were close together. Unfortunately, these depth values depend on the scene, and we cannot choose them the way we want.

The property that allows us to shift depth values together is that the outcome of filtering does not depend on the actual depths, but rather on the comparison with the reference depth $\tilde{z}$. The exact same result is obtained if all depth samples closer to the light than $\tilde{z}$ are moved to the depth $\tilde{z} - \varepsilon$. The actual distance from which the depth samples are away from a receiver depth $\tilde{z} = \mathbf{p}_{\tilde{z}}^{\mathrm{L}}$ is not interesting, only whether they are above or below. This insight led to the idea of a warping function that will adjust the depth values in order to make the approximation via Equation (5.11) more accurate.

Imagine that all depth samples in the shadow map were warped by

$$\varphi_d(z) = \begin{cases} 1, & \text{if } z \geq d, \\ 0, & \text{if } z < d, \end{cases} \tag{5.15}$$

then the result for a reference depth d using VSM would be equivalent to the accurate result of PCF filtering. It would be costly to perform this warping per view sample. Basically, we would again have to go over all samples in the PCF window. Hence, instead the scene is sliced into depth intervals $\{[d_i, d_{i+1}]\}_{i=0}^{n}$. Inside each such layer, the original depth values are warped linearly, whereas outside they are clamped:

$$\varphi_i(z) = \begin{cases} 1, & \text{if } z \geq d_{i+1}, \\ (z - d_i)/(d_{i+1} - d_i), & \text{if } z \in [d_i, d_{i+1}), \\ 0, & \text{if } z < d_i. \end{cases} \tag{5.16}$$

This leads to smaller variance estimates and, thus, better shadow behavior. In particular, the linear warping ensures that the quick momentum computation remains valid.

One could uniformly space the layer depth bounds d_i, but the authors also propose an algorithm to estimate the light bleeding based on the current depth map. The interested reader is referred to the original paper [Lauritzen08] for more details.

The method is very efficient because, for evaluation, each sample only needs to test the layer into which it is projecting. The algorithm leads to much better results than standard VSM, but to avoid light bleeding completely, many layers are needed and, hence, many filtering operations.

Further, many layers increase the memory usage, although it is possible to reduce the texture's precision with respect to VSM: 16 bits are sufficient, but often, even 8 bits lead to an artifact-free solution.

5.3.4   Convolution Shadow Maps

Convolution shadow maps (CSM) [Annen07] are the first approach to allow filter precomputation based on a linear signal-theory framework as described in Section 5.3.1. To derive suitable basis functions for the approximations of the shadow-comparison function, Annen et al. use a Fourier expansion. In theory, this expansion has unlimited coefficients, but a truncation leads to an approximation of the final result. In contrast to variance shadow maps, the Fourier approximation converges to the correct result when more coefficients are added (Figure 5.6).

Recall the PCF evaluation from Equation (5.4):

$$f_{\text{filter}}(\mathbf{t}, \tilde{z}) = \sum_{\mathbf{t}_i \in \mathcal{K}} s(z(\mathbf{t}_i), \tilde{z}) k(\mathbf{t}_i - \mathbf{t}). \tag{5.17}$$

PCF

Convolution
Shadow Map

Figure 5.6. Convolution shadow maps lead to reasonable results (middle). The main problem are light leaks due to insufficient coefficients, such as under the foot. Nevertheless, the strong speed-up makes it an interesting alternative, especially for large sources (right).

As discussed in Section 5.3.1, we need to transform this equation in such a way that the filtering (convolution) can be performed beforehand. To do so, the shadow-map comparison function s is developed into a series of basis functions B_k (Equation (5.8)) that are separable in $\tilde{z}$ and z:

$$s(z, \tilde{z}) = \sum_k a_k(\tilde{z}) B_k(z). \tag{5.18}$$

Through this expansion, the depth test becomes linear with respect to separable terms. Using Equation (5.18), one can conclude

$$f_{\text{filter}}(\mathbf{t}, \tilde{z}) = \sum_k a_k(\tilde{z}) \sum_{\mathbf{t}_i \in \mathcal{K}} k(\mathbf{t}_i - \mathbf{t}) B_k(z(\mathbf{t}_i)). \tag{5.19}$$

The resulting formulation is a weighted sum of convolutions. By looking at the terms, we see that it amounts to applying the basis function B_k to the depth map and blurring the result values with the kernel function k.

The main question is how to choose B_k and a_k. The authors tested several possibilities and concluded that a solution via Fourier analysis is the best choice. The shadow-comparison function is a step function $s(z, \tilde{z}) = H(z - \tilde{z})$, which is now approximated by a smooth function $\widehat{H}$ (e.g., $0.5\,\text{sigm}(z - \tilde{z}) + 0.5$, where sigm is a sigmoid (s-shaped) function). A Fourier expansion leads to an equation of form Equation (5.18). More precisely, we exploit the fact that the function is a real function and has no imaginary component. This avoids the complex exponential function and allows a decomposition into cosine and sine terms. The final equation truncated to M terms is

$$s(z, \tilde{z}) \approx \widehat{H}(z - \tilde{z})$$
$$\approx \frac{1}{2} + 2 \sum_{k=1}^{M} \frac{1}{c_k} \cos(c_k \tilde{z}) \sin(c_k z) - 2 \sum_{k=1}^{M} \frac{1}{c_k} \sin(c_k \tilde{z}) \cos(c_k z). \tag{5.20}$$

The precise coefficients c_k can be found in Section 3.1 of the original paper [Annen07]. In practice, the sum is usually truncated at 16 coefficients stored using

Figure 5.7. Convolution shadow maps can show light leaks due to an insufficient number of coefficients. The image illustrates the shadow result on a cube illuminated from the top scaled by a factor of four. Where four coefficients show strong ringing and significant light leaking at the top of the cube (left), 16 coefficients result in a much better estimate (middle). Nevertheless, the difference to the reference (right) remains visible.

8-bit values. Nevertheless, it should be kept in mind that $\sin(c_k z)$ and $\cos(c_k z)$ need to be stored separately, hence, 16 coefficients result in 32 values to store.

Ringing Artifacts

Any Fourier truncation can lead to ringing artifacts, which reflect the sinusoidal nature of the representation (Gibbs phenomenon). Figure 5.7 shows this effect on a real scene. The ringing artifacts cause light to be propagated into the shadow.

To hide the ringing artifact, the coefficients of higher frequencies are attenuated, but there is no guarantee that the ringing disappears. The red curve in Figure 5.8 shows the result of these damped coefficients for $M = 8$.

Light Leaking

There is still some significant light leaking and shadow leaking. In particular, the approximation $\widehat{H}$ always results in a C^∞-continuous function, whereas a step function is not even C^0-continuous. This has important consequences. On the exact shadow boundary ($\widehat{H}(0)$), we will encounter a value of 0.5 due to symmetry, leading to a reduced intensity for actually visible surfaces and, more generally, to shadow and light leaking.

The authors decided that light leaking is less objectionable. Their solution is to virtually shift the function by applying an offset o: $\widehat{H}_o(x) = \widehat{H}(x - o)$ (Figure 5.8, left). A second improvement results from scaling $\widehat{H}$ and clamping the shadow result (Figure 5.8, right). This gives a steeper approximation that sharpens shadows and can potentially reintroduce aliasing. Using a scaling by two ensures that view samples no longer shade themselves.

Usually, the method needs to rely on at least four 8-bit RGBA textures (16 coefficients) to achieve a good quality. For this setting, the method is reasonably

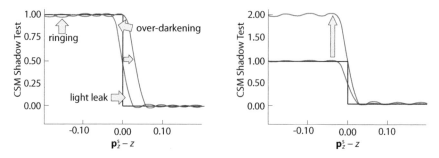

Figure 5.8. Damping the coefficients is not sufficient to avoid artifacts. The example shows the result of an approximation with 8 coefficients. To improve the solution, one can shift (left) or scale (right) the approximated step function.

fast for complex scenes and gives good antialiasing because mipmapping or even anisotropic filtering are meaningful when applied to the basis functions.

5.3.5   Exponential Shadow Maps

In concurrent work, Annen et al. [Annen08b] and Salvi [Salvi08] (who developed a similar solution that was presented slightly earlier at GDC) proposed new basis functions for the CSM approach. They suggested replacing the Fourier expansion by a simple exponential. This choice voids much of the storage requirements and thus addresses one of the major issues.

The main insight is that the depth map stores the nearest surface, thus, any view sample or point in the scene should project on or behind, but never in front of, any stored depth sample. With this assumption, $z - \tilde{z} \leq 0$. Hence, Equation (5.21) (below) behaves almost like a step function that becomes steeper for an increasing constant c:

$$s(z, \tilde{z}) = \widehat{H}(z - \tilde{z}) = \exp\left(-c(z - \tilde{z})\right). \tag{5.21}$$

In practice, $c = 80$ seems to be a good choice. Larger values can lead to an overflow due to numerical inaccuracies. Applying the filtering operation to this function leads to

$$f_{\text{filter}}(\mathbf{t}, \tilde{z}) = \exp(c\tilde{z}) \sum_{\mathbf{t}_i \in \mathcal{K}} k(\mathbf{t}_i - \mathbf{t}) \exp(-cz(\mathbf{t}_i)).$$

Thus, the two terms are again separated, but a single 32-bit information is sufficient this time.

Unfortunately, for a $\mathbf{t}_i$ coming out of a *neighborhood* of $\tilde{z}$, the assumption $z(\mathbf{t}_i) - \tilde{z} \leq 0$ does not necessarily hold. As a consequence, large positive values can occur. This is a problem because it invalidates the summation: the exponential no

---

Link to Image Processing

Convolution shadow maps show a resemblance to methods [Paris06] focusing on image processing with the bilateral filter [Tomasi98, Smith95], which found many applications in computational photography. It is actually interesting to see that PCF can be linked to these filter accelerations, and it gives a new way of looking at the problem.

The goal of fast bilateral upsampling [Paris06] is to provide an approximation for the bilateral filter:

$$\text{bilateral}(\mathbf{x}) = \frac{\sum_{\mathbf{y}\in\mathcal{N}(\mathbf{x})} I(\mathbf{y})\, g(\mathbf{y}-\mathbf{x})\, h(I(\mathbf{y})-I(\mathbf{x}))}{\sum_{\mathbf{y}\in\mathcal{N}(\mathbf{x})} g(\mathbf{y}-\mathbf{x})\, h(I(\mathbf{y})-I(\mathbf{x}))},$$

where $I(\mathbf{y})$ describes the value of the image at position $\mathbf{y}$. The variables g, h are usually Gaussian kernels. The filter thus combines pixels that are not only close in distance (g) but, further, have similar color (h). Paris and Durand compute the numerator and denominator separately. Let's first look at the denominator. It bears some similarity to CSM. We see that $g(\mathbf{y}-\mathbf{x})$ takes the place of k. But if h is chosen to be a step function, then it is similar to

$$s(z, \tilde{z}) = H(z - \tilde{z}).$$

We thus obtain the same equation.

Paris and Durand then use a similar key insight to replace h by an approximation via basis functions:

$$h(I(\mathbf{y}) - I(\mathbf{x})) = \sum_i \delta(I(\mathbf{x}) - I_i) h(I_i - I(\mathbf{x})),$$

where δ is measuring the similarity between $I(\mathbf{x})$ and the fixed samples I_i. This equation is already of the same form as Equation (5.18). The computation is thus separable, and both approaches perform similar computations. In a shadow context, this weight is already the final output. It describes how many pixels participate in the computation (let light pass). However, the derivation of the basis functions does differ. Paris and Durand rely on a linearization similar to previous work by Durand and Dorsey [Durand02], which *slices* the function with respect to a set of reference values. It could be interesting to see whether one approach could benefit from the other's solution.

---

longer behaves like a step function. Even though for many pixels this assumption does hold, the larger the kernel size, the less likely it is that artifacts can be avoided. This makes exponential shadow maps less usable for large kernels, and it mostly finds application to smooth the boundary of hard shadows without achieving penumbra-like effects.

In order to address this robustness issue, Annen et al. propose detecting those pixels where the assumption might fail. For these, a standard PCF filtering is applied. This PCF filtering can still be performed with the exponential map by simply clamping each single value before the summation.

Two possibilities are presented to classify erroneous pixels. A first strategy tests if the filtered value exceeds one. This solution is very approximate, but fast. A better classification can be performed by creating a lookup texture that gives the maximum z-value in each filtering window. This could be done using a min/max mipmap approach. This is conservative, but costly in practice.

Although (using the approximate classification) this approach leads to an approximate speed-up of two to three over CSM, the performance depends highly on the scene and the kernel size. For example, whenever silhouettes from the light are visible in the camera view, these will need to be evaluated with PCF. Grass on the ground, unstructured surfaces, or other fine geometry can result in many pixels being treated with PCF up to the point that the gained speed-up can completely vanish. Memory costs, on the other hand, are always improved by an important factor of around eight. For simpler models with less details, this method is a very good choice.

PCF Extension

Related, but more general than PCF, are multiple-depth shadow maps [Pagot04]; despite little practical relevance, the idea is intriguing. Instead of using all samples in a neighborhood of size l, a best selection of k elements is chosen (e.g., smallest/largest depth values). These samples are then evaluated with PCF. If k is small compared to l, then there is a potential gain. Unfortunately, the selection of the k elements is usually costly and the paper further limits the choice to $k = 2, 3$. Nevertheless, such a selection process is an idea to keep in mind for the future.

Exponential Layered Variance Shadow Maps without Layers

Surprisingly, the concurrently published layered variance shadow-map paper by Lauritzen and McCool [Lauritzen08] proposes an alternative warping based on exponential functions and without the need for layers.

They suggest using the variance shadow-map approach (see Section 5.3.2) and applying it to depth maps that were warped by an exponential function. They propose to use two such warped depth maps, using the functions $-\exp(-cz)$ and $\exp(cz)$. Both functions map the depth values monotonically, hence allowing them to use the standard variance shadow-map framework, and the mentioned Chebyshev inequality related to Equation (5.11) gives valid bounds in both cases. Consequently, for both functions, corresponding bounds p_-, p_+ are computed and the shadow is finally defined by $p := \min\{p_-, p_+\}$.

In practice, this method has little memory overhead, is the easiest to implement, and performs very well. For the case of antialiased shadows, this seems currently a very good choice.

VSM	LVSM	CSM	ESM
$2 \times$ F32	$n \times 16$	$2M \times 8$	F32
$2 \times$ F32	4×16	16×8	F32

Table 5.1. Comparison of memory requirements of different precomputed filtering approaches, in bits. For LVSM, n is the number of layers; for CSM, M is the expansion order. The last row compares typical configurations listed in the respective papers. The abbreviation F32 refers to a 32-bit floating-point component, 8 to an 8-bit byte component, and 16 to a 16-bit fixed point component.

5.3.6 Comparison

Common Observations

One aspect that needs to be taken into account for all filter precomputation methods is that shadow receivers have to be rendered into the shadow map even if they do not cast shadows themselves (e.g., a ground plane). The reason is that otherwise, the precomputation step would calculate an average based on depth values that are at the light far plane. For example, in VSM, this would imply a very large standard deviation and thus light bleeding.

Memory Requirements

The presented methods differ in the amount of memory they require for storing the approximation to the shadow-comparison function. In all cases, multiple targets can be created simultaneously by writing a full-screen quad to a multiple render target (MRT). Currently, in one render pass, four 8-bit or 32-bit RGBA-render targets can be written simultaneously. According to Table 5.1, all methods can be created in a single pass, except CSM with $M = 8$, which requires two rendering passes.

Tradeoffs

The different methods offer different parameters that need to be tweaked in order to achieve good results. For VSM, the minimum allowable variance and a bleeding reduction factor have to be set. LVSM introduce the number of layers as parameter. In CSM, the approximation order M has to be chosen, as well as the absorption factor to avoid ringing. ESM requires setting the scale factor to tune the falloff of the approximated step function. The original algorithms, like VSM and CSM, are particularly prone to light bleeding (see Figure 5.9), while newer algorithms like LVSM and ESM can be tweaked to reduce these artifacts significantly.

Figure 5.9. CSM (left pair) and VSM (right pair) show light bleeding artifacts. This can be made more visible when scaling the light intensity by a factor of four (right of each pair). Newer approaches are able to reduce these artifacts significantly, hence, such solutions are a good choice when high performance is needed.

5.4 Summary

In this chapter, we investigated the use of filtering hard shadows in order to create smooth shadow boundaries. Although not physically accurate, the methods can provide smooth transitions and visually pleasing results. In practice, these methods and their extensions to soft shadows that we will visit in Section 6.5.3 are relevant for practical real-time applications.

One advantage we did not point out sufficiently is the fact that filtering approaches like convolution, variance, or exponential shadow maps all support multisampling and can address aliasing due to foreshortening. When looking up values from the filtered textures, one can use anisotropy, supported natively as a texture-filtering mode, to reflect the pixel's projected footprint. This allows us to fight another source of aliasing.

The drawback is that the light source cannot be too large, otherwise the drawbacks of the constant filtering size become very obvious and contact shadows can suffer significantly. The methods are intended to fight aliasing, not to simulate soft shadows. The fact that aliasing removal can result in a pleasing and soft-shadow-like appearance is a welcome side effect.

CHAPTER 6

Image-Based Soft-Shadow Methods

6.1 Introduction

While exploring various aspects of computing shadows in the previous chapters, we have always restricted ourselves to point lights as the source of illumination. However, when you look around, you will notice that one rarely encounters point lights in the real world; instead, most light sources have a certain spatial extent. They come in several flavors, ranging from huge, distant environmental lights, like an overcast sky, to spatially well-confined area lights, like the sun or the ceiling lighting in an office. Whereas a point light can only be occluded either entirely or not at all, such extended light sources may additionally be partially visible. Therefore, cast shadows are not necessarily "hard" but may feature transition regions of intermediate illumination levels.

Such soft shadows are tougher and more costly to compute, and hence, a wide spectrum of approaches have been proposed that serve different needs, varying in aspects like the accuracy provided, the attainable speed, and the supported kind of light source. Exploring these methods, we first focus exclusively on nearby lights of simple shape, like rectangular or spherical light sources, in this and the next chapter, not least because it is often such kinds of lights that are responsible for producing visually dominating and distinctly recognizable soft shadows. Techniques for dealing with environmental light sources, like the skylight, will then be covered in Sections 10.5 and 10.6.

When determining the shading for a scene point $\mathbf{p}$, a point light merely requires considering the resulting simple point-to-point relationship for evaluating the direct illumination and checking for occlusion. By contrast, a whole light region has to be accounted for when dealing with area lights. To make the computation of the according integral

$$L_o(\mathbf{p}, \omega) = \int_{\mathcal{L}} \underbrace{f_r(\mathbf{p}, \omega, \mathbf{p} \to \mathbf{l}) \, L_e(\mathbf{l}, \mathbf{l} \to \mathbf{p}) \, G(\mathbf{p}, \mathbf{l})}_{\text{Shading}} \, \underbrace{V(\mathbf{p}, \mathbf{l})}_{\text{Visibility}} \, d\mathbf{l}, \qquad (6.1)$$

as introduced in Section 1.1.3, more tractable, typically two main approximations are made. First, visibility is separated from shading, enabling the independent computation of both terms. Second, the shading computation is simplified to treat the extended light as a single point light, that is, only some point $\mathbf{l}'$ of the extended light source, usually its center, is considered. Consequently, we are left with the task of determining the fraction of the light source visible to the scene point $\mathbf{p}$ and simply using the resulting *visibility factor*

$$V_{\mathcal{L}}(\mathbf{p}) = \frac{1}{|\mathcal{L}|} \int_{\mathcal{L}} V(\mathbf{p}, \mathbf{l}) \, d\mathbf{l} \qquad (6.2)$$

to modulate the direct illumination term computed for a point light at $\mathbf{l}'$:

$$L_o(\mathbf{p}, \omega) = \underbrace{\text{directIllum}(\mathbf{p}, \omega, \mathbf{l}')}_{\substack{\text{Point-light shading}}} \cdot \underbrace{V_{\mathcal{L}}(\mathbf{p})}_{\substack{\text{Extended-light} \\ \text{visibility factor}}}.$$

In this and the subsequent chapter, we will explore various approaches for determining this visibility factor efficiently. Some of these methods also readily support computing the accurate integral from Equation (6.1), and we briefly cover how to do this in Section 10.1.2.

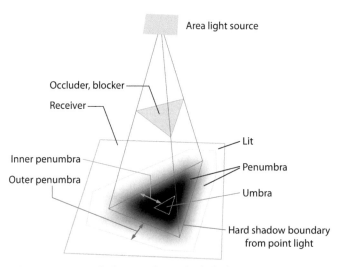

Figure 6.1. Terms encountered when speaking of soft shadows.

6.1.1 Properties and Terms

With soft shadows cast by extended light sources, three different kinds of illumination regions can be distinguished (see Figure 6.1):

- the *umbra*, where the light source is completely occluded and which, hence, comprises scene points entirely in shadow;

- the *lit region*, from which the light source is fully visible;

- the *penumbra*, the intermediate transition region where the light is only partially occluded and, hence, still some partial illumination is received.

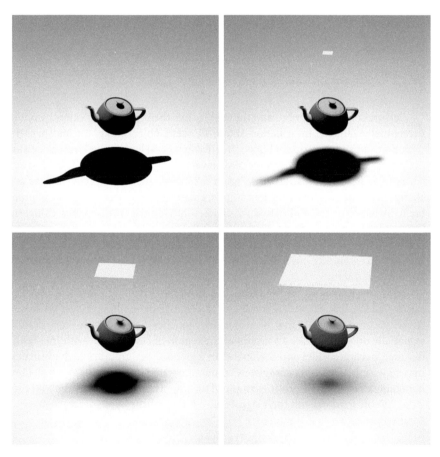

Figure 6.2. The size of the light source influences the shadow cast by a blocker. Shadows become wider and softer as the light's size increases.

Figure 6.3. Soft shadows harden towards regions of contact.

Features of the penumbra and the umbra, like their shapes and extents, convey perceptually valuable information about the scene objects, like, for instance, the directional position or size of lights, the silhouette and location of shadow-casting occluders, or the surface geometry of receivers.

For example, as illustrated in Figure 6.2, a soft shadow directly reflects any change in the size of its casting light source; enlarging the source causes the penumbra to increase and the umbra to shrink and eventually even to disappear. Concerning terminology (see Figure 6.1), the part of the penumbra growing outwards with respect to the umbra at point-light size is sometimes called *outer penumbra*, while the portion extending inwards and successively replacing the umbra is referred to as *inner penumbra*.

Similarly, if we keep the light fixed but move the occluder towards the receiver, the overall shadow size gets reduced and the relative penumbra portion decreases. A direct consequence is that if an occluder touches a receiver, the cast shadow essentially only comprises an umbra at the region of contact but, with increasing distance, becomes wider and dominated by a growing penumbra, which ultimately may supersede the umbra completely, as demonstrated in Figure 6.3. Such shadow *hardening on contact* is a prime example of the important cues [Mamassian98] provided by soft shadows and their significance for a realistic appearance.

6.1.2 Classification of Approaches

Given the large spectrum of different approaches for computing soft shadows, naturally several aspects exist for which various options have been explored and which thus may serve as basis for a classification. For instance, approaches may be distinguished according to[1]

- which set of occluders is considered (e.g., not all but only those visible from the light's center);

- in which space visibility computations are performed (e.g., in screen space);

- in which order occluder information is processed (e.g., looping over all receiver samples potentially affected by an occluder);

- how information about occluders is provided (e.g., by rendering a primitive for each occluder that covers all affected receiver samples);

- what kind of visibility information is determined (e.g., visibility of selected sample points on the light source).

Typically, however, the occluder representation is chosen as the primary categorization criterion. One major class of algorithms utilizes an *image-based* representation of the considered occluding scene objects. By contrast, *geometry-based* methods employ an explicit geometric primitive for each processed occluder to derive the soft shadows. Following this line of distinction, which also corresponds to how we organized the presentation in Chapter 2, we first cover image-based approaches in the remainder of this chapter. The following chapter is then dedicated to geometry-based methods, including hybrid approaches that feature both image-based and geometry-based components.

Image-based algorithms offer several advantages. First, current graphics hardware offers direct support for both the generation and the query of shadow maps, which are pivotal to many such techniques. Second, they typically scale better with scene complexity than geometry-based approaches. Third, such methods can readily deal with geometry altered in the fragment stage via alpha masking, pixel kills, or depth modifications. Especially the selective discarding of fragments is fundamental to many recent techniques for ray casting surfaces [Loop06, Stoll06] and for adapting the silhouette in per-pixel displacement-mapping algorithms [Oliveira05, Chen08]. On the other hand, an image-based representation involves sampling, leading to aliasing problems. In particular, fine structures may be missed, and silhouettes are easily captured at a too coarse resolution. Moreover, biasing of the depth values recorded in a shadow map is required to avoid surface-acne artifacts due to incorrect self-shadowing (see Section 2.2.3).

By contrast, geometry-based approaches avoid aliasing problems thanks to working with the exact occluding geometry. However, such algorithms are typically slower than image-based methods and may also suffer from numerical precision problems.

---

[1]A more detailed discussion is provided in our SIGGRAPH Asia 2009 course notes [Eisemann09, Section 5.1.1].

6.1.3   Section Guide

Before we start elaborating on any concrete soft-shadow algorithm, we will first spend Section 6.2 discussing some basic concepts that are repeatedly encountered as important elements in various algorithms and that thus highlight some general solution strategies. They also find application in the geometry-based approaches covered in the next chapter.

Then, in Section 6.3, we describe a rather slow but simple-to-implement, brute-force method and variants thereof for computing a high-quality solution, which commonly establishes the reference against which computationally cheaper and faster methods are compared. Such less accurate but often real-time algorithms are subsequently discussed in detail, with the order of the sections roughly corresponding to increasing degrees of physical correctness and hence agreement with the reference.

We begin with approaches that start off with hard shadows and augment them with inner and/or outer penumbrae, but which are nowadays mainly of historical interest (Section 6.4). By contrast, the family of spatially adaptive shadow-filtering approaches covered next (Section 6.5), which likewise is only aiming at phenomenologically plausible soft shadows, is extremely popular, not least due to ease of implementation, and is utilized in many games. These methods actually can produce (close to) accurate results, but only in a very restricted setting—for which faster approaches based on convolution exist. We cover them and their application to general scenes in Section 6.6.

Making a significant leap in attainable physical correctness, we then turn to algorithms that reconstruct occluder approximations from a shadow map and back-project them onto the light source (Section 6.7). When using information from multiple shadow maps, even better results can be obtained, and several related methods are briefly described in Section 6.8. Finally, we close the chapter with a summary of the techniques covered (Section 6.9).

6.2   Basics

With the plethora of soft-shadow algorithms around, there are some basic, recurring principles and strategies, which we discuss in this section, so that the reader is already armed with knowledge about common solution components and their properties and an understanding of limitations and challenges when delving into the description of actual algorithms.

6.2.1   Penumbra-Width Estimation

Several soft-shadow algorithms make use of the size of the penumbra effected by (a silhouette of) a blocker, for instance, to choose the amount of blurring accordingly

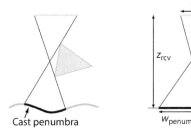

Figure 6.4. Computing the penumbra size in a general configuration (left) is nontrivial even in two dimensions, but it becomes straightforward in a simplified, restricted setup (right).

(see Section 6.5). While in a general setting the penumbra width can become quite involved to compute, a reasonable estimate is easily derived by assuming a planar light source, planar occluder, and planar receiver and that all of them are parallel to each other. In that case, the intercept theorem (or equivalently, looking at similar triangles) yields the relationship

$$w_{\text{penumbra}} = \frac{z_{\text{rcv}} - z_{\text{occl}}}{z_{\text{occl}}} w_{\text{light}}, \tag{6.3}$$

where z_{occl} and z_{rcv} are the distances from the light to the occluder and receiver planes, respectively, and where w_{light} denotes the size of the light source (see Figure 6.4).

6.2.2   Occluder Back Projection

While knowing the size and the boundaries of the penumbra may suffice for computing soft shadows accurately in some very restricted configurations, like the one assumed in the previous subsection, in general, more action is required for correctly determining the light visibility factor $V_{\mathcal{L}}(\mathbf{p})$ from Equation (6.2) for an arbitrary receiver point $\mathbf{p}$. Recalling that this factor reflects the fraction of the light source $\mathcal{L}$ that is visible to $\mathbf{p}$, one seemingly natural approach is to take the point of view of $\mathbf{p}$ and project all blockers that occlude some part of the light from $\mathbf{p}$ onto the light and measure the remaining unoccluded light area $A_{\text{unoccl}}(\mathbf{p})$. Putting this in relation to the overall light area $A_{\mathcal{L}} = |\mathcal{L}|$ then directly yields the sought-after visibility factor

$$V_{\mathcal{L}}(\mathbf{p}) = \frac{A_{\text{unoccl}}(\mathbf{p})}{A_{\mathcal{L}}}.$$

The projection onto the light source is often referred to as *back projection*, and we, too, adopt this term in the following, allowing for easy distinction from other types of projections.

In practice, two general computational orders exist for determining $A_{\text{unoccl}}(\mathbf{p})$ via occluder back projection:

- *Gathering* (of occluder information by receiver points):

  All receiver points are visited in an outer loop. For each point, all relevant occluders are then back-projected in an inner loop and the final visibility factor is determined.

  > For each receiver point $\mathbf{p}$
  >   For each (relevant) occluder $\mathcal{B}$
  >   Back-project $\mathcal{B}$ onto light $\mathcal{L}$
  >   Update information about unoccluded light parts
  >   Compute visibility factor $V_{\mathcal{L}}(\mathbf{p})$

  Since running the inner loop in a fragment shader mandates having access to some representation of all the (relevant) occluders in the scene, this strategy is primarily adopted by image-based approaches, where often some sort of shadow map provides this scene information.

- *Scattering* (of occluder information to receiver points):

  Essentially reversing the loop order, all occluders are processed in the outer loop. For each, all receiver points whose light visibility might be affected by the occluder are considered in the inner loop, updating their light visibility factors.

  > For each occluder $\mathcal{B}$
  >   For each (potentially affected) receiver point $\mathbf{p}$
  >   Back-project $\mathcal{B}$ onto light $\mathcal{L}$
  >   Update information about unoccluded light parts
  > For each receiver point $\mathbf{p}$
  >   Compute visibility factor $V_{\mathcal{L}}(\mathbf{p})$

  This approach is often realized by rendering a geometric primitive for each occluder that covers at least all those pixels where the corresponding receiver point is shadowed by this occluder. Consequently, one often encounters this strategy in geometry-based soft-shadow algorithms.

  Note that unlike before, where the information about unoccluded light parts only needs to be maintained for the currently considered receiver point and hence can be kept in shader registers, this computational order necessitates storing such intermediate visibility information for all receiver samples in some buffer.

Concerning the actual data stored about unoccluded light parts, various representations are encountered in practice, including

- a single, accumulated visibility factor, which, however, prevents accurate results, as we will see in the next subsection;

- per-sample values for multiple light-source samples (see Section 6.2.4 below);

- explicit geometric descriptions of the unoccluded parts [Drettakis94, Stewart94].

Since back-projecting an occluder identifies the concrete part of the light source that gets occluded, this technique directly supports accounting for nonuniform, multicolored light sources, which we cover separately in Section 10.1.

Conceptually, the back-projection approach is equivalent to rendering all blockers from the viewpoint of the receiver point onto the light's surface, constituting a "visibility image," and several algorithms actually adopt such a strategy. The earliest such algorithm is probably the hemi-cube method [Cohen85] from 1985, often used in radiosity systems [Cohen93, Sillion94]. A more recent example that targets modern graphics hardware is the bitmask-soft-shadows algorithm [Schwarz07], which we will discuss in Section 6.7.

6.2.3   Occluder Fusion

When multiple occluders block light from a receiver, the same light region may be occluded by more than one occluder, causing their back projections to overlap and hence these occluders to "fuse" from the perspective of the receiver. Generally, three basic scenarios can be distinguished in case of multiple occluders (see Figure 6.5):

(a) All blockers occlude disjoint parts of the light source.

(b) There is one master blocker whose back projection comprises the back projections of all other blockers.

(c) At least two back projections overlap partially.

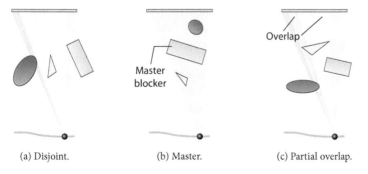

(a) Disjoint.   (b) Master.   (c) Partial overlap.

Figure 6.5. When multiple blockers occlude the light source, three general configurations concerning their back projections can be differentiated.

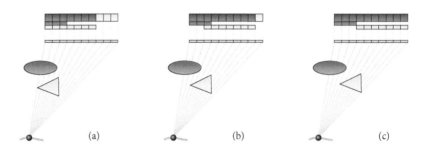

Figure 6.6. The aggregate occlusion factor for multiple blockers generally cannot be derived from the individual blockers' occlusion factors alone, as the same light region may be occluded by several blockers. In all three depicted cases, the red ellipse occludes 30% of the light and the green triangle occludes 70%. However, the overall occlusion due to these two blockers is different each time, ranging from (a) 70% to (b) 90% to (c) 100%.

Let's assume there are n occluders $\mathcal{B}_i$, with the fraction of the light area that the back projection of blocker $\mathcal{B}_i$ occludes being $O_i \in [0, 1]$. In scenario (a), the overall visibility factor is then directly computed from these *occlusion factors* O_i as

$$V = 1 - \sum_i O_i, \qquad (6.4)$$

and in scenario (b), we have

$$V = 1 - \max_i O_i. \qquad (6.5)$$

Note, however, that given just the occlusion factors, we cannot know which scenario applies and hence which formula to use. And for the more general scenario (c), an expression utilizing merely the occlusion factors does not even exist.

In practice, this means that accurate soft shadows cannot be computed by simply combining individual occlusion factors for all occluders (see Figure 6.6). Instead, the spatial relationship of the back projections on the light area has to be taken into account. On the other hand, working just with occlusion factors is easy to implement and runs faster than more accurate variants. Consequently, many real-time algorithms are based on utilizing individual occlusion factors and adopt some heuristic to derive an estimate of the overall visibility factor from them.

Most assume disjoint occluders and hence simply accumulate the occlusion factors (Equation (6.4)). Rarely, the master blocker scenario is adopted, picking the maximum occlusion factor (Equation (6.5)). Noticing that these two extremal cases establish lower and upper bounds on the accurate visibility factor, it has also been suggested to use some weighted average of them, for example [Soler98b],

$$V = 1 - \frac{1}{2}\sum_i O_i - \frac{1}{2}\max_i O_i.$$

Another proposed heuristic [Eisemann06b] takes the probability that an arbitrary point on the light source is unoccluded as the visibility factor estimate, treating the occlusion factors as such probabilities and combining them:

$$V = \prod_i (1 - O_i).$$

6.2.4 Point Sampling of Light Visibility

Computing accurate soft shadows requires that occluder fusion be correctly accounted for. One powerful approach that makes this manageable and avoids having to deal with complicated geometric representations of occluded regions is using Monte Carlo integration for computing the visibility integral from Equation (6.2):

$$V_{\mathcal{L}}(\mathbf{p}) = \frac{1}{|\mathcal{L}|} \int_{\mathcal{L}} V(\mathbf{p}, \mathbf{l}) \, d\mathbf{l} \approx \sum_i w_i \, V(\mathbf{p}, \mathbf{l}_i). \tag{6.6}$$

That is, visibility is only determined at n light sample points $\mathbf{l}_i \in \mathcal{L}$ with associated weights w_i, where $\sum_i w_i = 1$. The weighted average of these visibility samples is then used as estimate of the visibility factor $V_{\mathcal{L}}(\mathbf{p})$. With increasing sample count n, this Monte Carlo estimator converges to the accurate solution.

This reduction of the challenging light-area visibility problem to a set of simpler binary light-point visibility problems can be traced back to at least 1984 [Cook84, Brotman84]. It is often encountered in high-quality offline rendering systems, constituting the standard approach in ray tracing (see also Section 10.4). However, only in 2007 had graphics hardware grown powerful enough for real-time approaches to appear [Schwarz07, Eisemann07]. Since then, multiple GPU-based algorithms have been proposed and, for moderately complex scenes, it is now possible to compute accurate soft shadows at highly interactive frame rates, as we will see in Section 7.4.

Obviously, the number n of considered sample points $\mathbf{l}_i$ directly influences speed and quality. An optimal choice depends on many factors, like the width of the penumbra, the utilized sampling pattern, and the complexity of the surface texture. For very thin shadows on dark surfaces with high texture masking, even 16 sample points, providing just 17 discrete degrees of shadowing, may yield excellent visual results. On the other hand, wide penumbrae on a smooth white surface may still suffer from some undersampling artifacts, even with 4,096 sample points. In our experience, choices between 256 and 1,024 sample points typically work very well for most scenes if an appropriate sampling pattern is used.

Generally, regular, uniform sampling patterns should be avoided, as they are susceptible to causing banding artifacts. In particular, if an occluder edge is aligned with the sampling grid, a tiny change in the edge's position may affect a whole row of sampling points, drastically reducing the effective number of discrete visibility factors encountered in a certain penumbra. Instead, a stratified, jittered sampling

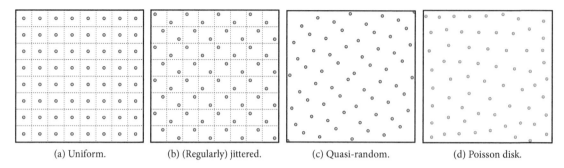

| (a) Uniform. | (b) (Regularly) jittered. | (c) Quasi-random. | (d) Poisson disk. |

Figure 6.7. Examples of sampling patterns (64 samples).

pattern, a pattern constructed from a quasi-random sequence like the Hammersley sequence, or a Poisson disk pattern should be employed (see Figure 6.7). With them, a minor translation of an occluder edge usually affects just one sampling point; moreover, undersampling manifests itself as noise in the final image, which is far less objectionable than stepping artifacts and also more easily masked by surface textures.

6.3   A Reference Solution

The point-sampling approach of treating an area light source as a collection of point lights enables leveraging techniques developed for hard shadows for computing accurate soft shadows. First note that the Monte Carlo estimate for the visibility factor $V_{\mathcal{L}}(\mathbf{p})$ from Equation (6.6) essentially boils down to determining, for each light sample point $\mathbf{l}_i$, the hard shadow cast by a point light source located at $\mathbf{l}_i$, and averaging these shadow values together. Naturally, shadow maps may be used to compute these hard shadows for all visible receiver points $\mathbf{p}$ in parallel. This leads us to the following simple algorithm:

```
1   Clear screen-sized visibility buffer
2   For each light sample point lᵢ
3       Compute shadow map for point light at lᵢ
4       Determine hard shadow using shadow map for all receiver pixels (view samples)
5       Add shadow result to visibility buffer
6   Apply visibility buffer to shaded scene
```

Here, the visibility for each screen pixel, corresponding to a receiver point, is accumulated in a visibility buffer, for which typically a single-channel 16- or 32-bit floating-point texture is used. The accumulation is realized by outputting the determined hard-shadow visibility value in the fragment shader and using additive blending to incorporate the result into the visibility buffer.

While the algorithm yields accurate soft shadows, it is rather costly because n shadow maps have to be computed in case of n light sample points, and each shadow-map generation involves rendering the scene, that is, overall, the scene needs to be rendered n times. To avoid having to render the scene another n times to apply the shadow maps (line 4), typically a deferred shading approach is pursued. Initially, the scene is rendered from the camera into a G-buffer (see Appendix E.1) recording either the position in world space or, even better, just the depth in camera space, from which the world-space position is quickly computed given the inverse view-projection matrix. Then, to apply the shadow map and determine visibility, merely a screen-sized quad needs to be rendered. In the triggered fragment shader, the receiver point's world position is determined from the G-buffer, transformed into light space, and compared against the corresponding shadow-map data, yielding the visibility value. Similarly, drawing a quad suffices to eventually use the computed visibility value for shading the scene (line 6).

Even though the presented algorithm is routinely used for producing reference solutions and we consider it to yield "accurate shadows," one should be aware that some inaccuracies may occur due to being based on shadow mapping, like surface-acne issues. However, if the light-sample count n is sufficiently high, such inaccuracies typically remain basically imperceptible, as they usually only occur for a subset of the samples at a certain point and thus don't contribute enough to the final visibility factor to evoke a noticeable artifact.

Towards Real-Time Performance

Despite the tremendous advances in graphics hardware performance, rendering the scene n times to produce the shadow maps may still consume seconds except for simple scenes or low sample counts, where interactive frame rates are attainable. Since not only hardware performance keeps growing but also scene complexity, we are supposedly still a very long way from making this brute force approach generally applicable to real-time rendering.

Till then, one may resort to progressively computing and displaying the soft shadows. By distributing the shadow-map generation over multiple frames, real-time feedback is feasible but requires the user to wait many frames to get a sufficiently converged result. Scherzer et al. [Scherzer09] build on this strategy and determine one shadow map per frame, each time choosing a different light sample point. For each pixel, the resulting visibility values are successively aggregated, providing a continuously improving estimate. In order to provide a good initial visibility value for fragments that become visible for the first time, they don't use the hard shadow result for the currently processed light sample, but utilize the shadow map to compute an approximate visibility value with the PCSS algorithm, discussed later in Section 6.5. Furthermore, to suppress flickering due to jumps in visibility factors during convergence, some smoothing is performed in screen space.

Recently, it was also suggested [Schwärzler09] to start with only four sample points at the corners of a rectangular light source and to incrementally add new points until a metric indicates convergence. The proposed metric looks at two opposing light samples and compares their associated shadow maps, checking the pixel-wise depth differences after reprojection in camera space. If some of them exceed a threshold, an adaptive subdivision of the light is performed and new sample points are added. Unfortunately, the simple metric may easily fail, stopping refinement too early. Moreover, the resulting regular placement of the sample points is typically undesirable, as discussed in Section 6.2.4. Nevertheless, such incremental approaches will evolve and may eventually prove pretty relevant. For instance, more involved refinement strategies are already successfully employed in offline global-illumination rendering techniques.

Variants

We should note that, historically, it was the advent of the accumulation buffer [Haeberli90] that introduced the general approach of averaging shadow-map results on graphics hardware. The proposed original algorithm rendered and shaded the scene once for each point light, computing not only the shadow-map–based visibility factor but also the direct illumination for this light, and accumulated the results. That is, the whole lighting integral from Equation (6.1) was computed with Monte Carlo integration and not just the isolated visibility factor, producing physically correct results (if the shading part in Equation (6.1) is computed correctly). We will come back to solving the lighting integral in Section 10.1.2.

Also nowadays only of historical interest is the variant proposed by Herf and Heckbert [Herf96, Heckbert97, Herf97]. Instead of using shadow maps and computing light visibility for all pixels in screen space, they generate a soft-shadow texture for each receiver that is then applied during rendering. To this end, for a given receiver face and a light sample point l_i, the pyramidal frustum with apex l_i and the receiver face as base is picked as viewing volume. All scene objects inside this volume are then rendered in black, effectively yielding the hard shadow on the considered receiver face in a surface texture. This step is performed for all light sample points, combining the individual results to yield the face-specific soft-shadow texture. Overall, the scene has thus to be rendered $n \cdot n_{\text{rcv}}$ times, where n is the number of light samples and n_{rcv} denotes the number of receiver faces in the scene. This quadratic complexity makes the method prohibitive already for moderately complex scenes.

6.4   Augmenting Hard Shadows with Penumbrae

Phenomenologically, it is primarily the existence of a penumbra that distinguishes a soft from a hard shadow. Exploiting this insight, early methods aiming for pro-

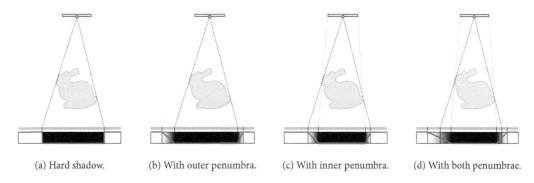

(a) Hard shadow. (b) With outer penumbra. (c) With inner penumbra. (d) With both penumbrae.

Figure 6.8. Plausible soft shadows may be created by augmenting hard shadows with outer and/or inner penumbrae.

ducing soft-shadow effects in real time concentrated on introducing some kind of penumbra, thus trying to fake soft shadows in a phenomenologically plausible way. The algorithms we are considering in this section all start with the hard shadow obtained for a point light source placed at the center of the extended light and then enlarge this shadow outwards [Parker98] and/or inwards to generate a penumbra region (see Figure 6.8 and also Section 7.1). To this end, for each receiver point $\mathbf{p}$ all algorithms basically search for hard-shadow boundaries in the point's vicinity and then determine which occluder sample (i.e., which shadow map texel) is responsible for this hard shadow. With this information, the penumbra's extent can be estimated (see Section 6.2.1), and the relative placement of $\mathbf{p}$ within the penumbra is determined to yield a visibility factor.

Before looking at concrete strategies to realize this basic approach, we should note that at the time the first algorithms were developed, the targeted consumer graphics hardware was still in its infancy. In particular, the programmability nowadays taken for granted was rudimentary at best. Consequently, the sophistication of the algorithms was limited by hardware features and most steps could nowadays be implemented in an easier and more direct way than presented in the original papers.

6.4.1 Light-Space Search

The first algorithm was presented by Brabec and Seidel [Brabec02c]. After creating a standard shadow map, they query this map to determine whether a receiver point $\mathbf{p}$ is lit or in (hard) shadow. If it is lit, a radial search in the shadow map (executed on the CPU) is initiated to find the closest shadow-map texel whose light-space depth is smaller than $\mathbf{p}$'s and which hence corresponds to an occluder. The search radius r is successively increased up to $r_{\max}$, which is chosen as a function of the distance from $\mathbf{p}$ to the light's center (i.e., the shadow-map origin). Once an occluding shadow-map texel is found, the visibility factor is computed as $\frac{1}{2}\, r/r'_{\max}$, where r'_{max} is obtained by shrinking r_{max} as a function of the distance from the found blocker to the light. This establishes an outer penumbra. Analogously, if **p** is initially determined to be in shadow, the closest nonblocking shadow-map texel is searched for to derive the inner penumbra. Note that by construction, the original hard-shadow boundary, where inner and outer penumbrae meet, is assigned a visibility factor of 50% (see Figure 6.8(d)).

To avoid wrong self-shadowing, object IDs are used (see Section 2.2.4); on the downside, this also prevents correct self-shadowing. The major problem of the algorithm, however, is its greedy approach. Once a blocker is found, the search is stopped. Consequently, only the occlusion to one single blocker is accounted for, and this blocker might not even be the one responsible for most of the receiver point's shadowing. Shadow quality is further affected by the way the visibility factor is computed from the found occluder, which makes several approximations. Finally note that the maximum width of penumbra regions is limited by the chosen maximum search radius.

Restructuring the search step, Kirsch and Döllner [Kirsch03] move all involved computations to the GPU. As a side effect, their method is restricted to handling only inner penumbrae, that is, the resulting faked soft shadow is not larger than but has the same extent as the hard shadow, which easily looks unrealistic unless the penumbra is rather thin.

In their algorithm, once a shadow map has been determined, a so-called *shadow width map* is constructed iteratively in light space; it essentially encodes the distance to the closest lit pixel (with respect to a plane below all occluders). The iteration starts by recording a 1 for blockers and 0 otherwise. Subsequently, the (normalized) distance to the lit region is propagated to a texel's neighbors, increasing it by Δ. That neighbor's value is only updated if the propagated value is smaller, that is, if it reduces the current distance estimate. In practice, the propagation is realized by rendering a quad and gathering values from four neighbors in the x- and y-directions (incremented by Δ) from the previous shadow width map in a fragment shader, resulting in a new shadow width map. This is repeated several times, each iteration doubling the neighbor distance and the increment Δ.

After the shadow width map is constructed, the visibility factor for a receiver point **p** that is in hard shadow can be computed as a function of the shadow width, queried from the shadow width map, and the distance from **p** to its hard-shadow occluder. That is, the radial search from Brabec and Seidel's algorithm has been replaced by a lookup in the shadow width map. On the downside, outer penumbrae are no longer supported. Note that it is now the number of iterations in the shadow width map construction that bounds the maximum size of penumbra regions.

A more advanced strategy is pursued by de Boer [deBoer06], which yields both inner and outer penumbrae. First, blocker silhouettes are determined in light space by applying an edge detection filter to the shadow map, yielding a *skirt buffer* that stores a 1 for edge pixels and 0 otherwise. Subsequently, these edges are widened to *skirts* by applying a 3×3 filter for r times, with r being the light's radius. Moreover, the minimum shadow-map depth encountered during filtering is recorded for each texel. The final skirt buffer thus provides an estimate of relative placement within the penumbra as well as a conservative light-space depth estimate of the responsible occluder (see also Section 7.2.1).

During rendering of the scene, this information is leveraged for computing the visibility factor. If the shadow map indicates that a receiver point **p** is lit, the skirt buffer is queried to check whether **p** might be in an outer penumbra. In that case, a visibility factor is computed from the skirt-buffer data and **p**'s light-space depth. An analogous procedure is pursued if **p** is in hard shadow according to the shadow map, except for one addition to avoid wrong inner penumbrae with some concave objects: if the skirt buffer indicates that **p** might lie in an inner penumbra, a disk centered on **p** (whose radius is chosen according to the blocker depth from the skirt buffer) is tested for being completely in hard shadow. if this is the case, **p** is assumed to be in umbra; otherwise, the visibility factor is computed analogously to the lit case.

6.4.2   Screen-Space Search

In slightly earlier work, Arvo et al. [Arvo04b] spread information about blockers outwards from blocker silhouettes in screen space instead of in light space. First, they determine a shadow map and compute hard shadows with it. By applying a Laplacian filter kernel, boundary pixels are detected.[2] The remaining pixels are classified as outer (outside the hard-shadow boundary) and inner pixels, again using the shadow map.

In the next phase, the boundary pixels propagate their shadow-map coordinates to their surrounding nonboundary pixels. To this end, conceptually, an eight-connected recursive flood-fill in screen space is performed. In practice, however, several iterations of a gathering approach are pursued, where instead of spreading the information to neighbors, it is the neighbors that actually collect this information. Initially, the visibility factor for all boundary pixels is computed and these pixels are marked as processed. In each subsequent iteration, a screen-filling quad is rendered, and for each unmarked pixel **p**, the eight neighbors surrounding the pixel are inspected in the invoked fragment shader. If such a neighbor is a marked pixel, its shadow-map coordinates are used to compute a visibility factor for **p**. Eventually, that visibility factor is picked which is highest or lowest, depending on whether **p** is an inner or an outer pixel, respectively, corresponding to an extremal occluder-fusion heuristic. In that case, the processed pixel is marked and attributed

---

[2]As they are found in screen space, they may not correspond to silhouettes in the shadow map but can also be due to occlusion in camera space. Therefore, an edge-detection filter is applied to the shadow map to verify that the screen-space shadow border is caused by a blocker silhouette in the shadow map, before marking a pixel as boundary pixel. However, as noted by Rong et al. [Rong06], this additional verification is not always sufficient.

with the shadow-map coordinates used for determining the picked visibility factor. That way, the boundary pixels' occluder information is spread outwards. The whole procedure is executed until all newly marked pixels are completely lit or a maximum number of iterations has been reached.

Visibility is computed by shooting a ray from the pixel **p** through the point specified by the considered boundary pixel's shadow-map coordinates and the corresponding shadow-map depth and determining the intersection with the light-source plane. The light is split into two parts at the intersection point via a line perpendicular to the direction from the intersection point to the light's center, and the fraction of the unoccluded part of the light area is computed.

Note that only hard-shadow borders visible in screen space can give rise to penumbrae. To avoid artifacts at the screen's border, all screen-space computations should be performed with an appropriately enlarged camera frustum. As with the light-space techniques discussed before, the number of iterations performed for propagating the boundary information limits the maximum width of the penumbra.

Rong et al. [Rong06] show that their jump flooding approach can be applied to reduce the number of iterations. However, in some settings, light holes in the shadow regions may wrongly occur. They also introduce a variant that operates in light space, but it only produces outer penumbrae.

6.5   Blurring Hard-Shadow-Test Results

As we have seen in Chapter 5, blurring the results of the shadow-map test with PCF can produce shadow results that appear like soft shadows. Actually, some games and game engines implement just this and call it "soft shadows." However, irrespective of the physical incorrectness of such an approach, using a fixed-size filter window is unable to reproduce varying penumbra widths and, hence, visually prominent soft-shadow behavior, like hardening on contact. However, this major shortcoming can be alleviated by adaptively varying the filter window size. In this section, we explore several algorithms that perform such an adaptive blurring and are thus often able to yield visually plausible soft shadows.

6.5.1   Projected Soft-Shadow Textures

Some very simple algorithms don't even use shadow maps but build on shadow textures (see Section 2.1.2). Mitchell's *Poisson shadow blur* [Mitchell04b], for instance, assumes that the occluder is illuminated from the side by the light, causing the part of the occluder touching the ground to appear at the bottom of the shadow texture. He then simply blurs the shadow texture using a Poisson disk sampling pattern, varying the filter width from almost no blurring at the bottom, simulating contact shadows, to strong blurring at the top, thus replicating the widening of the penumbra with increasing distance to the region of contact. As usual, this filtered shadow texture is finally applied to the shadow receivers. A related, less ad-hoc approach is *soft projected shadows* [Pranckevičius06], where the filter width is chosen according to the distance between the blocker and the receiver.

6.5.2   Fractional-Disk Soft Shadows

Most algorithms are based on shadow maps, however. One of the earliest published methods was *fractional-disk soft shadows* by Valient and de Boer [Valient04], which assume a circular light source with radius r_{light}. Following the considerations from Section 6.2.1, in the presence of a single occluder at light-space depth z_{occl}, this light basically gives rise to a penumbra of half-width,

$$r_{\text{penumbra}} = \frac{z_{\text{rcv}} - z_{\text{occl}}}{z_{\text{occl}}} r_{\text{light}}, \tag{6.7}$$

on a planar receiver parallel to the light at depth z_{rcv}. This observation is utilized to derive an approximation of the visibility factor for a receiver point $\mathbf{p}$ by considering a disk of radius r_{penumbra} centered on $\mathbf{p}$ (with $z_{\text{rcv}} = \mathbf{p}_z^{\text{l}}$) and determining the fraction of the disk that is unoccluded as seen from the center $\mathbf{l}'$ of the light source. Computing this fraction boils down to performing percentage-closer filtering on a shadow map obtained from $\mathbf{l}'$ using a circular kernel of radius

$$r = \frac{z_{\text{near}}}{z_{\text{rcv}}} r_{\text{penumbra}}, \tag{6.8}$$

where z_{near} denotes the shadow map's near-plane distance.

To obtain the occluder depth z_{occl} and avoid redundant PCF operations, this basic approach is pursued within a more involved algorithm. At first, a shadow map is computed, and for each texel $\mathbf{t}$, the distance $d(\mathbf{t})$ to the nearest edge (eventually corresponding to a hard-shadow boundary) and the occluder depth $z_{\text{e}}(\mathbf{t})$ at this edge are determined. This is achieved using edge detection and a propagation process similar to what we have encountered in the previous section. Utilizing this augmented shadow map, the visibility factor can subsequently be determined in a fragment shader as follows: First, the processed receiver point $\mathbf{p}$ is tested for being in hard shadow with a standard shadow-map test. If it is inside the hard shadow, z_{occl} is taken from $\mathbf{p}$'s shadow-map entry; otherwise, the previously determined occluder depth $z_{\text{e}}(\mathbf{p}^{\text{s}})$ for the closest shadow edge is picked (in case no closeby shadow edge could be found while preprocessing the shadow map, $\mathbf{p}$ is considered to be lit). With this occluder depth, the disk radius r can be computed using Equations (6.7) and (6.8). If r is larger than the distance $d(\mathbf{p}^{\text{s}})$ to the nearest hard-shadow boundary, $\mathbf{p}$ is either in umbra or completely lit, depending on whether it is in hard shadow or not, respectively. Only if this is not the case, PCF has to be performed to determine the unoccluded disk fraction.

Valient and de Boer also propose an alternative algorithm that doesn't necessitate augmenting the shadow map with $d(\mathbf{t})$ and $z_e(\mathbf{t})$. One main difference is that without the distance to the nearest hard-shadow boundary being available, one can now no longer directly detect umbra or lit regions, and hence, PCF is always performed. Moreover, in case $\mathbf{p}$ is outside the hard shadow, the occluder depth z_{occl} used for deriving the disk radius has to be determined on the fly, which involves sampling the shadow map within an appropriately sized disk.

6.5.3   Percentage-Closer Soft Shadows

Pursuing a similar approach as this latter algorithm, but also building on earlier work of his own [Fernando02], Fernando [Fernando05] introduced *percentage-closer soft shadows* (PCSS) in a one-page sketch. Designed to merely require the substitution of the standard shadow-map test in an existing code base to turn hard shadows into visually plausible soft shadows, the algorithm is simple both to understand and to implement. Hence, it is no wonder that PCSS and its variants enjoy popularity in many real-time applications (e.g., games).

After acquiring a shadow map for the scene, PCSS queries this shadow map to identify blockers that affect the receiver point $\mathbf{p}$ and derives a representative (virtual) planar blocker. Utilizing the penumbra-width estimate from Section 6.2.1, a filter size is determined, and the shadow map is sampled again to perform percentage-closer filtering accordingly. We will now have a closer look at these steps (see Figure 6.9).

Blocker search. At first, the shadow-map region $\mathcal{R}_s$ containing samples of relevant occluders is determined. It is defined by the intersection of the light–receiver-point pyramid (with the area light as base and the receiver point $\mathbf{p}$ as apex) with the shadow map's near plane. This region is then searched for blockers. These are simply identified by performing a standard shadow-map test, that is, all shadow-map entries that are closer to the light source than $\mathbf{p}$ are considered to be blockers.

Penumbra-width estimation. To derive the penumbra width required for blurring the shadow-test results, PCSS makes the simplifying assumption that there is only one occluder that is furthermore planar and parallel to the area light source's plane. This planar blocker is chosen to lie at the average depth z_{avg} of the blockers encountered in the blocker search. Further assuming that the receiver point $\mathbf{p}$ belongs to a planar receiver that is likewise parallel to the planar occluder, Equation (6.3) from Section 6.2.1 can be applied, yielding

$$w_{penumbra} = \frac{\mathbf{p}_{\bar{z}}^{L} - z_{avg}}{z_{avg}} w_{light}, \tag{6.9}$$

where w_{light} denotes the size of the light source.

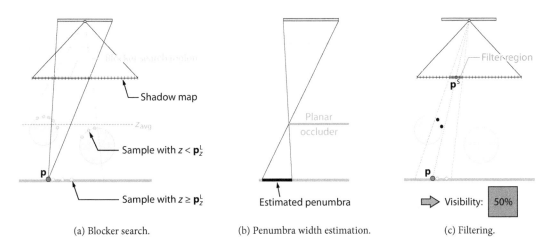

(a) Blocker search.   (b) Penumbra width estimation.   (c) Filtering.

Figure 6.9. Percentage-closer soft shadows first search the shadow map for blockers. Assuming a single planar occluder at the found blockers' average depth z_{avg}, an estimate of the penumbra width is derived, and the corresponding filter window size is determined. Finally, the shadow-map results are filtered accordingly to get approximate soft shadows.

Filtering. Given the penumbra width $w_{penumbra}$, a suitable PCF window width w_f is then derived. This can be achieved by projecting the penumbra width onto the shadow map's near plane:

$$w_f = \frac{z_{near}}{\mathbf{p}_{\tilde{z}}^L} w_{penumbra}. \qquad (6.10)$$

Finally, the shadow map is queried and filtered according to this window size.

Wrap-Up

In summary, the following fragment shader code has to be executed for each receiver point $\mathbf{p}$:

```
// Blocker search
Determine shadow-map region R_s of relevant occluders
z_avg ← 0, n_occl ← 0
For each texel t in R_s
    If s(z(t), p_ẑ^L) = 0, i.e., if z(t) < p_ẑ^L
        z_avg ← z_avg + z(t)
        n_occl ← n_occl + 1

// Penumbra-width estimation and filtering
Return 1 (= lit) if n_occl = 0
z_avg ← z_avg/n_occl
Determine w_f using Equations (6.9) and (6.10)
Perform PCF with filter size w_f
```

Limitations

The PCSS approach can produce visually pleasing results, especially for simple settings. However, one should be aware that the created soft shadows are typically not correct (except for some special cases). One major reason is the assumption of a single planar occluder parallel to the shadow map's near plane. While it enables simple processing, it is not always a good approximation. Moreover, when determining the average blocker depth z_{avg}, occluders are identified by a simple shadow-map test. Consequently, shadow-map entries that are outside the light–point pyramid and hence don't block the light at all from **p** are wrongly considered as occluders if they are closer to the light than the receiver point **p**. This can easily lead to incorrect estimates for z_{avg}.

The same imprecision occurs during filtering, manifesting itself in wrong visibility values (see Figure 6.10). Furthermore, filtering essentially assumes that the fraction of the light source that is occluded by a blocking shadow-map sample equals its PCF filter weight, which is generally not true.

Another line of problems arise from the fact that both searching the shadow map for occluders as well as performing percentage-closer filtering requires many shadow-map accesses, thus limiting the achievable performance. Consequently, in practice, the relevant shadow-map region $\mathcal{R}_s$ is not searched exhaustively, but the

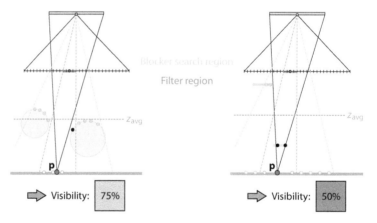

Figure 6.10. Percentage-closer soft shadows can easily lead to wrong results. In the left example, all samples considered as occluding (colored blue and black) during the blocker search are actually not blocking any light from the receiver point; analogously, the black sample in the resulting filter window is wrongly treated as occluding in the filtering step. Consequently, the algorithm erroneously yields a penumbra response (75% visibility, one sample blocking, three not) for the entirely lit receiver point **p**. Similarly, in the setup on the right side, the receiver point is wrongly considered to be in penumbra (50% visibility, two samples blocking, two not) instead of in umbra.

blocker-depth estimation takes just a limited number of samples into account. The resulting subsampling in case of large search windows $\mathcal{R}_s$ can cause neighboring pixels to choose largely varying average blocker depths, leading to different PCF window sizes and hence degrees of shadowing. Similar issues can arise if the number of samples employed for PCF is smaller than the number of texels in the filter window.

Fortunately, solutions to these latter, performance-related problems have been devised, ultimately rendering PCSS a constant-time algorithm. We cover them in the next two subsections.

Practical Quality Enhancement

A method rather similar to PCSS, developed independently and earlier in-house at Walt Disney Feature Animation, was presented by Burley [Burley06]. It offers several improvements to enhance the soft-shadow quality.

Since in practice the receiver will rarely be planar and parallel to the shadow map's near plane, biasing is required to alleviate incorrect self-shadowing (see Section 2.2.3). In principle, the farther the considered shadow-map sample is away from the receiver point's projection into the shadow map, the larger a bias has to be chosen. Consequently, using wide filters necessitates prescribing large bias values. But such large bias values can significantly affect the soft shadow's appearance, for example, by precluding contact shadows. Burley hence suggests not using a fixed bias but increasing the bias linearly with distance from $\mathbf{p}$, describing a "bias cone."

Furthermore, he notes that both subsampling and the unweighted averaging of blocker depths in determining z_{avg} foster missing regions of shadow contact. As a simple remedy, Burley advocates concentrating the taken shadow-map samples near $\mathbf{p}$ and reducing the sample weights with increasing distance from $\mathbf{p}$.

6.5.4   Accelerating Adaptive Filtering

As we discussed in Chapter 5, several alternative shadow-map representations exist that allow for prefiltering (i.e., precomputing the filter response). Hence, it is rather obvious that the filtering cost in the PCSS algorithm can be reduced significantly by resorting to a technique like VSM or CSM. Note, however, that since the filter window size is chosen separately for each receiver point and thus varies across screen to accommodate different penumbra sizes, prefiltering has to support variable window sizes. To this end, typically one of the following two approaches is adopted: mipmapping or summed-area tables (see also Appendix D).

Mipmapping.   The easiest and cheapest option is to create a mipmap chain of the shadow map representation (e.g., of the VSM), with each coarser level resulting from blurring the next finer one with a fixed-size filter kernel and downsampling. Filtering with a certain window size is then simply approximated by appropriately sampling this mipmap with trilinear interpolation.

On the downside, mipmapping provides only prefiltering for several discrete filter sizes and requires filtering with intermediate sizes to be approximated by interpolation. Moreover, the spatial resolution of the prefiltering solution decreases with increasing filter sizes, which can easily cause artifacts. This particular shortcoming can be alleviated by employing an N-buffer-like representation [Décoret05, Eisemann06b], which, however, consumes more memory and is more costly to build.

Summed-area table. Superior results can be achieved by constructing a summed-area table (SAT) [Crow84], which supports box filtering for arbitrary rectangular filter windows—utilizing just four texture fetches. However, SATs require more memory and are more expensive to create than mipmaps. An important issue is that summing up vast amounts of a certain quantity (e.g., the first moment in the case of VSMs) can easily lead to a loss of numerical precision. Therefore, starting at a certain shadow map resolution, it becomes necessary to adopt a 32-bit integer/fixed-point (or, if available, 64-bit floating-point) representation to avoid related artifacts. Lauritzen [Lauritzen07] provides more detail and discusses using SATs together with VSMs.

6.5.5   Accelerating Blocker Search

CSMs and VSMs are not only helpful for accelerating the filtering step but can also be adapted to speed up the derivation of the average blocker depth z_{avg}. Even more, the resulting methods actually search the relevant shadow-map region $\mathcal{R}_{\mathrm{s}}$ exhaustively, that is, in contrast to subsampling none of the blockers within $\mathcal{R}_{\mathrm{s}}$ is omitted from consideration. This is beneficial for the shadow quality, as it avoids subsampling-related spatial and temporal inconsistencies that can easily show up as artifacts.

Convolution Soft Shadows

Utilizing the machinery of CSM, Annen et al. [Annen08a] observe that averaging the depths $z(\mathbf{t})$ of all entries $\mathbf{t}$ within $\mathcal{R}_{\mathrm{s}}$ that are closer to the light and hence pass the complementary shadow test

$$\bar{s}(z, \mathbf{p}_{\tilde{z}}^{\mathrm{L}}) = 1 - s(z, \mathbf{p}_{\tilde{z}}^{\mathrm{L}}) = 1 - H(z - \mathbf{p}_{\tilde{z}}^{\mathrm{L}}) = \begin{cases} 1, & z < \mathbf{p}_{\tilde{z}}^{\mathrm{L}}, \\ 0, & z \geq \mathbf{p}_{\tilde{z}}^{\mathrm{L}}, \end{cases}$$

can be expressed as a convolution:

$$z_{\mathrm{avg}}(\mathbf{p}) = \frac{\sum_{\mathbf{t} \in \mathcal{R}_{\mathrm{s}}} k_{\mathrm{avg}}(\mathbf{t} - \mathbf{p}^{\mathrm{s}}) \cdot \left(\bar{s}(z(\mathbf{t}), \mathbf{p}_{\tilde{z}}^{\mathrm{L}}) \cdot z(\mathbf{t}) \right)}{\sum_{\mathbf{t} \in \mathcal{R}_{\mathrm{s}}} k_{\mathrm{avg}}(\mathbf{t} - \mathbf{p}^{\mathrm{s}}) \cdot \bar{s}(z(\mathbf{t}), \mathbf{p}_{\tilde{z}}^{\mathrm{L}})},$$

where k_{avg} is the averaging kernel and the denominator performs normalization.

While the denominator can readily reuse the basis images from the regular CSM (since it essentially equals $1 - f_{\text{filter}}(\mathbf{p}^s, \mathbf{p}_z^L)$ from Equation (5.19) on page 154), the numerator requires computing additional basis images for the product $\bar{s}(z(\mathbf{t}), \mathbf{p}_{\bar{z}}^L) \cdot z(\mathbf{t})$. With these, the blocker search boils down to performing a linear combination of basis images, thus becoming a constant-time operation like CSM-based filtering. However, this improvement in execution complexity comes at the price of necessitating many basis images, which incur both additional storage and creation cost compared to the original PCSS approach of simply sampling the shadow map for blockers.

Variance Soft Shadow Mapping

Dong et al. [Dong10, Yang10a] show that an estimate of the average blocker depth z_{avg} can also be obtained solely from the information contained in a (prefiltered) VSM. Assuming the shadow-map region $\mathcal{R}_s$ comprises n texels and n_{occl} of them are closer to the light than the receiver point $\mathbf{p}$, the average depth within $\mathcal{R}_s$ can be expressed as

$$\bar{z}_{\mathcal{R}_s} = \frac{n_{\text{occl}}}{n} z_{\text{avg}} + \left(1 - \frac{n_{\text{occl}}}{n}\right) \bar{z}_{\overline{\text{occl}}}.$$

The fraction n_{occl}/n of blocker samples corresponds to the probability $Pr(z < \mathbf{p}_{\bar{z}}^L) = 1 - Pr(z \geq \mathbf{p}_{\bar{z}}^L)$, $z \in \mathcal{R}_s$, a lower bound of which can be estimated with the Chebyshev inequality from Equation (5.11) on page 150. The involved mean $\mu = \bar{z}_{\mathcal{R}_s}$ and variance σ^2 can be obtained from a prefiltered VSM representation. Further assuming that all nonblocker samples and $\mathbf{p}$ lie on a common planar receiver parallel to the light source (i.e., the nonblocker samples' average depth $\bar{z}_{\overline{\text{occl}}} = \mathbf{p}_{\bar{z}}^L$), solving for z_{avg} yields the estimate

$$z_{\text{avg}} = \frac{\bar{z}_{\mathcal{R}_s} - Pr(z \geq \mathbf{p}_{\bar{z}}^L) \mathbf{p}_{\bar{z}}^L}{1 - Pr(z \geq \mathbf{p}_{\bar{z}}^L)}. \tag{6.11}$$

As discussed in Section 5.3.2, VSMs easily suffer from light-leaking artifacts, especially when using larger filter kernels. Since this negatively affects soft-shadow quality, Dong et al. embed their average blocker-depth estimation scheme within a larger algorithm, termed *variance soft shadow mapping* (VSSM), that pays special attention to alleviating the light-leaking problem.

Recall that with VSMs, the probability of interest $Pr(z \geq \mathbf{p}_{\bar{z}}^L)$ is estimated using the Chebyshev inequality, which provides an upper bound, thus tending to underestimate occlusion. Furthermore, if the average depth $\mu = \bar{z}_{\mathcal{R}}$ within a VSM region $\mathcal{R}$ is larger than the receiver point's depth $\mathbf{p}_{\bar{z}}^L$, the Chebyshev inequality is no longer valid and a value of one is assumed, meaning lit. However, unless the region $\mathcal{R}$ is rather small, it is not that unlikely that some samples in this region have a depth smaller than $\mathbf{p}_{\bar{z}}^L$ and, hence, that some occlusion indeed occurs, rendering the conservative lit assumption wrong. Building on this insight, Dong et al. propose to subdivide $\mathcal{R}$ if $\overline{z}_\mathcal{R} \geq \mathbf{p}_{\hat{z}}^{\mathrm{L}}$ and then work on the resulting subregions $\mathcal{R}_i$. Those subregions $\mathcal{R}_i$ for which $\overline{z}_{\mathcal{R}_i} < \mathbf{p}_{\hat{z}}^{\mathrm{L}}$ holds can readily be processed with the Chebyshev inequality. Any other subregion $\mathcal{R}_i$, for which this inequality is still not applicable because its average depth $\overline{z}_{\mathcal{R}_i} \geq \mathbf{p}_{\hat{z}}^{\mathrm{L}}$, is handled by performing ordinary PCF with a 2×2 kernel.

After having created the VSM, the VSSM algorithm constructs a summed-area table for it as well as a hierarchical shadow map (HSM), which we will cover later in Section 6.7.4. For each receiver point $\mathbf{p}$, a blocker search area $\mathcal{R}_s$ is then determined. Utilizing the HSM, it is first checked whether the samples within $\mathcal{R}_s$ are either all closer to the light than the receiver point $\mathbf{p}$, causing $\mathbf{p}$ to be in umbra, or all farther (or equally far) away, making $\mathbf{p}$ be lit. If this is the case, we are already done. Otherwise, the average blocker depth z_{avg} is computed according to Equation (6.11), subdividing $\mathcal{R}_s$ if necessary (i.e., if $\overline{z}_{\mathcal{R}_s} \geq \mathbf{p}_{\hat{z}}^{\mathrm{L}}$ holds). Subsequently, the filter kernel size is computed, and the visibility factor is derived for the resulting VSM filter region $\mathcal{R}_f$ by consulting the SAT and evaluating the Chebyshev inequality. Again, subdivision of $\mathcal{R}_f$ is performed if necessary.

6.5.6   Screen-Space Approaches

While PCSS and its variants operate on some shadow-map representation, there exist also a few algorithms that work directly on shadow information in screen space. Adopting PCSS's general strategy, they perform an initial blocker search to estimate the penumbra width, followed by an adaptive blurring of hard shadows. To this end, edge-ware filtering techniques are employed, for instance, some kind of bilateral filter (see also Appendix E.2.2).

Image-Space Gathering.   In their *image-space gathering* (ISG) approach, Robison and Shirley [Robison09] assume a screen-space map as input that encodes, for each view sample, the distance to the closest occluder towards the light center as well as whether the view sample is in hard shadow or not. This map can be generated, for instance, by applying a shadow map or invoking a ray tracer. To determine the soft shadow response for a view sample $\mathbf{p}$, at first, a search radius is determined based on the light's size and $\mathbf{p}$'s depth, and an accordingly sized bilateral filter is applied on the distance part of the input map. This filter ignores texels that are not in hard shadow and weights the remaining ones according to how close the corresponding view samples are to $\mathbf{p}$ in world space, favoring nearby samples. The resulting estimate of the soft-shadow–casting (virtual, planar) occluder's distance is then used to derive the penumbra width and an according filter radius for the hard shadow blurring. This spatially varying blurring is subsequently performed with a similar bilateral filter as before, this time operating on the hard shadow part of the input map.

Screen-Space PCSS. Similarly, it has been proposed [MohammadBagher10] to start with a conventional shadow map and derive from it both a screen-space hard shadow map, storing for each view sample whether it is in shadow or not, and a screen-space projected shadow map, recording for each view sample in hard shadow the occluder's depth. The blocker search is then performed in the projected shadow map, and, after determining a penumbra estimate, filtering is applied to the hard shadow map, yielding the final visibility value. Each time, a bilateral filter is used that takes camera-space depth differences into account. It is also suggested to use a separable approximation of the bilateral filter, resulting in significant performance benefits. Note, however, that as the filter size is not constant but varies across screen, separability does not hold (i.e., it is incorrect to first filter horizontally and then vertically, or vice versa).

Overall, PCSS-like screen-space approaches don't really offer a performance advantage over the classical PCSS, let alone more advanced variants like VSSM. This is not surprising given that essentially the same costly sampling steps (i.e., blocker search and filtering) have to be executed. Since they rely solely on screen-space information, and hence on less information than the non-screen-space algorithms, they also don't manage to excel when it comes to soft shadow quality. Consequently, such approaches are mainly useful in those niche scenarios where no light-space information (e.g., a shadow map) is available but only screen-space information, like when wanting to turn ray-traced hard shadows into plausible soft shadows.

6.6 Filtering Planar Occluder Images

While PCSS and its variants can often produce plausible soft shadows, they are typically not physically correct. A notable exception where these methods fare pretty well when it comes to accuracy is exactly the setup assumed in PCSS's derivation: a planar area light, a single planar occluder parallel to the light as well as a planar occluder, also parallel to the light. However, for this special case, a nice theoretical result exists that enables a more rapid computation of correct soft shadows (Section 6.6.1). Moreover, it also gives rise to a fast real-time soft shadow algorithm that is applicable to more general scenes (Section 6.6.2).

6.6.1 Convolution-Based Soft Shadow Textures

Let us consider an arbitrarily shaped planar occluder $\mathcal{B}$. It can be fully described by its supporting plane $\Pi_{\mathcal{B}}$ and the characteristic function

$$\delta_{\mathcal{B}} : \Pi_{\mathcal{B}} \mapsto \{0, 1\} \qquad \text{with} \qquad \delta_{\mathcal{B}}(\mathbf{x}) = \begin{cases} 1, & \text{if } \mathbf{x} \in \mathcal{B}, \\ 0, & \text{otherwise.} \end{cases}$$

Analogously, a planar area light $\mathcal{L}$ may be specified by its plane $\Pi_\mathcal{L}$ and a characteristic function $\delta_\mathcal{L}$. If the planes $\Pi_\mathcal{L}$ and $\Pi_\mathcal{B}$ are parallel, then the visibility factor at a point $\mathbf{p}$ on a planar receiver parallel to $\Pi_\mathcal{L}$ can be computed as

$$V_\mathcal{L}(\mathbf{p}) = 1 - \frac{1}{|\mathcal{L}|} \int_\mathcal{L} \delta_\mathcal{B} \left(\frac{(z_{\mathrm{rcv}} - z_{\mathrm{occl}})\, \mathbf{l}_{xy}^\Pi + z_{\mathrm{occl}}\, \mathbf{p}_{xy}^\Pi}{z_{\mathrm{rcv}}} \right) d\mathbf{l}, \qquad (6.12)$$

where $\mathbf{p}_{xy}^\Pi$ are $\mathbf{p}$'s in-plane coordinates (we make all planes use the same 2D coordinate system), z_{occl} denotes the distance between $\Pi_\mathcal{L}$ and $\Pi_\mathcal{B}$, and z_{rcv} is the distance between $\Pi_\mathcal{L}$ and the planar receiver. That is, we integrate over $\mathcal{L}$ and, for each considered light point $\mathbf{l}$, query $\delta_\mathcal{B}$ at the intersection of the occluder plane $\Pi_\mathcal{B}$ with the line from $\mathbf{p}$ to $\mathbf{l}$ to check whether the occluder blocks $\mathbf{l}$.

As shown by Soler and Sillion [Soler98b], Equation (6.12) can be expressed as a convolution:

$$V_\mathcal{L}(\mathbf{p}) = \frac{1}{\int_{\mathbf{R}^2} l(\mathbf{x})\, d\mathbf{x}} \int_{\mathbf{R}^2} l(\mathbf{x})\, o(\mathbf{p}_{xy}^\Pi - \mathbf{x})\, d\mathbf{x}, \qquad (6.13)$$

where

$$l(\mathbf{x}) = \delta_\mathcal{L} \left(-\frac{z_{\mathrm{occl}}}{z_{\mathrm{rcv}} - z_{\mathrm{occl}}}\, \mathbf{x} \right) \qquad \text{and} \qquad o(\mathbf{x}) = 1 - \delta_\mathcal{B} \left(\frac{z_{\mathrm{occl}}}{z_{\mathrm{rcv}}}\, \mathbf{x} \right)$$

are scaled versions of the light's and the occluder's characteristic functions.

This result directly leads to an efficient algorithm to compute soft shadows in such a restricted setup. First, a sampled representation of the involved characteristic functions is created by encoding the binary function $\delta_\mathcal{L}$ in a *source image* and the function $1 - \delta_\mathcal{B}$ in a *blocker image*. Subsequently, these two images are convolved according to Equation (6.13), yielding a soft shadow texture for the planar receiver that stores a regular sampling of the visibility factors for the points on this receiver. The convolution can be carried out by multiplication in Fourier space, involving two forward 2D fast Fourier transforms (FFTs) and one inverse 2D FFT.

General Setup

In a general setup where, in particular, occluders are not planar, the convolution formula from Equation (6.13) can obviously no longer be applied directly. To support such configurations, Soler and Sillion [Soler98b] suggest establishing a virtual planar light, a virtual occluder, and a virtual receiver; projecting the real entities onto them; and performing the convolution-based computation on these virtual elements. The obtained soft shadow texture can then be projected onto the real receiver.

Since the projection onto virtual, parallel planes is only an approximation of the real situation, the computed soft shadows are generally no longer accurate. Especially, occluders with a larger extent orthogonal to the plane can cause quality problems, like with contact shadows. These may be alleviated to some degree by subdividing the occluder and/or receiver, thus breaking the setup into multiple simpler configurations where the approximation with virtual planar entities may be more accurate. However, combining these partial solutions can be challenging. On the pro side, the algorithm's speed essentially doesn't depend on the light's size and, thanks to filtering the blocker image with the light's footprint, smooth penumbrae are produced in the soft shadow texture.

6.6.2 Occlusion Textures

Not least because computing a general convolution of two images is rather costly, even if performed by multiplication in Fourier space, the discussed algorithm is not really suitable for real-time setups. However, by assuming a rectangular area light, the computation becomes significantly simpler, eventually enabling a faster approach that can more easily deal with general setups.

More precisely, if $\mathcal{L}$ is an axis-aligned rectangular light source, then the convolution in Equation (6.13) boils down to applying a box filter to the blocker image, that is,

$$V_{\mathcal{L}}(\mathbf{p}) = \frac{1}{|\mathcal{K}(\mathbf{p})|} \int_{\mathcal{K}(\mathbf{p})} \left(1 - \delta_{\mathcal{B}}(\mathbf{x})\right) d\mathbf{x},$$

where $\mathcal{K}(\mathbf{p})$ is the rectangular region in the plane $\Pi_{\mathcal{B}}$ resulting from intersecting this plane with the light–receiver-point pyramid (see Figure 6.11). The size of $\mathcal{K}(\mathbf{p})$ (and hence of the box filter) can easily be determined by scaling the light's size according to the ratio of distances of $\mathbf{p}$ to the occluder and the light, that is,

$$\text{size}\left(\mathcal{K}(\mathbf{p})\right) = \frac{\text{dist}(\mathbf{p}, \Pi_{\mathcal{B}})}{\text{dist}(\mathbf{p}, \mathcal{L})} \, \text{size}(\mathcal{L}) = \frac{z_{\text{rcv}} - z_{\text{occl}}}{z_{\text{rcv}}} \, \text{size}(\mathcal{L}).$$

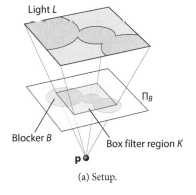

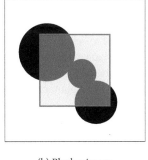

(a) Setup.   (b) Blocker image.   (c) Filtered blocker image.

Figure 6.11. Occlusion textures build on the observation that for a rectangular light and a parallely aligned planar occluder, the light visibility from a receiver point $\mathbf{p}$ corresponds to a box filter response.

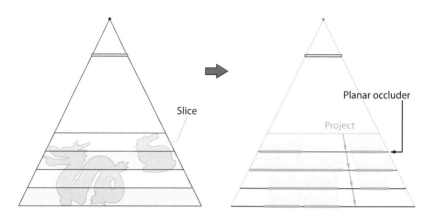

Figure 6.12. Occlusion textures are constructed by slicing the scene and projecting a slice's content to its bottom plane, recording covered parts.

Since a box filter is separable, the filter response can be computed rapidly for a planar receiver parallel to the light source, where all points have the same distance to the light and, therefore, the filter size is constant. Alternatively, by constructing a summed-area table for the blocker image, box filter responses of arbitrary size can be determined in constant time. This means that we are no longer restricted to a planar receiver but can quickly determine the visibility factors for arbitrary receiver points $\mathbf{p}$. Note that instead of an SAT, cheaper approximations may be employed in practice, as discussed in Section 6.5.4 (see also Appendix D).

Algorithm

Describing and leveraging these simplifications, Eisemann and Décoret [Eisemann06b, Eisemann08b] devised a real-time algorithm, termed *occlusion textures*, that can deal with general scenes. To this end, a given scene is approximated by a set of planar occluders. These are established by slicing the scene parallel to the light source and projecting the geometry inside a slice away from the light onto the slice's bottom plane, with the covered parts being recorded in a (binary) blocker image per slice, referred to as an occlusion texture (see Figure 6.12). Note that since each layer is treated as a planar occluder, intraslice shadowing cannot be captured correctly.

In practice, between 4 and 16 slices are typically chosen. Each slice is stored in a separate color channel of one to four RGBA textures, as this allows for easy creation: rendering to these textures simultaneously via multiple rendering targets and performing additive blending, one merely has to choose the appropriate color channel based on the fragment's light-space depth in the fragment shader.

Once the occlusion textures have been determined, prefiltered versions are computed, resorting either to mipmapping, to N-buffers, or to summed-area tables. While mipmapping potentially leads to noticeable artifacts, using the accurate SATs is costly. N-buffers are hence advocated by the algorithm's authors as a currently best option.

The shadow at a receiver point $\mathbf{p}$ can then easily be determined by processing all slices lying in between the light and $\mathbf{p}$. For each slice of occluders, the box-filter size $\mathcal{K}(\mathbf{p})$ is determined, and the corresponding occlusion texture's prefiltered representation is sampled accordingly to obtain the approximate occlusion caused by the slice. The resulting visibility values for all planes are finally combined multiplicatively, thus performing occluder fusion heuristically (see Section 6.2.3).

The occlusion-textures algorithm often manages to yield plausible shadows but generally doesn't produce accurate ones. Apart from not treating occluder fusion correctly, this is mainly due to the discretization of the scene into some small number of slices. This approximation can also lead to light leaks, especially in the case of thin structures, although a heuristic to combat them was devised. On the other hand, the algorithm's performance is independent of the light's and the penumbra's sizes, routinely achieving real-time frame rates. Note that occlusion textures are one of the rare algorithms available with this property (PCSS with CSM-accelerated blocker search and filtering as well as VSSM are two others; see Section 6.5). Altogether, this renders the technique attractive for compact indoor environments illuminated by a large area light.

6.7 Reconstructing and Back-Projecting Occluders

So far, we have only encountered approaches throughout the previous three sections that employ some gross approximations (at least for general scenes). While often managing to yield visually plausible soft shadows, they hence may easily fail to produce physically correct ones.

This situation is significantly improved by a group of algorithms that are often subsumed under the term *soft shadow mapping* or are alternatively referred to as *back-projection* methods.[3] Being shadow-map–based like most other techniques, they attain more physically precise results than the previously covered approaches, mainly thanks to two reasons. First, they utilize a more accurate approximation of the occluding geometry than just one or a few planar occluders. Second, the contribution of shadow map samples to light occlusion is treated more precisely. In particular, samples of geometry not occluding the light source at all are ignored

---

[3]Both terms are rather fuzzy. Actually, only one algorithm of this class [Atty06] creates a "soft shadow map," but all algorithms utilize a shadow map to compute soft shadows—like most other image-based techniques discussed in this chapter. Concerning back projection, again, several other algorithms perform some kind of projection onto the light (see Section 6.2.2), particularly most geometry-based techniques covered in the next chapter.

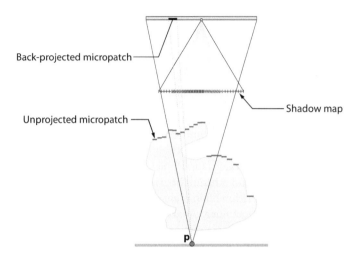

Figure 6.13. Basic soft shadow mapping derives occluder approximations by unprojecting shadow-map texels into world space. The resulting micropatches are then utilized to compute a visibility factor by back-projecting them onto the light source and accumulating the occluded areas.

correctly. By contrast, recall that PCSS, for instance, simply takes a sample's light-space depth as the sole occlusion criterion.

In a nutshell, soft-shadow-mapping algorithms employ a shadow map obtained from the light source's center and reconstruct potential occluders in world space from it. These are then back-projected from the currently considered receiver point **p** onto the light's plane to estimate the visible fraction of the light area (see Section 6.2.2). The various methods mainly differ in what kind of occluder approximation is employed, how the computations are organized, and how the occluded light area is derived. Among others, these choices directly influence performance, generality, robustness, and visual quality.

The general approach was initially introduced by Atty et al. [Atty06]. They adopt shadow map texels unprojected into world space as micro-occluders, termed *micropatches*. Looping over all micropatches, the occlusion caused by them is then distributed to all affected pixels in a so-called soft shadow map, which finally gets projected onto the scene. However, such a light-space computation of the scene shadowing has major shortcomings and limitations, like requiring a separation of objects into shadow casters and shadow receivers. Therefore, all other subsequently devised techniques choose to operate in screen space and reverse the computational order, making each receiver point process all occluders relevant to it, instead.[4] According approaches have been concurrently published by

---

[4]This corresponds to a change in computational order from scattering to gathering, as described in Section 6.2.2.

Guennebaud et al. [Guennebaud06], Bavoil and Silva [Bavoil06], and Aszódi and Szirmay-Kalos [Aszódi06], with all following soft-shadow-mapping papers essentially building and improving on them.

In the following, we initially detail the basic approach, concentrating on the variant introduced by Guennebaud et al. [Guennebaud06]. Serving as the foundation for more advanced techniques, we then look closer at the largely orthogonal aspects of visibility determination, occluder approximations, and acceleration strategies in the subsequent subsections.

6.7.1   Basic Approach

At first, a standard shadow map is generated from the center of the extended light source.[5] This depth map provides a point sampling of the scene geometry visible from the light center, and hence a representation of a subset of the occluders. An approximation of the captured geometry is generated by constructing a micro-occluder for each shadow map element. Typically, the whole texel is just unprojected into world space, resulting in a rectangular micropatch parallel to the shadow map's near plane, as illustrated in Figure 6.13. Alternative occluder approximations have been devised and are discussed below in Section 6.7.3.

The light visibility for a receiver point $\mathbf{p}$ is then computed in a fragment shader, where the shadow map is traversed, and for each texel, a micropatch is constructed on the fly. If a micropatch is closer to the light source than $\mathbf{p}$, it potentially blocks some part of the light. In this case, the micropatch is back-projected from $\mathbf{p}$ onto the light plane and clipped against the light's extent to determine the occluded light area. The individual covered light areas of all back-projected micropatches are summed to get an estimate of the overall occluded light area. Relating this to the total light area $A_\mathcal{L}$ yields a visibility factor describing the percentage of light visible to $\mathbf{p}$.

Overall, we end up with the following basic algorithm, to be executed in a fragment shader for each receiver point $\mathbf{p}$:

$A_{\mathrm{occl}} \leftarrow 0$
For each (relevant) shadow map texel
    If texel is closer to light than $\mathbf{p}$
        Construct micropatch and back-project it onto light $\mathcal{L}$
        Determine light area A_i covered by micropatch
        $A_{\mathrm{occl}} \leftarrow A_{\mathrm{occl}} + A_i$
$V_\mathcal{L}(\mathbf{p}) = \max(0, 1 - A_{\mathrm{occl}})/A_\mathcal{L}$

6.7.2   Visibility Determination with Occlusion Bitmasks

The simple approach of combining the occlusion of individual micropatches by accumulating the light areas covered by them is only correct if the projections of the

---

[5]In principle, any sample point on (or behind) the light source may be used instead of the center.

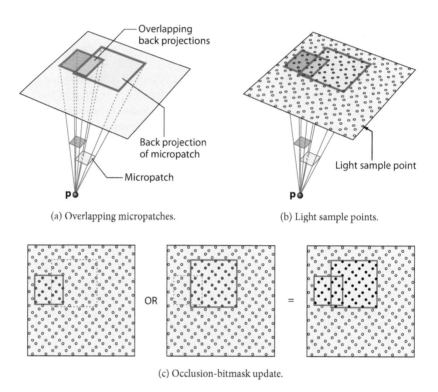

(c) Occlusion-bitmask update.

Figure 6.14. (a) The back projections of multiple micropatches often overlap. (b) This can be correctly dealt with by considering the binary visibilities at many light sample points. (c) These are efficiently encoded in a bit field; this occlusion bitmask is successively updated by ORing in the samples occluded by a certain micropatch.

micropatches onto the light source don't overlap (see Section 6.2.3). This, however, is typically not the case (see Figure 6.14(a)), although initially recording only occluders visible from the light's center surely helps obviate overlaps. The resulting incorrect occluder fusion leads to overestimating light occlusion and may cause clearly objectionable artifacts.

Occlusion Bitmasks

A robust solution for visibility determination that properly deals with arbitrary such overlaps was introduced by Schwarz and Stamminger [Schwarz07]. In their *bitmask soft shadows* (BMSS) algorithm, the visibility determination is approached via point sampling (see Section 6.2.4). Concretely, sample points are placed on the light source, and a bit field is used to track which of them are occluded. The resulting *occlusion bitmask* provides a discrete representation of which light area parts are occluded. By counting the set bits (see Section 10.1.3), the visibility factor can easily be determined (see Equation (6.6)).

The occlusion bitmask for a receiver point $\mathbf{p}$ is computed as follows. First, it is initialized by unsetting all bits, indicating that all light samples are visible. Subsequently, all relevant micro-occluders are processed. When back-projecting a micro-occluder, rather than computing the light area covered by it, a bitmask reflecting which light samples are occluded by it is determined. This is then incorporated into the existing occlusion bitmask with a bitwise OR, thus marking all light samples blocked by the processed micro-occluder as occluded. In case of overlapping micro-occluders, the same bit gets set multiple times, that is, occluder fusion is automatically dealt with correctly. Obviously, as it realizes the point-sampling strategy from Section 6.2.4, this technique is not restricted to soft shadow mapping but provides a general, practical solution to the occluder-fusion problem.

Sampling pattern. In principle, the sample points can be placed arbitrarily on the light source. However, for performance reasons, Schwarz and Stamminger suggest restricting the positioning and number of sample points such that fast updates of the occlusion bitmask are possible using only arithmetic operations, exploiting the fact that a micropatch's back projection is just an axis-aligned rectangle on a rectangular light source. Concretely, they advocate a sampling pattern with 256 regularly jittered sample points corresponding to an 8×8 tiling of the 2×2 rotated grid supersampling (RGSS) pattern commonly used for antialiasing [Akenine-Möller08].

Note that arbitrary sampling patterns are possible but require three texture lookups per micropatch [Schwarz09][6] (or one lookup per edge of the back projection in case of other occluder approximations like microquads, detailed below) and hence lead to a significantly lower performance.

Since visibility is determined by point sampling, encountered light visibility factors can only take on a limited number of different discrete values, defined by the size of the bit field. Recall from Section 6.2.4 that consequently discretization artifacts may arise and that it is hence pertinent to employ a large enough number of light samples, with 256 usually sufficing (if jittered).

Advanced Applications

Since occlusion bitmasks can correctly handle arbitrarily overlapping micro-occluders and also provide explicit information about which parts of the light source are blocked instead of offering just a visibility factor, new applications beyond standard soft shadow mapping become possible.

Most notably, occluder information from multiple shadow maps (e.g., obtained via depth peeling) can easily be incorporated, thus basically enabling capturing all

---

[6]Since the back projection is an axis-aligned rectangle, a strategy similar to summed-area tables can be used (see Appendix D.3).

occluders instead of just the subset visible from the center of the light.[7] Note, however, that rendering cost increases essentially linearly with the number of considered shadow maps.

Leveraging the provided spatial information about the occluded parts of the light source, it further becomes possible to correctly deal with multicolored light sources (see Section 10.1) and even evaluate the area lighting equation from Equation (6.1).

6.7.3   Occluder Approximations

Reconstructing an approximation of the captured occluders from the point sampling provided by the shadow map is central to soft-shadow-mapping approaches. Various options with different strengths and weaknesses have been proposed, which we briefly review in the following (see also Figure 6.15).

Micropatches

Let us first look closer at the historically first option already introduced above, micropatches, before covering alternatives that try to improve on them. Recall that a micropatch is constructed by unprojecting a shadow map texel into world space. Together, micropatches provide a piecewise-constant approximation of the captured occluders. Since they are parallel to the light plane, such that their back projections are axis-aligned rectangles, many operations are rather simple and hence fast to execute. However, this simplicity also causes micropatches to suffer from several problems. For instance, occluders are frequently overestimated, potentially leading to noticeable enlargements of the penumbra's extent. On the other hand, potentially overestimating an occluder's extent helps to capture fine structures.

A major issue is that gaps can occur between neighboring micropatches. Usually, such gaps are not actual occluder-free regions but undesired holes in the reconstruction of surfaces, which lead to disturbing light leaks. Given the lack of information allowing a correct discrimination, it is hence reasonable to try to close gaps. To this end, Guennebaud et al. [Guennebaud06] consider the left and bottom neighbors in the shadow map for each micropatch, dynamically extending it appropriately to the borders of these neighbors (see Figure 6.16(a)). However, gaps towards the diagonal neighbor may still exist [Schwarz07], which can be alleviated by explicitly accounting for this neighbor, too [Bavoil08a]. As a significantly more expensive alternative, Bavoil et al. [Bavoil08b] advocate using a multilayered shadow map obtained via depth peeling and, for a given texel, using only the layer

---

[7]Another option to capture more occluders and hence decrease artifacts due to ignored occluders is to split the light into multiple sublights and treat each sublight separately [Assarsson03b, Yang09] (see also Section 7.3.4). However, this comes at the cost of rendering a shadow map (and creating an according multiscale representation; see Section 6.7.4) multiple times. Moreover, while this approach is orthogonal to the chosen visibility determination technique, overlapping-related artifacts still occur unless occlusion bitmasks are used.

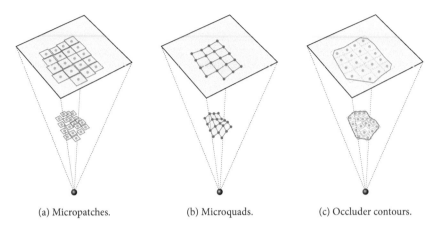

(a) Micropatches.   (b) Microquads.   (c) Occluder contours.

Figure 6.15. Examples of occluder approximations that can be derived from a shadow map.

farthest away from the light that is still closer to the light than the receiver point for micropatch construction.

Furthermore, micropatches easily lead to surface acne and require biasing to alleviate such self-shadowing artifacts. Using a midpoint shadow map (see Section 2.2.4) for depth comparisons [Bavoil08b] helps but incurs additional costs.

Finally, note that Bavoil and Silva [Bavoil06] employ the bounding sphere of a micropatch as occluder and compute the subtended solid angle to determine visibility of a spherical light source.

Microquads and Microtris

A more complex micro-occluder is proposed by Schwarz and Stamminger [Schwarz07]. They take the unprojected centers of the shadow map texels as vertices, which, along with their texture-space adjacencies, implicitly define a regular quad mesh. Each face serves as a micro-occluder, called a *microquad*. It is created from four vertices corresponding to 2×2 neighboring texels and gets taken into account during visibility determination only if all four vertices are closer to the light source than the point for which light visibility is computed.

Microquads provide a piecewise-(bi)linear approximation and hence adapt better to the actual geometry than micropatches. They are thus less prone to causing surface acne. Another advantage is that because adjacent microquads share a common boundary, no unwanted gaps occur in the first place (see Figure 6.16(b)), and hence, light leaks are avoided. Moreover, because two neighboring microquads are connected by an edge, their back projections usually don't overlap. This is in strong contrast to the situation with micropatches, which are just isolated primitives. But overlaps can still occur, and hence, utilizing occlusion bitmasks is still advisable for high quality.

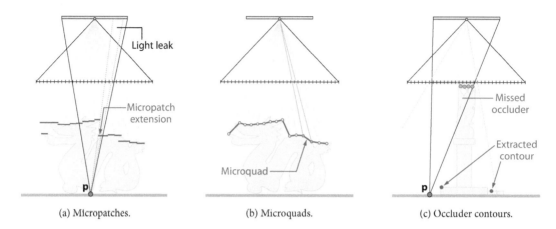

(a) Micropatches.   (b) Microquads.   (c) Occluder contours.

Figure 6.16. The various occluder approximations have different characteristics. (a) Micropatches suffer from light leaks, which can be (approximately) closed by dynamically extending them. (b) By contrast, microquads implicitly avoid such gaps in the occluder reconstruction but can miss thin structures. (c) Occluder contours are also essentially gap-free but may ignore occluders captured by the shadow map.

Since a quad's back projection onto the light area does not yield an axis-aligned rectangle in general, correct clipping and area determination as well as occlusion-bitmask updates are complicated. While accurate solutions have been devised [Schwarz08a], they are rather expensive. Therefore, in practice, usually the simple approximate approach by Schwarz and Stamminger [Schwarz07] is employed, which yields results that are visually hardly distinguishable and which is roughly as fast as micropatch processing.

In contrast to micropatches, microquads have a tendency to underestimate occluders and miss thin geometry, like twigs and branches covering only a single shadow map texel in width. Augmenting microquads with microtris [Schwarz08a] helps reduce the underestimation and also improves smoothness at features lying diagonal in shadow map space. A *microtri* is simply a triangle that is constructed if a microquad gets ignored because only three of its four vertices pass the distance test, using these three vertices. However, this often merely slight visual-quality improvement incurs a considerable performance impact.

Occluder Contours

Another, rather different occluder approximation was introduced by Guennebaud et al. [Guennebaud07], who construct an *occluder contour* for each connected region of shadow map texels that pass the depth test. To this end, they slide a window of 2×2 adjacent texels across the relevant shadow-map region $\mathcal{R}_s$. For each window position, the corresponding binary depth-test results are determined. These are then employed to consult a lookup texture for deriving a set of oriented edges,

> ### Treating Gaps as Reconstruction Errors
>
> Invariably closing gaps is a necessary approximation. It knowingly accepts over-occlusion artifacts due to blockers that are wrongly introduced by assuming that two adjacent shadow map texels sample the same surface. Actually, correctly dealing with such gaps in absence of further information is a general problem also encountered in ray tracing of depth images [Lischinski98, Keating99]. While heuristics were developed, like performing gap filling between two adjacent micropatches only if their depth difference is below a user-specified threshold [Agrawala00], they are far from robust.

which together ultimately form the contours. Each edge is back-projected, and the signed areas of the resulting radial segments with respect to the light center are accumulated to derive light visibility.[8] Because only contour edges have to be back-projected, and their number is typically smaller than the equivalent micropatch count, some computations are saved. However, all shadow map texels within the considered region $\mathcal{R}_s$ still have to be accessed, nevertheless.

Since a contour encompasses all neighboring shadow map samples passing the depth test, light leaks are implicitly avoided. However, because contours are extracted in 2D instead of 3D space, occluders recorded in the shadow map may be missed (see Figure 6.16(c)). This can lead to noticeable popping artifacts, as the depth values at the 2D contour may jump when the light moves relative to the occluder (even if the triggering occluder is captured in both the old and the new shadow map).

On the other hand, the way contours are constructed often causes neighboring receiver pixels to exclusively process the same occluder contours. This coherence is exploited by Yang et al. [Yang09] in their packet-based approach to speed up visibility determination. They group $N \times M$ receiver points to a packet and treat them at the same time (allocating a single GPU thread per packet, unlike packet-based ray-tracing methods), sharing the time-dominating contour-extraction computation among them. In case the receiver points of a packet don't have identical contours, the packet-based evaluation is aborted and all NM points are processed independently.

6.7.4 Acceleration with Multiscale Representations

For a reasonably high performance, it is essential to avoid useless computations, like processing micro-occluders that don't affect the result. An effective tool for approaching this obvious goal are multiscale representations of the shadow map (see also Appendix D), which can yield significant acceleration.

---

[8]This radial area integration bears some resemblance to how visibility is computed with penumbra wedges, covered later in Section 7.3.3.

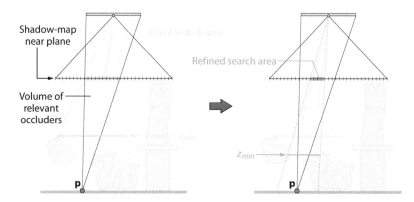

Figure 6.17. The intersection of the shadow map's near plane with the light–point pyramid yields an initial search area for extracting occluder approximations. If the minimum depth z_{min} of this area is known, it becomes possible to refine the search area iteratively.

Search-Area Determination

Instead of naively looping over all shadow map texels, ideally only those micro-occluders that actually project onto the light source and hence block some light are processed for a certain receiver point. In practice, a corresponding rectangular shadow-map *search area* encompassing these relevant micro-occluders is determined, and only the shadow map texels in the search area are considered. Note that we already silently assumed such a procedure in our exposition so far, unspecifically speaking of relevant shadow map texels and of a relevant shadow-map region $\mathcal{R}_s$, which we now can define to equal the search area.

A conservative first estimate of the search area is given by intersecting the shadow map's near plane with the light–point pyramid defined by the point $\mathbf{p}$. It can be further tightened if the depth range $[z_{min}, z_{max}]$ of the samples within the search area is known [Guennebaud06]: by intersecting the plane $z = z_{min}$ with the pyramid and projecting the result onto the near plane (from the light center), a refined search area is obtained (see Figure 6.17). This procedure may then be applied iteratively.

Knowledge about the depth range of the search area further allows identifying fragments in umbra and lit regions, where no micro-occluders need to be processed at all [Guennebaud06]. More precisely, if $\mathbf{p}_{\tilde{z}}^{\mathtext{L}} > z_{max}$ holds, it can safely be assumed that the light is totally blocked. Similarly, $\mathbf{p}_{\tilde{z}}^{\mathext{L}} \leq z_{min}$ ensures that the whole light source is visible.

Hierarchical Shadow Map

To quickly determine a conservative bound of the depth range of a shadow-map region, a multiscale representation of the shadow map proves useful. The *hierar-*

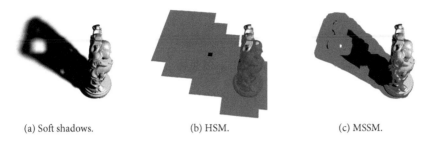

| (a) Soft shadows. | (b) HSM. | (c) MSSM. |

Figure 6.18. While an HSM is cheaper to create than an MSSM, the latter offers significantly better classification results, considerably reducing the number of pixels where back projection has to be actually performed to determine light visibility (colored reddish).

chical shadow map (HSM) [Guennebaud06], which essentially equals a hierarchical z-buffer [Greene93], is a mipmap-like pyramid for the original shadow map that stores successively aggregated minimum and maximum depth values at each coarser level. To answer a depth-range query, typically the finest level is chosen where up to 2×2 adjacent texels conservatively cover the area in question. While this keeps the number of required texture fetches constant, the actually considered shadow-map area is usually larger than the specified area, resulting in looser depth bounds. As a consequence, the search area is often unnecessarily large, and classifications as entirely shadowed or completely lit may be prevented.

Multiscale Shadow Map

An alternative multiscale representation that allows for much more fine-grained area queries than the HSM, thus drastically reducing the amount of soft shadow computations, is the multiscale shadow map (MSSM) [Schwarz07]. Here, a texel at level i (with $i = 0$ denoting the finest level) stores the minimum and maximum depth values in a neighborhood region of size $2^i \times 2^i$ centered on the texel (see Appendix D.2.2). Typically, an MSSM gets stored in a 2D array texture, enabling the dynamic selection of the sampled level within a shader.

Key to the improved results obtained with the MSSM is its ability to directly support queries for arbitrarily placed squares of power-of-two size. By contrast, the HSM, essentially being a quadtree constructed over the shadow map, is restricted to squares corresponding to quadtree tiles. Therefore, an arbitrary power-of-two-sized square typically has to be grown to the next-coarser encompassing tile, quadrupling its size. Consequently, the depth range is looser, often precluding a classification as completely lit or in umbra (see Figure 6.18).

Hybrid Y Shadow Map

Unfortunately, both its construction and its memory footprint render the MSSM too expensive for shadow map sizes greater than $1,024^2$ because the resolution is not reduced across levels. By contrast, the HSM entails significantly lower costs thanks to its pyramidal nature, which, however, is also responsible for the usually much more conservative results. To get the best of both approaches, a hybrid between the HSM and the MSSM, the *Y shadow map* (YSM) [Schwarz08b], is a good choice in practice. It is constructed by combining the first n levels of the HSM with an MSSM built from level $n - 1$ of the HSM.

Hierarchical Occluder-Approximation Extraction

Since the HSM constitutes a quadtree constructed over the shadow map, it is also possible to hierarchically traverse this tree to identify and process relevant micropatches [Dmitriev07] instead of determining a tight search area and looping over all texels within it. Similarly, the MSSM can be used to hierarchically extract occluder contours [Yang09].

6.7.5   Acceleration by Adapting Accuracy

Another popular and effective possibility to speed up shadow computations is to adapt the accuracy, typically by reducing the sampling density.

Micro-occluder Subsampling

Even if only relevant shadow map texels are considered, their number can easily reach and exceed several thousand for a single receiver point. Such large counts take a considerable amount of time to process, frequently preventing real-time performance. One simple possibility to deal with this situation is to restrict the number of micro-occluders that are actually processed and perform an according subsampling of the search area. Proposed variants include sampling according to a center-biased Poisson-disk sampling pattern [Bavoil06] and regular subsampling [Bavoil08b].

Coarser Occluder Approximations

Another possibility to limit the number of processed shadow map entries is to resort to a coarser-resolution shadow map for constructing the occluder approximation. To avoid overhead and allow a different effective shadow map resolution per receiver point, in practice, simply the minimum channel of an appropriate level of the HSM is employed [Guennebaud06], instead of actually rendering additional shadow maps. Given an imposed upper bound on the number of shadow map texels considered during visibility determination, typically the finest HSM level is selected where the search area comprises few-enough texels to meet this budget (see Figure 6.19). Note that an MSSM can be used equally well, as the information stored in the MSSM is essentially a superset of that in the HSM.

Picking the minimum depth value of 2×2 adjacent shadow map texels as their representative is simple and also conservative in that it ensures that if at least one

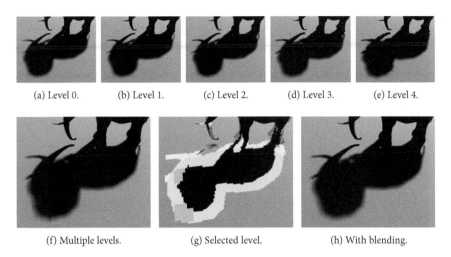

(a) Level 0.   (b) Level 1.   (c) Level 2.   (d) Level 3.   (e) Level 4.

(f) Multiple levels.   (g) Selected level.   (h) With blending.

Figure 6.19. (a)–(e) Coarser micropatches can be constructed by utilizing a coarser HSM level. (f)–(g) In practice, each receiver pixel chooses the finest level that still satisfies an imposed upper bound on the number of micropatches. (f) This, however, leads to noticeable transition artifacts. (h) These can be alleviated by adopting a blending strategy, which incurs some overhead, though.

of the original samples passes the depth test, then the coarser texel does so as well. Generally, this strategy preserves the tendency of micropatches and microquads to over- and underestimate occluders, respectively. In particular, fine structures are implicitly enlarged with micropatches at each coarser level, whereas microquads increasingly miss thin occluders. Occluder contours behave similar to micropatches in this respect, but they may be moved inwards to reduce the occluder-approximation size and hence counter some overestimation; however, this may at the same time also introduce some underestimation.

In addition to that, approximation quality is negatively affected by the missing flexibility of the micro-occluders, entailed by their simplicity. Since, for instance, micropatches have a uniform size in texture space, with them it is often not possible to represent the occluder samples from the original shadow map well at coarser levels. Better results can be achieved by generalizing micropatches, as demonstrated with the so-called *microrects* [Schwarz08b], but this naturally incurs some additional overhead due to more expensive generation and representation.

Another source of problems, especially when using an occluder approximation that provides merely a piecewise-constant approximation, is the depth-bias determination for the coarser levels. In particular, simply using the same bias value for all levels can lead to visual artifacts, like surface acne or missing contact shadows.[9]

---

[9]Note that this effectively precludes adding a bias during shadow map generation, which should be avoided anyway, as it affects the back projection's position and size, leading to inaccurate shadowing results.

Furthermore, selecting the level for constructing the occluder approximation individually per receiver point can lead to noticeable transition artifacts (see Figure 6.19(f)). If different levels are used for two adjacent pixels, different occluder approximations get employed, and these generally yield an unequal amount of light blocking. To alleviate related artifacts, the employed level can be made a continuous quantity. The visibility is then determined by considering the two closest integer levels and combining the results obtained for them via alpha blending [Guennebaud07, Schwarz08b] (see Figure 6.19(h)). Note that this involves processing more shadow map texels, causing some overhead. Furthermore, a scheme has been suggested by Schwarz and Stamminger [Schwarz08b] where the budget of shadow map texels to process can be specified locally in screen space, for instance, lowering it in regions of high texture masking. This effectively allows smoothly varying the soft shadow level of quality (LOQ) across screen.

Subsampling in Screen Space

Apart from adapting the sampling of the occluders, performance further profits from reducing the sampling density in screen space. Guennebaud et al. [Guennebaud07], for instance, suggest an according sparse sampling scheme for their soft-shadow-mapping algorithm, enabling high speed-ups. They derive an estimate of the penumbra's screen-space footprint and employ it to adjust the sampling density by appropriately skipping visibility computations for some pixels. The resulting subsampled visibility solution is then subjected to a pyramidal pull-push reconstruction to determine the final soft shadows. On the downside, with increasing sparseness, objectionable patterns can appear. Moreover, because the underlying sparse sampling pattern is fixed in screen space, these patterns can be expected to become particularly noticeable in animated scenes.

6.8   Using Multiple Depth Maps

A single shadow map only captures the occluders closest to a dedicated light point. Since we are dealing with area lights, though, further occluders may actually influence the light visibility. However, these are incorrectly ignored when relying on just one shadow map for occluder identification, which basically all algorithms covered so far do. While they still often manage to produce pleasing soft shadows, accurate results require that all contributing occluders be taken into account.

The situation can be significantly improved by computing additional shadow maps and processing all of them during visibility computation. Basically, any algorithm can be augmented accordingly if it is capable of performing correct occluder fusion, like bitmask soft shadows (see Section 6.7.2).

Furthermore, there also exist several dedicated approaches. They typically employ a single extended shadow map for the light center $\mathbf{l}'$. At each texel, it en-

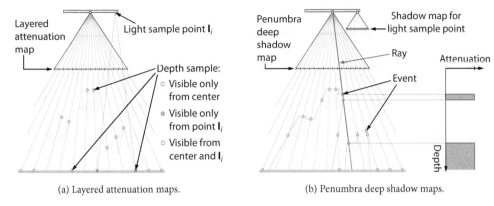

(a) Layered attenuation maps.   (b) Penumbra deep shadow maps.

Figure 6.20. (a) Layered attenuation maps store multiple depth samples per texel (obtained from warped shadow maps from multiple light sample points) and the resulting attenuation at these samples. (b) Similarly, penumbra deep shadow maps encode attenuation as a function of depth (only contribution from one light sample shown). It is derived from the visibility events encountered along a ray from the light center.

codes several occluder samples encountered along the ray emanating from $\mathbf{l}'$ and passing through the texel's center. This map is constructed by generating shadow maps from multiple points on the light source and subsequently merging them. Two basic options for the representation have been utilized: layered depth images [Shade98] and deep shadow maps [Lokovic00].[10]

Layered attenuation maps. Agrawala et al. [Agrawala00] chose layered depth images (LDIs) as representation for their layered attenuation maps (see Figure 6.20(a)). An LDI stores at each pixel a list of depth samples (i.e., several depth layers). For each recorded depth sample, the depth value as well as a counter reflecting the number of shadow maps and hence light points from which the sample is visible are maintained. In a preprocess, for all sample points on the light source, shadow maps are successively rendered and warped into the reference view from the light's center, with the warped samples being added to the LDI. If the LDI pixel already features an entry whose depth matches the warped sample's one within some small tolerance ε, the entry's counter is incremented. Otherwise, a new layer is inserted, with its counter being initialized to one. Finally, an attenuation map is computed by dividing all counters by the number of considered light points.

During rendering, this attenuation map is consulted to determine whether a depth sample has been recorded for the receiver point (again within tolerance ε), with the accompanying attenuation value indicating the fraction of the light (i.e.,

---

[10]Occlusion textures (see Section 6.6.2) also employ a multilayered occluder representation. However, unlike extended shadow maps, the layers do not correspond to per-texel depth samples but result from slicing the scene. Consequently, they store whether any occluder exists in the corresponding slice, and not at which light-space depth an occluder is located.

> ### Ray Tracing against Multilayered Shadow Maps
>
> Extended shadow maps storing several depth values per texel provide an augmented image-based scene representation compared to ordinary shadow maps. This is exploited by several (offline) methods that compute soft shadows by casting rays from the receiver point to sample points on the light source, utilizing such multilayered shadow maps to determine intersections with the scene. Early examples include the works by Lischinski and Rappoport [Lischinski98], as well as Keating and Max [Keating99]. Agrawala et al. [Agrawala00] introduced several quality and performance improvements with their coherence-based ray-tracing technique. More recently, Xie et al. [Xie07] presented an algorithm that further supports semitransparent objects.

the percentage of light sample points) from which the receiver point is visible. If no entry is found in the attenuation map, the receiver point cannot be seen from any (considered sample) point on the light source and, hence, is in umbra.

Penumbra deep shadow maps.   By contrast, St-Amour et al. [St-Amour05] adopt deep shadow maps (see Section 8.1), storing occlusion as a function of depth for each texel. For each light point, a shadow map is rendered. To incorporate its information, for each texel of the deep shadow map, a ray is cast against the shadow map, recording changes in visibility (events) along the ray (see Figure 6.20(b)). More precisely, the ray from the light center through the texel's center is considered and projected onto the shadow map, with all covered shadow map texels being processed. Finally, attenuation as a function of depth is computed by integrating the visibility changes. The function is subsequently compressed by reducing the number of stored function samples such that a prescribed bound on the approximation error is respected. During rendering, the receiver point is projected into light space and the according attenuation factor is read from the penumbra deep shadow map.

Although such methods allow for rendering rather accurate soft shadows in real time once the extended shadow map has been created, the generation of this structure is typically only possible at interactive rates, at best. In particular, high quality usually requires considering many light sample points and thus acquiring and incorporating a large number of shadow maps. Consequently, these approaches are limited to static scenes in practice.

6.9   Summary

In this chapter, we covered a wide range of different algorithms for producing soft shadows. While all of them employ some image-based representation, they differ significantly in their complexity, speed, and accuracy. Generally, a higher quality is paid for with a slower performance, but clever formulations, prefiltering techniques, and multiscale representations can provide a competitive edge.

The phenomenologically motivated approach of adaptively blurring hard-shadow-test results (Section 6.5) often yields visually satisfying soft shadows. Its most prominent representative, PCSS, is extremely simple to implement and, hence, frequently employed in real-time applications. However, as the blocker search and the filtering steps involve sampling the shadow map, the attainable performance is quite limited if many samples are taken. To avoid this, the light size should be kept rather small, which is also advisable to prevent inaccuracies due to the underlying approximations made to become too pronounced. Alternatively, subsampling may be performed, which negatively affects quality, though. Consequently, if both speed and quality matter, a more advanced variant should be adopted. A prime candidate is VSSM, whose performance is almost independent from the scene complexity and the light size once a VSM has been created. However, it is considerably more complex than PCSS.

For scenes of smaller extent, occlusion textures (Section 6.6.2) offer another practical solution with high performance and reasonable soft shadow quality. Building on prefiltering like CSSM and VSSM, this algorithm's running time is essentially independent of the light's size, rendering it a good solution for interior scenes with large light sources. Note, however, that the method does not scale well for large scenes.

If more accurate results are desired, soft-shadow-mapping algorithms (Section 6.7) are a natural choice. Generally, the highest quality is obtained when using occlusion bitmasks, ideally combined with microquads. Occluder contours and simple area accumulation usually also yield good results and further allow for a rather fast implementation by adopting hierarchical contour extraction and packet-based processing [Yang09]. Often, achieving high performance may necessitate resorting to coarser occluder approximations, though. This requires care to avoid artifacts, like noticeable transitions. Otherwise, one may easily end up with visually less-pleasing shadows compared to the approximate solution obtained with simple PCSS.

Finally, if required, accuracy can be further improved by considering multiple shadow maps. However, this entails a significant cost that is supposedly only justifiable in very few cases. But even then, the sampling-related limitations of the employed image-based representation generally preclude producing completely accurate soft shadows. To overcome these restrictions, we turn to geometry-based approaches in the next chapter, which are often slower, though.

CHAPTER 7
Geometry-Based
Soft-Shadow Methods

This chapter presents soft shadow methods that are based on creating the geometry for the penumbra regions rather than purely relying on images of the scene sampled from the light source. These algorithms come in several flavors, where we generally will move to higher and higher correctness. Geometry-based soft shadow approaches are build upon the idea of creating geometry for the penumbra regions and rasterizing these to compute smooth shadows for receivers (see Figure 7.1). They typically do not share the aliasing and visibility problems of image-based methods. On the other hand, they are usually more computationally expensive.

First, we will describe some simple and highly approximate, but very fast, methods to add a soft appearance to hard shadows. Then, we will go into more accurate but slower methods that belong to a type of algorithm called *soft shadow volumes*. The chapter will end with a class of methods called *view-sample mapping*, which, if desired, can produce correct sample-based light visibility for each point on the screen.

7.1 Plausible Shadows by Generating Outer Penumbra

We will start by describing a category of techniques that we classify as outer penumbra methods. Image-based equivalents have been covered in Section 6.4. The common denominator is that these methods first compute a hard shadow that is then smoothed outwards to simulate the penumbra (see Figure 7.1, left). The first geometry-based algorithms were designed to work either without pixel shaders, or with very rudimentary shaders, since pixel shaders just started to appear around

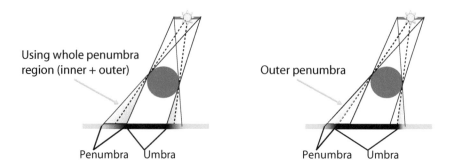

Figure 7.1. The geometry-based soft-shadow methods create polygons for the penumbra regions, which then are rasterized with fragment shaders that compute soft-shadow values for receivers inside the penumbra. There are two categories of approaches — one that creates polygons for the whole penumbra region, generally slower but resulting in higher quality (left), and the other that only considers the outer half of the penumbra region (right), since this is considerably simpler. For both approaches, the umbra part is filled in by a standard method for hard shadows, such as shadow maps or shadow volumes.

2002. Most of the techniques described in this section can be considered obsolete, nowadays, but have historical interest. The techniques that we will cover are single-sample soft shadows [Parker98], soft planar shadows using plateaus [Haines01], penumbra maps [Wyman03], and smoothies [Chan03].

7.1.1   Single-Sample Soft Shadows

Single-sample soft shadows presented by Parker et al. [Parker98] provide a simple technique to achieve a soft-shadow–like effect in the context of ray tracing. The main principle is to derive shadow intensity from a single-sample ray based on how closely the ray passes to the original object. To find this distance, each object is surrounded by an englobing geometry that is tested for intersection (see Figure 7.2). The paper states that each triangle is enlarged per ray. Many people, however, assumed or proposed the less costly approach with bounding shapes that were chosen conservatively in advance.

The assumption is that the shadow-casting surface is locally a plane hiding a part of a spherical source (as illustrated in Figure 7.2, right, where the plane is outlined in red).

Parker et al. derived the following formula that describes the amount of the light source that is hidden:

$$s(\tau) = \frac{1 + \sin\left(\pi\tau - \frac{\pi}{2}\right)}{2},$$

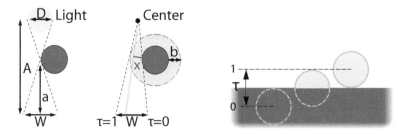

Figure 7.2. Single-sample soft shadows [Parker98]. A light source, blocker (red), and corresponding penumbra region (left). The blocker is virtually enlarged before shooting a shadow ray (green) to create outer penumbra (middle). Looking from the view sample to the light source, the blocker is assumed locally to be a plane that partially hides the light source (right).

where τ corresponds to the relative location in the penumbra region of the shadow ray, which is shot from the point to be shaded to the light-source center. They point out that a polynomial matching (of values and derivatives at the extremities) gives the simple expression $s(\tau) = 3\tau^2 - 2\tau^3$. To further reduce computational costs, the value can be precomputed and stored in a texture [Haines01, Chan03].

Another contribution was the way to approximate the penumbra region. This is illustrated in Figure 7.2 (middle). The goal is to provide a smooth variation of size equivalent to W on the left side. The light source is replaced by a point light and each view sample shoots a single ray towards it. Inside the hard shadow, the illumination is still assumed to be zero (only an outer penumbra is added). Otherwise, the shortest distance x of the ray to the object is computed. The variable b should be aD/A because $W \approx aD/(A - a)$; τ can then be set to x/b to achieve the wanted behavior.

7.1.2 Soft Planar Shadows Using Plateaus

Soft planar shadows using plateaus [Haines01] avoid ray tracing by attaching the outer-penumbra region to shadow boundaries on a planar ground. The camera is placed orthogonally to the planar receiver to create a shadow texture for the ground. Each vertex and silhouette of an occluder are transformed into a three-dimensional shape that, when projected onto the ground, delivers a quad or triangle for a silhouette edge and a circular approximation to outline the penumbra, according to Figure 7.3. One smaller problem is that the construction of the plateau volumes may contain hyperbolic surfaces if, for example, two vertices adjacent to an edge are not at the same distance from the light. The algorithm was adapted to graphics hardware when shaders were still not supported.

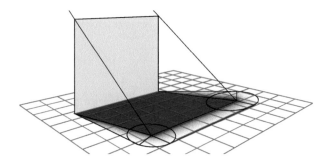

Figure 7.3. Soft planar shadows using plateaus [Haines01].

7.1.3   Penumbra Maps

Wyman and Hansen later proposed a related solution, called penumbra maps, for arbitrary receivers, that exploits the fragment-shader capability that recently had appeared at the time [Wyman03] . Penumbra maps are based on the observation that, by definition, the outer-penumbra region is always visible from the light center (while the inner-penumbra region is not). This allows for rasterizing the soft shadows directly into a texture that can then be applied just like a shadow map. The algorithm starts by computing a standard shadow map. In a second pass, the *penumbra map* is created by rasterizing outer-penumbra geometry into a separate buffer, still from the light's point of view and using the same depth buffer, but with

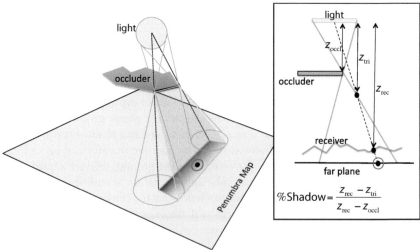

Figure 7.4. Construction of the penumbra maps—a texture storing the soft-shadow values for the scene.

further depth writes disabled (see Figure 7.4). Each vertex on the silhouette is extruded to a cone corresponding to the spherical light source projected through the vertex. Silhouette edges are transformed to sheets connecting these cones tangentially, which is a similar construct as used for the accurate penumbra-region determination.

While rasterizing these sheets in the light's view, a shadow intensity is derived and stored in the penumbra map. To compute this value, they rely on an ad-hoc formula that combines the current height of the rasterized sheet, z_{tri}; the receiver point from the underlying depth map, z_{rec}; and the distance of the occluding element from light, z_{occl} (see Figure 7.4).

Finally, the scene is rendered from the camera, and for each rasterized pixel, the soft-shadow value is looked up in the penumbra map, while the hard-shadow value is looked up in the shadow map.

The approach delivers overestimated shadows and uses a discretized map despite the geometry extraction.

Penumbra Map Construction

As depicted in Figure 7.4, the penumbra map is created in the following way from the scene geometry for every frame. For each silhouette edge of an occluder (blue), shadow influence cones (light blue) are extruded for the two vertices, all the way to a plane (gray) at an appropriate distance beyond all shadow-receiving objects. An outer quad between the cones is created per edge (orange). In addition, special polygons are added for the outer-cone boundaries to connect adjacent quads. These quads and polygons are then projected, from the light position, down onto the far plane to rasterize shadow into the penumbra map. The fragment shader computes a shadow-percentage value that varies linearly from the hard shadow border to the outer-penumbra limit by using the relationship between the occluding edge's z-value (interpolated between the edge vertices), the quad-fragment's z, and the receiver's z-value, according to the formula shown on the right in the figure.

7.1.4   Smoothies

Smoothies [Chan03] are theoretically very similar to penumbra maps. However, instead of polygonizing the outer-penumbra borders, they use small quads called *smoothies*, produced per frame and attached at each silhouette and vertex. These small quads are parallel to the light plane and of constant extension in the penumbra direction in the light's view. Nevertheless, the amount of rasterization work is the same for penumbra maps and smoothies, since the smoothie quads and penumbra polygons have equally large footprints in the light's view.

The main difference between smoothies and penumbra maps is that the penumbra maps create three-dimensional cones and sheets for the penumbra re-

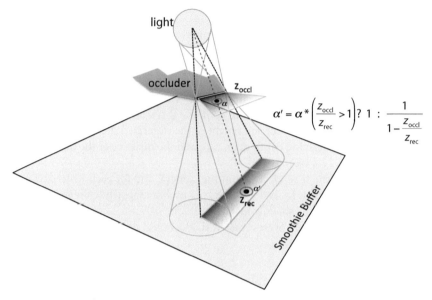

$$\alpha' = \alpha * \left(\frac{z_{occl}}{z_{rec}} > 1 \right)?\ 1\ :\ \frac{1}{1 - \frac{z_{occl}}{z_{rec}}}$$

Figure 7.5. Smoothie construction.

gions, while smoothies create only flat quads parallel to the light plane (see Figure 7.5). Penumbra maps store only the depth of the blocker, while smoothies also store softness as an α-value. To deal with superposition of smoothies, a *min blending* is used to keep the lowest penumbra value per pixel. The resulting mask can then be queried via texture lookups.

Since smoothies and penumbra maps produce a soft shadow texture as seen from the light, the algorithms inherit similar resolution artifacts and biasing problems as shadow maps. Nevertheless, as long as the resolution is adequate, the nature of soft shadows often hide aliasing along sharp shadow borders well. Biasing can be a problem where a blocker is close to the receiver.

The smoothies method is related to the method used by Crytek in their game engine CryENGINE for the game Far Cry, from 2004.[1]

Smoothie Construction

Figure 7.5 illustrates the process for creating the smoothies and how these are used to create a soft shadow texture that is then used in runtime to look up penumbra values when rendering the scene from the camera. (A shadow map is used for the umbra.)

[1]That method is described in US patent application no. US 2003/0112237A1, filed by Marco Corbetta on behalf of Crytek GmbH in December 2001.

The smoothies algorithm creates a soft shadow texture, the *smoothie buffer*, by extending a fin (top orange outline) outwards from each occluder's silhouette edge horizontally (i.e., parallel to the light plane). The amount of extension is equal for all fins, and they are all textured by the same shadow falloff texture. Special fins are created to patch the corners (not shown in the figure). Then, each fin is projected onto a plane (gray) (i.e., the smoothie buffer), where the fragment shader looks up the falloff α from the fin texture and rescales the value to α', according to the given formula in the figure, to create a varying penumbra width. Furthermore, z_{rec} is the receiver's z-value from a depth map (the shadow map) that also has been created from the light's view. Finally, when the scene is rendered from the camera, the smoothie buffer is used to look up the shadow values as follows: for each rasterized potential shadow-receiving fragment, if $z_{fragment} > z_{occl}$, where z_{occl} is the occluder's z-value (stored together with the α' value in the smoothie buffer), the soft-shadow value α' is applied.

7.2   Inner and Outer Penumbra

In this section, we will treat methods that are similar to the outer-penumbra methods in the sense that they use silhouette-edge information to create a separate buffer used for soft shadows. The first two methods are *skirt buffers* and *multi-layered shadow fins*, which are nearly identical to smoothies and penumbra maps, although they are capable of producing both inner and outer penumbra. Secondly, we will describe the *soft shadow occlusion camera*.

7.2.1   Skirt Buffers

De Boer has presented an algorithm that is very similar to penumbra maps and smoothies [deBoer06]. The main difference is that it uses image-based methods to construct the equivalent to *fins* in the smoothies method or penumbra regions in the penumbra-maps method. In addition, it produces both inner and outer penumbrae. This method was also partially covered in Section 6.4.1.

Starting with the depth values of a standard shadow map and applying an edge-detection filter on this, the silhouette edges as seen from the light source are outlined and the result is stored in a new buffer—still in light space. Each silhouette edge is then grown inwards and outwards, by repeatedly using an image-based 3 × 3 filter where the number of iterations depends on the light source's radius. The rationale is to create a penumbra skirt for each silhouette edge, and the corresponding buffer is called the skirt buffer. This skirt buffer is then used in a final render pass from the camera to apply a soft-shadow value per pixel that depends on the ratio of distances between the receiving pixel, the occluder, and the light source in an identical manner as in the penumbra-maps method.

7.2.2 Multilayered Shadow Fins

Cai et al. [Cai06] extend the idea of using smoothie fins to not only extend them outwards but also inwards in order to handle inner penumbra. In other words, both an inner- and an outer-penumbra map is created. Another important advantage of this method is that by using multiple layers of fins, they ameliorate the problems of overlapping penumbrae that afflicts the other methods. Cai et al. use 16 layers of fins, unequally distributed in depth from the light source. This is achieved by first sorting the fins into 1,024 equally distributed layers of depth from the light and then merging the layers in such a way that each of the 16 final layers afterwards holds approximately the same number of fins.

An illuminance buffer is created for each of the 16 fin layers, storing the amount of soft shadow per pixel in light space. Since a fin of one layer affects all illuminance buffers of layers further from the light source, each buffer is computed incrementally in order from the light and copying the result of the previous layer's illuminance buffer.

7.2.3 The Soft Shadow Occlusion Camera

Mo et al. present the soft shadow occlusion camera [Mo07]. This method has similarities with the fin-related methods in the sense that quads are rendered for each silhouette edge into a special buffer (here called a distortion map) so that both inner- and outer-penumbra regions can be handled.

The idea is to create a camera that sees around edges. Such a camera has been suggested by Popescu and Aliaga [Popescu06]. A shadow map does not contain enough information to determine visibility for the full penumbral regions. For instance, the inner-penumbra regions are never represented. Therefore, the occlusion camera warps the input geometry in the vertex and fragment shaders in such a way that geometry in the penumbral regions (i.e., near silhouette edges) become fully visible.

The algorithm starts by detecting silhouette edges on the CPU in light space. For each edge, a quad (much like a skirt, or two fins—one on each side of the edge) is extruded perpendicular to the light's view direction. This quad is rendered into the distortion map, storing the required amount of warp for the geometry in the edge's neighborhood. This information is stored as the image-space coordinate for the nearest point on the silhouette edge, the two-dimensional edge surface normal and the magnitude of the depth discontinuity z_{near} and z_{far}.

A standard shadow map is also created. Then, the main principle for computing soft shadows goes as follows: A fragment shader computes the amount of shadow intensity by, for each pixel, checking if it lies near a depth discontinuity in the distortion map. If not, the shadow map is used for determining visibility. Otherwise, the fragment position is warped according to the distortion map. If the point is still in hard shadow, then it is completely shadowed. If it is no longer near a discontinuity, then it is completely lit. Otherwise, the visibility is approximated by the distortion magnitude. The rationale for the latter is that there is some relationship between the penumbra value and the amount of distortion.

Like for skirt buffers and the outer-penumbra methods, the algorithm has problems when multiple penumbrae overlap, resulting in visible artifacts. But for well-behaved objects, all these methods are capable of creating nice-looking soft shadows very rapidly.

7.3   Soft Shadow Volumes

The algorithms of this class are also capable of creating inner and outer penumbrae. Silhouette edges are used here as well, but the main difference lies in how the visibility values are computed. For these methods, the soft-shadow value for a view sample is computed by calculating the occluded area of the light source by integrating over the silhouette edges. In addition, the renderings are typically done in eye space instead of light space.

7.3.1   Overview

Geometry-based soft shadows were launched into quite a different direction by a series of methods that led to the soft shadow volume algorithm, which will be described in this section. The soft shadow volume algorithm stems from the concept of using *penumbra wedges* [Akenine-Möller02, Assarsson04].

The initial penumbra-wedge approach suggests encapsulating the penumbra regions by geometrically creating a wedge from each silhouette edge, where the wedge encloses the penumbra cast by the corresponding edge (Figure 7.6). Shadow-receiving points that lie inside the wedge receive a shadow value solely

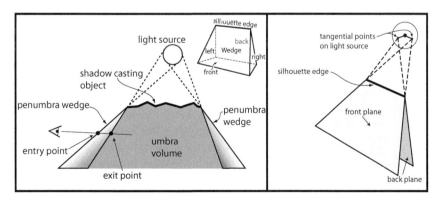

Figure 7.6. Penumbra wedges are tangent to silhouette edges and the source.

based on interpolation between the inner and outer wedge borders. Wedges are not allowed to overlap or artifacts appear, which leads to several complicated wedge situations (Figure 7.7). The soft shadow volume technique lifts this restriction of the penumbra-wedge algorithm by proposing a method to split the shadow contribution unambiguously between all edges [Assarsson03a]. The penumbra wedges then only need to be conservative. A nice feature is that soft shadow volumes create shadows without any discretization artifacts or undesirable discontinuities, which often leads to a visually pleasing result. Later approaches improve on the speed [Assarsson03b, Lengyel05, Johnson09], ameliorate the approximations [Forest06], and also show how to get correct sample-based results [Laine05c, Lehtinen06, Forest08]. We will now treat the different approaches in more detail.

7.3.2   Penumbra Wedges

The major idea of penumbra wedges is to adapt the shadow-volume separation into umbra and lit regions for soft shadows. The observation is that silhouette edges as seen from the light source should contain all the information that is needed to derive shadows. Therefore, the algorithm starts by creating a hard shadow in the scene. Then, wherever a light silhouette is interacting with the shadow, the initial solution is overwritten. To compute the influence region of each light-silhouette edge (determined from the center of the source), the concept of penumbra wedges is introduced (Figure 7.6). For each silhouette edge, two tangential points are found on the source that correspond to light-tangent planes containing the edge. The penumbra wedges are then defined by the shadow volumes created from the tangential points on the light. On the sides, two infinite triangles close these tangent faces to a volume. The first algorithm exploiting this representation was introduced for graphics cards without shader support [Akenine-Möller02]. Consequently, the shadow computation was necessarily simple, since CPU rasterization was used. The authors decided to linearly vary intensity inside of the penumbra wedges (not unlike [Wyman03]). To achieve a continuous behavior in this scenario, care has to be taken for adjacent silhouette edges. The penumbra-wedge side triangles should be shared, and this results in a very involved construction that needs to distinguish between several geometrical situations that can occur. Figure 7.7 depicts some of the problematic light-source/edge configurations that could not easily be handled. The interested reader is referred to the paper by Akenine-Möller and Assarsson [Akenine-Möller02] and its amelioration [Assarsson04]. Because these methods can be considered outdated due to their successors, we will not discuss them in more detail here. The important message is that a simple scheme to interpolate the penumbra contribution between the inside and outside of the penumbra wedge quickly runs into insurmountable robustness problems. Overlapping wedges have to be dealt with. Clipping the wedges against each other only works for very simple shadow casters. All these problems called for a solution where the wedges can be constructed per silhouette edge, in a streaming fashion, disregard-

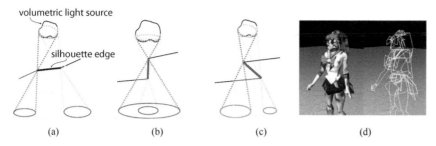

Figure 7.7. Problematic penumbra-wedge situations. (a) A standard nonproblematic case. (b) Here, the edge lies totally within the penumbra, cast by the edge itself. (c) The edge is inside the penumbra cast by its adjacent (upper) neighboring edge, which makes a geometrical separation between the wedges very complicated. This illustrates the desire to separate the geometrical wedges from the penumbra computation and motivates the soft shadow volume technique, described in Section 7.3.3. (d) Example showing that silhouettes from real objects can be complicated, making it virtually impossible to create reasonably nonoverlapping wedges that separate adjacent wedges with a shared side plane.

ing other wedges and where the penumbra contribution only depends on the edge itself and not adjacent edges. This leads us into the next topic—the soft shadow volume algorithm.

7.3.3   Basic Approach

The main principle of soft shadow volumes is very similar to the penumbra-wedges approach. Each light silhouette gives rise to a penumbra wedge. The main difference is that they are now constructed independently for each light-silhouette edge or adjacent edge (see Figure 7.8). For each penumbra wedge, shadows are no longer determined by interpolation; instead, a fragment program is executed on the contained view samples. Each view sample projects the silhouette onto the light source and computes its blocking contribution. This degradation of penumbra wedges to *enclosing volumes* of the transitional shadow region allows us to simplify construction of the wedges substantially because they can be allowed to be very coarse bounding volumes. They are no longer used to directly interpolate shading. Many of the complex cases (e.g., (almost) alignment with the source—see Figure 7.7(b))—can be circumvented by shifting the wedges' vertices (see Figure 7.8(a)).

Wedge Construction

The construction is as follows: both silhouette vertices are lifted to the same height (the nearest distance to the light), and the front and back quads are constructed as before. The sides are based on tangential planes to the light, which contain the

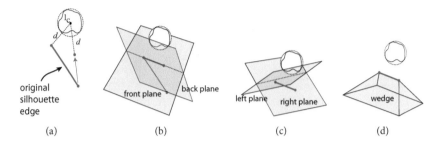

Figure 7.8. Wedge-construction steps. (a) Move the vertex furthest from the light center l_c towards l_c to the same distance as the other vertex. (b) Create the front and back planes. (c) Create the left and right planes. (d) The final wedge is the volume inside the front, back, left, and right planes.

edge extremity and the cross product of the edge and the vector connecting the extremity with the light's center. The resulting volume is a conservative bound for the penumbra region generated by the light silhouette edge. Nevertheless, their determination is performed from the light's center, which is an approximation and can even result in temporal incoherence when an edge is suddenly becoming a silhouette (see Figure 7.10, left).

Computing the Soft-Shadow Value

The next step is to compute the actual shadow intensity. This works almost like the approach for computing the area of a polygonal closed shape: choose an arbitrary reference point (e.g., the center of the light source) and sum up the *signed* areas of all triangles defined by edges and the reference point. The nice observation is that, as long as the edges have a consistent orientation, the final sum can be computed by treating the edges independently and accumulating the result.

This is actually an example of using Green's theorem in a plane to compute an area by integrating over the curve enclosing the area. In our case here, the curve consists of the silhouette edges projected onto the light-source plane. The resulting area is divided by the light-source area to get an occlusion value between [0,1]. The integration constant is measured using shadow volumes constructed from the center of the light source. This measures how many shadow volumes the view sample is located within, and this value is added to the result from the integration. The shadow-volume pass is also used to create hard shadows for the umbra regions in the image.

One minor detail is worth noticing. We only want to compute the area inside the light source, and thus, we can clamp the edges to the light-source borders. Then, the computation becomes much simpler if, instead, one sums the opposites, meaning the sector inside the light source (described by the two clamped-edge extremities and the center) minus the triangle formed by the clamped edge itself

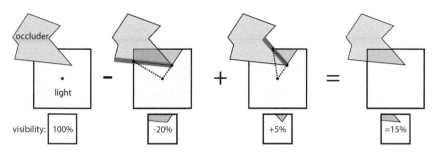

Figure 7.9. Computing the blocked area for an occluder at a shadow-receiving view sample. Each silhouette edge is treated separately. The blocking contribution of an edge is the intersection of the light source with the sector described by the center of the light source and excluding the triangle described by the edge and the center. Depending on the edge's orientation, the area is subtracted or added. This leads to an integration of the occlusion area once all light-intersecting edges are processed.

and the reference point. (Figure 7.9 shows an example of the process.) The solution works because the sector area is restricted to the light-source region resulting in a finite value.

The projected edge orientation, which defines the sign of the integration contribution, is chosen according to the view sample and the light's center. For this, each penumbra wedge is virtually divided into an inner and outer half-wedge by a hard-shadow quad created from the light's center. If the view sample is outside the hard shadow quad, then the contribution is positive since we add light-source occlusion; otherwise, the contribution is negative to add visibility. This classification is equivalent to whether the light center is in the "blocked" half-space by the edge or not. To compute the covered light area efficiently, a four-dimensional texture can be derived in a precomputation (four dimensions because it is queried by a pair of two-dimensional endpoints of the projected and clamped edges). Then the blocking contribution of each clamped edge boils down to a single lookup. This is especially efficient for textured light sources, which is covered in Section 10.1.1.

Problems

Some shortcomings of this solution are that occluders are necessarily additively combined (see Figure 7.10, right). Otherwise, a more expensive method is needed where the shadow information for each occluder is derived separately [Assarsson03b] (see Section 7.3.4). Unfortunately, this can lead to a strong umbra overestimation. On the other hand, for nonoverlapping silhouettes, the method derives an accurate solution. The main reason it has not yet been used in practice is the cost of the approach. It inherits the deficits of shadow volumes with strong overdraw. Historically, silhouette determination was also considered costly, and corresponding wedges need to be created.

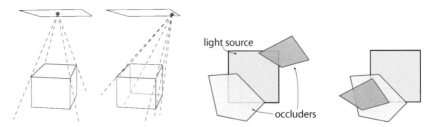

Figure 7.10. Approximations: When finding the silhouette edges, the silhouette is assumed as seen from the center of the light source, which is an approximation, since the true silhouette varies over the light source (left). The original soft shadow volume algorithm ignores correct treating of overlap between different occluders (i.e., incorrect occluder fusion), since each silhouette contributes a constant amount, disregarding which part it occludes (right). Thus, the left and right situation will incorrectly produce the same amount of shadow. This is solved in more recent soft shadow volume algorithms.

7.3.4   Improvements

Several improvements have been presented since the first soft shadow volume algorithm, both in terms of speed and quality.

Lengyel [Lengyel05] presents a way to use orientation and z-tests to optimize the penumbra-wedge rendering. He also passes the plane equations for the inner, outer, and hard-shadow planes into the fragment shader to classify the samples based on their plane distances.

The quality of the shadows can easily be improved by splitting the light source into smaller patches and using the algorithm for each light patch [Assarsson03b]. This is somewhat similar to an approximation via several point lights but here using small patches. By splitting the light source into 2×2 or 3×3 patches, the artifacts from both using only the silhouette edges as seen from the center of the light patch and ignoring correct treating of overlapping occluders, are significantly improved. However, the execution time grows roughly linear with the square root of the number of patches. Splitting the light source is actually an approach that can be used in general—even for image-based methods—to improve the shadow quality.

Forest et al. [Forest06] provide an amelioration over the several passes (for each region of the light). They break the light virtually into four regions and compute the blocking contributions during a single pass for all four regions (the key is that the silhouettes are detected for the common corner of all four light regions). Further, they keep track of already-created blocker surfaces by maintaining a bounding box. Whenever a new silhouette is added, the overlap of the bounding boxes is tested and the shadow contribution is decreased by a relative amount, according to the detected intersection. Of course, this is a coarse heuristic, but it results in better-looking, lighter shadows.

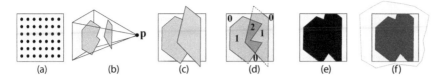

Figure 7.11. Illustration of the depth-complexity function. (a) Each sample point on the light source (typically 256 to 1,024 samples) is represented with a depth counter. (b) Two occluders are located between point **p** and the light source. (c) The occluders projected on the light source from **p**. (d) The depth-complexity function tells us the number of surfaces that overlap a point on the light source. During the integration, when adding the contribution from each silhouette edge, the affected depth counters are increased or decreased accordingly. (e) The visibility function is reconstructed from the depth-complexity function. (f) Finally, a ray is shot towards any unoccluded sample to determine whether the light source happens to be fully covered by any object whose silhouette edges do not intersect the light source.

Depth-Complexity Sampling

Soft shadow volumes have also been used successfully in the context of offline rendering using ray tracing. Just like for image-based methods, the light visibility can be point sampled (see Section 6.2.4). Laine et al. [Laine05c] use several light samples, each with a counter that counts the number of layers of occlusion, instead of only an occlusion value for the whole light (see Figure 7.11). After integration of all silhouette edges, the result indicates, up to some offset that is the unknown integration constant, how many surfaces are intersected by a ray from the view sample to each light sample. As a result, only one final ray needs to be shot per view sample to derive the correct values for all light samples. Mathematically, this corresponds to finding the integration constant, which is still ambiguous after just having done the covered-region integration from the silhouette edges. To illustrate the necessity of this last ray, imagine that not a single penumbra wedge interacted with a view sample. This does not necessarily mean that the sample cannot lie in shadow; for instance, it can lie deep in the umbra region (see Figure 7.11(f)). To find silhouette edges related to view samples, they use a hierarchical hemicube-like structure. Then each view sample finds potential silhouette edges from this structure and tests which ones of these are actual silhouettes that will be integrated in the process.

The work by Lehtinen et al. [Lehtinen06] improved the method by taking advantage of the fact that locally clamping penumbra wedges based on the adjacent triangles can significantly reduce their size (see Figure 7.12). Futher, they use a three-dimensional kd-tree to recover the potential light silhouette edges that are also silhouette edges for the view sample in question. The point of using a three-dimensional kd-tree is that, compared to the original two-dimensional grid used

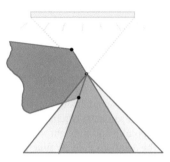

Figure 7.12. The green region is the wedge from standard creation [Laine05c] . The wedge can, however, be cropped by the planes of the adjacent triangle planes, since the silhouette (red dot) is only a silhouette for points in the blue region [Lehtinen06].

by Laine et al., when questioning the data structure for potential silhouette edges from a certain point in space, the returned set of edges is significantly less conservative, which both reduces memory usage and improves speed.

Depth-Complexity Sampling for Real-Time Rendering

Forest et al. present an algorithm that can be seen as an adaptation of the work by Laine et al. [Laine05c] for the GPU [Forest08]. No hierarchical structures are used. Instead, penumbra wedges are directly involved to determine the view samples with which the light silhouette edges interact. The counters are packed into bits of floating-point numbers, allowing maintaining several counters in a single variable. Nevertheless, care has to be taken to ensure that there is no overflow because it would pollute the neighboring counters. Lookup tables are used to evaluate the result, but imprecisions can lead to stronger artifacts in this case. The solution achieves interactive performance if the number of light samples is low (typically 16) because of the necessity to maintain counters. Instead of tracing a reference ray, in order to find the integration constant [Laine05c], Forrest et al. use shadow volumes, like the original soft shadow volume algorithm [Assarsson03a]. This is, however, not fully robust here, since imprecisions from using 32-bit floating-point operations in the projection of edges onto the light source could cause nonrobust (inconsistent) results for light samples very close to the edge. If the value for the reference sample becomes wrong, all light-sample values will be wrong. Therefore, preferably, the reference sample should be chosen from safe samples. No such safe samples are guaranteed to exist, but more care could be achieved by using shadow volumes from more than just one sample position on the light source and using voting to find a value that is correct with a higher probability.

Soft textured shadow volumes. Forest et al. combine textured shadow volumes (see Section 2.5) with soft shadow volumes to achieve *soft textured shadow vol-*

umes [Forest09]. Like for textured shadow volumes, a shadow volume is created per triangle that can cast a textured shadow. These are then rendered one by one, where the fragment shader looks up a colored shadow value per light-source sample using the triangle's texture. This is particularly efficient for few large textured objects that represent complicated fine-grained geometry, such as a net or metal fence. The textures need to have a binary transparency value—so a texel is either fully transparent or fully opaque.

7.4 View-Sample Mapping

7.4.1 Rasterizing in Light Space

One of the major problems with soft shadow volumes reaching high frame rates, together with the fairly expensive fragment shader, is the fact that *soft* shadow volumes have the same tendency to produce a huge amount of fill due to large elongated polygons as *hard* shadows do. One way to avoid this is to do the rendering of the wedges in light space instead of screen space. Thus, each wedge's influence region only becomes a polygon corresponding to the bottom face of the wedge, which typically results in a significantly smaller rasterized area. This is related to how penumbra maps and smoothies work, as described in Section 7.1, but without using their highly approximate approach. Two algorithms that utilize this idea are the ones by Sintorn et al. [Sintorn08b] and Johnson et al. [Johnson09]. But before we describe these methods, we will explain the concept of view-sample mapping, which is used by these two and more shadow algorithms. The basic concept is to store view samples in a light-space map (hence the name view-sample mapping) and perform the shadow computations for these sample points with respect to one or many light samples. We have already briefly encountered this for hard shadows, in Section 4.5. The advantage is that the shadow map stores the exact points that we want to sample in screen space, eliminating resolution and biasing problems, and at the same time, trying to avoid the high fill-rate demands of shadow volumes.

7.4.2 Theory

View-sample mapping methods compute accurate visibility relationships between a set of light-source samples $\mathbf{s}_i$, $1 \leq i \leq s$, placed on the light and a set of view samples $\mathbf{r}_j$, $1 \leq j \leq r$ (points for which we want to determine the shadow) in the presence of occluding triangles T_k, $1 \leq k \leq t$. The situation is illustrated in Figure 7.13 (left).

Such methods derive a discretized solution of the initial shadow definition in Equation (1.1); that is, for each view sample $\mathbf{r}_j$, the set of light-source samples not

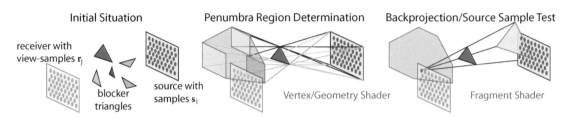

Figure 7.13. Eisemann and Décoret consider a sampled planar light-source patch, a sampled planar receiver patch, and a set of triangular occluders placed between them (left) [Eisemann07]. For each triangle separately, they produce a conservative penumbra approximation on the receiver plane (middle). For each view sample inside this estimated region, the triangle is back-projected onto the light-source plane and all light samples are tested against it (right). The occluded samples are then added to the blocked-sample set stored in the view sample.

visible from view sample $\mathbf{r}_j$ is computed. This can be written formally as

$$\mathcal{B}_j := \left\{ \mathbf{s}_i \mid \exists k \, [\mathbf{s}_i, \mathbf{r}_j] \cap T_k \neq \varnothing \right\}, \qquad (7.1)$$

which is read out loud as $\mathcal{B}_j$ is the set of all light-source samples, $\mathbf{s}_i$, such that there exists a k for which the intersection between the triangle T_k and the closed (line) segment between $\mathbf{s}_i$ and $\mathbf{r}_j$ is nonzero. One thing to notice is that if the light is uniformly sampled, the ratio of the set's cardinality $|\mathcal{B}_j|$ (i.e., the number of samples in the set) and the total number of light samples s gives an approximation of the blocked light as seen from sample $\mathbf{r}_j$ and, hence, of the visibility integral from Equation (1.6); that is, the percentage of occluded light samples corresponds to the amount of shadow in $\mathbf{r}_j$. In fact, it should be pointed out that the set in Equation (7.1) also contains all information necessary to sample Equation (1.4) to produce truly physically based shadows.

Despite this major precision benefit, computing this set is challenging. Fundamentally, computing $\mathcal{B}_j$ requires a triple loop with an inner intersection test, which can be expressed as

$$\forall i \quad \forall j \quad \forall k \quad [\mathbf{s}_i, \mathbf{r}_j] \cap T_k \overset{?}{\neq} \varnothing, \qquad (7.2)$$

which in pseudocode becomes:

For each light-source sample $\mathbf{s}_i$
    For each view sample $\mathbf{r}_j$
        For each triangle T_k
            Test if triangle T_k intersects ray between $\mathbf{s}_i$ and $\mathbf{r}_j$

The commutativity of the "for each" operators results in six different ways of organizing the computations. In fact, due to the reciprocity of view and light samples, only three major algorithmic choices arise. For $\mathbf{s}_i$ and $\mathbf{r}_j$ fixed, testing intersections against triangles is basically equivalent to ray tracing. For $\mathbf{s}_i$ and T_k fixed, finding the $\mathbf{r}_j$s that pass the intersection test is very similar to the idea of creating a shadow map from $\mathbf{s}_i$ with all triangles T_k. Testing the shadow status of $\mathbf{r}_j$ then amounts to performing a shadow-map test. The same computation structure was at the basis of the algorithm in [Heckbert97]. An off-center perspective view of the occluders is rendered from each light sample to obtain a black and white occlusion mask. These views are accumulated to obtain an image that represents exactly $|\mathcal{B}_j|$. In fact, by drawing a shaded occlusion mask, it is further possible to sample the physically based integral in Equation (1.4).

Even though highly precise, this latter approach has some limitations. First, it only computes the cardinal numbers of the sets, not the sets themselves, and is thus limited to visibility-only integrals like in Equation (1.6). Second, it requires as many renderings as there are light samples. For 1,024 samples, this can drastically impact performance. Third, all view samples $\mathbf{r}_j$ are located on a receiver plane.

In the following, we will show how view-sample–mapping algorithms can evaluate visibility by performing a single rendering pass. The principle is to compute all blocking contributions of a single triangle while it is processed by graphics hardware. This corresponds to the third algorithmic permutation derivable from Equation (7.2).

7.4.3   Triangle-Based Approach

Basic Principle

To facilitate explanations of this method, we will first focus on the particular case of a *receiver plane* that contains all samples $\mathbf{r}_j$ arranged on a regular grid (hence the name view-sample mapping) and a *light-source plane* that contains all samples $\mathbf{s}_i$. We will explain later in this section how this assumption was removed in [Sintorn08b] to allow a computation for a general placement of view samples and, hence, arbitrary scenes.

Laine and Aila [Laine05b] utilized the idea that it can be efficient to perform all computations involving a particular triangle while it is at hand instead of traversing the geometry several times. Their suggestion was to work on the Cartesian product[2] between the set of light and view samples, resulting in all possible combinations between elements of the two sets. Each entity in this set can then be associated to a segment running from a light sample to a view sample. In their approach, they successively cull elements from this set that correspond to segments that would intersect the triangle at hand. After having looped over all triangles, the remaining elements describe the visibility relationships.

Even though their algorithm did not aim at real time and would be hard to realize on graphics hardware, it laid important groundwork for more adapted GPU

---

[2]The Cartesian product of two sets X and Y is the set of all possible pairs where the first pair element is from X and the second element is from Y.

computations [Eisemann07,Sintorn08b]. Eisemann and Décoret proposed the following algorithm:

1. Traverse all triangles.

2. Traverse all view samples that are potentially affected by the current triangle.

3. Find light samples that are hidden by the current triangle from the current receiver sample.

4. Accumulate result with the result determined by previously treated triangles.

This approach requires a single rendering pass and can be implemented using vertex, geometry, and fragment shaders. An overview of the steps is illustrated in Figure 7.13.

The viewport of rendering is chosen to coincide with the planar receiver patch. Hence, the receiver samples correspond to pixels on the screen and the view samples are mapped into a texture. Each of these pixels will be used to store the blocked sample list of the corresponding view sample. The algorithm proceeds by treating each triangle separately. First, the triangle is projected in this view, such as to cover all view samples whose visibility of the light is potentially affected by this triangle. For each of these view samples, the actual set of light samples that are blocked by this triangle is derived. This result is encoded as a bit pattern in the form of a color, and the blending capacities of the hardware allow updating the current set of the blocked light samples. Proceeding in this way, once all triangles are treated, the correct blocked sample set is represented in the form of a color at each view sample's position.

Determining Potentially Affected View Samples

For a single triangle, the region where occlusion can occur contains those view samples for which the triangle is hiding a part of the light source. This region can be equivalently defined as the union of all projections of the triangle from the light samples on the receiver plane or as the shadow produced by the light source and the triangle. To compute the influence region of a triangle, one can use the soft shadow volume wedges that were described in Section 7.3.3. These wedges are guaranteed to enclose the penumbra region cast by the triangle. It is enough to compute the intersection of the three wedges with the receiver plane and then compute the convex hull of this intersection. An efficient CUDA implementation for this convex hull is described by Sintorn et al. [Sintorn08b].

Since blocked light samples will be determined in a second pass, it is enough to find a conservative penumbra estimate. Therefore, one simpler choice is to compute an axis-aligned bounding quadrilateral [Eisemann07]. In the particular case of a planar receiver, there is a special reason why a bounding quad is a good idea: it enables an efficient interpolation of values from the vertices of this quad and therefore avoids some of the costly computations in the second part of the algorithm (i.e., where the blocked light samples are computed). Such a solution would be more expensive if many corners were present. For a nonplanar receiver, however, the overly conservative shape of a bounding quad would be too inefficient in terms of fragment-shader invocations, not to motivate using a more precise penumbra estimate.

Back Projection on a Planar Light Source

For each potentially affected view sample, one needs to find which light samples are hidden by the triangle. In a first step, the triangle is back-projected onto the light source.[3] As explained below, each light sample is subsequently tested for containment in the triangle's projection. Note that the back-projection matrix depends on the view sample and can, therefore, not be passed as a uniform. Hence, in general, the projection matrix needs to be built in the fragment shader, but it is worth mentioning that in the particular case of a planar receiver, a more efficient computation is possible because more values can be interpolated across view samples [Eisemann07].

To enable a simpler computation of the blocked light samples in the next step, the back-projection matrix is defined such that the coordinates of the back-projected triangle are in a *normalized clip space* for the light, where the light is a square $x = \pm 0.5$, $y = \pm 0.5$, $z = 0$. This naturally allows handling rectangular light sources by reverting their stretch in the projection matrices. This is achieved by scaling the entire scene according to the light such that the rectangular light is of unit size. This can be done with a matrix. Thus, from now on, we can simply assume that our light is of uniform size.

At this stage, fragments corresponding to view samples inside the triangle's penumbra have computed the coordinates of the triangle's back projection. The next step is to find the light samples inside the back-projected triangle.

Determining Blocked Source Samples

The first idea is to store the set of blocked light samples as a color. To make this possible, each light sample is associated to one bit of the output color. Typically, for RGBA8, this means that 32 light samples can be treated (but on today's hardware using multiple render targets and integer textures, 1,024 samples are possible). A light sample is blocked if the corresponding bit is one; otherwise, it is visible for the current view sample.

One solution to produce the blocked sample set is to loop over all light samples and perform a containment test against the back-projected triangle. Depending on the outcome, the bits are set accordingly. Though conceptually simple, it is

---

[3]Back projection was also covered in Section 6.2.2 but in the context of image-based methods.

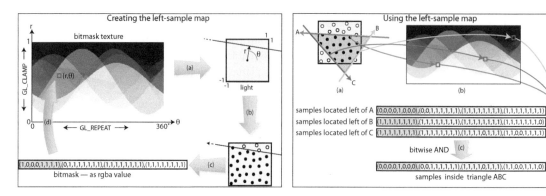

Figure 7.14. Overview of the light-sample evaluation. Preprocessing the left-sample map for a set of 32 light-source samples (left): For every texel (θ, r), (a) the line corresponding to this Hough space value is built and (b) samples located on the left of it are determined. These samples are then (c) encoded as a bitmask in the form of (d) the color of the texel. (The sine wave in the resulting textures corresponds to the Hough dual of the sample points.) Using the left-sample map (right): To find the light samples within (a) the back projection of a triangle, one can use the bitmask texture. (b) Looking up bitmasks for each edge and (c) combining them using a bitwise AND results in the contained samples.

highly inefficient for a general triangle. Instead, a precomputation allows a parallel execution of this test for multiple samples.

The set of samples inside a two-dimensional triangle is the intersection of the set of samples on the left of the supporting line of each (oriented) edge. This allows us to devise a better method based on a precomputed texture.

An oriented line in the two-dimensional plane of the normalized light space can be represented by its Hough transform [Duda72], that is, an angle $\theta \in [-\pi, \pi]$ and a distance r to the origin. The distance can be negative because the lines are oriented. However, only those lines intersecting the normalized light square are needed. In consequence, it is possible to restrict the domain to $r \in [-\sqrt{2}/2, +\sqrt{2}/2]$. In a preprocess, the Hough space is then sampled in a two-dimensional texture called the *left-sample map*. For every texel (θ, r), the samples located on the left of the corresponding line are found and encoded as a color (Figure 7.14, left).

At runtime, the fragment shader evaluates which samples lie within the back projection as follows. First, one ensures that the back projection is in counter-clockwise orientation, reversing its vertices if not. Then the lines supporting the three edges of the back projection are transformed into their Hough coordinates, normalized so that $[-\pi, \pi] \times [-\sqrt{2}/2, +\sqrt{2}/2]$ maps to $[0, 1] \times [0, 1]$. These coordinates are used to look up three bitmasks (one for each edge). Each bitmask encodes the samples that lie on the left of each edge. The Hough dual is periodic on θ. Thus, the correct wrapping modes are GL_REPEAT for θ and GL_CLAMP for r. The latter correctly results in either none or all samples for lines not intersecting the normalized light square. These three bitmasks are ANDed together. This logical operation is available on Direct3D 10–class graphics cards. The result is a single bitmask representing the samples inside the back projection, which is then output as the fragment's color (Figure 7.14, right).

Combining the Occlusion of All Triangles

As explained above, for each scene triangle, a polygon covering the shadow influence region is created and rasterized onto the shadow receiver. For each such generated fragment during the rasterization, the fragment shader sets the receiver's bits for the light samples occluded by the scene triangle. The set output by the fragment shader for a receiver sample $\mathbf{r}_j$ and a triangle T_k can be formally written as

$$\mathcal{B}_{j,k} \equiv \left\{ i \mid [\mathbf{s}_i, \mathbf{r}_j] \cap T_k \neq \varnothing \right\}. \tag{7.3}$$

It can be seen that $\mathcal{B}_j = \bigcup_k \mathcal{B}_{j,k}$. In other words, the blocked samples can be computed for each triangle separately, and the resulting sets only need to be combined. Performing this union is possible using graphics hardware again. Because the blocked samples are stored as a bitmask, indicating with ones the light samples that were blocked, a union between two such sets can be realized by ORing the bitmasks. To perform this operation on the graphics card, one can rely on a *logical operation* blending mode. Note that this mode is currently only exposed in OpenGL but not in Direct3D up to version 11. Setting the blending to OR will ensure that the previously stored set of blocked samples is combined with the incoming set of blocked samples for the current triangle. Once all triangles are processed, the bitmask stored in the view sample then reflects the samples blocked by the geometry of the entire scene.

Once having the bitmask, it is easy to count the number of set bits to receive the visibility percentage of the light source (see Section 10.1.3).

Light Source

One feature of precomputing the left-sample maps is that the light samples can be arranged in an arbitrary way without performance penalty. This offers an interesting option for better sampling by using more irregular distributions of the light samples between pixels. One can choose from a set of precomputed light-sample textures depending on the current view sample. This increases quality if particular alignments are present in the scene or for very large light sources. Also, the method allows working with colored light sources by clustering the samples in groups of constant colors that are passed as uniform values.

Volumetric light source. To work with volumetric light sources, Sintorn et al. [Sintorn08b] mentioned a different way of evaluating the shadows. Instead of a back projection, they construct the frustum defined by the triangle's edges and the view sample. The resulting plane equations can also be transformed into a three-dimensional Hough space (resulting in two spherical angles describing the normal

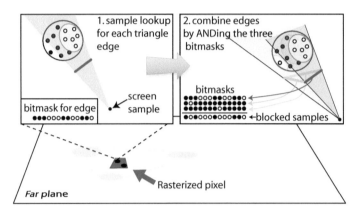

Figure 7.15. Efficient determination of visible light samples for volumetric light sources.

of the plane and its distance to the light source). The left-sample map then corresponds to a three-dimensional texture encoding the samples lying on the same side of the plane as the triangle. This is illustrated in Figure 7.15. It also relates to [Kautz04], where the light source is assumed to be an environment map and hence only the plane normal is used to look up the blocked samples.

Receiver

To lift the restriction of a planar receiver, Sintorn et al. [Sintorn08b] proposed an efficient algorithm to store a list of view samples in each pixel. We have already reviewed this technique in the context of hard shadows in Section 4.5, and the same principle can be applied for soft-shadow rendering, too.

We here quickly repeat the main steps, which are outlined in Figure 7.15. First, all view samples are transformed from view space into light space and stored in a light-space buffer, where each pixel holds a list of the view samples that fall into its position (in the figure, two view samples (black) are stored in the same pixel (red)). Details on these lists were also given in Section 4.5. Then, for each shadow-casting scene triangle, a conservative shadow influence footprint (light blue at bottom) into this buffer is created. This footprint is polygonized and rasterized into the light-space buffer, and for each fragment, the fragment shader loops over the lists of view samples (here two for the red pixel). For each view sample, the fragment shader computes the occluded light-source samples according to steps 1 and 2 in the top left and right parts of Figure 7.15. Step 1 illustrates a plane through the view sample and one of the triangle edges. A lookup is done into a three-dimensional texture for this plane to find which light samples are inside the plane. Step 2 illustrates that three such lookups (one per triangle edge) is performed and the result is ANDed to receive the light samples that are inside all three planes (i.e., occluded by the triangle). The fragment shader outputs this bitmask to the view sample with logical OR blending. Thus, the view samples' lists of occlusion bits per light sample is updated by the occlusion from the triangle. In this way, after all shadow-casting triangles have been processed, each view sample's bitmask will identify its occluded light samples.

Optimizations

In general scenes, shadows only need to be computed for light-facing view samples. In addition, if the caster is watertight (i.e., it encloses a volume), one can perform a front-face culling. In consequence, every triangle that is front facing for all points on the light source can be ignored as a caster. Indeed, a ray blocked by such a triangle is necessarily blocked by a non-front-facing one (it must enter and exit the volume). Culling the front faces is more interesting because it yields smaller influence regions. In the geometry shader, triangles are tested by checking if it is front facing for the four corners of the light source. If yes, it is safe to let the geometry shader discard it. This optimization eliminates roughly half the faces, and thus doubles the frame rate for watertight objects.

Implementation on Direct3D 9–Class Cards

The algorithm for planar receivers (and even height-field surfaces) can be implemented also on older hardware lacking a geometry shader [Eisemann08a]. The solution is to create a *shadow mesh* from the original triangle mesh. For this structure, each triangle is replaced by a quad, storing in its texture coordinates the three vertex positions of the original triangle. The position information of each vertex indicates what corner of the bounding quad it is supposed to represent (there are four entries in the position vector; setting the corresponding component to one defines what corner the vertex will correspond to). With this representation, it is possible to determine the bounding quad of the triangle in the vertex shader using the texture coordinates and to select the corresponding corner. The other obstacle is the sample evaluation. Bitwise operations are not supported, and one needs to resort to texture-based evaluations to encode the AND operation. Performing a bitwise logical AND between three values in the fragment shader requires integer arithmetic. However, if not available, it can be emulated [Eisemann06a] using a precomputed 256^3 texture such that

$$\text{opMap}[i, j, k] = i \text{ AND } j \text{ AND } k. \qquad (7.4)$$

Then, to perform the AND between three RGBA8 values obtained from the left-sample map, a three-dimensional texture lookup is sufficient. This approach is general: any logical operation can be evaluated using the appropriate opMap texture. Further, 32-bit textures do not support blending, but this restriction can be overcome by using multiple render passes and computing 128 samples (four color channels each with 8 bits and four MRTs) per pass.

7.4.4   Silhouette-Based Approach

Soft Irregular Shadow Mapping

Johnson et al. present a combination of image-based and geometry-based methods [Johnson09]. They essentially use an irregular shadow map to compute the umbra contribution. Then, for each silhouette edge (as seen from the center of the light source), a penumbra wedge is created that is projected, in light space, onto a representation of the screen-space samples that we want to compute shadows for. This representation is a light-view spatial acceleration structure in the form of a three-dimensional grid shaped as the light frustum. The cells of the grid contains the screen-space samples. For each projected wedge, the affected screen-space samples are tested for penumbral occlusion against this silhouette edge, like previous real-time soft shadow volume algorithms. In other words, the penumbra contribution is computed by integrating the occluded light-source area from the shadow silhouette edges. One difference, though, is that they note that doing an inverse cosine function call is faster than using a lookup table of inverse tangent values [Assarsson03b]. Like the faster real-time shadow volume algorithms, this approach only uses the silhouettes as seen from one point on the light source, while the true silhouettes actually vary between light samples. Also, penumbrae from separate occluders are just added instead of accounting for the situation that they may cover the same parts of the light source (see Figure 7.10). On the other hand, this comes with the advantage of higher performance compared to the more exact view-sample–mapping methods. To measure the integration constant, Johnson et al. use a modification of their irregular shadow-map method that computes the total depth complexity between a receiver point and the light. Johnson's method was highly adapted for Intel's Larrabee graphics card that was expected to arrive but later was cancelled by Intel. Nevertheless, real-time performance was expected for modern game scenes (~30 fps is reported).

On a high level, the algorithm by Johnson et al. and the one by Sintorn et al. have several similarities in that they both utilize light space and an irregular z-buffer for computing umbra. By moving this to light space, the algorithms come closer to shadow maps, which normally have a considerable lower fill-rate demand. One major difference is that Sintorn et al. use the triangles to compute visibility per pixel, whereas Johnson et al. use the silhouette edges.

7.5   Tradeoffs

When selecting an appropriate geometry-based or view-sample-mapping–based soft shadow algorithm, there are several choices to consider.

Triangles or Silhouette Edges

Visibility can be determined either from all shadow-casting triangles or by integration from all silhouette edges plus measuring the integration constant. The integration constant can be computed by either shooting a shadow ray (most efficiently to a sample with the lowest depth complexity) [Laine05c], using shadow volumes [Forest08], or using an irregular shadow map [Johnson09] that calculates the total depth complexity from a sample on the light source to all shadow-receiving points. Using silhouette edges has the advantage that they typically are much fewer in number than all scene triangles. The average number of silhouette edges in a mesh of n triangles is around $n^{0.8}$ [McGuire04b]. The disadvantage is that probing for the integration constant is prone to robustness problems, whereas computing the visibility from the triangles is not. The shadow ray has to be shot towards a light sample that is some epsilon distance away from all edges that are projected onto the light source [Laine05c]. Numerical imprecision may cause an edge to end up on the wrong side of the sample after projection. This is particularly bad, since the outcome of the integration constant affects all sample values for a pixel, which typically results in a totally black or white shadow value at the wrong place. Nevertheless, careful treatment of this problem by choosing a light sample not too close to a projected edge results in a fully robust algorithm [Laine05c].

The same rule applies when using shadow volumes or irregular shadow maps to sample the depth and selecting a suitable light sample. If the true silhouette edges are used for each shadow-receiving point (instead of only the silhouettes as seen from the light center), then it is most likely hard to find a light sample that lies at least a distance epsilon from all silhouette edges for all shadow-receiving points. Instead, as partially hinted upon in Section 7.3.4, shadow volumes or irregular shadow maps could be created, for example, for three samples and voting could be used to select the integration constant. We believe this is enough to lower the error rate to less than one faulty shadow value per frame, but it has yet not been tried, to the best of our knowledge.

Number of Light Samples

Choosing only one light sample obviously provides the cheapest fragment shader, but also has the advantage of providing smooth penumbrae without undesirable discontinuities. The problem lies in the occluder fusion, where the shadow contributions from overlapping occluders are simply added. This can easily result in too dark penumbra regions.

Using four or more light samples is more expensive but drastically improves the quality and often becomes indistinguishable from the ground truth (see Section 7.3.4).

The view-sample–mapping techniques reviewed in this chapter typically use a huge number (256 to 1,024) of light samples but only compute a binary visibility value per sample, in contrast to computing a smooth value in the range [0,1] per sample. Thus, the number of samples typically needs to be much higher than 256 in order to avoid visible discretization artifacts. Storing the intermediate result for all light samples per pixel during rendering comes with a higher memory cost. On the other hand, fully correct sample-based visibility values are produced.

Light-Space Rasterization of Wedges

Rasterizing the wedges or triangles' shadow footprint in light space instead of eye space reduces the number of rasterized fragments and significantly reduces the amount of generated fill. On the other hand, currently, it comes with the disadvantage of more complicated rasterization algorithms, since a list of view samples needs to be stored per pixel in light space and then be checked during the wedge rasterization.

7.6   Summary of Soft-Shadow Algorithms

Soft shadows are more pleasing to the eye than hard shadows. They increase realism in scenes but are much more difficult to compute.

Image-Based Methods

Image-based solutions are generally faster than geometry-based methods. The varying interpretations of the shadow map allow us to eliminate many of the aliasing artifacts. The shadows look good for smaller light sources, but can become less convincing for larger lights because, in many cases, only a single depth map is used. One such depth layer contains insufficient information about the scene. One possibility is depth peeling, but this implies that one pass is needed per layer, which can quickly outweigh the performance advantage of using image-based approaches.

Geometry-Based Methods

The main directions in the field of geometry-based approaches include soft shadow volumes, which create shadow-volume-like primitives bounding the penumbra region with wedges. This delivers alias-free shadows. On the other hand, a problem is that incorrect occluder fusion can result in disturbing artifacts. While later approaches deal with this problem, it requires more computations, which lowers the frame rate. The cost of creating shadow volume primitives makes the methods rather expensive and, even on the latest hardware, acceptable runtimes are difficult to achieve even for average-sized scenes.

View-Sample Mapping

View-sample mapping computes visibility between a set of view samples and a set of light samples, and it is part of more recent soft shadow algorithms. Since the soft shadows are sample based, the number of light samples has to be high to avoid visible sampling artifacts. An advantage is that the method can compute visibility between one view sample and several light samples for a potentially blocking triangle very fast using lookup tables. Nevertheless, the overall costs of current algorithms are still high, and acceptable frame rates are only achieved for moderate scene complexities.

CHAPTER 8
Image-Based Transparency

Computing shadows in the presence of semitransparent objects or even gaseous phenomena is a difficult challenge. Currently, there is no algorithm that is capable of doing so in real time for a scene with arbitrarily colored semitransparent occluders. In this chapter, we will present techniques that made significant advances in this direction.

Early methods dealing with transparency effects in combination with shadows often relied on a precomputation step and stored the result in a memory-intensive three-dimensional texture [Behrens98]. A less costly approach was proposed by Lokovic and Veach [Lokovic00], which created the basis of many of the recent techniques to address semitransparent objects. The major simplifying assumption was to restrict light paths to straight lines. By excluding any kind of scattering, it is possible to utilize a simplified representation of the attenuation that is inflicted by the occluders. In other words, when thinking in terms of a shadow map, each pixel does not store a depth, but a one-dimensional *transmittance function*.

In the case of standard shadow maps, we have seen (Chapter 2) that the shadow test can be seen as a step function. In the presence of semitransparent occluders, the situation can be more complex because it encodes visibility as a function of distance to the light. In other words, it represents how much an element at a given distance will be visible from the light. Depending on the nature of the occluders, this function can vary significantly. Figure 8.2 illustrates some different cases.

In this chapter, we will examine several methods to construct, represent, and exploit the transmittance function efficiently. We will explain the background behind the transmittance function and illustrate how to extend it to arbitrarily colored materials in the next section. Interestingly, we will show that this function is also useful to composite semitransparent objects from the viewpoint. We then present various approximations and efficient real-time execution schemes (Section 8.2).

Figure 8.1. The images illustrate the importance of taking transparency into account while computing shadows (images use the method by [Sintorn08a]).

8.1 Deep Shadow Maps

The goal of deep shadow maps [Lokovic00] is to compute shadows from a point light in the presence of nonopaque occluders. A simplifying assumption is that light will pass straight through each occluder. Light is attenuated on its way, but it does not change direction. Figure 8.2 illustrates this principle and an example showing the outcome of this simulation.

Deep shadow maps are a specialized shadow map. Instead of storing a single depth value, each pixel holds a one-dimensional function that describes the attenuation of light along the corresponding ray.

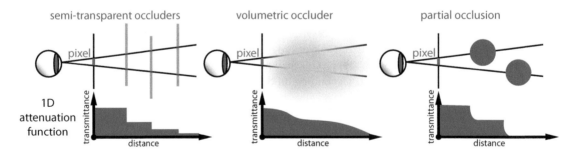

Figure 8.2. Deep shadow maps store in each pixel of the shadow map a one-dimensional attenuation function. Depending on the nature of the scene, these functions exhibit different shapes: semitransparent occluders result in steps in the transmittance function (left), volumetric occluders result in a more continuous attenuation (middle), and partial occlusion inside the pixel can lead to both (right).

8.1.1 Light Attenuation of Semitransparent Occluders

To understand this function better, let's first assume semitransparent surfaces. Semitransparent surfaces are usually defined by a transmittance function that encodes how light is attenuated when passing through the surface. These functions can be complex (just like reflectance functions for reflected light; see Appendix C). A simplifying assumption is to use a single value, or an RGB-tuple (for colored shadows), basically encoding a per-channel opacity (zero being totally transparent, one totally opaque). Let $a^0 := (a_r^0, a_g^0, a_b^0), \ldots, a^n := (a_r^n, a_g^n, a_b^n)$ be the values encountered by a ray from the point light towards a point $\mathbf{p}$. The incoming radiance at $\mathbf{p}$ is then defined by the light's emitted energy c_l, while taking the light interaction at the intersection points into account. The final radiance arriving at $\mathbf{p}$ is given by $c_l \prod_{i=0}^n (1 - a^i)$. This expression is a well-known result from volume rendering (e.g., [Max95]) and also exists as a continuous version that we ignore here for the sake of simplicity and relevance for our purposes, to some extent, we will come back to this in Chapter 9.

Let's illustrate the expression with a simple example. Imagine two semitransparent occluders, one being $a_0 := (0.5, 0.5, 1)$, which lets past yellow light with half-intensity and a second surface being $a_1 := (0.75, 1, 1)$, which implies that it is red and blocks one-quarter of the light. When light encounters the first surface, 50% will be reflected (because the surface is 50% opaque), 50% will pass, but the blue component is blocked by the material. After this interaction, the light's energy (l_r, l_g, l_b) will become $(l_r * (1-0.5), l_g * (1-0.5), l_b * (1-1)) = (l_r * 0.5, l_g * 0.5, 0)$. The next interaction then modifies the remaining energy again. This time, the surface is only 25% transparent and only lets past red light. In other words, 75% of the red channel will be blocked, leading to $(l_r * 0.5 * (1 - 0.75), 0, 0)$. This reasoning results in the aforementioned formula $c_l \prod_{i=0}^n (1 - a_i)$.

8.1.2 Accumulation of Semitransparent Surfaces from the Eye

Although we have not explained yet how to perform the computations efficiently, we have seen how light is attenuated on its way from the light. Still, when drawing an actual scene with transparent objects, it is important to be able to render the light response on each surface correctly and take their interaction from the point of view into account. If an observer looks through the set of $n + 1$ semitransparent materials, their reflected light also plays a role. Let c_k be the RGB-tuple encoding the color of the $k + 1$th surface. Usually, because the light that is not reflected passes through the surface and vice versa, this color is often defined as $a_k c_k$. That is the color of the object modulated by its opacity. Then the formula to compute the observed color, which is a combination of all surfaces, is given by

$$\sum_{k=0}^n \left(\prod_{i=0}^{k-1} (1 - a_i) \right) a_k c_k. \tag{8.1}$$

Let's explain this expression step by step. Let's look at one term in the sum $(\prod_{i=0}^{k-1}(1 - a_i))a_k c_k$. The term $a_k c_k$ encodes the color at the kth surface that has to pass through all surfaces in front of it to reach the eye. The term $\prod_{i=0}^{k-1}(1 - a_i)$ encodes exactly this attenuation, precisely, how the light is attenuated after passing through the first k surfaces towards the eye. All these light contributions are additive, which explains the sum that leads to the above formula.

Usually, the transparent objects are combined in an iterative manner. If all surfaces are sorted, then Equation (8.1) can be obtained by iteratively adding contributions based on a blending formula; in the case where all absorption values are the same for all components, standard alpha blending is an option. The scene is drawn back to front and each incoming fragment is evaluated to $a_k c_k$ and combined with the framebuffer value f via

$$a_k c_k + (1 - a_k)f.$$

Sorting is a very costly process, but as observed in [Sintorn09] and [Patney10], the sorting is not needed. Instead, if we could compute each incoming fragment's visibility attenuation $\prod_{i=0}^{k-1}(1 - a_i)$, Equation (8.1) becomes commutative, and each incoming fragment can be treated independent of the others. We simply multiply the color $a_k c_k$ with the corresponding visibility $\prod_{i=0}^{k-1}(1 - a_i)$ to obtain $\prod_{i=0}^{k-1}(1-a_i)a_k c_k$, which is exactly one of the terms in the sum. Now, all we need to do is sum up these contributions to obtain the correct result, which is independent of the order of these fragments.

While solutions have been proposed to hierarchically compute these terms in an efficient manner [Patney10], we will pursue a more general observation [Enderton10]. When looking at the coefficients $\prod_{i=0}^{k-1}(1 - a_i)$ that are applied to each surface color, we realize that it is the same term that we need to compute the attenuation from the light. Our goal in this chapter is to present solutions to encode these terms as a transmittance function [Lokovic00]. In other words, for a given distance d, the transmittance function is

$$vis(d) := \prod_{d<z_i}(1 - a_i),$$

where z_i are the distances of the semitransparent surfaces to the observer/light. In other words, for a given distance d, the function returns the visibility through all surfaces nearer to the camera/light than the distance d [Lokovic00].

In the following, we will concentrate on computing the transmittance function from the light because we focus on shadows, but the reader should be aware that the same function computed from the camera can be used to composite the final results from the semitransparent surfaces.

8.2   Approximating the Transmittance Function

A precise representation of the transmittance function could be derived by depth peeling [Everitt01] (see Appendix A) from the light, but such an approach is too costly in practice. If we stick to the case of semitransparent surfaces, each single such occluder introduces a step in the transmittance function. For complex objects, such as hair, grass, or smoke particles, quickly hundreds of such primitives can overlap in a pixel, leading to a very complex result. Instead, it can make sense to represent the transmittance function in an approximate but efficient way. In this section, we will present several such solutions.

There are different types of algorithms. *Reconstruction-based* approaches start by creating lists in each pixel. Each fragment that is produced in a pixel and not occluded by opaque objects is attached to its list. These fragments are then used to approximate the transmittance function. The second type is *layer-based* approaches. Here, the transmittance function is captured directly from the scene in a discretized form. The third type is *stochastic* methods, where stochastic rendering is used to approximate transparency. Finally, specialized *function-based* solutions that project the influence of each primitive into a specialized set of basis functions can be used. The projection leads to varying coefficients for each primitive. The coefficients, as they correspond to the same basis functions, can then be added to yield a complete representation of visibility expressed in terms of the function basis.

8.2.1   Reconstruction-Based Approaches

The main principle of reconstruction-based solutions is to first capture all transparent fragments that are not occluded by opaque surfaces. To perform this operation, a first depth-only rendering pass fills the depth buffer with all opaque objects. The second pass does perform a depth test, but no depth writes, and renders all transparent objects. All produced fragments are then attached to a list, which can be implemented in various manners. 2More on this topic can be found in Section 4.5. Here, we assume that such a list per pixel is given.

Per-View-Sample Evaluation

Irregular rasterization [Aila04b, Johnson05, Sintorn08b] (see Section 4.5) approaches can also be used for semitransparent shadow casters. The list of all view samples is stored in each shadow map pixel and the incoming semitransparent fragments are then directly attributed to the view samples. In this particular case, we do not even need to store a list of the incoming semitransparent fragments but can directly accumulate their contribution. Precisely, each view sample stores a transparency value, which is initialized to fully transparent. Whenever a semitransparent shadow caster is rasterized and lies in front of a view sample, the transparency value of that view sample is multiplied with the transparency of the caster.

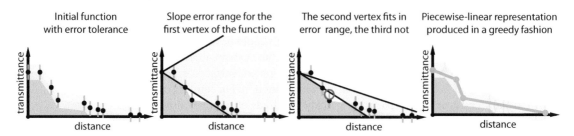

Figure 8.3. The deep-shadow-map algorithm simplifies the transmittance function in an iterative and greedy fashion. Iteratively new segments are added until the piecewise-linear representation well describes the function.

Colored transparency requires a full RGB transparency value to be stored with each view sample. However, for an efficient GPU implementation [Johnson05, Sintorn08b], the number of used bits per view sample should be kept low, so that only a few levels of transparency are possible.

Deep Shadow Maps

The approach that introduced the transmittance function [Lokovic00] did not store an accurate representation of the transmittance. Instead, an optimization scheme was used to reduce the complexity of the function.

Representation. Given some error threshold ε, the optimization scheme approximates the original function vis with a piecewise-linear representation vis_{lin}, such that $|vis(d) - vis_{\text{lin}}(d)| \leq \varepsilon$ for all depths d. In other words, the approximation differs from the original function never more than some given value ε.

Construction. While optimal solutions could be used, it proved more efficient to rely on a greedy solution. The approach first sorts all list elements by depth and then processes them in ascending order. Initially, a starting point $\mathbf{p}$ is chosen at depth zero and full visibility (one). For each new element, the algorithm tries to define a line segment with starting point $\mathbf{p}$ that ensures that all values between the depth of $\mathbf{p}$ and the newest element stay within the given error threshold ε. Precisely, an interval with the minimum and maximum slope $[m_{\text{low}}, m_{\text{high}}]$ that satisfies the distance condition is maintained. At some point, this interval becomes empty. Let $\{v_i, v_{i+1}, ..., v_{j-1}, v_j\}$ be the list of processed list elements since the last starting point. The algorithm then defines the line segment with the values $\{v_i, v_{i+1}, ..., v_{j-1}\}$ (all but the last, which broke the property) by using the slope $(m_{\text{low}} + m_{\text{high}})/2$. Its endpoint becomes the new starting point for the next linear segment, which will be matched against v_j and all following list elements (Figure 8.3).

Adaptive Volumetric Shadow Maps

The simplification scheme of deep shadow maps was also ported on the GPU [Hadwiger06] in the context of volume rendering. Here, it is particularly important to consider the transfer function from density to opacity. Similar to pre-integrated volume rendering [Engel01], where one stores the variation between two density samples in a precomputed texture, the opacity variations need to be taken into account to avoid artifacts when applying the deep shadow map. The process is iterative, as above, and can require several rendering passes to obtain the simplified transmittance function.

While the GPU mapping seems straightforward, the approach benefits drastically from the fact that volume rendering is used because the correct order of surface samples encountered on the rays from the light is naturally ensured by a ray-tracing method. For general scenes based on triangles, a fragment-sorting step is needed. This sorting is usually costly. Furthermore, the original transmittance approximation can lead to varying memory consumption. These reasons make it difficult to apply the original deep-shadow-map solution efficiently to real-time applications and triangle-based scenes. A more GPU-adapted solution has been proposed [Salvi10] that we discuss in the following.

Representation. Here, the representation of *vis* is also based on a piecewise-linear approximation, but this time only a fixed number of segments (defined by endpoints) is used. Consequently, the error of this approximation can no longer be bounded, but construction and evaluation time, as well as memory consumption are reduced drastically.

Construction. In a first pass, a single segment approximation of the entire function *vis* is computed. The starting point is implicitly defined at zero with visibility one, and the endpoint is defined explicitly by the depth of the farthest list element and the sum of all opacity values. These two points will not move during the refinement of the approximation. The last endpoint is particularly important to ensure that any projected shadows are always correct (e.g., smoke shadowing a ground).

For N inner-segment endpoints, the algorithm makes use of $2N$ 16-bit values stored and written in textures per pixel. One value represents the depth, the other the actual occlusion. The inner-segment endpoints are first initialized with the first N list elements. Unfortunately, this strategy can no longer be applied when list element $N + 1$ is processed because the approximation only allows for N inner-segment endpoints. To decide how to modify the transmittance-function representation, we first *virtually* include its value, so that the resulting approximation has one node more than allowed. We then update the piecewise-linear function. We test all combinations one by one to decide which endpoint to remove based on how much each potential removal changes the piecewise-linear function's shape. Precisely, this change is captured by evaluating the area of the triangle formed by

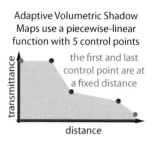

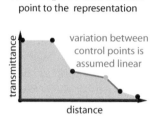

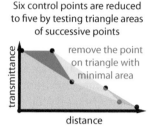

Figure 8.4. The approximation of the transmittance function is updated for every incoming fragment. Once all fragments are treated, a simple piecewise-linear approximation is obtained.

the removed point and its immediate neighbors (Figure 8.4). Finally, the endpoint removal that induced the smallest impact is performed. The other endpoints are kept and the algorithm is ready to process the next list element.

While the construction is very fast, a limitation lies in the fact that the algorithm is greedy. This implies that the solution might not be optimal, and the lack of sorting can introduce temporal inconsistencies. Nonetheless, the approach is very fast and results in a good rendering quality.

8.2.2   Layer-Based Approaches

As an alternative, layer-based approaches approximate the transmittance function implicitly. Instead of directly storing the resulting visibility, one records the encountered surfaces along each ray through the pixel and light's camera center. Because this would amount to a depth-peeling-like approach (see Appendix A), instead the depth along this ray is discretized into bins. These bins are filled with the visible semitransparent surfaces of the scene. Because the bins are ordered, it is a valid approximation to not sort the contained primitives, but simply accumulate them. We will refer to this representation as the *discretized absorption function*.

In some cases, the discretized absorption function is not transformed into a transmittance function, but instead, the visibility is derived on the fly. From the given position in space, the contribution of all bins is accumulated towards the source (Figure 8.5). While the evaluation of the transmittance function is, hence, often slightly more costly, the construction of this representation is so much more efficient than previous solutions that the cost usually balances out.

Opacity Shadow Maps

One of the first solutions in this direction is *opacity shadow maps* (OSM) [Kim01].

Representation.   The idea is to divide the view frustum of the light according to certain distances. These distances, $d_0 < \ldots < d_{n+1}$, can be chosen uniformly,

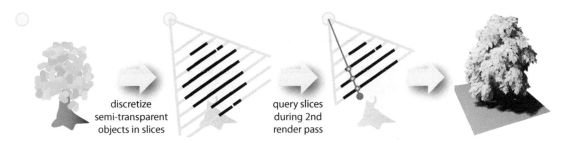

Figure 8.5. The discretization of the semitransparent elements in the scene can be used to derive a layer-based representation that can then be queried to derive the shadow effect in each point of the scene.

but adaptive solutions are also possible [Kim01]. To each depth interval $I_i :=$ $[d_i, d_{i+1})$, an opacity map is associated. This texture captures the opacity of all primitives whose distance to the light lies in the interval I_i. The set of these opacity textures $\{O_0, ..., O_n\}$ can be used as the discretized absorption function. To query the resulting absorption value for a given point $\mathbf{p}$, the point is simply projected into light space $\mathbf{p}^L$. Its z-coordinate can be used to determine its depth interval I_i and, hence, the corresponding opacity texture O_i. Its x, y-coordinates are used to look up the absorption value in O_i and the other opacity-texture layers towards the light.

Construction. In the original approach, the rendering of these maps was done in a two-step process. First, all elements were attributed to their corresponding interval. Then, the opacity texture of each interval was computed by rendering only the associated elements and blending their contributions together into a texture using the hardware's blending functionality `glBlendFunc(GL_ONE, GL_ONE)`. On today's hardware, it is often also acceptable to perform multiple render passes over the entire geometry to produce the opacity textures. In each pass, clipping planes are placed at the depth bounds of the corresponding interval. A more modern solution is to directly redirect the triangles into a layered texture, using the geometry shader [Lee09]. For the latter, care has to be taken when triangles cross depth intervals. In this case, the primitive has to be cut in the geometry shader against the planes that divide the frustum according to the depth bounds.

It is relatively simple to transform opacity maps into an approximation of the transmittance function. This transformation boils down to replacing the ith opacity map O_i by the sum over all opacity maps O_k, with $k < i$. This step is an image-based operation and, thus, very effective. Let V_i be the resulting OSM. Then, during the final rendering, the shadow values can be directly queried. Alternatively, the absorption can be produced directly during construction, by drawing primitives not in a single, but all intervals closer to the light. Nonetheless, this process implies more geometry and fragment processing and can easily become more costly.

OSM are usually 8-bit luminance textures. This choice implies that all elements can be rendered using quality-improving rendering solutions such as antialiasing, which is crucial for hair rendering. Furthermore, lookups can be performed with linear or even mipmap interpolation to avoid pixel artifacts. In particular, it is also possible to linearly interpolate between different OSM textures depending on the position of the query point with respect to the depth bounds. Hereby, a smooth variation can be achieved inside of each depth interval, but occasional unwanted self-shadowing can occur.

Opacity shadow maps presented a milestone in realistic rendering of hair, smoke, and other complex objects. The downside is that for an efficient implementation 2one needs to first derive all layers of the OSM, before being able to compute the shadow response. Consequently, the memory consumption can be relatively high, especially for a larger scene where their number can be elevated; 16 is usually a minimum requirement, and only for very localized effects (e.g., hair) can fewer be sufficient. Furthermore, the global depth-interval bounds are not always appropriate because, for some pixels, many of these intervals stay empty.

Slice Maps

A more compact representation is *slice maps* [Dong04, Eisemann06a, Eisemann08c]. These maps encode a three-dimensional voxel grid of the scene. While slice maps are very versatile, one particular application is to use them as a discretized absorption function [Eisemann06a] in the form of *transmittance shadow maps*.

Representation. To voxelize a scene, it is placed in a grid of cells. Each cell can hold information about the contained surfaces. In the simplest case, this information might just be a single bit indicating the presence (one) or absence (zero) of matter. Usually, it is quite costly to fill such a voxel grid with all primitives, but the use of graphics hardware allows for an efficient construction and a compact representation in the context of binary voxelization. In this process, two observations are exploited: First, the pixels of an image implicitly define a two-dimensional grid. Hence, when rendering from the light, primitives in the form of fragments are already sorted into this two-dimensional grid, which extends along the view frustum of the camera. The grid's resolution along the x- and y-axes corresponds directly to the resolution of the rendering. The camera can be orthographic or perspective and can be placed at any position.

To encode the third dimension of the voxel grid along the z-axis, a special encoding in the color channels of the pixels is used. The colors of a pixel (x, y) represent a column in the grid. The cells within this column are encoded via the RGBA value of the pixel. Each color channel is represented as a number, which in turn is represented via a bit sequence. The idea is to interpret the RGBA value as a single long bit vector2, whose bits are associated to voxel cells along the z-axis in space. With modern hardware, 128-bit vectors can be obtained by using 32-bit data types per color component. Using several such textures, their number can be further increased. The name *slice maps* comes from the idea that when considering only the ith bit in all pixels, the result is a single voxel-grid slice of the original scene.

In comparison to OSM, each slice is only binary and does not contain float values. This restriction also implies that each blocker has to share the same transmittance properties because they can no longer be distinguished. Furthermore, two blockers that fall into the same voxel are only captured once. Despite these disadvantages, slice maps lead to a much higher resolution with respect to OSM and deliver this result at a lower rendering cost.

Construction. One important feature of slice maps is that the representation is not only well suited but also easy to construct. The construction is performed in a single rendering pass.

For each primitive, we have to find the intersected voxels and set the corresponding bits to one. During the rasterization, the primitive is transformed into fragments, each in its corresponding intersected column. Its linear depth d (distance from the light) is used to determine the slice it falls into. A fragment program then transforms this depth into a 32-bit mask with zeroes everywhere except for a one in the bit corresponding to the slice. The result is then fused with the framebuffer using an OR operation to keep all active bits. This OR blending is part of the standard pipeline and activated via `glLogicOp(GL_OR)` (a discussion of Direct3D implementations can be found on page 251). While it is possible to compute the bitmask for a fragment arithmetically [Eisemann08a], it is currently more efficient to rely on a texture (128 RGBA 32-bit texels). The texture directly converts a given depth d with a single lookup into its corresponding bitmask.

In the case of such a boundary voxelization, a fragment only fills a single voxel, while the represented surface part often covers more than one voxel. This undersampling routinely leads to holes, which are especially pronounced for almost orthogonal faces. To understand this effect, imagine a single cube where the camera view aligns perfectly with one of its sides. Consequently, this wall cannot appear in the voxelization because it does not produce any fragments. To alleviate such artifacts, Dong et al. [Dong04] proposed to associate each triangle to one of three views (along each axis) according to its normal. The view that most aligns with the normal direction is chosen. Finally, these separate voxel grids are fused together in a postprocess. Instead of choosing a view for each triangle, one can also use the geometry shader [Forest10] to produce three copies of each triangle that are transformed into the three views and redirected to different voxelization textures (e.g., using the layered-texture mechanism).

Note, however, that keeping multiple voxel grids and merging them comes with some overhead. Moreover, even these more costly approaches still suffer from gaps. This originates in the fact that a fragment is only generated if the triangle it belongs to overlaps the pixel's center. But to capture all surface parts, a fragment would also have to be generated if any other part of the pixel is overlapped. Since such conservative rasterization is not supported by the graphics pipeline, it has to be performed manually [Hasselgren05]. An according conservative voxelization approach that yields a slice map has been proposed by Zhang et al. [Zhang07b]. Unfortunately, it is generally too slow to be of practical relevance for our context.

Another alternative is to resort to a compute language like CUDA to perform the voxelization. As has been shown recently [Schwarz10], this enables generating accurate conservative voxelizations, where all voxels overlapped by a surface are set, at high speed.

Evaluating visibility. Even though the representation is efficient, using the representation to compute a transmittance-function value can still be costly. Basically, to query the result at a point **p**, one would need to project it into the light's view and look up the corresponding voxel column. Given the point's distance to the light and corresponding bit entry i in the voxel column, one would need to count all activated bits between bit i and bit 0, which represent the voxels between **p** and the light source. Then this number is an approximation of the number of surfaces that are traversed on the way to the light. Unfortunately, such a loop would be very costly.

A simple observation accelerates the evaluation. First, to only consider bits below the ith bit, it is enough to perform a mod operation in the shader with the number 2^i that can be obtained by a simple bit shift. Such an operation successfully sets all bits above the ith position to zero. To count the remaining bits, one can employ the solutions of Section 10.1.

The number of bits can be transformed into a transmittance-function value using a power function, exponentiating the user-defined absorption value for the semitransparent scene elements. A final observation is that it is possible to produce a voxelization per different type of material to even create a few differently colored shadows. This extension can still be achieved in a single construction pass [Eisemann06a].

Extensions. Solid voxelization that fills the interior of watertight objects is also possible [Eisemann08c]. Thereby, appropriate shadows from solid transparent objects can be emulated.

To decide whether a voxel is inside of the object, one could shoot a ray towards the light and count the number of intersections with the objects. If it is odd, the voxel lies inside the object. This is similar to the counting step of shadow volumes (Section 2.4). Shooting a ray per voxel would be very costly on current GPUs. But there is a minor modification to the previous algorithm that allows us to compute this solution efficiently.

We precompute masks such that a fragment recovers a bitmask that does not only have a single activated bit at its corresponding depth but also all other bits further from the light are activated as well. The intuition behind this mask relates to the observation that was already applied in the context of stencil shadow volumes (Section 2.4). Intuitively, if one imagines shooting a ray from all the voxels that

---

Voxelization in Direct3D

One catch is that bitwise blending does not exist in recent versions of Direct3D. This makes the implementation of slice maps somewhat cumbersome.

An unsatisfying solution around this issue is to use additive blending instead and sum up the bitmask. Unfortunately, using one bit per voxel implies that if two fragments end up in the same voxel, the sum can no longer be stored and will affect adjacent voxels in the voxel column. To remedy this effect, instead of using a single bit, several bits can be associated to a voxel. In this case, summing up several fragments inside a voxel does not directly *pollute* adjacent bits (e.g., allocating 2 (4) bits per voxel means that up to 3 (15) fragments can be summed before the highest bit will affect the next voxel entry in the column). This solution can be implemented with Direct3D but lowers robustness and resolution.

Producing a solid voxelization is actually very tricky because using additive blend would result in sums that easily exceed their limits. Instead, there is a better solution that exploits the orientation of the triangles. If the face is back-facing, the mask is multiplied by -1 before being blended additively. In practice, this corresponds to a substraction that simulates the XOR operation. Other alternatives with potentially higher precision exist [Eisemann06a] but are more complex to implement.

With Direct3D 11, two further implementation alternatives became possible, which allow for accurate bitmask updates. The simpler one is to harness the new ability to write to textures from within the pixel shader and use atomic bitwise operations to perform these writes. The second more powerful and flexible, but also more laborious, alternative is to implement the voxelization with compute shaders.

---

are activated in this mask towards the light, each of these rays would intersect the fragment and, hence, the surface. Therefore, if we would have a counter in each voxel and we would add the incoming bits, the final sum would correspond exactly to the number of surfaces that would be intersected by a ray to the light.

Counting is not possible in an efficient manner, but ultimately, we do not care about the actual sum, only the number's parity. Hence, it would be enough to initially set all bits to zero and then toggle them whenever an activated bit comes in. This behavior is achieved when blending the masks with a XOR operation. Consequently, after rendering the entire scene, a voxel's bit is one if the number of intersections of a ray towards the source is $2odd$. An $2odd$ number of intersections means that the corresponding voxel is inside the object's volume.

To improve precision, it is further possible to increase the precision of each voxel column [Eisemann06a]. The idea is to first compute a near and far depth map of the visible transparent objects. These two per-pixel depth bounds then define the interval in which the uniform voxelization should take place. The modification to the above algorithm is tiny. Instead of using d directly for the bitmask lookup, it is first transformed by $(d - n)/(f - n)$, where n is the near value and f the far value in the pixel to rescale it into the interval $[0, 1]$ between n and f.

Stochastic Approaches

Another way to represent visibility is through stochastic approaches [Kircher09, McGuire10b, Enderton10, McGuire10c]. The basic observation is that the opacity of a semitransparent surface corresponds to the ratio of energy that is blocked (reflected) by the surface. The idea of stochastic approaches is to cast opacity into a probabilistic framework. By using a special rendering of the scene that discards fragments based on a probability that is defined by the surfaces' opacity, the resulting image contains a stochastic representation of the transparent scene.

Before explaining the details, we will first introduce the relationship between probability and opacity, then we explain how to use this probabilistic interpretation to spatially resolve transparency. Further, we explain how to exploit this representation to compute an approximation of the transmittance function.

Opacity and probability.   Let's first clarify the intuition behind the relationship of opacity and probability. Imagine a ray through a single semitransparent surface with opacity α and color c and a background color b. The correct color response for this ray would be $\alpha c + (1 - \alpha)b$.

Now let's assume we do not shoot this ray only once but N times along the same path, but this time, we modify the computation as follows. When we hit the surface, we draw a random number $r \in [0, 1]$. If r is smaller than the surface's opacity α, the ray is stopped and we report c; otherwise, we continue along the ray and hit the background and we report b. Because the probability that a ray is stopped corresponds exactly to the surface's opacity, the number of times that we report c should be roughly αN, whereas the number of times we find b is $(1-\alpha)N$. Hence, if we average the result of all rays, we obtain again

$$((\alpha N)c + ((1 - \alpha)N)b)/N = \alpha c + (1 - \alpha)b.$$

The above example for a single surface generalizes to several surfaces and results in a valid compositing (according to Equation (8.1)).

The transmittance function for the above example with one surface should return 1 then $1 - \alpha$ after crossing the surface. It is implicitly computed by evaluating all the rays. Basically, counting the ratio of rays that arrive at a certain distance d is an approximation of the result of the transmittance function for distance d.

Stochastic rasterization.   We have just seen that the shooting of many rays can allow us to derive an approximation of the transmittance function. While this solution does not sound efficient because many rays are involved, we will see that it is the key to a fast, yet relatively accurate algorithm.

The main observation is that the above probabilistic formulation ensures that each ray will at most hit a *single* surface. We never actually need to consider any attenuation or scaling along the ray. We will see that this is the basis to defining a special stochastic rasterization technique of the surfaces to obtain an equivalent result. We will derive this technique in the following paragraphs.

Let's imagine that we applied the probabilistic approach from above with S rays; we further arrange their impact points (depth) in a small $\sqrt{S} \times \sqrt{S}$ window of an image. We will refer to such a window as a *transparency-pixel window*.

In a first step, we will assume a single semitransparent occluder f_0 with opacity o_0. Because rays were stopped with a probability of o_0, the window will contain roughly So_0 pixels that contain the depth of f_0. Consequently, $S(1-o_0)$ pixels contain the background. Alternatively to shooting rays, we could have drawn f_0 into all S pixels while discarding fragments with a probability of o_0 (e.g., for $o_0 = 0.25$, only every fourth pixel is drawn). We will call this kind of rasterization *stochastic rasterization*. We will now show that this strategy of rasterization generalizes to several semitransparent occluders $\{f_0, \ldots, f_n\}$.

Let $f_0, \ldots, f_n$ be the sorted surfaces encountered along the ray, and $o_0, \ldots, o_n$ be their corresponding opacities. Let's assume all surfaces are stochastically rasterized based on their opacity. A depth value of the ith surface that is written to a pixel inside a transparency-pixel window will prevail during the stochastic rasterization of all other surfaces if and only if it is not directly discarded by the depth test (which happens if a pixel from $f_0, \ldots, f_{i-1}$ was already output at the same location before), and if it is not overwritten by a pixel at a later point (which happens if a pixel from $f_0, \ldots, f_{i-1}$ is afterwards written to the same location). The surfaces $f_{i+1}, \ldots, f_n$ behind f_i cannot affect its pixels.

The probability that a pixel never contains a depth value from $f_0, \ldots, f_{i-1}$ is $\prod_{k=0}^{i-1}(1-o_k)$ because all surfaces are independently stochastically rasterized based on their own opacity. Consequently, roughly $S \prod_{k=0}^{i-1}(1 - o_k)$ pixels remain that can actually receive depth values from f_i, but because f_i is rasterized itself with a probability of o_i, only roughly $S \prod_{k=0}^{i-1}(1 - o_k)o_i$ will receive its values. Looking closely at $\prod_{k=0}^{i-1}(1 - o_k)o_i$, we realize that it is the exact probability we aimed for, namely, the probability of a ray passing through the first $i-1$ surfaces to be blocked by the ith.

In other words, if we render a scene with stochastic rasterization, the transmittance function inside a transparency-pixel window can be approximated by

$$vis(d) \approx \text{count}(d \leq z_i)/S,$$

where S is the number of pixels and z_i the depth values inside the considered transparency-pixel window.

In conclusion, we have seen that the transmittance function can be approximated by ratios of rays arriving at a given distance without being stopped by a surface, which happens with a probability based on the surface's opacity. Here, we have seen that a stochastic rasterization that discards fragments of a surface according to its opacity can be used instead. To then evaluate the transmittance function in a transparency-pixel window p_T for distance d, one only needs to calculate the

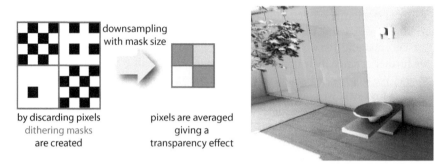

Figure 8.6. By discarding fragments, one can produce dithered transparency. The resulting dithering masks can then be filtered (left). The resulting image gives the illusion of semi-transparent materials (right).

ratio of pixels farther from the light inside p_T. This evaluation is very similar to the computation applied in percentage-closer filtering (compare PCF, Chapter 5).

Implementation. Implementing stochastic rasterization on a GPU is not straightforward because of the lack of a random value function. Hence, we cannot simply discard fragments with a certain probability. Instead, one can predetermine *dithering masks* that are accessed in the shader to decide which fragments to delete, leading to a two-dimensional stippling pattern. A dithering mask is a binary mask that is created in accordance to an opacity value. It indicates which pixels should be kept and which should be thrown away to fulfill the probability criterion. Consequently, each opacity value has a different dithering mask, or rather, each dithering mask corresponds to a certain opacity (the ratio of pixels that are kept). Figure 8.6 shows a dithered scene and, next to it, the final result after filtering.

Care has to be taken to avoid that two surfaces share the same mask in the same transparency-pixel window. Otherwise, the mask of the first will completely occlude the mask of the second. Consequently, the method fails. The reason is that stochastic rasterization would actually no longer be really random.

To solve the issue of the same mask, several versions are produced for a given opacity value. All these versions are stored in a two-dimensional lookup table, one dimension for the various alpha values, the other for the different versions of dithering masks. During rendering, each surface (e.g., via its primitive ID) uses a random seed to decide on the mask version.

Extensions. In [Enderton10], several modifications are presented to improve the above approximation, but they are out of the scope of this book. They point out that a first pass can be used to compute an accurate full accumulation alpha via additive blending. They suggest a solution for antialiasing and also analyze how to proceed for arbitrary opacity values for which one cannot construct a corresponding dithering mask because its resolution is insufficient. Finally, they also show how to exploit multisample buffers during the transparency pass to gain performance.

While the algorithm is relatively fast compared to its good results, problems can occur if many different opacity values are in the scene. For example, a 2×2 dithering mask basically enables only five different opacity levels. Also, if many transparent surfaces overlap, the dithering-mask resolution is rarely sufficient. Increasing the resolution of the entire image and the dithering mask would be an option, but the downside is that the high variance in the z-buffer can affect performance because it leads to incoherent shader executions. This problem can be avoided if one relies on multisample buffers. A transparency-pixel window then corresponds to a color pixel, and its contained pixels to the subpixel depth values. Consequently, only a single shader execution is performed for all depth samples. Unfortunately, the number of depth samples per pixel is currently limited to eight, which makes it necessary to execute several rendering passes for a higher image quality.

Overall, this technique is the only currently available for high-performance colored shadows, which makes it the first choice in this area.

8.2.3 Function-Based Approaches

The idea of function-based approaches is to represent the transmittance function as a linear combination of simpler basis functions (such as sine/cosine representations in Fourier analysis). The use of basis functions has an important implication. Any general function can be projected into such a basis and be approximated as a vector of coefficients. The advantage is that if we want to combine several such functions, we can simply sum up the coefficients to derive the representation of their sum. In other words, each primitive will define a function representation of its impact on the visibility, and we can, by summing the coefficients, derive a function representation of the impact on visibility of all primitives together. This fusion operation does not rely on any sorting, nor is it necessary to otherwise interpret the respective functions.

The major approach making use of such a solution is *Fourier opacity shadow maps* by Jansen and Bavoil [Jansen10]. The applied techniques are strongly related to convolution shadow maps [Annen07], and the reader might find it helpful to read up on Section 5.3.4.

The basic idea is to use a Fourier decomposition to find an appropriate representation of the transmittance function. It turns out that instead of decomposing the transmittance function itself, it is more helpful to decompose the absorption function. Absorption and transmittance are both related. In the context of semitransparent occluders, the transmittance function can be rewritten as

$$vis(d) := \prod_{d < z_i} (1 - \alpha_i)$$

$$= \exp\left(\sum_{d < z_i} \log(1 - \alpha_i) \right)$$

$$= \exp\left(\int_0^d \sum_{i=0}^n \log(1 - \alpha_i)\delta(d - z_i) \right). \qquad (8.2)$$

We will see that this reformulation renders all occluders independent of each other. For the moment, we will focus on a single term: $\log(1 - \alpha_i)\delta(d - z_i)$. We want to represent this function in a Fourier basis. As in Section 5.3.4, the Fourier parameter is scaled such that d is assumed to be in the range $[0, 1]$, which leads to a representation of the form [Jansen10]

$$\log(1 - \alpha_i)\delta(d - z_i) \approx \frac{a_0^i}{2} + \sum_{k=1}^n a_k^i \cos(2\pi k d) + \sum_{k=1}^n b_k^i \sin(2\pi k d), \qquad (8.3)$$

where

$$a_k^i := \int_0^1 \log(1 - \alpha_i)\delta(z - z_i)\cos(2\pi k z)dz = -2\log(1 - a_i)\cos(2\pi k z_i),$$

$$b_k^i := \int_0^1 \log(1 - \alpha_i)\delta(z - z_i)\sin(2\pi k z)dz = -2\log(1 - a_i)\sin(2\pi k z_i).$$

If we plug this representation in Equation (8.2), we obtain:

$$vis(d) := \exp\left(\int_0^d \sum_{i=0}^n \frac{a_0^i}{2} + \sum_{k=1}^n a_k^i \cos(2\pi k d) + \sum_{k=1}^n b_k^i \sin(2\pi k d) \right)$$

$$= \exp\left(\sum_{i=0}^n \left(\frac{a_0^i d}{2} + \sum_{k=1}^n \frac{a_k^i}{2\pi k}\sin(2\pi k d) + \sum_{k=1}^n \frac{b_k^i}{2\pi k}(1 - \cos(2\pi k d)) \right) \right)$$

$$= \exp\left(\left(\sum_{i=0}^n \frac{a_0^i d}{2} \right) + \sum_{k=1}^n \left(\sum_{i=0}^n \frac{a_k^i}{2\pi k} \right)\sin(2\pi k d) \right.$$

$$\left. + \sum_{k=1}^n \left(\sum_{i=0}^n \frac{b_k^i}{2\pi k} \right)(1 - \cos(2\pi k d)) \right)$$

$$= \exp\left(\frac{a_0^{\text{all}} d}{2} + \sum_{k=1}^n a_k^{\text{all}}\sin(2\pi k d) + \sum_{k=1}^n b_k^{\text{all}}(1 - \cos(2\pi k d)) \right), \qquad (8.4)$$

where $a_k^{\text{all}} := \sum_{i=0}^n a_k^i/(2\pi k)$ and $b_k^{\text{all}} := \sum_{i=0}^n b_k^i/(2\pi k)$.

| opacity 0 | opacity 0.25 | opacity 0.5 |

Figure 8.7. A few examples for semitransparent objects. Especially for clouds and smoke-like structures, the appearance is relatively smooth and convincing.

The above reformulation shows two things. First, the integration can be applied to the basis functions only. This is something that is computed once and independent of the coefficients. Second, the rearranging of the terms shows that all coefficients can be summed up to a_k^{all} and b_k^{all} to derive a valid approximation of the transmittance function. These results are useful because, for all semitransparent surfaces i, we can compute the coefficients a_j^i and b_j^i using Equation (8.3) and then simply sum up all coefficients of these functions independent of any ordering. Finally, given the sum of all coefficients, Equation (8.4) delivers a valid representation of the transmittance function.

On the GPU, the implementation is straightforward. Each incoming semitransparent fragment is transformed into its coefficients vector using Equation (8.3). The coefficients are written to multiple textures. The more coefficients one uses, the better the approximation. To ensure that the coefficients of all incoming fragments are combined properly, the result is blended in the framebuffer using `glBlendFunc(GL_ONE, GL_ONE)`. After having processed all these fragments, the approximated transmittance function is ready to use. To query the transmittance function for a depth d, one fetches the summed-up coefficients a_k^{all} and b_k^{all} that are used to evaluate Equation (8.4).

The approach of Fourier opacity shadow maps is very elegant and relatively efficient. The problem is that Fourier analysis is best applied to smooth functions. Therefore, if many elements with small opacities are in the scene (e.g., particles representing a cloud), the resulting visibility function is usually well approximated. Even a few coefficients (such as 15) can result in visually convincing renditions. The performance in such cases remains high, making this method a good choice for such scenarios. Figure 8.7 shows some examples obtained with this approach.

8.3   Summary

The use of transparent objects augments the image quality drastically; for example, glass elements appear significantly more convincing. The choice of the algorithm depends heavily on the scene and quality that is considered. If only one or a few different types of semitransparent materials are used, but these are applied to many objects, layer-based solutions seem appropriate.

For a few different materials, stochastic approaches perform well and efficient implementations are possible on modern hardware. One issue is that only a few different opacity levels are possible because one needs to associate a proper dithering pattern or randomized process. Especially, superposing elements can cause trouble. Finally, for volumetric objects, it can sometimes be helpful to rely on more continuous function-based solutions.

CHAPTER 9
Volumetric Shadows

The concept of volumetric shadows is part of the huge topic of light scattering in participating media that gives rise to phenomena such as shadows in clouds, gas, smoke, and hair and shafts of light in air and water. Shafts of light in air are also known as God rays due to the analogy of how God often was visualized in older movies. In this section, we will only focus on real-time methods for shadows in homogeneous participating media, such as air. Shadows in nonhomogeneous media (clouds, gas, smoke, and hair) are also feasible today in real time, to some extent [Salvi10, Sintorn09, Biri06, Zinke08], while simulation of multiple light scattering generally is too time consuming to be performed for other than offline rendering. We refer the reader to Cerezo et al. [Cerezo05] for a detailed survey on rendering techniques for participating media—both real-time and non-real-time, and for both single and multiple scattering.

In this section, we will focus on what are probably currently the most practically usable approaches for volumetric shadows with single scattering in participating media for real-time purposes. First, shadow mapping based methods with ray marching are described. This is followed by approaches that replace the ray marching by using shadow volumes.

9.1 Real-Time Single Scattering in Homogeneous Participating Media

Participating media (e.g., clouds, fog, smoke, or dusty air) are media that participate in the light interaction. The light does not pass through the medium without being affected. The media may absorb and scatter the light rays due to reflections and refractions at microscopic particles (e.g., water drops). Computing the true

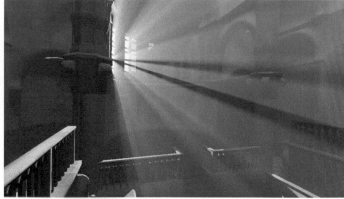

Figure 9.1. The Sibenik scene with volumetric shadows in homogeneous participating media. The phenomenon also goes by the name *shafts of light* or *airlight*. The scene here uses two light sources in real time [Billeter10].

scattering effects, with multiple reflections or refractions as the light passes within the medium, is still too time consuming for real-time applications. However, limiting the scattering to a single reflection simplifies computations, which allows for real-time applications while achieving visually pleasing results (see Figure 9.1).

In single light scattering, the dominant visual effect is assumed to be when light travels from the light source into the medium and then undergoes one in-scattering along the view ray (see Figure 9.2). This assumption is true when the participating medium is optically thin (i.e., the transmittance is close to 100%); the light transmits through the medium fairly undisturbed, which is true for highly transparent materials such as air. Then, the primary visual factor comes from the single in-scattering along the view ray, making it more reasonable to ignore the subordinate and complex multiple scattering effects. Clouds and smoke have a very high albedo,[1] making single scattering a crude approximation. The albedo for cumulus and stratus clouds are 0.7 to 0.9 [Nishita96]. Nevertheless, for air containing a relatively low amount of small particles such as dust or thin fog, single scattering produces plausible and eye-pleasing results. In particular, the single-scattering model convincingly captures the effects of halos around light sources. Light that is scattered towards the viewer, making the participating medium visible, is often referred to as *airlight*.

It is also common to consider the light attenuation due to absorption and out-scattering during the light's traversal through the medium, both along the ray path from the light source to the point of in-scattering and along the remaining way to the eye. These extra calculations are both simple and often have a dramatic impact on the visual result.

---

[1]The albedo is the fraction of the light that is reflected by the object.

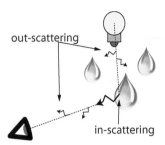

Figure 9.2. Illustration of single light scattering. Light is in-scattered from the surroundings (here by a water drop) into the view ray. In single scattering, the dominant in-scattering is assumed to be from the direction of the light source. The fact that light can be in-scattered from other directions as well is ignored. Light is also out-scattered (e.g., by other water drops not visualized here) on its way from the light source to the event of in-scattering and then on its way to the eye. This out-scattering leads to attenuation of the light intensity.

Next to the single light scattering, we assume that the participating medium is homogeneous. In other words, the medium fills the whole scene of interest. For a scene with a homogeneous medium, the in-scattering along an eye ray is determined by the parts of the ray that are directly visible from the light source. In other words, the problem transforms into computing the shadowed parts of the view rays. Nonhomogeneous media, such as a gas cloud, would require also considering what parts of the light traversal happen inside the medium, that is, which parts of the view rays that have in-scattering—due to being nonshadowed and lying within the medium—and how much attenuation there is along those separate parts of the ray paths.

9.2   Ray Marching a Shadow Map

Figure 9.3(a) illustrates a popular method for computing single scattering in homogeneous media. Using a shadow map from the light's position, it is possible to find out which parts of each view ray are visible from the light source and have in-scattering. For each delta step along the view rays, the shadow map is checked for visibility of the light, and in-scattering is added with proper absorption along the path from the light and path to the eye.

Following the definitions of Figure 9.3(a), a brute force algorithm becomes

For every pixel in screen space (A)
   Step along ray, from the eye to a surface point **p**, using ray marching
      For each sample position x_j
         Check in shadow map (B) if light source is visible
         If so: add in-scattered light contribution with attenuation to the pixel's color.

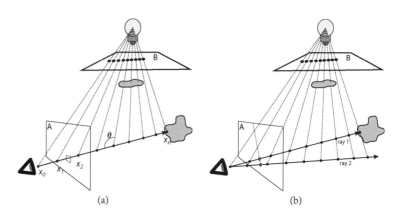

Figure 9.3. (a) The image illustrates how to compute the airlight along a view ray through one pixel (red). The in-scattering, including attenuation, is integrated over the view ray by sampling at regular intervals x_j and checking for shadows against a shadow map (B). (b) Baran et al. note that the result for a ray (here marked as ray 2) that lies below and in the same plane as a ray 1 and the light source can be computed incrementally from ray 1, resulting in significant speed improvement [Baran10, Chen11].

In addition to computing the airlight contribution, it should be noted that the surface shading of the point **p** should also be attenuated depending on its distances between **p** and the light and **p** and the eye. This contribution is, however, easy to add to the shading computations in the fragment shader when initially rendering the scene geometry to the screen (i.e., before doing the ray-marching pass).

9.2.1 General Airlight Approximation

While the light is attenuated on its way to a surface point **p**, the surface point also receives in-scattering from the surrounding participating media, enhancing the light intensity. This latter term is, however, as computationally expensive to compute per pixel as the full in-scattering towards the eye for the whole image. Therefore, a plausible approximation is to assume that the attenuation from the light to the surface point is low compared to the attenuation from the point to the eye. Thus, the in-scattering that would affect the surface shading is usually ignored, in order to gain real-time performance. This is, however, an approximation.

9.2.2 Airlight Contribution

The formula for the airlight contribution (in-scattering and attenuation) from a to b along a view ray is computed as follows:

$$L = \int_a^b \beta \varphi(\theta) \frac{I_0 e^{-\beta d(x)}}{d(x)^2} e^{-\beta x} dx, \tag{9.1}$$

where $d(x)$ is the distance from point x to the light source; β is the optical thickness of the medium; the $I_0 e^{-\beta d(x)}$ factor is the attenuation of the intensity from the light to x due to out-scattering; the dividend $d(x)^2$ is the decrease in intensity with the square of the distance due to a radial light source; the $e^{-\beta x}$ factor is the attenuation from x to the eye due to out-scattering; and the $\varphi(\theta)$ factor is the phase function that tells what portion of the light intensity is in-scattered for various angles θ (see Figure 9.3(a)). In practice, a constant phase function of $1/4\pi$ can be used [Baran10, Blinn82].

The in-scattered light contribution at each point x_j only varies with the distance to the light and angle θ. The rest of the factors are constant for a certain medium. Therefore, this formula can be calculated efficiently using precomputed lookup tables stored as textures [Sun05, Pegoraro09b, Pegoraro09a]. A purely analytical method also exists [Pegoraro10].

9.2.3   Ray-Marching Approaches

Ray marching along the view rays can be done on the GPU, either by drawing alpha-blended planes [Dobashi02, Imagire07, Mitchell04a], by explicitly looping in a fragment shader [Gautron09, Tóth09, Engelhardt10], or by implementing the full ray marching in OpenCL or CUDA [Baran10, Chen11]. Since the ray marching constitutes the expensive part of the algorithm, several optimizations have been suggested. Wyman [Wyman08] adds bounding planes of the ray marching using shadow volumes. Along each view ray, the front-most shadow-volume plane and farthest shadow-volume plane clamps the region for which ray marching with visibility testing against the shadow map is necessary. This may significantly reduce the parts along the view rays that need to be ray marched. Tóth and Umenhoffer [Tóth09] suggest that only a few ray-marched samples x_j are taken for each pixel, and nearby pixels may borrow results from each other. They use interleaved sampling, where a block of $M \times M$ pixels on the screen evaluates only N samples (i.e., to determine if the sample position along the eye ray is in shadow or if in-scattering occurs). The algorithm is implemented in a fragment shader, executed as a postprocess using the shadow map.

Engelhardt and Dachsbacher [Engelhardt10] sample sparsely along the epipolar lines in screen space (see Figure 9.4). In addition, they linearly search along the epipolar lines for discontinuities in the depth buffer (i.e., where the in-scattered radiance changes abruptly) and place samples just before and after such positions (see red points on box in Figure 9.4). In between sample points along an epipolar line, linear filtering is used. Between other sample points (e.g., between epipolar lines), bilateral filtering is used. The rationale is to keep the number of samples for the single scattering to a minimum since this is expensive. In-scattering at a sample point is computed using ray marching. In addition, Engelhardt and Dachsbacher handle textured light sources.

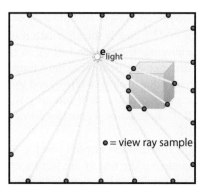

Figure 9.4. *Epipolar lines*, here visualized in screen space. The light position is an epipole, e_{light}, in screen space—not necessarily inside the screen as here (vice versa, the eye is also an epipole in shadow map space). The lines through the epipole are called epipolar lines. The red dots illustrate Engelhardt and Dachsbacher's [Engelhardt10] sparse sampling of view rays. Samples are taken along the image border and also at discontinuities in the depth buffer (see samples at the box). That is, ray marching is only performed for view rays at the these positions. Interpolation and filtering are used for results in between sample positions.

Baran et al. [Baran10] notice that the in-scattering for a ray can be computed incrementally from a ray along the same epipolar line but closer to the light source. The reason is that in-scattering can only monotonically decrease with the ray's distance from the light source (see rays 1 and 2 in Figure 9.3(b)). They perform a hierarchical update based on partial sum trees. In this way, the cost for integrating the in-scattering along a view ray on average becomes only logarithmical. The algorithm is clever but involved, and we have to refer to the original paper for the details. In short, the steps include ray marching, epipolar sampling, incremental hierarchy integration, rectification and unrectification, and solving a singular value decomposition (SVD) per frame for a 64×64 matrix. The rectification here means that the view rays and light rays are transformed into a coordinate system where they are orthogonal to each other.

The implementation was also optimized by noting that the traversed path of an eye ray over the shadow map results in the traversal of a one-dimensional height field [Chen11]. The shadow map first undergoes epipolar rectification, meaning that every ray traverses along one single row in the shadow map. Chen et al. accelerate their method by replacing the partial sum tree with a one-dimensional min-max mipmap computation of the shadow map. For every slice of eye rays over the same shadow-map row, the same one-dimensional mipmap section is used for finding lit parts of the ray's traversal, when computing the in-scattering for that ray. This method is relatively fast for high-resolution shadow maps (e.g., $4k \times 4k$), but at the same time, the discretization requires high resolution to avoid visible artifacts.

Wyman [Wyman10] replaces the ray marching with one texture operation per view ray. He voxelizes the shadow casters in epipolar space. To understand how this is done, we will first quickly explain epipolar space in more detail. Epipolar space slices the scene into planes that all go through the light and the eye position. One such slice is visualized in Figure 9.3(a). Each view ray lies in a specific plane. Every point in the scene has a coordinate in epipolar space, such that the x-coordinate defines the epipolar plane in which the point lies, the y-coordinate is the distance from the light source, and the z-coordinate is the distance from the eye.

Wyman voxelizes the shadow casters into a grid of one bit per voxel (Chapter 8.2.2 describes how to do this rapidly). A bit equal to one represents light-blocking geometry in that cell. Then, he performs a parallel scan on the grid columns, such that each bit will be set if any of the bits that are closer to the light source in the same column is set. To find the blocked samples x_j along a view ray, it is enough to do a texture lookup returning the bits along the view ray. Up to 128 bits along a view ray can be fetched per texture lookup. The voxelization and bit lookups are extremely fast and can be done at frame rates of over hundreds of fps, even for scenes of over a million polygons. Nevertheless, the method is not demonstrated for scenes that include single scattering—only shadows.

9.3   Shadow-Volume–Based Approaches

It should not come as a surprise to the reader by now that there are also shadow-volume–based approaches for computing the volumetric shadows. The shadow volumes are used to solve the integration instead of using ray marching in the shadow map.

If shadow volumes are guaranteed not to overlap, then the integration of the in-scattering along each view ray can be computed as a sum of order-independent terms by adding the in-scattering up to each front-facing shadow volume plane and subtracting the in-scattering along each back-facing shadow volume plane (see Figure 9.5). In order to achieve nonoverlapping shadow volumes, and thus avoid casting volumetric shadows from edges that are already in shadow (shadows in shadows), Biri et al. [Biri06] use sorting of shadow volume quads in back-to-front order from the camera. James [James03] orders the shadow planes using depth peeling instead.

Another alternative to guarantee that the shadow volumes do not overlap is to construct them from a shadow map [Billeter10], in the same spirit as McCool [McCool00] suggests for hard shadows (see Section 2.4.7). A polygonal mesh is created from the shadow map, with one vertex per shadow map sample, where the vertex position is the shadow map's sample position in world space (see Figure 9.6). The mesh can also be adaptively coarsened, only keeping refined tessellation along the edges in the shadow map, in order to limit the polygon count for the mesh.

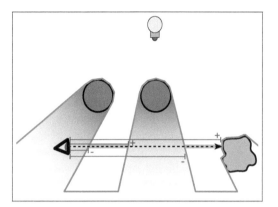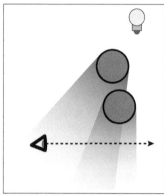

Figure 9.5. Computing the in-scattering (or airlight, which includes the attenuation) along a partially shadowed view ray (dashed black). The airlight for a view ray up to the visible surface (orange) can be computed by adding/subtracting the contribution along an unshadowed view ray up to each front/back-facing shadow mesh polygon (dark blue). Blue represents segments of positive airlight contribution, added for each front-facing shadow volume-mesh polygon, while red represents the negative contribution from each back-facing mesh polygon. This correctly sums up to the nonshadowed airlight contribution (green) (left). This is, however, only true if shadow volumes are nonintersecting (image illustrating failure case), which can be guaranteed by creating the shadow-volume mesh from a shadow map (right).

The shadow-volume–based algorithm by Billeter et al. consists of the following steps [Billeter10]:

1. Create the shadow map by rendering the scene into a depth buffer.
2. Render scene from the camera with diffuse lighting, attenuating incoming and outgoing light due to absorption and scattering in media. Hard shadows on surfaces can be calculated in this step using standard shadow mapping.
3. Construct the mesh from the shadow map, with or without adaptive tesselation.

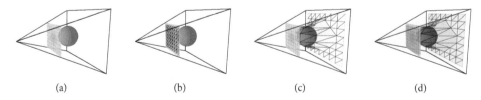

(a)   (b)   (c)   (d)

Figure 9.6. Creation of the shadow-volume mesh from the shadow map. (a) First, the shadow map is rendered. (b) Then, the mesh is constructed with one vertex per shadow-map pixel. The mesh triangles should face the light source. (c) The mesh vertices are displaced by the depth values in the shadow map so that each vertex is the corresponding shadow map pixel's world-space coordinate. (d) Finally, the mesh is closed by the four light-frustum planes.

4. Render the mesh with depth testing disabled and additive blending enabled. The fragment shader evaluates the in-scattering, including attenuation, for a nonshadowed ray from the eye to the fragment's position. If fragment belongs to a back-facing mesh polygon, the contribution is negated.

There are several options for the implementation of the in-scattering and attenuation computations, and therefore, we will next explain the details of one efficient way to perform the airlight computations in steps 2 and 4 of the pseudocode above.

9.3.1 Airlight Contribution for Shadow-Volume–Based Approaches

Figure 9.7(a) shows the computation of the light-attenuation factor of the surface-shading contribution from a view sample (point on a scene object) to the eye used in step 2. Figure 9.7(b) illustrates the airlight contribution between this surface point and the eye, including the attenuation, which is used in step 4.

Since airlight$_a$ and airlight$_b$ (see Figure 9.7(b)) only depend on a', b', and c', they are precomputed into a two-dimensional texture and looked up in runtime by step 4. The contribution is split into two parts to simplify storage in the lookup table. The first part (red) is between the eye up to the point of projection of the light onto the view ray, and the second part is the remaining distance up to the point **p**. The airlight for each part is the integration for each z-value of the attenuated light reaching z, scaled by the square of the distance to the light source and then attenuated by the distance z to the eye (see formulas for airlight$_a$ and airlight$_b$). Since a and b could be negative—if the projection of the light source is behind the eye or beyond **p**—the fragment shader deals with these two special cases as well.

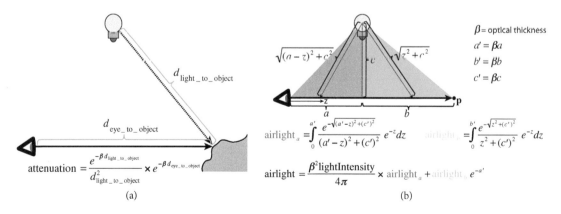

Figure 9.7. (a) Illustration of the light-attenuation factor used after the lighting computations for standard surface shading (see step 2). (b) Computation of airlight contribution (in-scattering and attenuation) along an unoccluded ray, from the viewpoint to a certain position **p** (used in step 4).

The total airlight for the ray is the sum of the airlight contribution for a and b, where the latter is also scaled by the attenuation for distance a' to the eye. The total is also multiplied by the phase function $1/4\pi$ and the optical thickness β (see the definition of Equation (9.1)) and finally multiplied by $\beta \times$ lightIntensity.

Brief History

There has been research on rendering volumetric shadows since the early 1980s. Blinn [Blinn82] was the first to introduce a single-scattering model to computer graphics by describing a light-reflection function for clouds and dusty surfaces made up of many small particles. The earliest approaches on shadows in and by participating media, such as clouds, were based on ray tracing [Kajiya84]. Max [Max86b, Max86a] was the first to use shadow volumes for atmospheric shadows (e.g., shafts of light) as early as 1986. He used a scan-line algorithm and epipolar lines. Nishita et al. [Nishita87] also used shadow volumes and a scan-line algorithm.

9.4 Summary

Wyman [Wyman10] has demonstrated a very fast method to create shadows in homogeneous participating media. Chen et al. [Chen11] consider single light scattering, in addition to just the shadows—at a higher cost but still at real-time frame rates for impressive scenes. The shadow-volume–based approach for single scattering by Billeter et al. [Billeter10] is the simpler one to implement and has similar frame rates as the ray-marching approaches. However, for textured light sources, the texture values must somehow be considered (e.g., sampled at regular intervals), and for this, the ray-marching algorithms right now stand out as the natural option.

Nevertheless, at the time of writing this book, this area is undergoing a rapid evolution, and it is still an open issue what technique will be the most fruitful during the next years. For game scenes, it is not uncommon that the frame rates already are in the order of 100 fps with any of these three methods.

CHAPTER 10
Advanced Shadow Topics

The previous chapters have given an overview of the most important shadow techniques and explained many of these approaches in detail. While we covered many subjects, visibility is used in a large variety of other contexts as well.

In this chapter, we will provide a glimpse on advanced visibility techniques. We give explanations on how to deal with multicolored light sources (Section 10.1) and how to perform shadow antialiasing (Section 10.2). Other advanced methods include specialized algorithms for particular data structures, with a focus on voxel representations (Section 10.3), and different rendering paradigms in the form of ray casting (Section 10.4), and we discuss how to use shadow algorithms for general environment lighting (Section 10.5). In this context, we further added a discussion of precomputed radiance transfer (Section 10.6). It is a very useful real-time global illumination method that also has found its way into movie productions.

In contrast to the other chapters, the presentation here will be less profound than for previous parts of this book. The reason is that each of the topics is very general and each one could fill an entire book. Here, we only want to provide a global overview that gives some indications and pointers to the interested reader.

10.1 Multicolored Light Sources

In this section, we will cover techniques when using textured light sources. The texture could, for instance, represent a fire, possibly animated, or an image of several smaller light sources, perhaps with complex shapes (see Figure 10.1).

There are two classes of methods for managing textured light sources. The first class is based on an analytic visibility computation that provides a continuous, non-sample-based, light-occlusion result. Soft shadow volumes (see Section 7.3) and soft shadow mapping by back projection [Guennebaud06] (see Section 6.7) belong

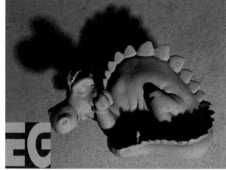

Figure 10.1. Examples of real-time shadows from textured light sources. In left to right order, images are from [Assarsson03a] and [Schwarz07].

to this class. The second class is based on having a bitmask with a set bit for each occluded light sample. This is the result of visibility sampling [Eisemann07, Sintorn08b] and bitmask soft shadows [Schwarz07], which were presented in Sections 7.4.2 and 6.7.2, respectively. A bitmask is also the result when integrating the visibility from the silhouette edges using a set of binary light samples [Forest08, Laine05c], which is covered in Section 7.3.4.

10.1.1 Textured Lights Using Continuous Visibility Evaluation

Soft Shadow Volumes

Soft shadow volumes compute the visibility of the light source by integrating over the silhouette edges. For each view sample, the silhouette edges of occluding geometry are projected onto the light and clipped against the light-source borders. The occluded area is integrated from the edges by using Green's theorem (see Figure 7.9). Instead of using just the ratio of the occluded area to the total light-source area as the amount of shadow, we can compute how much of the red, green, and blue light is occluded. Assume that (x_1, y_1) and (x_2, y_2) are the endpoints of an edge that has been projected onto the light and clipped against its borders. Then, this edge's contribution to the integration is totally determined by (x_1, y_1) and (x_2, y_2) (see Figure 10.2, left). For each combination of x_1, y_1 and x_2, y_2, a lookup table can be precomputed that returns the amount of occluded light for red, green, and blue. Thus, the amount of occluded light can be accumulated for each view sample, for instance, into a separate buffer.

When doing shading for a view sample (see Appendix C), the light color to be used is the total sum of all light texels minus the amount of occluded light for the view sample. In practice, you will likely also want to scale the light intensity to a suitable range, for instance, if a texture or framebuffer with 8-bit channels is used.

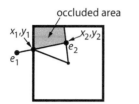 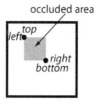

Figure 10.2. Calculating occluded area per edge (left) and per shadow-map pixel (right) for soft shadow volumes and soft shadow maps for back projection respectively. Instead of just an area value, for textured lights, the occlusion is a triplet of the amount of occluded red, green, and blue light.

In case shading is done before the shadows are applied, an ad hoc but less accurate method is to simply multiply the color value from the shading with (1 − the sum of all occluded light). This will most noticeably be wrong where there are specular highlight contributions in regions that are supposed to be fully in shadow.

Soft Shadow Mapping by Back Projection

As described by Guennebaud et al. [Guennebaud06], for each view sample, the shadow map samples within a search neighborhood are back-projected onto the light source to accumulate occlusion (see also Section 6.7). This gives a continuous soft shadow value per view sample. Instead of just computing a scalar occlusion value, colored shadows from a textured light can be achieved in the following way. If a shadow sample covers a rectangular region of the light source corresponding to {*top, bottom, left, right*} (see Figure 10.2, right), a four-dimensional texture can encode for all combinations of a discrete range of values (e.g., 32 per parameter) how much of the red, green, and blue light is occluded. Thus, when accumulating occlusion, the amount of occlusion for red, green, and blue light is computed separately, and the shadow color can be set accordingly.

10.1.2 Textured Lights Using an Occlusion Bitmask

For the class of methods where an occlusion bitmask is available, the assumption is that each bit corresponds to one light sample that in turn corresponds to one texel of the light texture. The brute-force way to compute lighting for a certain view sample is to, for each clear bit in the bitmask, compute lighting contribution from the corresponding light sample by essentially treating it as a colored point light source. Shadows are thus implicit, since light is not accumulated for occluded light samples. Such an accurate computation is done by solving the direct-lighting equation (see Equation (1.4) on page 10) for the shadow-receiving point **p**, but as a sum over the contribution from each light sample, as follows:

$$L_o(\mathbf{p}, \omega) \approx |\mathcal{L}| \sum_i w_i \, f_r(\mathbf{p}, \omega, \mathbf{p} \to \mathbf{l}_i) \, L_e(\mathbf{l}_i, \mathbf{l}_i \to \mathbf{p}) \, G(\mathbf{p}, \mathbf{l}_i) \, V(\mathbf{p}, \mathbf{l}_i),$$

where $\mathbf{l}_i \in \mathcal{L}$ is a light sample i with associated weight w_i, $\sum_i w_i = 1$, and $V(\mathbf{p}, \mathbf{l}_i)$ is the visibility information from the bitmask for light sample i. It should be noted that for a nonuniform distribution of the light samples, the weights w_i also become nonuniform, inversely proportional to the density of samples in the neighborhood of each sample. An example implementation is presented by Forest et al. [Forest08].

Evaluating shading for each nonoccluded light sample is the only way to compute accurate shadow results, and not just visibility. A faster and very common method, much more feasible for real-time performance, is to simply scale the shading from the center position of the light source by the visibility of the light (i.e., the fraction of visible light samples versus occluded ones). This, however, leads to an approximation of the true shadows.

Computing this fraction could, for instance, be done by lookup tables. For each group of, let's say, eight light samples, a lookup table is generated, storing the amount of occluded light for each possible bit combination of the corresponding 8 bits of the occlusion mask. Each entry stores the amount of occluded red, green, and blue light in a triplet. Such a lookup table is typically quite cheap to compute even in runtime for each frame, for instance, in the case of an animated light texture. When computing lighting for a view sample, lookups are done for each group of 8 bits in the occlusion bitmask in order to accumulate the total amount of occluded light. However, this will only be reasonably fast for a smaller number of light samples (e.g., up to 16×16), since the number of lookups corresponds to the number of light samples divided by the number of groups. Each lookup table for a group size of eight consumes 256×4 bytes for an RGBA-texture.

If the light texture contains only a few number of different colors, a faster method is to precompute a bitmask per unique texture color that identifies all light samples corresponding to this color. When computing the shadow for a view sample, for each unique color, its precomputed bitmask is ANDed with the occlusion bitmask for all light samples. Then, the resulting number of set bits is counted. The amount of occluded light for this color is then given by the count times the color. The contribution is summed for each unique texture color to get the total amount of occluded light for the view sample.

10.1.3   Counting Set Bits

Counting the number of set bits in a bitmask is useful not only for textures of a few unique colors. It is also the default method for converting an occlusion bitmask into a visibility value used for computing shadows for a constant colored (nontextured) light source. For these two reasons, we will here briefly mention how to efficiently perform such bit counting.

Bit Counting Using Lookup Tables

It is possible to count the number of set bits in, for instance, a byte by computing a lookup table of 256 entries that for each possible bit combination encodes the number of set bits. In this way, the bits are counted for each chunk of 8 bits of the bitmask. Naturally, larger lookup tables could be used at an increased memory cost in order to loop fewer times over the bitmask. Nevertheless, lookup tables for 32 bits are unfeasible since that requires storage of four billion entries.

Bit Counting in Parallel

There is, however, a method that allows us to compute the number of set bits in a word in logarithmic time, as long as the word matches the size of a machine word. On the GPU, this allows us to count the number of set bits for a 32-bit word in five steps.

The idea is to count bits in parallel inside the word. In the first step, each 2 bits of the bitmask are used to sum those 2 bits and store the result in the same 2 bits. Secondly, every group of 4 bits is summed into the group's own 4 bits. In the third step, every group of 8 bits is summed into the group's 8 bits, and so on.

Even more efficient is to count in only three steps, up to each separate byte, and then use one multiplication to sum all bytes together in the left byte of the 32-bit word.[1] It turns out that this requires equally many instructions (i.e., 12) as using a lookup table for 8 bits, but the advantage is that we do not need the lookup table, which avoids expensive memory reads and potential cache misses.

This results in the following snippet of code [Anderson], which is generally the best way to sum the number of bits in a 32-bit word, if there is not a specific hardware assembler instruction for it:

```
int popcount(uint32 v) {
    // put count of each 2 bits into those 2 bits
    v = v - ((v >> 1) & 0x55555555);
    // put count of each 4 bits into those 4 bits
    v = (v & 0x33333333) + ((v >> 2) & 0x33333333);
    // put count of each 8 bits into those 8 bits
    v = (v + (v >> 4)) & 0x0f0f0f0f;
    // returns left 8 bits of x + (x << 8) + (x << 16) + (x << 24)
    return (v * 0x01010101) >> 24;
}
```

On many CPUs, and also on later GPUs, there is a native population count instruction for counting the number of set bits in a 32- or 64-bit word. This is typically called popc. It is exposed through bitCount() in GLSL and countbits() in HLSL.

In addition, the most optimal way to then sum the series of counts (one count per 32-bit word) is to use a prefix sum on the stream.

---

[1]http://en.wikipedia.org/wiki/Hamming_weight

10.2   Multisample Antialiasing

All image-based representations are susceptible to aliasing artifacts, and it is not just shadow maps (see Chapter 3) but also the final rendered image that falls into this category. Diagonal edges leading to staircasing artifacts are a common example encountered here. An effective means to combat such artifacts is multisample antialiasing (MSAA), which is supported by all current graphics hardware and typically incurs only a minor overhead. It requires the use of an according multisample texture or framebuffer, which maintains multiple so-called *multisamples* per pixel. These directly correspond to sample points placed across the pixel (all pixels use the same sampling pattern). When a triangle is rendered, for each covered pixel, the multisamples overlapped by the triangle are determined. If any of them is overlapped, the fragment shader is executed once (typically at the center of the pixel), and the shader result is assigned to all covered multisamples. This means that pixel coverage is determined at a higher resolution, reducing staircasing artifacts, while the potentially expensive shader execution is only performed once per fragment, like in single-sample rendering. To present a multisample framebuffer to the user, it needs to be resolved, which involves deriving a color value for each pixel from its multisamples.

Using MSAA together with shadow algorithms is trivial if the algorithm runs in the fragment shader as part of a triangle's shading computation, as for instance in shadow mapping. In this case, no change to the shader has to be made. The situation is more challenging when the algorithm works on view samples recorded in a multisample G-buffer (see also Appendix E.1 on deferred shading) and produces some kind of visibility map, where a visibility factor (or some related information) is stored for each pixel. One straightforward solution is to record the result in a multisample texture and run the algorithm for each multisample, which is possible since Direct3D 10.1, by running the fragment shader at sample frequency (exposed in OpenGL via the `GL_ARB_sample_shading` extension). However, this is quite expensive as the shadow algorithm is run multiple times per pixel (e.g., four times in case of 4 × MSAA). While it can be a viable approach if the shader is extremely simple and cheap to execute, it is definitely not reasonable if the shadow calculations are more costly, like when running PCSS or reconstructing and back-projecting occluders.

A large improvement is obtained by restricting the multisample-level shader execution to pixels overlapped by triangle edges [Thibieroz09]. The other pixels, where the multisamples don't differ, are then processed by running the algorithm only once per pixel. However, the runtime overhead compared to a single-sampled setting can still be significant, especially when the number of pixels overlapped by edges is high, like with finely tessellated assets. Determining pixels with screen-space discontinuities in a separate pass (flagging them in the stencil buffer, for instance) and then running the shader only on those pixels at sample frequency can provide some relief in the latter case.

Another problem of such an approach is that using a multisample texture for capturing the result further increases the memory footprint compared to single-sample rendering, as data (like visibility) are not only stored once per pixel but once per multisample. To avoid the overhead of both this extra memory consumption and the multisample-level shader execution, one may opt to derive a representative multisample per pixel and only operate on this multisample. The result can then be output to a single-sample visibility map. To apply it to the multisample G-buffer (as part of the resolve step, for instance), a multisample visibility signal has to be reconstructed from the visibility map [Schwarz08b]. To this end, the best candidate from a small neighborhood in the single-sample visibility map can be chosen. One criterion that often works very well in practice is the light-space depth distance between the candidate multisample from the visibility map and the target multisample from the G-buffer. Furthermore, one might take additional information like normals into account. Overall, compared to single-sample rendering, this approach incurs only a minor overhead owing to deriving the representative and to signal reconstruction; moreover, this overhead is basically independent of scene complexity.

10.3   Voxels and Shadows

With the advances of graphics hardware, alternative representations become increasingly common. Further, it is very uncommon that plain flat triangle scenes are an optimal choice, and other data representations or scene structures can be very useful considerations. Because many of the alternative primitives often involve customized rendering schemes, it is out of the scope of this book to give an exhaustive overview. The particular type that we are going to focus on are voxels because this rendering primitive has recently received much attention in the context of direct illumination.

We will present two types of voxel shadow algorithms. The first will focus on binary-voxel data, which can be constructed efficiently on the fly (Chapter 8.2.2). The second kind of algorithm will directly address scene content that is represented in a voxel format. Future game engines seem to make use of this option [Lefohn08], which is reason enough to address this topic briefly.

10.3.1   On-the-Fly Voxelization

It is possible to create a binary-voxel–based scene representation for each frame at a high frame rate (Section 8.2.2). Even though just binary, this information is sufficient for visibility computations in opaque scenes. In fact, a binary voxelization can be seen as a grid of which each cell indicates the presence of matter with a single bit. Based on such a representation, it is easy to compute shadows. For each view sample, one can shoot rays towards the source. Along each ray, one tests the entries in the voxel grid and if one of them is nonzero, the ray is assumed to be blocked by the geometry. Note that to not miss thin structures, like twigs of a tree, and to not suffer from light bleeding through surfaces due to holes, ideally a conservative scene voxelization should be employed.

This ray-tracing approach gets close to reference shadow quality with increasing voxel resolution. Unfortunately, this precision comes with a double price: the memory cost grows with the number of voxels (a 2048^3 binary grid already represents 1 GB of memory) and the ray-tracing step needs to visit an increasing amount of cells. In practice, for typical game scenes and larger light sources, 512^3 (16 MB) can often be sufficient. Furthermore, recent solutions in sparse voxelization [Schwarz10] can efficiently compress empty space by directly voxelizing into a sparse spatial data structure. This not only saves space but also accelerates ray traversal as empty regions can be skipped efficiently, and, hence, it constitutes a promising outlook for the here-presented solutions.

Hierarchical Voxel Grids

Forest et al. [Forest10] propose to voxelize the scene from the light source and to build a hierarchical representation to accelerate ray tracing (Figure 10.3). The rays are shot towards an area source to efficiently sample the light's visibility. Their idea to accelerate this tracing step is to perform a mipmap-like resolution reduction of the binary voxel data; on lower-resolution versions, a large neighborhood can quickly be tested for the presence of a filled voxel. In each level, a 2×2-voxel-column neighborhood is fused, where a column is actually represented by a pixel because the z-axis is stored in the bits of the pixel's color. While standard mipmapping usually computes an average value, Forest et al. propose to use an OR operation to derive a hierarchical representation. The observation is that if one of the voxel columns contained a scene triangle, let's say in its ith bit, the resulting value for the fused columns at bit i will be one as well. Only if the ith voxel of all columns is empty is the resulting value zero. Therefore, a single bit in a higher level of the hierachical representation allows us to draw conclusions about several vox-

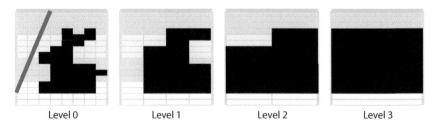

| Level 0 | Level 1 | Level 2 | Level 3 |

Figure 10.3. Neighboring voxel columns are fused with a bitwise OR operation. The resolution along the z-axis is, thus, not reduced.

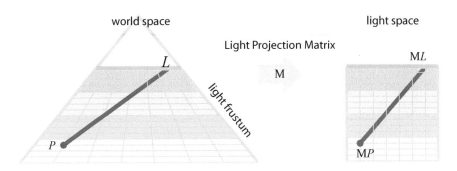

Figure 10.4. Instead of traversing the potentially deformed voxel grid in world space, one can project the segment in light space and consider a uniform grid instead.

els. We will refer to a *node* as the pixel of this hierarchical representation. During ray tracing, these nodes, when empty, can be used to quickly skip large areas.

It should be underlined again that no fusion is performed along the z-direction. The z-axis maintains its full resolution. The compression along the z-axis can be used to gain some memory if needed because less bits would need to be stored. In practice, this reduction is usually omitted because it leads to a higher precision and, therefore, acceleration of the ray-tracing step, as we will see next.

Ray Tracing for Shadow Computations

To compute the shadows in the scene, the algorithm launches several rays per pixel towards the light source from where the voxelization was done. Consequently, the z-axis of the voxelization that is encoded in the form of bits aligns with the light's view frustum. The rays are tested against the hierarchical voxel representation using an adaptation of the intersection test in [Revelles00], as described hereafter.

The idea is to intersect the ray with the voxel frustum to compute a segment that is then tested against the voxelized geometry. While the voxelization from the light is typically done with a perspective projection (leading to a perspectively deformed frustum), it is possible to project the segment into light space (Chapter 2) where one can assume that the voxelization is uniform and the frustum itself is a cube (Figure 10.4).

The intersection test itself is performed recursively, starting with the highest mipmap entry. In each step, the segment is tested against a voxel mipmap entry. Each entry reflects, by construction, an entire voxel column v_c. 2To test whether a segment potentially intersects the scene, the entry and exit points of the segment into the column are computed, in other words, the endpoints of the subsegment that lies entirely in the voxel column. These two points span a certain z-voxel interval in the column; that is, between entry and exit points lies a certain set of voxels $i, \ldots, j$. (See Figure 10.5.) This voxel interval corresponds to a *voxel-segment*

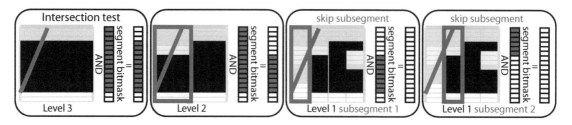

Figure 10.5. The hierarchy was illustrated in Figure 10.3. The segment is first tested against the highest level. If there is a bit overlap, the algorithm descends in the hierarchy. The second descend enforces a cut on the segment. The part closer to the origin is treated first. Here, the bitmask for this second step is zero, implying that there are no intersections. The same holds for the second part of the segment.

bitmask v_s that can be easily computed by $(2^{j+1} - 1) - (2^i - 1)$. In v_s, all bits are zero except those between bit i to j. If one computes v_s AND v_c, where AND is the logical bitwise AND operation, the special mask v_s will extract exactly the bits i through j from v_c. In other words, if $(v_s$ AND $v_c)$ equals zero, one can conclude that no intersection between the segment and the voxelized scene occurred. If $(v_s$ AND $v_c) \neq 0$, the algorithm recursively refines the computation.

To refine computations, the mipmap level is lowered, leading to four new nodes. The segment is then cut at each node boundary, and the new subsegments are tested in a depth-first manner. This means that the algorithm continues with the segment closest to the view sample (from where the ray was shot), and only if this subsegment does not intersect the scene are the remaining ones processed.

Discussion

The 2method achieves high quality when a high voxel resolution is used, but then the intersection test is prohibitively expensive. In practice, not more than 128 bits should be allocated per voxel column to ensure a fast execution at real-time rates. In this case, a column fits conveniently in an RGBA integer value. Unfortunately, especially when approaching objects, the resolution can become insufficient.

Extensions

To increase the details for nearby objects, Nichols et al. [Nichols10] proposed to perform the voxelization from the camera, but, consequently, geometry outside the view frustum will not produce shadows. This can lead to important inconsistencies.

A better solution is to keep a high voxel resolution, but to accelerate computations by relying on upsampling strategies (Appendix E). The shadow computation is only executed for some pixels, where illumination changes occur; thereby, the computation is concentrated on the variations of the shadows that are faithfully captured. In particular, one criteria for this refinement can be a comparison of the visible source samples between two neighboring pixels. This can be done efficiently when storing them in bitmasks (Section 7.4) because, then, finding differences amounts to comparing bits. This operation can be swiftly done using a bitwise XOR followed by a bitcount (Section 10.1). In practice, for 128 light samples, if at least 64 differ, the computation should be refined [Nichols10] and the resolution is locally 2augmented.

10.3.2 Voxel-Based Scene Representations

Voxel representations are often the standard format in medical applications. Data captured with magnetic resonance imaging (MRI) and computed tomography scans (CT) are usually transformed into large voxel grids. These scans lead to significant memory requirements that often exceed the GPU's capacities. In order to address this issue, various out-of-core rendering methods have been proposed to efficiently stream or compress such data.

As even an introduction to this topic delivers enough material to fill an entire book (e.g., [Lichtenbelt98]), we only chose two examples for shadow-computation algorithms presented in recent publications. The first assumes that the entire data fit into GPU memory and deliver high image quality [Itkis06]. The second is based on the principle of ray differentials [Igehy99] and is well suited for out-of-core solutions. By no means do these particular choices provide a complete overview of the topic. Our intention is to propose two practical solutions for the two classes of volume-rendering approaches (in core and out of core). This presentation also serves as an entry point for further reading.

In-Core Methods

Voxel data are often difficult to render because all elements have potentially a certain transparency, which makes it difficult to find a suitable display method, just as for semitransparent objects (Chapter 8). To obtain a valid visualization, we need to accumulate several contributions in each pixel. There are two convenient solutions to composite data correctly. The first option is rasterization based and renders slices of the volume in a back-to-front or front-to-back order. All slice values are appropriately combined via blending operations. This solution was well suited for older graphics cards with less shader programmability. Today's technological advances enable a second option to be executed on the GPU, which is ray tracing. The ray traversal makes it easy to ensure a correct ordering. In this first approach, we will concentrate on the rasterization option.

Rendering. The shadows we want to compute will follow the deep-shadow-map principle (Chapter 8), which means that we assume that light always follows a straight path but is attenuated along the way. For this scenario, an efficient slic-

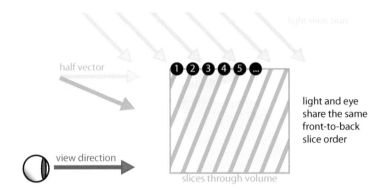

Figure 10.6. Slicing the volume according to the half-vector leads to a sorting of the slices that is valid from the light and the view. So incrementally, one can maintain the attenuated light from the source, apply it to the next slice, and correctly composite the contributions in the view.

ing and compositing method exists that advances along the light and view path in parallel [Itkis06].

The idea is to choose the slices through the voxel data according to the half-vector between the light and view direction (Figure 10.6). The slices are then rendered in a front-to-back order into the light and the view. The main observation is that the choice of the slice orientation ensures that the compositing order of the slices is the same for the light and the view. In other words, rays from the eye or the light towards slice i can only intersect the slices 0 to $i-1$. Hence, the idea is to render in parallel a view from the light (containing the light attenuation) and a view from the observer, rendering the accumulated scene where all shaded slices are composited. The light's view is used to compute the light attenuation (or shadow) onto the next slice that will be added to the observer's view. Precisely, in step i, slice i is shaded with the current light attenuation and then composited in the observer's framebuffer. After this step, the slice i is rendered a second time, now in the light's view. Here, it is composited with the attenuation of slices 0 to $i-1$ to yield the attenuation of slices 0 through i.

Discussion. In a single pass, the illumination and transparency are correctly handled. For translucency effects, one can even slightly blur the buffers to simulate scattering. The quality is high if enough slices are used, but the algorithm needs to perform a ping-pong rendering to correctly blend the contributions, which is costly. For in-core data, it is nevertheless a good tradeoff between performance and quality.

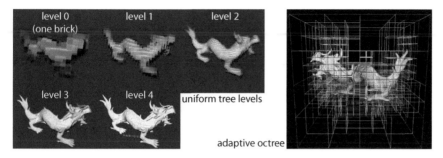

Figure 10.7. Brick hierarchy that allows a local refinement of the data according to the current view.

Out-of-Core Methods

For out-of-core methods, different solutions are more appropriate because the data are usually inhomogeneous, making slicing approaches difficult to use. Typically, such approaches rely on a hierarchically represented data set that is traversed with ray tracing.

Following [Gobbetti08, Crassin09], on each level, the data are represented by blocks of constant resolution (typically 16^3), so-called *bricks*. These bricks are structured in the form of an octree. Each parent node contains a brick that is a downsampled version of the data of its children nodes; in other words, the children's bricks are put together into a larger volume whose resolution is then reduced to yield the brick of the parent. Consequently, nodes in higher levels of the tree correspond to larger extents of the scene. Because their resolution is constant, the approximation is coarser if the extent is larger; for example, the root node contains a brick that represents the entire scene (Figure 10.7).

Based on this representation, it is possible to refine the data representation in certain regions by descending in the tree, while other regions are coarsely represented. Typically, data far away from the viewpoint can be represented at lower resolution and, thus, with bricks that cover a larger scene extent. In practice, bricks are selected such that their voxels roughly project to the size of a pixel. A nice side effect of this choice is that it implicitly performs an antialiasing because subpixel information is not displayed directly, but as a filtered value that is stored in a brick. The fact that this representation gives access to a filtered version of the data will be key in the shadow computation.

Because all bricks share the same resolution and, hence, memory consumption, it is easy to manage them in a data pool. In fact, not all bricks are always on the GPU (they would not fit anyway), but only those needed for the current view. Unused bricks (because their precision does not match the viewpoint) or invisible bricks are replaced by those that are currently needed. Thereby, the memory consumption is kept to a manageable level. To decide which elements are removed, a least-recently-

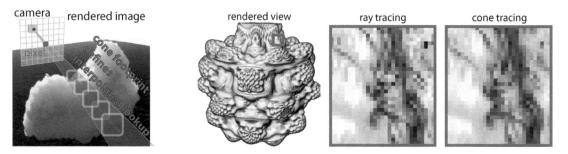

Figure 10.8. Approximate cone tracing for volume data. By adapting the kernel size according to the pixel, one can approximate a cone-tracing process (left) that leads to good antialiasing behavior (right). This solution is also useful for shadow computation, where an approximate cone is traced towards the source.

used cache scheme is often applied. As the view does usually not change much from one frame to the next, these updates are well behaved and only a few elements actually need to be replaced.

Rendering. To render the data structure, ray tracing is used. The ray traverses the octree and, in each node, its corresponding brick; hence, the ray-tracing step can also be seen as a ray marching. Because the projected brick voxels should roughly match the screen pixel size, the ray does not always descend into the leaf nodes. One can further interpolate between nodes of different tree levels if the size of a projected voxel falls between two levels. Thereby, brick voxel sizes effectively appear to be roughly of constant size.

Because elements are potentially transparent, shadow contributions need to be added for each position along the ray from the eye towards the scene. These shadow rays need to be shot towards the light source. For a point light, this corresponds to a single ray, but the fact that the data resolution is reduced with distance means that larger parts of the scene are grouped into a single voxel. Just shooting a ray to derive a shadow value will suffer from significant aliasing. Instead, the goal is to render an *average* shadow for all scene points that fall into a pixel.

In practice, this means that instead of a standard ray marching, a cone-tracing process is applied (Figure 10.8, left). Cone tracing does not consider a ray, but instead an entire bundle of rays, organized in a cone. This principle relates to ray differentials [Igehy99] and leads to much smoother results than standard ray tracing. In fact, the previous approach that kept the projected voxel size to one pixel can already be considered an approximate cone tracing [Crassin09], but it is cheaper than actual cone tracing. Hence, one should rely on the same principle for the shadow computations.

In other words, each position along the ray is associated with the volume of the corresponding voxel size. In order to achieve a better approximation for shadows, when performing a marching towards the light, the lookup size is chosen to roughly reflect the radius of the cone that has its apex on the point light and encompasses the data volume at the current view ray position.

In the same way, one can approximate area light sources by shooting an according cone (Figure 10.8, right). Instead of placing the apex on the source, it is simply shifted behind the source such that the cone contains both the data volume at the current view ray position and the light source. Interestingly, because larger cones imply lower data resolution, a large light source results in a faster computation. This contradicts the typical behavior that one encounters for standard soft-shadow algorithms.

Unfortunately, the larger the cone, the more approximate the result becomes because contributions along the ray are not integrated correctly. First, the filtering is uniform in space (due to the mipmap hierarchy) and not according to the viewpoint, as would be the case for a true cone tracing. Second, the evaluated visibility is only heuristically combined [Crassin10] (following the principle of occlusion textures; see Section 6.6.2) to avoid the high cost of shooting many rays. To illustrate this shortcoming, imagine a wall that has one red and one yellow side; at a certain distance, it is averaged into an orange result, although this is physically never possible.

Discussion. Although very approximate, the soft shadows based on voxelization are very smooth. The property that large sources are less costly is a nice side effect and allows us to quickly compute soft scene illumination without wasting much computational resources.

10.3.3   Summary

Voxels are a versatile data structure that seem to increase in importance. The fact that the representation is very regular makes it easy to employ out-of-core rendering methods. The other interesting observation is that level-of-detail mechanisms seamlessly integrate into such structures and are also suitable for the production of shadows. On the downside, the memory consumption is often very elevated, the alignment of the data might not always be suitable for the represented geometry, and the rendering speed is currently still lower than when using standard primitives. Nonetheless, complex phenomena such as semitransparent surfaces and volumes are gracefully handled, and even participating media can be easily represented with voxels. As such, it seems that voxels are a promising primitive for the future.

10.4   Ray-Casting Shadows

In real-time rendering, the primary approach for synthesizing images is rasterization, and it is the corresponding graphics pipeline that is implemented by graphics hardware (see Appendix A for a primer). Consequently, we concentrated on according techniques throughout the book. However, images and shadows may also be created using the competing approach of ray tracing. Thanks to recent advances, both algorithmically and with respect to leveraging SIMD units of multicore CPU systems as well as to employing increasingly powerful graphics hardware, real-time performance has now become possible, at least for restricted settings. Actually, ray-casting techniques are already successfully utilized in several hybrid systems where one or several rays are cast within a fragment shader to compute secondary effects, like in some of the voxel-based algorithms covered in the previous section. Foremost, however, ray tracing is at the core of many high-quality offline rendering solutions and is increasingly used in production rendering.

For a point light source, shadows are generally computed in ray tracing by casting a shadow ray from a scene point $\mathbf{p}$ towards the light point [Whitted80]. In case any object is hit, occlusion occurs and $\mathbf{p}$ is in shadow; otherwise, it is lit. Note that when testing for intersection with scene geometry, knowing that an intersection occurs suffices; it is not necessary to determine the closest intersection point along the ray, as for shading computations.

Area light sources are typically handled by distributed ray tracing [Cook84]. Pursuing a Monte Carlo integration approach , the light source is stochastically sampled, and a shadow ray is cast towards each sample point. A visibility factor can then be derived from the fraction of occluded sample points. Recall from Section 6.2.4 that such a sampling-based approach is also employed in several soft-shadow algorithms relying on rasterization. These, however, typically choose one or a few fixed sampling patterns for all receiver points, whereas the distributed ray-tracing method can easily adopt a different pattern for each receiver point and flexibly adjust the number of samples according to the solid angle subtended by the light.

Casting many rays towards a light source for each receiver point is expensive, though, especially if a generic ray-casting procedure is employed. Therefore, a few methods have been devised that explicitly target computing soft shadows from area lights, showing that such specialization enables considerable speed-ups. The most prominent algorithm actually takes inspiration from real-time rendering. As discussed in Section 7.3.4, Laine et al. [Laine05c] extended penumbra wedges to soft shadow volumes with depth-complexity sampling, such that all blockers are accounted for and correct occluder fusion is performed. While this offers significant performance increases, even further improvements are possible, as demonstrated by Lehtinen et al. [Lehtinen06].

Another proposed approach is multifrusta tracing [Benthin09], which pays special attention to enabling an efficient implementation on wide SIMD architectures like GPUs, aiming for real-time performance in the long run. Assuming an SIMD width of 16, a set of 16 receiver points are processed in parallel. For each, a pyramidal frustum originating at the receiver point is traced towards the area light. If the frustum intersects a triangle, rays towards different light samples are generated on the fly. These are tested for intersection with the triangle in groups of 16, recording the result in a binary occlusion bitmask.

Apart from such algorithmic and implementation-related improvements, performance can also be increased by resorting to an image-based scene representation, which sacrifices some accuracy, though. We have already encountered several according methods (utilizing multilayered shadow maps) in the context of Section 6.8.

10.5 Environmental Lighting

In this book, we have seen several methods that aim at the computation of shadows for a given light source. With recent advances in computational power, an increasing amount of light sources can and will be added to virtual scenes. Step by step, this trend will lead to the simulation of an entire environment that is integrated accurately in the illumination process. Ultimately, global illumination, where basically each element in the scene is considered a light source, might be simulated with all-frequency information. Until then, we still have a long way to go, but it is interesting to already take a peek at scenarios in which light sources are no longer well-defined entities with limited spatial extent but are, rather, entire hemispheres around a point. Such techniques have received much attention recently because they give the impression of global-illumination-like effects, without introducing the same costs. Several very efficient solutions exist that can enrich the appearance of the final rendering significantly. Even though such solutions are often approximate, they are sufficiently convincing and appealing to also be used in movie productions. Figure 10.9 shows an example for the influence of the different types of illumination on the appearance.

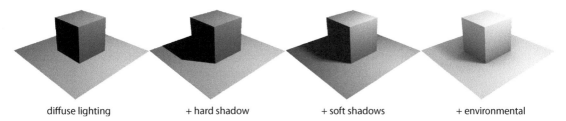

diffuse lighting   + hard shadow   + soft shadows   + environmental

Figure 10.9. Diffuse illumination is the standard way of lighting a scene (left); hard shadows add spatial cues (middle left), but soft shadows make the scene look much more realistic (middle right). Adding environmental illumination further enriches the appearance (right).

Figure 10.10. Convolution soft-shadow maps are relatively efficient to evaluate. This makes them well suited when an environment map is to be approximated by several area lights.

10.5.1   Environment Map Shadows

In principle, environmental illumination can be approximated by assuming an environment map that is a texture surrounding the scene and that encodes the incoming illumination from all directions. This environment map can then be decomposed into a set of distant area light sources or point light sources. This follows the same principle that allowed us to decompose an area light into smaller sources (as discussed in Section 1.3). Initially, we simply suggested decomposing the light into a set of uniformly spaced source samples, but several more efficient strategies have been developed (such as importance sampling [Hammersley64]). The idea is that it does not make sense to place sources at locations where there is not enough energy to actually contribute to the image. A simple example is an environment map with a single bright spot somewhere while the rest of it is black. Any source placed on the dark part will not emit any light.

For importance sampling, the distribution of points is chosen according to the energy that is emitted. When now attributing the same radiance to each source, such that the sum of all these values corresponds to the integral over the environment map, the resulting image lit by the point lights will deliver a good approximation of the lighting via the environment map. The multitude of the sources will balance out the fact that the incoming radiance is now a constant.

More advanced sampling methods exist, but such approaches are outside the scope of this book.

Instead of point approximations, it is also possible to rely on a decomposition into area light sources [Annen08a] (see Figure 10.10). This approximation is not limited to any particular soft-shadow algorithm and could be used in conjunction with any existing method. Nonetheless, it is not clear that such a decomposition is always of advantage with respect to a point-based solution. The outcome depends heavily on the content of the environment map.

10.5.2   Ambient Occlusion

A simpler scenario is ambient occlusion (AO). A survey of related techniques can be found in [Méndez-Feliu09]. It is an illumination method based on the assumption that light is locally impinging uniformly from all directions of the hemisphere onto each point of the scene. AO can also be seen as an accessibility value [Miller94]: the less a scene point is exposed to the environment, the darker it appears. In other words, AO can also be seen as a refinement of the often-employed ambient term (Appendix C), which is a simple constant to coarsely approximate reflected light in a scene.

In theory, the implementation of an AO algorithm is simple:

```
// Simple AO Algorithm
for each view sample (p)
  ambientOcclusion = 0
  for(i = 0; i < nbSamples; ++i)
    dir = choseARandomDirectionInHemisphere(p)
    if(intersectsScene(ray(p, dir)))
      ambientOcclusion += 1/nbSamples
```

The motivation behind this approach is that in many situations, light is not restricted to a single point or area light source, but instead, it comes from the environment, such as the light from the sky. In other words, this illumination comes from "everywhere" but is blocked by geometry. Basically, you can imagine an environmental illumination with an environment map of constant color. One difference is that distant geometry is usually assumed to have less blocking contribution, which often allows us to concentrate on occlusions near the impact point.[2] The latter observation is used to restrict the intersection test to a limited volume around each point by employing a falloff function, which can be exploited to obtain a significant performance improvement. Furthermore, indoor scenes would otherwise appear entirely black because any ray would intersect the geometry at some point. The falloff function is usually a smooth-step function[3] or an exponential falloff to avoid artifacts due to abrupt occlusion changes. An exponential function is usually a good choice. The pseudocode only needs to be changed insignificantly:

```
    if(dist = intersectsScene(ray(p, dir)))
      ambientOcclusion += 1/nbSamples * falloff(dist)
```

This technique might sound like a crude approximation, but it leads to convincing and especially smooth shading that resembles indirect illumination. Furthermore, AO can be precomputed and stored in textures, which is often done for static elements in games as well as movie productions. When evaluated at runtime, it can even provide shadow-like effects on nearby elements of the scene.

---

[2]The definition of ambient occlusion can vary and sometimes include the cosine of the angle between the incoming light, changing the contribution in the pseudocode to $1/nbSamples \mathbf{n_p} \cdot dir$. This change does not does not affect the discussion in this chapter.

[3]The smooth-step function is available in GPU shaders. A possible definition that smoothly varies between zero and one in the interval [edge0, edge1] can be computed by setting x := max(0, min(((x - edge0)/(edge1 - edge0),1))) and evaluating x*x*(3-2*x).

"Attached" Ambient Occlusion

One way to efficiently apply ambient occlusion in real-time applications is to "attach" an ambient-occlusion volume to objects. These volumes are used to trigger the occlusion effect of the object itself on the nearby surrounding.

One way to attach AO to an object is to precompute the ambient occlusion and encode it in a cube map placed at the object's center [Kontkanen05]. Each texel entry stores occlusion information in the form of three coefficients a, b, c of a quadratic rational function $AO(d) := 1/(ad^2 + bd + c)$, where d is the distance. The coefficients of these functions are matched in a preprocess to best represent the also precomputed and sampled AO function. To calculate the impact of the object onto a point $\mathbf{p}$ in the scene, a lookup retrieves the pixel that corresponds to $\mathbf{p}$'s projection into the cube map. The corresponding occlusion function is fetched and evaluated using the distance of $\mathbf{p}$. They further combine several occluders based on a uniform repartition heuristic, similar to the solution described in Section 6.6.2.

A faster and simpler way to store and retrieve AO is to directly rely on a three-dimensional texture surrounding the object [Malmer07]. Each view sample only needs to fetch the AO value depending on its relative position to the object center from the texture. Inherently, this method needs to assume a finite support, meaning that AO values need to be clamped and outside of a fixed radius (the limit of the three-dimensional texture); no shading is influenced anymore. As indicated before, this is a common assumption for AO and one can directly store the AO result (including the falloff function) in the three-dimensional texture. Figure 10.11 shows results achieved with this approach. The shadows are generally very blurry, which gives the images a nice feel but can also hide high-frequency influences. This is particularly visible on the object itself where the computation of blocked light is not always very successfully handled.

As these two first approaches are based on precomputation, it is not possible to deform objects in realtime. Nonetheless, each object can be moved dynamically, and it can cast shadows on other surrounding scene elements. Because the evaluation is basically a simple texture fetch, several hundreds of objects can be evaluated.

A more precise solution, called ambient occlusion volumes, for deforming dynamic scenes was presented recently by McGuire [McGuire10a]. The idea is to construct a volume on a per-triangle/polygon basis. These volumes are chosen such that all points in space that are potentially affected by the current triangle are included. Consequently, it is enough to test each view sample against the occlusion volume and if it is contained, the AO contribution of the triangle is attributed to the view sample.

In practice, the approach first starts off with deferred shading from the viewpoint. In each pixel, one stores the corresponding view-sample position, depth, and normal. The second pass then renders the triangles' occlusion volumes (constructed in the geometry shader). These volumes are rendered into the deferred

Figure 10.11. Ambient occlusion often looks very convincing and is even used in the industry for feature-film productions. It delivers smooth and visually pleasing shadows.

image and tested against the depth buffer, but without actually modifying it. Then, for each rasterized pixel, the fragment shader retrieves the covered view sample and tests whether it is located in the occlusion volume. If so, the shader computes the area obstructed by the occlusion volume's triangle on the hemisphere around the view sample. This step also employs the AO falloff function to this value. The blocking contribution of all triangles are accumulated via blending operations.

The use of blending implies that the final AO value corresponds to an additive fusion of all blocker contributions. This usually leads to a significant overestimation. In order to remedy these artifacts, McGuire proposes a heuristic to remap these values. This remapping function was derived by comparing several of the overestimated results against reference solutions. Roughly, it follows

$$\text{remap}(o) = \begin{cases} 0.8o, & \text{if } o \leq 0.5, \\ 0.4 + 0.5(o - 0.5) = 0.15 + 0.5o, & \text{if } o > 0.5. \end{cases} \quad (10.1)$$

Although this solution is purely heuristic, it delivers surprisingly good results.

While the first two presented solutions are fast, the third is a bit slower but of higher accuracy. All are temporally coherent and no high-frequency artifacts appear in the images. Unfortunately, even when used in a larger neighborhood, AO cannot replace shadows. Further, incoherences can show, and the shading might appear unrealistic.

Screen-Space Ambient Occlusion

Cheaper, more local approaches can avoid any preprocessing or specialized geometry treatment at all. One such example is screen-space ambient occlusion (SSAO), which deserves special attention as it is substantially used in games. The first appearance was in 2007 in Crysis by Crytek, described in more detail in [Akenine-Möller08]. Recently, similar solutions have been added as a default option in mod-

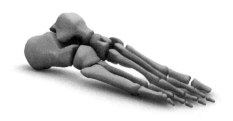

Figure 10.12. Screen-space ambient occlusion is a relatively cheap procedure that estimates the incoming light at each pixel. From the point of view, the algorithm extracts a depth map, which is an approximation of the surfaces in the form of a height field. The ambient-occlusion value is derived by investigating a neighborhood in this depth map. (Images were produced with [Bavoil08c] (left)) and [Huang11](right).)

ern graphics drivers. Figure 10.12 shows two results obtained with SSAO. Due to the many variants of this approach, we refer the interested reader to, for example, [Bunnell06, Hoberock07] and only concentrate on a few practical examples.

An early version was presented in [Shanmugam07]. The idea is to approximate ambient occlusion solely based on a depth map shot from the current point of view. For each view sample **p**, the surrounding pixels are transformed into spheres (meaning their center is defined by the view frustum, their radius via their projected size on the screen). These spheres are, one by one, projected on the hemisphere around **p**. The size of their projection defines their blocking contribution. These contributions are added up to define the final occlusion value for **p**. As before, the influence of distant spheres is not taken into account and only a local neighborhood is examined. Precisely, a local *ambient-occlusion sphere* (AOS) is defined around the view sample, and only spheres whose radius indicates an intersection with this sphere are taken into account. The approach can be refined by extracting a second layer from the viewpoint, but this choice is optional. Further, an extension is presented to deal with more distant scene elements. This computation is less interesting in our context, as more efficient solutions will be presented in the following. We refer the interested reader to the paper.

Interestingly, even simpler solutions based on an AOS can lead to convincing results (illustrations can be found in Figure 10.13). For every view sample, the occlusion is again estimated by sampling a pixel neighborhood, but the evaluation follows the principle of percentage-closer filtering (Chapter 5). The depth of the surrounding pixels inside the AOS is compared to the depth of the current view sample. Unfortunately, such a simple solution also shares typical PCF problems, such as biasing. A solution employed by Crytek's SSAO [Akenine-Möller08] is to sample uniform locations in the interior of the AOS and to compare these samples against the surface. If they fall locally below, they are counted as blocking, otherwise, as unblocked (as the depth map is created from the viewpoint, "below" refers to a distance that is farther from the camera than the view-sample distance).

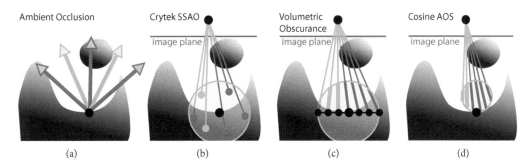

Figure 10.13. (a) Standard ambient occlusion (AO) relies on ray shooting, (b) Screen-space AO samples random points in an ambient-occlusion sphere (AOS) and compares these against the depth buffer, (c) to reduce noise, instead of a testing isolated points, one can derive unoccluded segments of rays through the pixels that lie in the AOS , (d) the AOS can also be modified to mimick a cosine falloff.

An even-better approximation can be achieved when considering volumetric obscurance [Loos10]. The idea is to estimate the empty space inside the AOS using line integrals. To employ this approximation, one recovers all the depth-map pixels that potentially lie inside the AOS. For each such sample **q**, one computes the line connecting it to the viewpoint. Then one computes the length of the line segment lying inside the AOS. The sum of all these lengths is an approximation of the free space in the AOS. This value can then be used to shade the sample. To some extent, one can see the use of these segment lengths as weights that determine the impact of each depth sample in the neighborhood of **q**. If a normal is incorporated, one can also use a hemisphere instead of the AOS. Because such an evaluation is more continuous, the result appears smoother, while having similar to less cost than SSAO.

In a similar approach, Szirmay-Kalos et al. [Szirmay-Kalos10] also proposed a modification to SSAO. The paper presents a very thorough analysis of AO computations and, further, provides one very distinct extension. When assuming not only that AO takes visibility into account but also that the contribution for each direction is actually weighted by a cosine, as would be the case if we would consider environmental illumination, the authors point out that this scaled influence can be mimicked by an AOS of radius R that corresponds to half the radius of the original AOS and centered at a distance R from the view sample in the direction of the normal (Figure 10.13). All previous solutions can be modified in this way to better represent the directional character of an environmental lighting.

In the same spirit, we should mention a last, slightly more costly, solution that uses an alternative to an AOS by relying on an occlusion cone. This cone is defined as the largest cone that does not intersect nearby depth samples, with the constraints that the apex lies on the view sample and its opening is in the direction of the normal. These cones are computed by shooting rays in all two-dimensional directions of the depth map. Along each ray, the steepest angle is measured. Hence, combining the result of all directions defines the cone opening. The larger the cone, the brighter the shading [Bavoil08c]. This estimation was already successfully used in the context of height-field illumination [Oat07]. It looks very convincing and leads to a smoothly varying AO estimate.

Extensions. To some extent, AO is related to global illumination. Simply, one assumes that light arrives from all directions. A small modification to the standard ambient occlusion allows us to approach this effect even further. In fact, instead of just storing an obscurance, one can sample with each AO ray a texel from an environment map. This results in colored shadows that further increase realism [Ritschel09, Landis02]. It is beneficial to choose the rays to shoot wisely, based on the environment map (i.e., one can rely on the aforementioned importance sampling to select appropriate ray directions). With respect to the above pseudocode, such a change can be easily incorporated as

```
if(intersectsScene(ray(p, dir)))
  ambientOcclusion += lookupRadiance(EnvMap, dir)
```

One drawback of screen-space ambient occlusion is that abrupt changes in the depth map can result in artifacts during animation. Especially, missing occluder information can lead to inconsistencies because, basically, only the first visible surfaces intervene. With this in mind, [Reinbothe09] applied a GPU voxelization technique [Eisemann06a] (see Chapter 8) to obtain a more faithful *hybrid ambient occlusion* that also considers hidden surfaces.

Improvements. For all AO applications, one general property holds: for high quality, many evaluations (samples) are necessary. In practice, varying sets of rays can be used per pixel and an edge-aware filtering can fuse the result of neighboring pixels in order to produce a smoother outcome (Appendix E). With such a method, as little as six samples or less can be sufficient.

Furthermore, instead of directly evaluating the pixels in the depth buffer, one can rely on hierarchical representations that group several depth samples depending on their distance from the considered view sample. In practice, this can be realized by computing a mipmap or Gaussian pyramid from the depth buffer.

One interesting observation is that SSAO shares many similarities with PCF evaluation (Chapter 5). Principles such as variance shadow maps [Lauritzen07] can be directly applied to AO [Loos10]. Even a separable approximation can be applied that filters first along a single axis and then blurs the result again in an orthogonal direction [Huang11], whereby the number of samples to evaluate is reduced drastically. Such choices can lead to an important acceleration.

Bent Normals for Cheap Ambient Occlusion

At the other end of the spectrum, the cheapest solution to fake AO is to rely on bent normals [Landis02]. The rough idea is to precompute the direction in which a point is most accessible (i.e., most rays that deviate only slightly from this main direction will be unblocked). The normal is then reoriented in precisely this direction. Thereby, even when lit with a standard illumination pipeline, the model with the so-transformed normals will appear as if some light blocking was actually taken into account. The algorithm to produce such normals is relatively straightforward and builds upon the standard AO code on page 287. Instead of summing up ambient occlusion, one sums up directions and normalizes the result to unit length to define the bent normal.

The approach is most effective for static objects, but even for animated models it can be convincing. Because the technique comes basically for free, it is always a useful addition to the rendering.

10.5.3 Summary

Image-based techniques have been shown to be particularly efficient and lead to a good overall quality compared to the cost. Furthermore, the implementation of such methods is particularly simple. Nonetheless, such solutions can result in some artifacts due to the ambiguous depth-map interpretations and view dependence. Consequently, occlusions might be missed and some temporal incoherence can occur.

While no far-field occlusions are considered, visually pleasing influences of nearby objects on their surrounding are captured, thereby mimicking almost shadow-like effects. Nevertheless, this effect should be seen as a quality-improving supplement, not as a replacement for soft-shadow computations. The missing directionality, globality, and its screen-space nature do not provide the same visual cues that shadows do (see Figure 10.14). As an additional effect, though, it is extremely useful and should be integrated to enhance scene details.

Ambient Occlusion   AO + HS   Hard Shadows

Figure 10.14. Ambient occlusion is a great way to complement direct illumination and shadows. For height fields the computation time for ambient occlusion is much faster than for general geometry.

10.6   Precomputed Radiance Transfer

While we have concentrated on shadows cast by point lights or area lights of rather small extent in the majority of the book, the last section turned to scenarios where light is impinging on a scene point from basically all directions and not just from one small light source or a few of these. Although ambient-occlusion methods are quite effective in providing visually satisfying results, they suffer from several limitations, not least due to the simplifying assumptions made. The fast screen-space methods, for instance, merely account for nearby occluders and are also only able to consider a quite small set of directions to remain real time, easily missing some occluders.

A different approach is taken by *precomputed radiance transfer* (PRT) techniques. Basically, they precompute a solution of the rendering equation (see Equation (1.2) in Section 1.1.2):

$$L_o(\mathbf{p}, \omega) = L_e(\mathbf{p}, \omega) + \int_{\Omega_+} f_r(\mathbf{p}, \omega, \hat{\omega}) \, L_i(\mathbf{p}, \hat{\omega}) \, \cos(\mathbf{n_p}, \hat{\omega}) \, d\hat{\omega},$$

or a simplified version of it. This is done in such a way that one or more components of it, like the material (i.e., the BRDF f_r) or the lighting, can be exchanged quickly and cheaply at runtime. To this end, (groups of) factors of the integrand, each constituting a (hemi)spherical function, are projected into adequate functional bases. That is, each factor is expressed as a weighted sum of basis functions. Since the number of basis functions can be extremely high, typically only the weights (also called basis coefficients) for a small set of basis functions that contribute most are retained, introducing some approximation error.[4] If the bases have been chosen carefully, then the integral can be computed efficiently from the retained coefficients for the factors. For instance, decomposing the integrand into two factors and selecting the same orthonormal basis for both of them reduces the integral to a simple dot product of the two factors' coefficient vectors.

There exist a plethora of PRT algorithms, and hence, a wide variety of bases and integrand decompositions have been investigated. Depending on the targeted applications, they also differ in whether they support the complete light transport according to the rendering equation, thus taking interreflections into account, or only a subset of it, like direct lighting. Moreover, while some of the integrand components, like an incident light from an environmental map, are shared by all considered scene points, others depend on the concrete scene point $\mathbf{p}$ and involve expensive precomputations. Not only may these easily take several hours, but the dependence on $\mathbf{p}$ also results in enormous amounts of coefficients, necessitating (lossy) compression schemes. As a consequence, usually several entities of the setup are considered static, as changing them would require expensive and long

---

[4]We already encountered such a truncation in the context of convolution shadow maps (Section 5.3.4) and Fourier opacity maps (Section 8.2.3).

recomputations. For instance, for cinematic relighting, both the view and the geometry are fixed. However, considerable work has been done to relax such restrictions. Unfortunately, a detailed treatment is beyond the scope of this book, and the reader is referred to Ramamoorthi's survey [Ramamoorthi09] for a broader overview.

In the following, we exemplarily focus on two dedicated approaches that primarily target shadows and that don't restrict the scene to be static. Both of them consider only the direct transport (see Equation (6.1)):

$$L_o(\mathbf{p}, \omega) = \int_{\Omega_+} f_r(\mathbf{p}, \omega, \hat{\omega}) \, L_i(\mathbf{p}, \hat{\omega}) \, \cos(\mathbf{n_p}, \hat{\omega}) \, V(\mathbf{p}, \hat{\omega}) d\hat{\omega},$$

where the incoming radiance $L_i(\mathbf{p}, \hat{\omega})$ stems from a light environment whose visibility is given by $V(\mathbf{p}, \hat{\omega})$. For real-time performance, both algorithms resort to the *spherical harmonics* (SH) basis to encode the integrand's factors. Basically, constituting the analogue to the Fourier series on the sphere, spherical harmonics are well suited to represent low-frequency signals, like a smoothly changing environment map. For these, a small number of coefficients suffices, where rarely more than 25 (corresponding to fifth-order SH) are employed in practice. However, that does not hold for high-frequency signals, including environment maps with a strong, spatially confined light or for visibility with its binary nature. These get significantly smoothed, essentially removing their higher-frequency content, if they are approximated by a low number of SH basis functions. Using considerably more basis functions is not an economical solution, though, because the SH basis functions have global support. Instead, other bases whose basis functions' spatial influence is more localized, like wavelets, are a better option. Nevertheless, supporting all-frequency signals incurs a noticeable overhead compared to considering only low-frequency content.

10.6.1   Precomputed Shadow Fields

Targeting scenes consisting of an environmental light, local light sources, and objects, where these light sources and objects are predetermined but can be arranged dynamically, Zhou et al. [Zhou05] precompute the influence of each light source and each object in the surrounding empty space. To this end, sample points on 16 concentric spherical shells are considered, placing 1,536 points on each shell. For a light source, a source radiance field (SRF) is computed, recording at each sample point the SH representation of the light incident from the light source. Using 16 SH coefficients per sample point and storing RGB values, an SRF requires $16 \times 1{,}536 \times 16 \times 3 = 1{,}152$ KB of memory. Similarly, an object occlusion field (OOF) is precomputed for each object, determining at each sample point the occlusion caused by the object. At runtime, computing the radiance L_o then only involves combining the SH representation of the environmental light, the SRFs, and the OOFs according to the actual scene configuration, which still requires quite some computational effort, though. Note that if a receiver point is outside the outmost spherical shell of an object whose radius is typically chosen as eight times the radius of the object's bounding sphere, the occlusion potentially caused by that object is ignored.

For higher performance, several optimizations have been presented [Tamura06], like adapting the sampling density. Furthermore, an extension exists that also accounts for light interreflections [Pan07].

10.6.2 Spherical Blocker Approximation

A different approach that mainly focuses on supporting articulated characters is pursued by Ren et al. [Ren06]. In a preprocess, a hierarchical sphere set approximation is constructed for each scene object. During runtime, visibility is then determined by accumulating the occlusion due to the spheres. Since each sphere subtends a circular solid angle, a corresponding generic pretabulated SH projection can easily be utilized. By multiplying the resulting visibility functions for the single spheres (or adding them in log space), correct occluder fusion is performed, even though the low-frequency nature of the SH representation prevents accurate results.[5] The method was later improved upon and extended to incorporate indirect lighting [Sloan07].

While the sphere approximation and the choice of the SH basis enable real-time performance, they also cause unrealistic and missing shadows in locations where rather higher frequencies occur (e.g., where a box touches the ground). In particular, contact shadows are often wrongly shaped and partially lose their contact, which is suboptimal since they constitute visually important features [Thompson98]. Inaccuracies like this would become especially noticeable if the environmental light featured a small region of high radiance, like the sun.

By contrast, such key lights are explicitly supported by Snyder and Nowrouzezahrai [Snyder08], who consider the special case of dynamic height fields. They approximate the horizon blocking the environmental light by visibility wedges and utilize pretabulated SH projections for them to determine the overall visibility. In a follow-up [Nowrouzezahrai09], this solution was accelerated and extended to indirect illumination.

---

[5]For any given direction ω, the resulting function V yields the product of the input functions V_i evaluated at ω. Consequently, if any $V_i(\omega) = 0$, indicating that the light is blocked in this direction by at least one occluder, the composite response $V(\omega)$ will be zero. Otherwise, meaning that no blocker occludes the incident direction ω (i.e., all $V_i(\omega) = 1$), $V(\omega)$ will return one. In practice, however, the projection to the SH basis causes the input functions V_i to take values close to but other than zero and one, resulting in a smoothed, nonbinary overall response.

CHAPTER 11

Conclusion

In practice, it is very frequent that people jump directly to conclusions. So if you did, you might as well continue reading because in this case, your choice of starting with the conclusion first indicates what you are after: solutions to a particular problem, not necessarily an exhaustive overview.

This book provides a sufficient amount of details to understand and implement the major techniques. We described many techniques in order to give a good overview of the state-of-the-art solutions. But why did we present so many methods? Why not just the best solution? In fact, some readers might even feel a little overwhelmed by the variety of possibilities. The simple reason is that there is no ultimate shadow algorithm at the current moment in time. We have many solutions that all address certain situations and needs. Further, it can make perfect sense to combine several methods to yield a system that provides an even better behavior. We saw such a situation in Chapters 3 and 4 where reparametrization of shadow maps and partitioning lead to a better overall behavior. We feel it is therefore of large benefit to have a good overview to find the most adequate solution for a particular situation.

In the following, we will investigate several application scenarios and point out which algorithms might be of high interest to you.

11.1   Hard Shadows

Algorithms for hard shadows are very interesting for real-time purposes and aim at the simulation of point light sources. The shadows look sharp, which might result in an artificial appearance. But it is easier to avoid artifacts than in the other shadow categories, making them still very interesting in the context of high-quality imagery.

11.1.1   Accurate

If accurate hard shadows are needed, geometry cannot be ignored and needs to be considered. Usually, this implies that culling should be applied to only consider casters that are necessary and, if used, shadow volumes should be clamped if possible. There is some work in this direction [Lloyd04], but it does not eliminate the problem of the actual shadow computation. Shadow volumes [Crow77] (Section 2.3) are a standard option to compute high-quality shadows. The overdraw and geometry processing can be prohibitive, but it has found practical application in the industry [Stich07].

Alternatively and more efficiently, accurate shadows can be computed with irregular z-buffer [Johnson05] strategies. Related CPU [Aila04b] and GPU [Sintorn08b] implementations exists; the CPU solutions have more hierarchical adaptation, whereas the GPU solutions are currently clearly faster. The downside is that omnidirectional lights require renderings in several directions, and the algorithms also become costly if the shadow map has to cover a large scene. Adaptations in the direction of light-space perspective shadow maps can improve the result significantly. Currently, it seems to be one of the more promising directions to go.

11.1.2   Approximately Accurate

When lowering the quality to only approximately accurate hard shadows, very efficient solutions move within reach. Adaptive subdivision approaches (Section 4.4.2) are most promising. These methods make a good guess for a partitioning of the shadow map in order to achieve a close-to-accurate result. One prominent example [Lefohn07] runs entirely on the GPU. But currently, it seems that putting some workload on the CPU slightly accelerates the process [Giegl07a]. Depending on the workload of the application, one might favor one or the other.

11.1.3   Approximate

When entering the realm of approximate hard shadows, the most important aspect is performance. The cheapest solutions are based on shadow-map parametrizations. Light perspective shadow maps [Wimmer04] (Section 4.2.1) are a very good option. They basically come at almost no cost because the only GPU-side change is to switch the original light matrix to a modified one. This makes it particularly appealing for games.

Only slightly more expensive, but significantly more general, are z-partitioning approaches [Engel06, Zhang06a], where the view frustum is decomposed into several distances, mimicking the optimal, logarithmic behavior. These techniques are a good compromise between quality and cost and are probably the most practical and most widely used hard-shadow algorithm today. They deliver even better quality when combined with the aforementioned parametrization techniques, and they can be greatly improved by analyzing the distribution of samples in the view frustum [Lauritzen11], although this already requires carrying out most of the work needed for the higher-quality adaptive subdivision methods.

If computation time remains to treat geometry, silhouette shadow maps [Sen03] are a valuable addition to hide some more of the pixel artifacts.

11.2   Filtered Hard Shadows

An improved shadow appearance can be achieved when considering a depth map as a discretized signal that one tries to reconstruct. In practice, a certain amount of blur is added to the shadow boundary that removes the artificial hard-shadow look. Currently, most real-time applications rely on shadows of this kind. In the case of small, smooth shadow boundaries, the good tradeoff between cost and visual quality makes filtered shadows a good option for convincing yet cheap solutions. Many methods aim at speeding up the computation of standard percentage-closer filtering [Reeves87] (Section 5.1.3), and the main differences are related to the memory budget.

If memory is an issue, the best approach is probably still a well-adapted implementation of variance shadow maps [Donnelly06] (Section 5.3.2). Light leaks may appear, which can be combatted through exponential shadow maps [Salvi08, Annen08b] or exponential warping [Lauritzen08] (Section 5.3.5).

The other advantage is that filtered shadows address aliasing due to foreshortening. This is a very good property that creates nice-looking shadows. In spite of the soft look of filtered shadows, the result is not to be confused with a physically correct soft-shadow solution, as the penumbra width does not change. But in some scenarios (e.g., in a game context), a designer is often able to tweak the scene in order to make these approaches look sufficient.

11.3   Soft Shadows

The highest physical plausibility is achieved by soft-shadow methods. These can be used to create convincing shadows, but are also of interest when actual physical simulations are a must, such as for the previsualization applied in the context of architectural design.

11.3.1   Accurate

Currently, the most efficient algorithm for animated scenes with reasonable light sources are view-sample mapping [Sintorn08b] solutions (Section 7.4). Depth-complexity sampling [Forest08], which belongs to the class of accurate soft shadow volume approaches (Section 7.3.4), is generally slower and would only become interesting for larger sources, for which view-sample mapping is costly. Unfortunately, for such a scenario, it is very important to consider generalized silhouette edges, not only those from the light's center. This increased workload results in a much higher computation cost and reduces the overall performance of soft-shadow volumes drastically. The principle does help though with more advanced data structures to perform more efficient ray tracing [Laine05c]. But currently, these optimizations head towards an offline scenario, and dynamic scene changes are problematic. For highest accuracy, beam tracing [Overbeck07] can be employed, but it is sensitive to complicated primitives. The topic of accurate soft shadows will occupy us for some time to come.

11.3.2   Approximate

This category of shadows is currently the most interesting for real-time applications. Relatively high quality can be achieved while keeping the computational overhead at levels that allow for reasonably high frame rates.

Methods based on adaptively blurring hard-shadow test results (Section 6.5) deliver satisfying soft shadows for smaller light sources and are rather easy to implement. Approaches from the PCSS family are especially widely used in interactive applications, such as games. For scenes of smaller extent, occlusion textures (Section 6.6.2) constitute another practical option, especially if the light source is relatively large. More accurate results can be obtained with soft-shadow-mapping algorithms (Section 6.7); even correct occluder fusion and using multiple shadow maps to capture more occluders are possible. However, each move towards higher quality typically comes along with a drop in performance, and speed-increasing adaptations (like subsampling or resorting to coarser occluder approximations) require care to not compromise quality so much that it drops below that of simpler methods.

As all these approaches are image based, they may suffer from aliasing artifacts. These are avoided by geometry-based methods, which are more costly, though. Moreover, all approximate algorithms like penumbra wedges (Section 7.3.2) suffer from incorrect occluder fusion, which is typically more pronounced than in image-based methods.

11.4   Advanced Methods

We have further analyzed advanced topics, including semitransparent shadow casters in Chapter 8. Stochastic methods are most promising in this context, as they are simple to implement and perform well in practice [Enderton10]. For volumetric shadow effects that result in God rays, the current state of the art [Chen11] combines high efficiency and quality.

11.4.1   Further Topics

Finally, we discussed various extensions beyond standard shadow computation in triangle-based scenes in Chapter 10. We analyzed voxel-based solutions, potential future solutions based on ray tracing, as well as more general lighting in the form of environmental light. In particular, PRT and very game-relevant screen-space ambient-occlusion computations are useful tools in any modern rendering engine.

11.5   Welcome Tomorrow

As always, when giving advice, it is based on the current conditions. At the moment, we rely on programmable graphics hardware following the rasterization pipeline. Hardware modifications can thus void our previous suggestions. For example, *Doom 3* was a game that relied on shadow volumes [Crow77], a technique that was previously considered too expensive because it does not scale well with geometry. But the new hardware made it possible to significantly reduce the polygon count by relying on new shading capabilities to simulate geometric detail via normal mapping. The resulting geometric simplification made shadow volumes again feasible. Today, shadow-map–based approaches are the first choice, and it is likely that this will stay true in the near future.

Nevertheless, we have reached a point in computer graphics where tremendous hardware changes might occur soon. More generalized computation units (regrouping several processors) or combinations of processors and graphics cards, similar to AMD's Fusion, are about to hit the market. Hardware like this might open up the road to ray tracing in the long run, and we discussed some first-adapted methods (Section 10.4). More close-to-hardware solutions are likely to appear soon. For the next years though, we believe that the above suggestions (mostly based on today's GPUs) will remain valid and of great help to guide you on your quest to find the most appropriate shadow technique. Furthermore, even if the hardware changes, many aspects of shadow algorithms are kept. Today, even in production, the use of shadow maps is extremely common, despite the fact that large clusters otherwise employ ray tracing or Reyes engines.

We hope you enjoyed this book, and we invite you to visit our webpage in the future: http://www.realtimeshadows.com/. Here, we will continue to provide you with more information on recent topics and future trends. The development will continue because as you know by now, no algorithm is perfect. Each one has advantages, as well as weaknesses. This situation can be very confusing, and we hope this book shed enough light on this topic to be of help.

"The true work of art is but a shadow of the divine perfection."

Michelangelo (*1475 -1564*)

Down the Graphics Pipeline

This chapter will give a short overview of the functioning of a graphics card and the associated so-called *graphics pipeline*.

We will not present the details of the classical graphics pipeline, which can be found in [Shreiner09]. Further, our presentation here is slightly simplified with respect to the reality, but it will make it easier to understand the way GPUs work and their properties, which are of interest throughout this book. Anyone familiar with graphics hardware is invited to skip this chapter.

For a much more complete and thorough overview of the development of DirectX and the corresponding hardware, we suggest taking a look at NVIDIA's Programming Guides that provide much information on different shader models.

A.1 Rendering

There are two fundamental algorithms for image synthesis: ray tracing and rasterization.

Shader Model/DX

Shader Models describe the minimum specifications of a graphics card. DirectX (DX) is a Microsoft library (or API) that gives access to hardware functionality, just like OpenGL. Often, Shader Model and DX are used interchangeably. Basically, DX11 gives access to Shader Model 5.0 extensions. We will follow this trend and talk, for instance, about DX10 when we mean the extensions that are described in Shader Model 4.0. Nevertheless, extensions remain accessible through OpenGL as well.

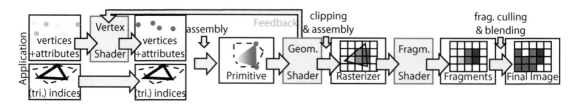

Figure A.1. Graphics pipeline. The application sends vertices and their attributes such as colors, texture coordinates, and other per-vertex parameters. The vertex shader modifies each single vertex. The modified vertices are combined to yield a primitive that is then altered in the geometry shader. Finally, the primitive is rasterized and the fragment shader works on each resulting fragment.

Ray tracing shoots one ray from the eye through each pixel and finds the first intersection with the scene. This impact point then defines the color of the pixel. This process is usually done using a local illumination model (Appendix C). For more complex illumination models, it is also possible to recursively cast rays to yield approximations of indirect illumination and effects such as refraction (i.e., view deformations through glass).

Rasterization is at the basis of the graphics hardware pipeline. The algorithm loops over all primitives (triangles, lines, points, . . .). The vertices of all triangles are first projected onto the screen. Using projective geometry, this can be achieved by a matrix multiplication (compare Chapter 2). The second step builds the projected primitives from the projected vertices. A rasterization unit then finds all those pixels whose center falls inside the projected primitive and invokes the so-called fragment shader on each of those pixels to compute a corresponding color. Nonetheless, not all pixel colors should be written to the screen (e.g., hidden objects should not appear in the final view). To this extent, graphics cards rely on a depth buffer, an image of the size of the screen containing the depth of previously written pixels. Now, whenever a new pixel is produced, its depth is compared to the already-present depth at the corresponding screen location. If the new pixel is nearer, the color value is written to the screen, and the depth value is updated.

Today, one can interact with this graphics pipeline through so-called *shaders*. These are basically small programs that modify the standard behavior of the pipeline (see Figure A.1). From OpenGL 3 on, the standard pipeline was even declared deprecated and all instances are implemented via shader programs.

Texel, Pixel, Fragment

Even though a texel refers to a texture, a pixel to the screen, and a fragment to the entity that is a candidate for being blended in the framebuffer (e.g., color and depth), we will not always make an exact distinction in order to simplify explanations.

- *Vertex shader.* The input of this step are vertices specified by the application. The latter usually needs to also define how these vertices define primitives, but this assembly information will only be used in the next stage of the pipeline. Here, isolated vertices are treated independently of the triangle it belongs to. Usually, in this step, the vertex's coordinates are multiplied with a matrix to project it onto the screen, according to the current point of view. Nevertheless, on newer graphics cards, it is possible to transform the vertex based on a program that can make use of the vertex's data or texture memory on the GPU, as well as an array of values sent from the CPU (uniform variables). One application is *displacement mapping*, where a vertex is shifted to a new location based on a texture. The output of the vertex shader is a single vertex.

- *Geometry shader.* This rather new element, since Shader Model 4.0, of the pipeline allows us to apply modifications to each primitive (e.g., triangles, lines, and points). The input data in this step are the primitives assembled from the vertices of the previous stage. During the transformation, access to uniform variables and texture memory is allowed. Interestingly, special data arrangements can further give limited access to a a neighborhood of the primitive. For example, given a triangle, its three neighboring triangles can be made accessible. It is currently not possible to extend this neighborhood further. The output of this phase is from none to even several primitives that are clipped to the camera frustum once this step is performed. Theoretically, 1,024 vertices can be produced, although, in practice, more than 6 to 18 results in a strong performance penalty.

- *Fragment shader.* The assembled primitive is rasterized (meaning scan converted to *fragments*) by a rasterization unit. The fragment shader allows modifying the fragment's color value and its depth before it is blended into the framebuffer. One can think of the framebuffer as an image/texture into which one writes—it could even be the screen. Besides the information of the current primitive that was rasterized, again uniform variables and texture memory can be involved. The way data are passed from the primitive to the fragment can be roughly specified via two categories: continuously varying data (interpolated from the vertices) and flat data (one value per triangle). Nonetheless, there are also some more advanced strategies that relate to supersampling. At the end of the fragment shader, the resulting depth value is tested against the depth buffer. If this test fails, the color-value computation can be skipped because the element will never show on the screen.[1] If it passes the test, its color is produced and blended with the information

---

[1]Graphics hardware usually supports early z-culling that hierarchically performs depth/stencil tests and delivers a strong speed-up. Unfortunately, this usually only works if the depth is not modified in the fragment shader.

already present in the framebuffer. Prior to Shader Model 5.0, it was not possible to interact with the blending process in a programmable manner. The methods can only be chosen from a set of operations. The operations include logical (bitwise) operations and the more general alpha blending. Alpha blending is used to combine the current color value with the current framebuffer content in a weighted manner based on a fourth color channel: the so-called alpha channel. This allows, for example, to sum up values.

- *Tessellation shader.* Since Shader Model 5.0, tessellation has been exposed to the programmers. This element in the pipeline is situated before the vertex shader and is itself organized into several pipeline steps. This stage is currently less involved in shadow computations and, therefore, we will not analyze it in detail here. The principle of tessellation is to subdivide primitives such as triangles into many small subtriangles. One advantage is that this process reduces the bandwidth: a small set of primitives can be augmented to a very smooth or detailed surface. When these subdivision strategies are applied in a view-dependent manner, it is even possible to achieve complex-looking scenes with a high efficiency.

A.2　Per-Fragment Processing—Culling and Blending

Correct rendering of transparent objects is not straightforward with alpha-blending operations. Elements would need to be sorted appropriately from back to front, which contradicts the parallelized design. Depth peeling [Everitt01] enforces a correct ordering by performing several render passes.

In the nth depth-peeling pass, the nth depth layer can be extracted by smartly discarding all fragments that are closer than the last extracted depth. In consequence, one obtains a depth map of all the scene parts that are one layer farther away. Newer, more efficient approaches use conservative read/write operations [Liu06] or order-independent transparency that make use of the append-buffer extension [Yang10b]. The latter is only available in Shader Model 5.0 but delivers a high efficiency. Unfortunately, it can result in high memory usage (theoretically unbound, but up to 600 MB are not uncommon for a full-HD scene).

Here, we will focus on the more common depth peeling. In pseudocode, the following OpenGL calls should be applied:

```
shader.activate();
for (int i=1; i<=passes;++i)
{
    fbo[i].activate();
    shader.attachTexture("LastLayer",
                         fbo[i-1].getDepthTexture());
    glClear(GL_COLOR_BUFFER_BIT|GL_DEPTH_BUFFER_BIT);
```

```
    renderScene();
}
shader.deactivate();
```

The class `fbo` represents an array of framebuffer objects with an attached depth and color buffer into which the scene is rendered. For `fbo[0]` it is assumed that its depth texture was cleared to zero. The idea is to render into depth texture i and discard the fragments closer than the depth value stored in texture $i-1$. The result of the previous step becomes the input of the next. Consequently, the shaders are relatively simple:

```
uniform Texture2D LastLayer;
uniform vec4f projectedPos;
void main()
{
    //...
    projectedPos.xyz/=projectedPos.w;
    float depth=texture2D(LastLayer, projectedPos.xy);
    if ((projectedPos.z+1.0)/2.0<depth)
        discard;
    //...
}
```

If the depth of the current fragment is closer than the depth stored in the last layer at this position, the fragment is discarded. We, hence, effectively peel off one layer at a time. The fragment shader can be further simplified by avoiding the depth normalization (Chapter 2).

Before a fragment is output, a variety of tests are applied. We already mentioned depth, but scissor tests (against a user-specified rectangle, useful for light sources with attenuation), depth extents, alpha tests (testing the alpha channel against a user-defined value), and the stencil test, to name the important ones, are all applied before accepting the fragment. The stencil test is the most complex one and is based on an 8-bit stencil buffer. For a given fragment, a depth test and a comparison between the pixel's stencil buffer value and a reference is performed. Based on the outcome, one can specify how the stencil-buffer value is altered thereafter. Prior to Shader Model 5.0, one had to choose from a set of predefined behaviors and the stencil buffer outcome was not accessible nor specifiable in a shader. If all the tests pass, then only the fragment arrives in the framebuffer.

A.3   The Framebuffer

The framebuffer that will contain the final image can hold a variety of data types: IEEE floats, integers, fixed point (8- or 16-bit), ...

Further, one can connect several attachments to which it is possible to write simultaneously (this is referred to as *multiple render targets (MRTs)*. Up to eight such buffers can currently be attached on cards such as NVIDIA's GTX480. The introduction of MRTs can be considered a small revolution. With a single geometry transformation, several color values can be produced per pixel. This possibility gave boost to *deferred shading*, which is a very powerful technique that is of interest if the bottleneck of the algorithm is the fragment shader—which is actually often the case for shadow computations. The principle is to render the scene once and, instead of producing the final color values, recover only scene data (normals, world position, materials, etc.). A subsequent pass, only on these values and no longer on the geometry, then produces the final image. A more detailed analysis is presented in Appendix E.

A.4   Geometry Representation

OpenGL offers the so-called *immediate mode*, where primitives with the per-vertex data can be sent directly to the GPU without being stored by the graphics API. While being a convenient way for the programmer to draw simple objects, this does not make sense from a performance perspective if the transferred data are the same in each frame.[2] In this case, it is much more useful to store the information directly in the graphics card's memory and thus only transfer it once. The mechanism for this is a *vertex buffer object (VBO)*. These are zones in a card's memory that contain the data to be rendered. The only CPU interaction is thus a call that tells the graphics card to process the data at a certain memory location.

The idea to free the CPU's workload is also reflected by the introduction of *instances*. Here, one single CPU call triggers multiple processing of a VBO. To enable the GPU to distinguish between the instances, a primitive ID is accessible in the shaders. This technique is particularly useful when crowds of similar objects need to be rendered.

There is another advantage of keeping the geometry on the GPU. On DirectX 10 cards, feedback mechanisms exist that enable us to reconnect the geometry shader's output to the vertex shader and, thereby, iterate over the data several times.

Mesh Representation

Basically, there are two possibilities: flat (*n* successive vertices define a primitive) or indexed (two buffers, one containing indices, the other the actual vertex data). The second solution is not only more memory efficient but also delivers increased performance. The reason is that the GPU can reuse computations of the vertex shader for several triangles.

---

[2]In fact, this is why this mode is deprecated since OpenGL 3.0. In DX this never existed.

A.5   Hardware

In previous generations, there was a clear distinction between the type of processors on the card. Some were fragment-, others vertex-shader units. Currently (as of NVIDIA's G80 and even earlier on the ATI-side with the XBox 360), this no longer applies. Today's stream processors can be scheduled to work on all three shader interactions depending on the workload of each. This much more general description also gave rise to APIs such as CUDA, OpenCL, and Compute Shaders (the latter since DirectX 11), which are programming libraries that allow us to use the graphics card as a parallelized multicore stream processor. It seems that future development will follow this trend of generalization. NVIDIA's TESLA cards are already directed towards general scientific computations and are similar to standard GPUs but do not contain any graphics components. Nevertheless, it is unlikely that the graphics pipeline will vanish soon because some of its performance relies on very specialized solutions. For example, scan conversion is supported by specialized raster units. Other elements are responsible for texture fetches and caches, and it will be hard to efficiently replace these by generalized mechanisms.

Brief Guide to Graphics APIs

In practice, the algorithms described in this book are typically implemented using one of the standard graphics APIs: OpenGL or Direct3D.[1] To facilitate such implementations for the reader, this appendix provides a structured overview of all the API commands and conventions relevant to shadow computations that have been covered in the book. As we have adopted OpenGL for the implementation hints throughout the book, in an effort to keep the description focused, consistent, and concise, this appendix also serves to help readers find the Direct3D equivalent of the mentioned OpenGL functionality.

OpenGL has evolved steadily since its introduction in 1992, and even very old code still runs under the newest versions. However, since the inception of OpenGL, both CPUs and graphics hardware have changed tremendously, rendering several design decisions suboptimal in today's hardware landscape. Therefore, in an effort to better adapt to the current environment, certain functionality became deprecated with the introduction of OpenGL 3.0—but to not break legacy code and allow a smooth transition, it is still fully supported in the *compatibility profile* (as opposed to the *core profile*). Even though the reader is encouraged to not use deprecated functions if developing in OpenGL, we are well aware that many developers still have not made the move to the "new" API and are more familiar with the "old" one. Therefore, we have adopted the older but more common OpenGL 2.1 in the book (referring to it as classic OpenGL), and highlight any relevant changes in OpenGL 3.0 and newer in the following sections.

Direct3D, by contrast, typically introduces a new API interface with every new major release. While this approach typically breaks old code, it helps to keep the API clean from legacy features and design decisions and the overhead incurred

---

[1]Direct3D is the graphics component of DirectX, and hence, often simply the more general term DirectX is used.

by supporting them. In particular, Direct3D 10 introduced a radical redesign [Blythe06] tailored to fit the highly programmable, high-performance GPUs that are in common use nowadays. Despite introducing many new features, the latest incarnation, Direct3D 11, is very close to Direct3D 10 concerning the API, and we will thus cover only Direct3D 11 in the following. Note that the Direct3D 10 equivalent is typically obtained by substituting `D3D11` or `D3DX11` in the name with `D3D10` or `D3DX10`. In contrast to OpenGL, where a number of procedures operate on a complex state machine, Direct3D has an object-oriented interface. At the core is an `ID3D11Device` object, which encapsulates a rendering device and is used for resource creation. The actual rendering-related functionality has moved to `ID3D11DeviceContext` objects with Direct3D 11, facilitating multithreaded rendering.

B.1   Transformation Matrices

When implementing and using transformation matrices, two aspects have to be considered: storage order and the layout of the vectors that are to be transformed by the matrix. The storage order determines how the elements of a two-dimensional matrix are stored linearly in memory. In *column-major order*, the matrix elements are serialized such that first all elements of the first column are stored, then those of the second column, and so on. Analogously, in *row-major order*, linearization proceeds row-wise. Note that interpreting a matrix in the wrong storage order yields the transpose of the matrix. In all of its API calls, OpenGL assumes that matrices are stored in column-major order, whereas Direct3D expects row-major order. Within shaders, however, the order is essentially arbitrary and can be specified with modifiers, with the default for uniforms being column-major order in both GLSL and HLSL.

In graphics nowadays, a vector $\mathbf{v}$ is typically considered a column vector that is transformed by multiplying it with a matrix $\mathbf{M}$ from the right:

$$\tilde{\mathbf{v}} = \mathbf{M}\mathbf{v} = \begin{pmatrix} m_{00} & m_{01} & \cdots \\ m_{10} & m_{11} & \cdots \\ \vdots & \vdots & \ddots \end{pmatrix} \begin{pmatrix} v_0 \\ v_1 \\ \vdots \end{pmatrix}.$$

Consequently, if $\mathbf{v}$ is supposed to be transformed first by $\mathbf{M}_1$, then by $\mathbf{M}_2$, and finally by $\mathbf{M}_3$, the multiplication order of these matrices is reversed, starting with $\mathbf{M}_3$:

$$\tilde{\mathbf{v}} = \mathbf{M}_3\left(\mathbf{M}_2(\mathbf{M}_1\mathbf{v})\right) = (\mathbf{M}_3\mathbf{M}_2\mathbf{M}_1)\mathbf{v}.$$

However, it is totally permissible to alternatively assume that vectors are row vectors. In that case, they are multiplied from the left:

$$\tilde{\mathbf{v}}^T = \mathbf{v}^T \mathbf{N} = \begin{pmatrix} v_0 & v_1 & \cdots \end{pmatrix} \begin{pmatrix} n_{00} & n_{01} & \cdots \\ n_{10} & n_{11} & \cdots \\ \vdots & \vdots & \ddots \end{pmatrix}.$$

Note that matrices $\mathbf{M}$ applied to column vectors and matrices $\mathbf{N}$ applied to row vectors are related by transposition (i.e., $\mathbf{N} = \mathbf{M}^T$). Consequently, when transforming vectors by multiple transformations, the multiplication order corresponds to the transformation order and is thus reversed with respect to the column vector setting:

$$\tilde{\mathbf{v}}^T = \mathbf{v}^T (\mathbf{M}_3 \mathbf{M}_2 \mathbf{M}_1)^T = \mathbf{v}^T (\mathbf{M}_1^T \mathbf{M}_2^T \mathbf{M}_3^T).$$

Classic OpenGL enforces the column-vector convention, which we also adopted for this book, and maintains matrix state for the model-view matrix (for the mapping from model to eye space), the projection matrix, and a texture-coordinate transformation matrix. These matrices can be modified by operations like `glLoadIdentity()`, `glMultMatrixf()`, or `gluLookAt()`, which operate on the matrix selected by the current matrix mode. It can be set via `glMatrixMode(mode)`, where mode is `GL_MODELVIEW` for the model-view matrix and `GL_PROJECTION` for the projection matrix. Within shaders, the current matrices can be accessed via predefined uniforms. In GLSL, for instance, these uniforms are called `gl_ModelViewMatrix` and `gl_ProjectionMatrix`. Moreover, several derived quantities are also predefined, like

- transposes (e.g., `gl_ModelViewMatrixTranspose`);

- inverses (e.g., `gl_ModelViewMatrixInverse`);

- transposed inverses (e.g., `gl_ModelViewMatrixInverseTranspose`);

- `gl_ModelViewProjectionMatrix` (the matrix product of `gl_ProjectionMatrix` and `gl_ModelViewMatrix`);

- `gl_NormalMatrix` (the transposed inverse of the upper left 3×3 submatrix of `gl_ModelViewMatrix`).

As this matrix state functionality is deprecated in core OpenGL 3.0 and later, it is up to the developer to write functions (or use some external library) for building matrices, multiplying them, transposing them, and inverting them; to define uniforms in the shaders; and to explicitly set these uniforms before the shader is invoked. Note that such a procedure is of course also possible (but not required) if using classic OpenGL. While this puts some burden on the developer, it also enables adopting other conventions, like row vectors instead of column vectors, if desired.

Similarly, Direct3D also requires the developer to define uniforms in the shader and update them before using the shader. However, with XNAMath,[2] a high-performance math library is provided as part of DirectX that encapsulates vectors and matrices, among others, and provides functions for setting up special matrices, for matrix multiplication, and for matrix inversion, for instance. The resulting matrices can then be directly used for setting the shader uniforms. Note, however, that because Direct3D adopts the row-vector convention, all matrix setup functions yield according matrices. The user is free, though, to transpose the matrix and work with the column-vector convention.

B.1.1   Handedness

Another aspect that often influences the matrix content is whether the used frame is right-handed or left-handed. OpenGL uses a right-handed coordinate system, and we also employ this convention in this book. By contrast, Direct3D prefers a left-handed frame,[3] but the developer is free to adopt a right-handed one. Actually, XNAMath (and the older D3DXMath library) provides functions for both left- and right-handed frames, indicating the handedness by the postfix (LH or RH).

Note that changing the handedness affects whether a triangle is front or back facing. Therefore, it is possible to define which vertex order (counterclockwise or clockwise) corresponds to front facing. In OpenGL, this is accomplished with the glFrontFace() command, whereas in Direct3D 11, it is controlled by the FrontCounterClockwise element of the D3D11_RASTERIZER_DESC structure describing an ID3D11RasterizerState object. Further note that changes in the handedness might also require changes in the assets, like flipping the normals' direction.

B.1.2   View Matrix

A view matrix is typically defined by the eye point $\mathbf{e}$, a point $\mathbf{p}$ to look at, and an up vector $\mathbf{y}'$. In classic OpenGL, the function gluLookAt() takes these parameters as input and sets the following matrix:

$$\mathbf{M}_v = \begin{pmatrix} \mathbf{a}_x & \mathbf{a}_y & \mathbf{a}_z & -(\mathbf{a} \cdot \mathbf{e}) \\ \mathbf{b}_x & \mathbf{b}_y & \mathbf{b}_z & -(\mathbf{b} \cdot \mathbf{e}) \\ \mathbf{c}_x & \mathbf{c}_y & \mathbf{c}_z & -(\mathbf{c} \cdot \mathbf{e}) \\ 0 & 0 & 0 & 1 \end{pmatrix}, \quad \text{where} \quad \begin{aligned} \mathbf{c} &= (\mathbf{e} - \mathbf{p})/\|\mathbf{e} - \mathbf{p}\|, \\ \mathbf{a} &= (\mathbf{y}' \times \mathbf{c})/\|\mathbf{y}'\|, \\ \mathbf{b} &= \mathbf{c} \times \mathbf{a}. \end{aligned}$$

Recall that in core OpenGL 3.0 and newer, you have to construct this matrix yourself.

---

[2]In DirectX 9 and 10, the D3DXMath library has been included instead, and it also can be used with DirectX 11. Typically, the names of corresponding XNAMath and D3DXMath functions only differ by the prefix: XM versus D3DX.

[3]Interestingly, Microsoft's XNA framework uses a right-handed frame.

In Direct3D, the `XMMatrixLookAtRH()` function produces the same matrix but transposed (due to the row-vector convention), that is, $\mathbf{M}_v^T$. The left-handed version is obtained via `XMMatrixLookAtLH()`.

B.1.3   Projection Matrix

The perspective projection matrix serves to transform the viewing frustum into a unit cube, mapping the frustum's left face to $x = -1$, the right face to $x = 1$, and the bottom and top faces to $y = -1$ and $y = 1$, respectively. Furthermore, the far clipping plane is mapped to $z = 1$. Depending on the API, the near plane is mapped to either $z = -1$ (OpenGL) or $z = 0$ (Direct3D).

The frustum can be conveniently specified by its vertical field of view $fovy$, the aspect ratio α, and the (unsigned) distances of the near and far planes, n and f. In classic OpenGL, `gluPerspective()` yields the following matrix for these parameters:

$$\mathbf{M}_p = \begin{pmatrix} \frac{1}{\alpha} \cot \frac{fovy}{2} & 0 & 0 & 0 \\ 0 & \cot \frac{fovy}{2} & 0 & 0 \\ 0 & 0 & \frac{n+f}{n-f} & \frac{2nf}{n-f} \\ 0 & 0 & -1 & 0 \end{pmatrix}. \tag{B.1}$$

Analogously, Direct3D's `XMMatrixPerspectiveFovRH()` produces

$$\mathbf{M}_p^T = \begin{pmatrix} \frac{1}{\alpha} \cot \frac{fovy}{2} & 0 & 0 & 0 \\ 0 & \cot \frac{fovy}{2} & 0 & 0 \\ 0 & 0 & \frac{f}{n-f} & -1 \\ 0 & 0 & \frac{nf}{n-f} & 0 \end{pmatrix}.$$

Note that the matrix is transposed due to the row-vector convention and only differs from the OpenGL version in the modified z-related elements, causing $z \in [-f, -n]$ to be mapped to $[0, 1]$ instead of $[-1, 1]$. The according left-handed variant is

$$\mathbf{M}_p^T = \begin{pmatrix} \frac{1}{\alpha} \cot \frac{fovy}{2} & 0 & 0 & 0 \\ 0 & \cot \frac{fovy}{2} & 0 & 0 \\ 0 & 0 & \frac{-f}{n-f} & 1 \\ 0 & 0 & \frac{nf}{n-f} & 0 \end{pmatrix}$$

and can be obtained with `XMMatrixPerspectiveFovLH()`.

Alternatively, the frustum can be specified by providing the width and height of the front face, along with near- and far-plane distances. XNAMath provides the

functions `XMMatrixPerspectiveRH()` and `XMMatrixPerspectiveLH()` to this end.
The most general way to define a frustum, however, is by giving the horizontal and
vertical ranges $x \in [l, r]$ and $y \in [b, t]$ of the front face and the near- and far-plane
distances. The `glFrustum()` takes such a specification and sets the matrix

$$
\mathbf{M}_{\mathrm{p}} = \begin{pmatrix} \frac{2n}{r-l} & 0 & \frac{r+l}{r-l} & 0 \\ 0 & \frac{2n}{t-b} & \frac{t+b}{t-b} & 0 \\ 0 & 0 & \frac{n+f}{n-f} & \frac{2nf}{n-f} \\ 0 & 0 & -1 & 0 \end{pmatrix}.
$$

The Direct3D analogs, again returning the transposed versions, are `XMMatrix
PerspectiveOffCenterRH()` and `XMMatrixPerspectiveOffCenterLH()`, with the
latter, left-handed one yielding

$$
\mathbf{M}_{\mathrm{p}}^{T} = \begin{pmatrix} \frac{2n}{r-l} & 0 & 0 & 0 \\ 0 & \frac{2n}{t-b} & 0 & 0 \\ -\frac{r+l}{r-l} & -\frac{t+b}{t-b} & -\frac{f}{n-f} & 1 \\ 0 & 0 & \frac{nf}{n-f} & 0 \end{pmatrix}.
$$

B.2   State

The graphics pipeline state controls the exact rendering behavior, covering aspects
ranging from which vertex order makes a triangle be considered as front facing (see
above, Section B.1.1), over how depth tests are to be performed, to which shader
is executed.

In OpenGL, binary state, like performing depth testing or not, is typically controlled by the functions `glEnable()` and `glDisable()`. Furthermore, a plethora of
functions exists to modify the huge amount of state parameters. Since, typically,
a function call is required for each individual state parameter to be changed, state
changes involving many parameters can become quite costly.

To address this problem, from which Direct3D 9 also suffers, Direct3D 10 and
11 organize state parameters into a few groups and only allow setting all parameters
of a group at once. Typically, the individual parameters of a group are captured
in a descriptor structure and an according state object is created (with a member
function of the device object). Changing the state then merely requires a single API
call to set the corresponding state object. In Direct3D 11, these setter functions are
members of the `ID3D11DeviceContext` interface, while in Direct3D 10, where the
context concept is not present, they are members of the `ID3D10Device` interface.

For the developer, the downside of this approach is that for each required combination of parameter values for a state group, a separate state object has to be created, which can make temporarily changing only one parameter value during development tedious. Note that to really benefit from this grouping, state objects should be created on initialization or on first use and then maintained for all following frames, and not created and destroyed every frame anew.

B.2.1   Depth-related State

Depth testing is enabled in OpenGL via glEnable(GL_DEPTH_TEST). The actual comparison performed can be specified with glDepthFunc(), and writing to the depth buffer can be controlled with the glDepthMask() function.

In Direct3D 11, the state related to depth testing and processing is set via the OMSetDepthStencilState() member function of a context object. It expects an ID3D11DepthStencilState object, which is described by a D3D11_DEPTH_STENCIL_DESC structure. Among this structure's members, DepthEnable controls whether depth testing is performed or not, with DepthFunc specifying the comparison function employed for depth testing. Writing to the depth buffer can be turned off by setting DepthWriteMask to D3D11_DEPTH_WRITE_MASK_ZERO.

Depth Bias

In OpenGL, biasing of depth values is activated by glEnable(GL_POLYGON_OFFSET_FILL), and glPolygonOffset() is used to specify the constant offset and slope-dependent bias to be applied (see Section 2.2.3).

Since biasing is performed during rasterization, in Direct3D 11, it is controlled by the ID3D11RasterizerState object set via RSSetState(). The relevant members of the describing D3D11_RASTERIZER_DESC structure are called DepthBias and SlopeScaledDepthBias. Unlike OpenGL, Direct3D 11 also allows capping the applied bias by specifying an according DepthBiasClamp value. This is useful, since a high triangle slope can result in large bias values, which often leads to problems.

Depth Clipping

Typically, fragments are clipped against the near and the far plane. This behavior can be disabled in OpenGL via glEnable(GL_DEPTH_CLAMP), causing fragments beyond the far plane and in front of the near plane[4] to not get discarded but to move on in the pipeline. Like with all fragments, their depth values are clamped to the valid depth range. The vendor-specific extension GL_AMD_depth_clamp_separate further allows disabling only the clipping against the near or the far plane.

---

[4]Note that a fragment is only generated in the first place if its homogeneous coordinate value $w > 0$. Therefore, in case of a perspective projection, no fragments are generated behind the eye point.

OpenGL	Direct3D 11	Description
GL_INCR_WRAP	D3D11_STENCIL_OP_INCR	Increment, wrap around to zero
GL_DECR_WRAP	D3D11_STENCIL_OP_DECR	Decrement, wrap around to maximum
GL_INCR	D3D11_STENCIL_OP_INCR_SAT	Increment, clamp to maximum
GL_DECR	D3D11_STENCIL_OP_DECR_SAT	Decrement, clamp to zero

Table B.1. Selection of stencil operations.

In Direct3D 11, fragment depth clipping is controlled via the DepthClip Enable member of the D3D11_RASTERIZER_DESC structure, used for describing an ID3D11RasterizerState object.

B.2.2   Stencil Test

The stencil test is enabled in OpenGL with glEnable(GL_STENCIL_TEST), with glStencilFunc() specifying the employed test function, the test reference value, and the mask indicating the bits that are employed in the test. The stencil operation (see Table B.1) that is performed according to the outcome of the test is selected by glStencilOp(), where the three cases "stencil test fails," "stencil test passes but depth test fails," and "both stencil and depth tests pass" are distinguished. It is also possible to specify the test and the operations individually for front- and back-facing triangles via glStencilFuncSeparate() and glStencilOpSeparate().

In Direct3D 11, stencil-related state is set with the context's OMSetDepth StencilState() member function, which expects an ID3D11DepthStencilState object and the reference value for the test. The state object is described by a D3D11_DEPTH_STENCIL_DESC structure (see above for depth-related members), whose StencilEnable enables the stencil test. The mask is specified by StencilRead Mask and StencilWriteMask, and the FrontFace and BackFace members control the face-orientation-specific actions, allowing the specification of the applied test function and the result-dependent operations (see Table B.1).

B.2.3   Blending

In OpenGL, blending is turned on with glEnable(GL_BLEND). The source and destination blending factors are specified with glBlendFunc() or, if separate factors are required for the color and the alpha channels, with glBlendFuncSeparate(). The employed blend operation (e.g., adding source and destination, scaled by their respective factors) is selected via glBlendEquation().

In Direct3D 11, the blending state is encapsulated by an ID3D11BlendState object and can be set with the context's OMSetBlendState() method. The state object is described by a D3D11_BLEND_DESC structure, which allows activating blending (via the RenderTarget[].BlendEnable member), specifying source and destination factors as well as choosing the blending operation (separately for color and alpha channels). These blending settings can also be done independently for each render target by setting `IndependentBlendEnable` to true.

Bitwise Blending

For several applications, like voxelization, bitwise blending (i.e., combining source and destination via bitwise operations like OR, AND, or XOR) can be useful. However, such blending operations are currently not supported with ordinary blending functionality. In OpenGL, they are exposed as logical pixel operations, instead. These are activated with `glEnable(GL_COLOR_LOGIC_OP)`, and the operation to apply is specified via `glLogicOp()`.

Unfortunately, recent versions of Direct3D don't provide that functionality, forcing the developer to adopt an alternative algorithm formulation to reach the intended goal. One possibility is to resort to compute shaders instead (as has been done in the case of voxelization). Another option is to directly update some writeable texture or buffer in the pixel shader by binding it via an unordered access view and applying atomic operations like `InterlockedXor()`.

B.3   Framebuffer and Render Targets

The rendering result is output to the current framebuffer, which typically consists of one color buffer and a combined depth and stencil buffer. However, it is also possible to use no color buffer, like when generating a shadow map, or multiple ones, like when recording attributes (like position, normal, and material properties) for deferred shading. Note that a color buffer does not necessarily store color, and its pixels can essentially have any format (e.g., two channels of 32-bit unsigned integers); it is hence often more appropriately referred to as *render target*. The individual buffers that make up the framebuffer are often just textures.

In OpenGL, a framebuffer is represented by a framebuffer object (FBO), to which individual buffers can be attached. It is generated with `glGenFramebuffers()` and destroyed with `glDeleteFramebuffers()`. Two-dimensional textures can be attached via `glFramebufferTexture2D()`, for instance. Notice that the attachment of color buffers alone does not imply that all of them are active and written to during rendering; instead, the desired set of attachments has to be specified via `glDrawBuffers()`. To make an FBO active, it has to be bound with `glBindFramebuffer()`. It is deactivated by binding another FBO or the default framebuffer (which corresponds to FBO name[5] 0). Note that updates to the FBO's state, like attaching render targets, require the FBO to be bound. Active buffers can (and should) be cleared via `glClear()`, with the clear value being specified with `glClearColor()`, `glClearDepth()`, and `glClearStencil()`, respectively.

---

[5]In OpenGL, objects are identified by so-called names, which are just unsigned integer IDs, though.

In Direct3D 11, the render targets and the depth/stencil buffer to use are set with the context's `OMSetRenderTargets()`, thus fully specifying the framebuffer. Render targets are represented by a render target view (`ID3D11RenderTargetView`) of some subresource, like a mipmap slice of a two-dimensional texture. Similarly, a depth/stencil view (`ID3D11DepthStencilView`) is utilized for the depth/stencil buffer. Note that to be able to create such views, an according bind flag has to be set when creating the resource (e.g., `D3D11_BIND_RENDER_TARGET` in `D3D11_TEXTURE2D_DESC`'s `BindFlags` member). Views can be cleared with `ClearRenderTargetView()` and `ClearDepthStencilView()`.

B.4 Texture Sampling

In OpenGL, textures are represented by texture objects, and sampling parameters are associated with a texture object. Once a texture object is bound via `glBindTexture()`, parameters related to sampling the texture within a shader can be specified with the family of `glTexParameter*()` functions. For instance, filtering is specified when using the parameters `GL_TEXTURE_MIN_FILTER` and `GL_TEXTURE_MAX_FILTER`. The interpretation of texture coordinates outside the normal range $[\varepsilon, 1 - \varepsilon]$, with ε denoting half a texel's extent, is governed by the wrap mode, which can be set with the parameters `GL_TEXTURE_WRAP_S`, `GL_TEXTURE_WRAP_T` and `GL_TEXTURE_WRAP_R`. If the wrap mode involves a border color, the one specified via the parameter `GL_TEXTURE_BORDER_COLOR` is used. For shadow map tests, the z-component of the texture coordinates should be compared against the texture value referenced by the x- and y-components and the comparison result be returned. This behavior can be turned on by setting the parameter `GL_TEXTURE_COMPARE_MODE` to `GL_COMPARE_REF_TO_TEXTURE`. The actual comparison function used is specified by the parameter `GL_TEXTURE_COMPARE_FUNC`.

In Direct3D 11, textures are made accessible to shaders by creating according shader resource views (`ID3D11ShaderResourceView`). The sampling behavior is encapsulated in a sampler state, which is orthogonal to the texture being sampled. Such states are represented by an `ID3D11SamplerState` object, which can be set in the individual shader stages via the context's `*SSetSamplers()` functions (e.g., with `PSSetSamplers()` for the pixel shader stage). The state object is described by a `D3D11_SAMPLER_DESC` structure. The filtering is specified by the `Filter` member, and the `AddressU`, `AddressV`, and `AddressW` members control the wrap mode for the texture coordinates (see Table B.2), with the border color being set with `BorderColor`. To enable comparing the sampling result with an arbitrary reference value and returning the comparison result, a corresponding comparison filter has to be specified in `Filter`. The comparison function can be selected by `ComparisonFunc`. Note that sampling is then performed in the HLSL shader with the `SampleCmp()` function, which expects the reference value for the comparison in

OpenGL	Direct3D 11
GL_REPEAT	D3D11_TEXTURE_ADDRESS_WRAP
GL_CLAMP_TO_EDGE	D3D11_TEXTURE_ADDRESS_CLAMP
GL_CLAMP_TO_BORDER	D3D11_TEXTURE_ADDRESS_BORDER
GL_MIRRORED_REPEAT	D3D11_TEXTURE_ADDRESS_MIRROR
GL_MIRROR_CLAMP_TO_EDGE_EXT	D3D11_TEXTURE_ADDRESS_MIRROR_ONCE

Table B.2. Overview of texture wrap/address modes.

addition to the texture coordinates. For shadow-map testing, this reference value is typically the light-space depth.

B.5   Shading Languages

In OpenGL, the prevalent shading language is GLSL, whereas HLSL is used in Direct3D 11. Since even a brief overview would be too long for this book, and GLSL is used throughout the book, we restrict ourselves to listing some nonobvious HLSL equivalents to mentioned GLSL terms.

The predefined GLSL variable gl_FrontFacing, indicating whether the triangle from which a fragment stems is front facing, corresponds to defining an input variable with semantic SV_IsFrontFace in HLSL. Similarly, GLSL's gl_FragCoord is equivalent to an input variable with semantic SV_Position in HLSL.

Concerning texture access, GLSL's ordinary texture() sampling function corresponds to the Sample() member function of the texture object in HLSL, and the equivalent of texelFetch() in GLSL, which allows accessing texels by their indices, is the Load() member function in HLSL.

A Word on Shading

This book focuses on shadow algorithms, whose main difficulty is to compute the visibility between the light source and each receiver point. We are less interested in the light interaction with the receiver surface itself. This interaction is usually caught in a BRDF (bidirectional reflectance distribution function) f_r (see Introduction). It is a four-dimensional function that associates to an incoming light direction $\hat{\omega}$ the reflected amount of energy in direction ω at a given point $\mathbf{p}$. Shading is crucial for the production of a convincing image because it contributes significantly to the appearance of the surfaces. To evaluate the shading response with respect to a given light source, one can sample the light source and evaluate the shading response for each point. Especially, if it is known which source samples are visible, one can restrict the shading evaluation to those visible samples, which ensures a physically based illumination. Such an evaluation integrates well with sample-based shadow algorithms (compare Chapter 10.1).

As shown in Equation (1.5) on page 10, the shading is often separated from the light-source visibility, but the evaluation of the shading part can even then be a costly task. Usually the idea is to restrict oneself to a point light source (often placed at the center of the original source). Consequently, in the following we will investigate the shading response for a point-light illumination scenario and give a brief overview of the most common shading models in this chapter.

C.1   Analytical Shading Models

A shading model is an approximation for the surface–light interaction. In our case, we will focus on BRDF representations. Depending on the material, this interaction can be very complex.

One efficient possibility to represent a BRDF is an analytical model. These functions try to grasp the essence of the physical processes and capture them in formulas. For real-time rendering, this solution is usually preferable because of the lower memory cost. Depending on the surface properties, the formulas can be more or less complex. In the following, we will present a few important ones. For more details, one can refer to an excellent survey [Schlick94] that we strongly suggest to any interested reader. Modern hardware often facilitates the implementation of the presented models in shaders, but other papers [Heidrich99b] even present implementation details for older graphics cards.

C.1.1   Notations

Analytical shading models are expressed with respect to a surface normal $\mathbf{n}$, a unit view vector ω, and a unit light vector $\mathbf{l}$. For a given surface point $\mathbf{p}$, the view vector ω is defined by the direction from $\mathbf{p}$ towards the observer. Similarly, $\mathbf{l}$ defines the direction from $\mathbf{p}$ towards the light.

Again, we want to underline that we will only consider a single light direction in the shading definition. This should not be confused with a restriction to a single light source. In fact, it is always possible to consider the incoming radiance over the entire hemisphere by integrating the shading over all light directions, similar to the rendering Equation (1.2) (see Chapter 1).

One important remark is that a light source can be colored. For the here-presented models, this can be easily integrated by modulating the shading by the colored light energy $\bar{L}_c$ to derive the resulting shading value. In practice, $\bar{L}_c$ is usually an RGB-tuple that is simply multiplied by the result of the formulae given below.

C.1.2   Diffuse Surfaces

One of the simplest BRDF models is for Lambertian shading. The assumption is that the surface is a totally diffuse reflector, meaning that the incoming light is scattered uniformly in all directions. In particular, this property implies that the appearance is independent of the observer's viewpoint; for example, unfinished wood gets relatively close to this model.

Mathematically, the shading is defined as follows:

$$L_o^d(\mathbf{p}, \omega) = \kappa_d \max(0, \mathbf{n} \cdot \mathbf{l}),$$

where κ_d is a scalar *reflectance* that encodes how much energy is absorbed by the surface and max returns the maximum of the two parameters. In this case, it basically encodes that we assume that the light comes from above the surface ($\mathbf{n} \cdot \mathbf{l} > 0$) and that the lighting contribution cannot be negative.

One can notice that the outgoing radiance does not depend on the point of view, which reflects the uniformity of the light scattering. The second observation

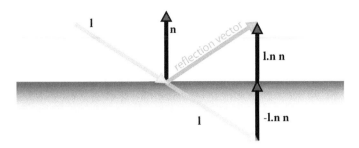

Figure C.1. Derivation of the reflection vector.

is that the dot product implicitly encodes that L_o will be lower when the light arrives at a grazing angle. This effect can be easily observed in reality when taking a flashlight. Pointing it straight downwards will illuminate a small area more than when lighting it from the side. Basically the light is relatively spread over a larger area, which is exactly captured by the dot product.[1]

C.1.3   Specular Surfaces

The Lambertian model falls short for many materials. General reflections are a highly view-dependent effect and, so far, not covered by the model. An extreme example is a mirror; every move of our head makes the reflected image move too. Such materials are very common in nature, and it is rather rare that a material does not exhibit a so-called *specular component*. Mostly, this property is perceived as view-dependent highlights on surfaces that basically show a more or less accurate reflection of the light source. The fact that the source is reflected also implies that, in most cases, highlights actually exhibit the color of the light, not the material. A typical example is plastic that shows white highlights under white light but has a colored diffuse appearance due to the light that is scattered by its pigments. The same holds for other so-called *dielectric* materials, such as glass, plastic, and water, while metals typically have colored highlights. In order to be able to integrate such effects properly, several models have been proposed.

Phong

The Phong model is based on the informal observation that highlights typically appear when the view vector aligns with the direction of the reflected-light vector $\mathbf{r} := \mathbf{l} - 2(\mathbf{n} \cdot \mathbf{l})\mathbf{n}$ (Figure C.1). As soon as the view vector deviates from $\mathbf{r}$, the highlight starts disappearing. Phong modeled the specular component of the material

---

[1]Please remember that both vectors $\mathbf{n}$ and $\mathbf{l}$ are of unit length and, hence, the dot product results in the cosine of the angle between the two.

with the following function:

$$L_o^s(\mathbf{p}, \omega) = \kappa_a + \kappa_d L_o^d(\mathbf{p}, \omega) + \kappa_s \max(0, \omega \cdot \mathbf{r})^\alpha,$$

where κ_s is the specular-reflection constant that defines the ratio of reflection and κ_d the ratio of the diffuse part L_o^d—usually $\kappa_s + \kappa_d < 1$. The constant term κ_a (ambient) can be used to emulate some indirect illumination. It is not physically based and is mostly a *hack* but can be used to avoid in-shadow objects appearing completely black. Finally, α defines the shininess of the material. The larger its value, the smaller and more focused the highlights on the surface will be.

Blinn-Phong

A modification of the Phong model has been suggested by Blinn. It is particularly interesting for real-time applications as it is cheap to compute but delivers a high visual quality. Instead of relying on a reflected-light vector, they define a unit halfway vector between the view and the light $\mathbf{h} := (\omega + \mathbf{l})/\|\omega + \mathbf{l}\|$, which is cheaper to compute. Interestingly, this new model is not only more efficient but is often also more accurate when reproducing measured BRDF surfaces [Ngan04], making it a very good choice for real-time graphics.

The mathematical formulation of the Blinn-Phong model reads as follows:

$$L_o^s(\mathbf{p}, \omega) = \kappa_a + \kappa_d L_o^d(\mathbf{p}, \omega) + \kappa_s \max(0, \mathbf{h} \cdot \mathbf{n})^\alpha.$$

Advanced Models

More advanced models, such as Cook-Torrance or the Ward model, simulate an even larger variety of materials. They build upon the assumption that the surface consists of small specular microfacets that reflect the light but that are not visible at the macroscale at which we observe the surface. In fact, these small microfacets can basically also be used to explain why highlights are often slightly blurred and the light is not perfectly reflected. Imagine that all microfacets point in different directions but are slightly oriented around the normal; the highlight will be brightest along the direction of the reflected-light vector based on the normal, but for small deviations, some of the microfacets will still perfectly reflect the light, leading to a halo around the highlight.

The Cook-Torrance model describes the microfacet orientation according to a Gaussian distribution and takes occlusion into account (the microfacets can block light from each other: incoming and reflected). Further extensions are possible and Ward proposed considering anisotropic orientation distributions to simulate materials with deformed highlights. Both models are out of the scope of this book. Figure C.2 shows the result of different shading models visually.

Figure C.2. Different materials produced with analytical BRDF models.

C.2 Approximating Incoming Radiance

We mentioned in the beginning of this chapter that all models concentrate on a single light direction but that one could integrate all incoming directions on the hemisphere above the receiver point and evaluate the shading model to derive the shading under a general illumination. Nonetheless, such integration can quickly become costly, for example, when evaluating shading for all points of an area light. Instead, especially for real-time applications, it is common to approximate the incoming radiance of an area light.

One solution to address this problem is to sample the shading for a few directions. In particular, it can even be very effective to approximate a whole area light with only a single point light. The idea is to add a few additional constraints that define how to alter its outgoing radiance with respect to the receiver point. This measure has also been integrated into OpenGL via the `glLight*()` command.

In theory, one realizes that a good approximation is to assume a radiance loss that relates to the squared distance. The insight behind this choice is that light travels along straight lines and the energy is conserved. In consequence, the energy on the surface of a sphere around a point light source (which grows quadratically with distance) should be constant.

Interestingly, OpenGL offers the possibility to attenuate the light's power according to its distance not only with a simple quadratic function but with a general quadratic polynomial. This may sound surprising and makes many people smile when they hear about this option for the first time, but it actually makes some sense to include this supplementary degree of freedom.

The situation is depicted in Figure C.3. Far away source samples will have very little influence on the final result due to their orientation with respect to

Figure C.3. For a large source, the change in incoming radiance is very small for slight perturbations of the source.

the receiving point. Following Equation (1.3) (on page 9), this is reflected in the $\cos(\mathbf{p} \rightarrow \mathbf{q}, \mathbf{n_p}) \cos(\mathbf{q} \rightarrow \mathbf{p}, \mathbf{n_q})$ term of $G(\mathbf{p}, \mathbf{q})$. In consequence—if the light is large with respect to the current receiving point—moving this source a little will have almost no impact on the received illumination. In other words, leaving the source at the same position and looking equivalently at adjacent receiver points, we will basically observe the same energy. From a certain distance, the orientation will be mostly constant, and thus, attenuation behaves in a quadratic manner as predicted. In between, the behavior passes through a linear stage. The more general polynomial that OpenGL offers provides the possibility to mimic some of this behavior. The definition of the actual coefficients of the light attenuation depends on the scene and light size. A bit of experimentation is needed to get this right, but the final evaluation is very efficient and can deliver a visually more pleasing outcome than a standard point-light illumination.

Fast GPU Filtering Techniques

In many shadow applications, it is necessary to find an average value of a region in a texture (e.g., Section 6.5.4 and Section 6.6). A brute-force computation that would look up these values individually can become very costly. Furthermore, we will see that this is usually unnecessary, in particular, when considering averaging values in a rectangular region. In practice, the shape is often effectively rectangular because of the assumptions that many algorithms rely on (e.g., a rectangular source).

In this chapter, we will analyze approximate, but also accurate, ways to accelerate the task of computing an average value in a rectangular window. Precisely, we will analyze common solutions such as mipmaps and also advanced techniques, such as N-buffers and summed-area tables.

Mathematically, we seek to compute

$$f_{\text{filter}}(\mathbf{t}) = \frac{1}{|\mathcal{K}(\mathbf{t})|} \sum_{\mathbf{t}_i \in \mathcal{K}(\mathbf{t})} I(\mathbf{t}_i), \qquad (\text{D.1})$$

where $\mathcal{K}(\mathbf{t})$ is the rectangular neighborhood around the pixel $\mathbf{t}$ and $|\mathcal{K}(\mathbf{t})|$ the number of its elements; I is the image containing the pixels. This is illustrated in Figure D.1.

D.1   Mipmap

A mipmapped texture is a texture that is structured as a pyramid. In each new level of this pyramid, the resolution of the previous level is divided by two along

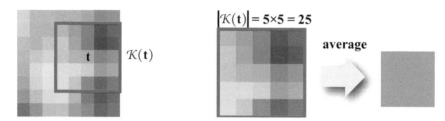

Figure D.1. The filtering process and notations.

each axis until only a single pixel remains. While the lowest level of the pyramid contains the original texture, in each intermediate level, four neighboring texels of the previous level are averaged together to produce a texture of half the resolution. In other words, each pixel contains the average of the 2×2 pixels that lie underneath it in the previous higher-resolution level (see Figure D.2). As an example, a mipmapped 512×512 texture exhibits ten levels, ranging from 512×512 to 1×1. In general, mipmaps have $1 + \log n$ levels, where n denotes the texture width (= height) and the final level only contains a single pixel.

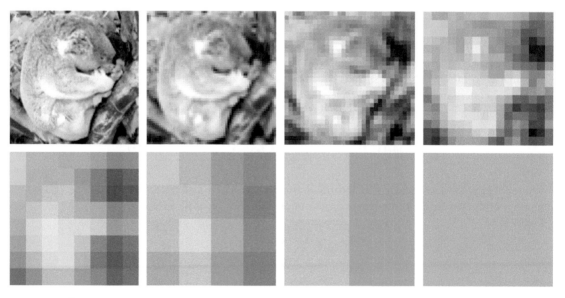

Figure D.2. The mipmap representation is an image pyramid, where each level has its resolution reduced by a factor of four (two along each axis). Four pixels of the previous level are averaged together.

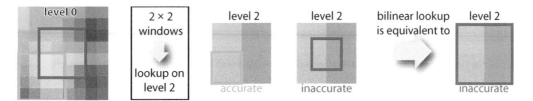

Figure D.3. Some power-of-two filter kernels are not representable in an accurate manner by mipmaps (red) while others are (green). Precisely, if the window position falls between pixels of the according level, no lookup delivers an accurate result.

D.1.1   Construction

Constructing mipmaps is very efficient. In fact, it is even hardware accelerated and directly accessible through the graphics APIs (in OpenGL: `glFramebuffer-MipMapEXT` or `gluBuildMipMap`). The construction happens in the order of milliseconds even for high-resolution textures. The different levels are all stored within the texture and not separately.

D.1.2   Filtering

Our goal is to find the average value in a rectangular neighborhood. To understand how to compute an approximation of this value with mipmaps, some additional analysis is needed. In each level, four texels are averaged. In other words, in level 1 we will find the 2×2-pixel averages of the original texture. Level 2 contains the 2×2-pixel averages of level 1—consequently, the 4×4 neighborhoods of the original texture. In general, level i contains the averages of $2^i \times 2^i$ pixels of the original texture. Unfortunately, because the resolution halves on each level, there are power-of-two squares for which we cannot find the average in the mipmap texture. Kernels of size 2^n are only present for each 2^nth texel (see Figure D.3).

Intertexel Interpolation

Following the above observation, mipmaps are useful to compute power-of-two squares, but because of the resolution reduction, it is not possible to achieve an *accurate* power-of-two box filter. Nonetheless, a cheap approximation exist. By activating linear texture filtering (`GL_LINEAR_MIPMAP_LINEAR`), the values of the neighboring texels will be interpolated at in-between texel positions. Thereby, the result for arbitrary window positions is simulated, but still it remains a strong approximation and block artifacts can occur.

Interlevel Interpolation

A second limitation is that only 2^n-texel squares are acceptably represented. For in-between sizes, one needs to introduce another approximation. Usually, one linearly interpolates between the two neighboring mipmap levels. For example, to approximate the average in a 3^2 square, one would interpolate (here, it is simply the mean) between the values of level 1 (2^2 texels) and level 2 (4^2 texels). This interpolation operation is supported directly when the aforementioned GL_LINEAR_MIPMAP_LINEAR-texture interpolation is activated. In a shader, the texture2DLod lookup function's level parameter determines the mipmap level from which the value is recovered and can be fractional.

Anisotropy

An interesting advantage of mipmaps is the support for anisotropic filtering. Here, with a simple API call (via the texture parameter GL_TEXTURE_MAX_ANISOTROPY_EXT), one can approximate rectangular regions. Internally, this is often implemented as up to 16 standard mipmap lookups that are placed along the line of anisotropy (the longest extent of the area) to well cover the quadrilateral region. Therefore, the quality is not extremely high, but it is a simple way in terms of hardware logic to improve the generality of the approach and makes it reasonably well suited for nonsquare filters. In a shader, the anisotropy is controlled via the derivative parameters of the texture2DGrad lookup function.

D.2   N-Buffer and Multiscale Map

An *N-buffer* [Décoret05] is a structure similar to mipmaps, but instead of reducing the resolution in each pyramid level, all levels of the N-buffer have the same resolution as the initial texture. In its original definition, a pixel in an N-buffer of level l holds the maximum of all pixels in a window of size 2^l for which the current pixel is the upper-left corner (see Figure D.4). It is also straightforward to store the average of this region instead. An N-buffer usually exhibits $\log(n)$-levels, like mipmaps, where n denotes the texture width (= height). In the highest level, the window size corresponds to the texture size.

D.2.1   Construction

The construction of N-buffers is relatively efficient because it can be done in an iterative manner. When constructing level i, one can make use of the values stored in level $i - 1$. In consequence, it is enough to apply a *ping-pong rendering*, where the texture computed in the last pass serves as an input for the new pass.

The algorithm is summarized in pseudocode as follows:

```
shader.attachTexture("SourceTexture", originalTexture);
for(int i = 0; i < levels; ++i) {
  shader.activate();
  shader.setUniform1f("PixelDistance", pow(2, i));
  fbo[i].activate();
```

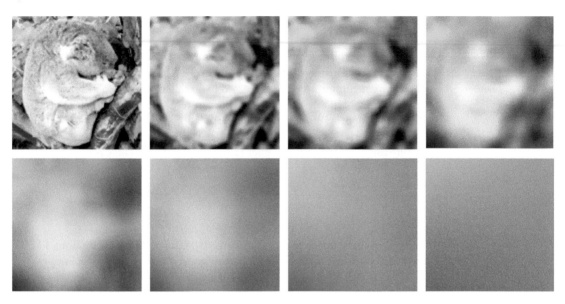

Figure D.4. The N-buffer representation keeps the same resolution on each level. In level i each pixel contains the average of a $2^i \times 2^i$-window of the pixels in level 0.

```
  renderQuad();
  shader.deactivate();
  shader.attachTexture("SourceTexture", fbo[i].getTexture());
}

//shader code
uniform Texture2D SourceTexture;
uniform float PixelDistance;
void main() {
  vec4 nbuffer = 0;
  for(int x = 0; x < 2; ++x) {
    for(int y = 0; y < 2; ++y) {
        nbuffer += texelFetch2D(SourceTexture, glFragCoords.xy + vec2u(
            x*PixelDistance, y*PixelDistance));
    }
  }
    //...
}
```

The efficiency of the construction lies in the fact that each level only relies on four lookups, which is relatively cheap in practice. The downside of N-buffers is the increased memory consumption. While mipmaps use only $1\frac{1}{3}$ times the amount of texture memory with respect to the original texture, N-buffers are much more costly. Each level adds the same memory cost as the original texture, resulting in $\log(n)$-times the original cost, where n is the width (= height).

As of 2007, the different N-buffer levels are not stored in separate textures anymore but rather inside slices of a texture array. The advantage is that only a single texture identifier needs to be passed to a shader in order to grant access to all levels of the N-buffer. Alternatively, one can rely on a three-dimensional texture that even supports automatic linear interpolation between the slices, but their implementation is, until now, often less efficient. In particular, a three-dimensional texture might impose much higher restrictions on the possible resolutions of each slice, whereas array textures share the resolution constraints of standard two-dimensional textures.

D.2.2   Multiscale Map

In the domain of image processing [Jähne05], multiscale representations, like discrete scale spaces, are employed in many applications. One simple but powerful representative is the Gaussian stack. For a given input image, it stores the filtered result by (truncated) Gaussians of increasing size w_i, with twice the size of level i being used for level $i + 1$ (i.e., $w_{i+1} = 2w_i$). This means that for a pixel position $\mathbf{t}$ at level i, the two-dimensional Gaussian-weighted average of the input image pixels within the $w_i \times w_i$ neighborhood centered on $\mathbf{t}$ is recorded.

We can also replace the two-dimensional Gaussian filtering by ordinary averaging or by computing the minimum or maximum, and we may also choose the initial neighborhood size to correspond to one pixel (i.e., $w_0 = 1$). These changes directly lead to a representation termed *multiscale (shadow) map* [Schwarz07] that provides filtered results for all scales with a power-of-two-sized square support. Put another way, the entry at position $\mathbf{t} = (x, y)$ and level i stores the filter response for the neighborhood region of size $2^i \times 2^i$ centered on $\mathbf{t}$, which is the square region

$$(x - \lfloor 2^{i-1} \rfloor, \ldots, x + \lceil 2^{i-1} - 1 \rceil) \times (y - \lfloor 2^{i-1} \rfloor, \ldots, y + \lceil 2^{i-1} - 1 \rceil).$$

A closer look reveals that this is similar to what we encountered with N-buffers. The major difference is that the considered neighborhood is shifted to be centered on the looked-up texel. This, however, results in supporting a significantly higher number of different rectangular regions if the neighborhood is clipped against the image extent, which applies in most applications. Because a multiscale map increases the neighborhood in all four directions when proceeding to the next level, the new neighborhood will differ from the old one even if clipped. By contrast, N-buffers expand the neighborhood only in the positive x- and y-directions, and hence, clipping can cause the new neighborhood to coincide with the old one, making the N-buffers store redundant information. This is particularly pronounced on the highest level, where a whole 25% of the texels in an N-buffer cover the same region as on the second highest level, thus redundantly storing the same values.

Consequently, it is advisable to use a multiscale map instead of N-buffers in practice.

D.2.3 Filtering

In contrast to the interpolated mipmap approximation, N-buffers deliver the correct result for power-of-two square windows. As for mipmaps, in-between filter sizes can be approximated by interpolating the two nearest power-of-two filter responses. While this is is not correct, it performs well in practice. In this scenario, N-buffers can provide the result with only one or two lookups, which leads to a high performance, similar to mipmaps.

Y Map

An important observation is that mipmaps actually do perform well for smaller windows, but for larger ones, the resolution reduction becomes very visible and leads to the aforementioned block artifacts. One possibility to exploit this observation is to rely on a hybrid scheme. While the first levels of the texture are handled like a mipmap, one can switch at later levels to a multiscale map. This *Y map* [Schwarz08b] combines the advantages of a high-quality N-buffer-like filtering with a relatively low memory consumption. Using a mipmap only for the first two levels already implies that 16 levels of succeeding N-buffers will fit in the original texture's amount of memory, making this extension a very valuable contribution.

Min/Max Computation

Finally, we quickly want to mention that the particular case of looking for minimums and maximums inside a rectangular region can be handled by N-buffers as well. In fact, N-buffers deliver the accurate result in an arbitrary square region with only four lookups. Basically, one covers the query square with four lookups from the one-level-below N-buffer texture (Figure D.5). Computing the maximum/minimum of these four values then results in the maximum/minimum of the entire square region.

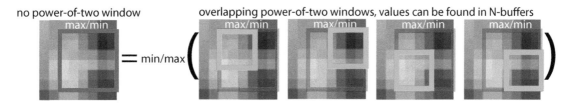

Figure D.5. Covering a square region with four square windows allows us to use N-buffers for an accurate min/max computation in arbitrary square regions.

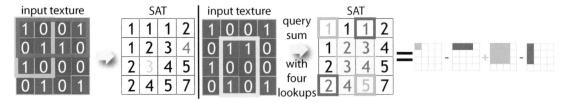

Figure D.6. To construct the SAT, one sums all values to the upper left of the considered pixel (left). Four lookups at the corners of a rectangle are enough to compute the sum of all its contained pixels.(right)

D.3   Summed-Area Table

A summed-area table (SAT) [Crow84] is a one-texture representation that allows us to accurately determine the average in an arbitrary rectangular region by using only four lookups into this texture. In each texel $\mathbf{t} := (x, y)$, we store the sum $SA(x, y) = \sum_{i \leq x \wedge j \leq y} I(i, j)$. Consequently, the average value A of a window defined by texels (x, y), (i, y), (i, j), and (x, j) with $x < i$ and $y < j$ is given by $SA(x, y) - SA(i, y) + SA(i, j) - SA(x, j)$ (see Figure D.6). The construction is very efficient [Hensley05], but a high data precision is needed to avoid artifacts. For a binary input texture, the summed-area table should be stored in a 32-bit integer texture, which ensures robust results.

D.3.1   Construction

A brute-force construction would simply loop for a given pixel over all pixels in the upper left quadrant. Such a scheme is, however, very expensive (e.g., for the pixel in the lower-right corner, one would need to loop over all pixels in the image). Instead, one can compute an SAT with an efficient recursive scheme.

One-Dimensional Case

Efficient construction algorithms [Hensley05] are slightly involved, and we will first concentrate only on a one-dimensional SAT that is a one-dimensional texture. In other words, it means that we want to store in a pixel x the sum of all pixels to its left: $SA(x) := \sum_{i=0}^{x} I(i)$. Equivalently to the two-dimensional case, one could retrieve the exact average in a pixel interval $[x, y]$ by computing $SA(y) - SA(x-1) = \sum_{i=x}^{y} I_i$.

The recursive construction is accomplished in several passes. We will denote S^k the resulting texture of pass k. For $k = 0$, this is just the original input image. After the first pass, each pixel will contain the sum of itself and its left neighbor: $S^1(x) := I(x) + I(x - 1)$. The second pass will derive a texture S^2 where each pixel contains the sum of itself and its three neighbors to the left: $S^2(x) := I(x) + I(x - 1) + I(x - 2) + I(x - 3)$. Generally, $S^k(x) := \sum_{i=0}^{2^k} I(x - i)$. We will see later how this construction is achieved. Let's first look at the resulting texture after $\log(n)$ passes, where n is the width of the texture. For a given pixel x, we have $S^{\log(n)}(x) := \sum_{i=0}^{n} I(x - i)$. Looking closely at $I^{\log(n)}$, one realizes that it is almost the actual SAT representation:

$$\sum_{i=0}^{n} I(x - i) = \sum_{i=0}^{x} I(i) + \sum_{i>x} I(x - i) = SA(x) + \sum_{i=1}^{n-x} I(-i).$$

If one assures that $I(i) = 0$ for all $i < 0$, the construction results directly in the SAT. In fact, this property is easy to ensure by relying on the standard graphics API and adding a black border to the input texture (GL_TEXTURE_BORDER_COLOR, see also Appendix B).

We have seen that $\log(n)$ passes are needed to compute the SAT representation (e.g., a 1024-texel-wide texture requires ten passes). But so far, we have not yet described how to produce S^k from S^{k-1} efficiently. While the first can obviously be performed with two lookups per pixel, the second pass seems to involve already four lookups in order to compute $S^2(x) := I(x) + I(x - 1) + I(x - 2) + I(x - 3)$. Fortunately, the second pass can actually be realized with only two lookups by relying on the result from the previous pass:

$$S^2(x) := (I(x) + I(x - 1)) + (I(x - 2) + I(x - 3)) := S^1(x) + S^1(x - 2).$$

This observation generalizes, and it is always possible to compute S^k by relying on S^{k-1} with just two lookups per pixel:

$$
\begin{aligned}
S^k(x) &= \sum_{i=0}^{2^k} I_{x-i} \\
&= \sum_{i=0}^{2^{k-1}} I(x - i) + \sum_{i=2^{k-1}}^{2^k} I(x - i) \\
&= \sum_{i=0}^{2^{k-1}} I(x - i) + \sum_{i=0}^{2^{k-1}} I(x - 2^{k-1} - i) \\
&= S^{k-1}(x) + S^{k-1}(x - 2^{k-1}).
\end{aligned}
$$

In other words, all one needs to do during the construction of a new level is to fetch two values from the previous level (for level one, these two texels are neighboring). For each level, the lookup distance between these two texels should be doubled.

Two-Dimensional Case

Finally, the extension of the previous algorithm to the two-dimensional case is surprisingly simple. First, one computes in parallel a one-dimensional summed-area table SAT^{1D} for each pixel row in the input texture I. Then, one computes one-dimensional SATs for each column of this texture SAT^{1D} to derive the two-dimensional version SAT^{2D}. To understand why this works, we can quickly look at the math behind these operations and illustrate that SAT^{2D} is nothing else but a one-dimensional row SAT of the one-dimensional column summed-area table SAT^{1D}:

$$SAT^{2D}(x, y) := \sum_{i=0,j=0}^{n} I(x - i, y - j) = \sum_{i=0}^{n}\sum_{j=0}^{n} I(x - i, y - j) = \sum_{i=0}^{n} SAT^{1D}(x - i, y).$$

Implementation

While the overall algorithm is relatively efficient, the process is still more involved than for the N-buffer computation. In particular, it is due to the fact that one needs to rely on high-precision textures. Summing all pixels can quickly lead to an overflow when working with 8-bit values. Instead 16, often even 32, bits might be necessary.

It is important to notice though that, in contrast to N-buffers, the intermediate textures do not need to be stored and can be discarded. The effective memory cost corresponds only to a single texture. Although in practice, two such textures are often allocated to allow ping-pong rendering during the construction. The below pseudocode summarizes the construction steps.

```
shader.attachTexture("SourceTexture", originalTexture);
//INPUT -> 1D SAT
int lastI;
for(int i = 0; i <= passes; ++i) {
  shader.activate();
  //lookup in x direction
  shader.setUniform2f("LookUpDir", pow(2,i), 0);
  fbo[i%2].activate();
  renderQuad();
  shader.deactivate();
  shader.attachTexture("SourceTexture", fbo[i%2].getTexture());
  lastI = i;
}
//1D SAT -> 2D SAT
for(int i = lastI; i <= passes + lastI; ++i) {
  shader.activate();
  //lookup in y direction
  shader.setUniform2f("LookUpDir", 0, pow(2,i));
  fbo[i%2].activate();
  renderQuad();
  shader.deactivate();
  shader.attachTexture("SourceTexture", fbo[i%2].getTexture());
}
```

```
//shader code
uniform Texture2D SourceTexture;
uniform vec2 LookUpDir;
void main() {
  vec4f sat
    = texelFetch2D(SourceTexture, gl_FragCoord.xy)
    + texelFetch2D(SourceTexture, gl_FragCoord.xy+LookUpDir);
  //...
  }
```

Details

In order to reduce the needed bit depth, two strategies can be employed: centering and origin-centering [Hensley05].

Centering. Centering tries to optimize bit usage by shifting all image values. By substracting the average from all pixels, values become generally smaller and the sum of all pixels will be zero. This operations can be easily inversed: one computes the size of the filtering rectangle in pixels and multiplies this area by the average value. The resulting correction value is added to the result.

Origin centering. Origin centering reduces numerical issues by cutting a texture into four quadrants and by computing the SAT in such a way that a pixel stores the sum of all pixels in the same quadrant towards the center of the image. One can still compute the correct filter result, but at most one-fourth of all pixels in the initial texture are summed, which often enables the use of a cheaper data format.

Practical example: binary images. For shadow computations, it is sometimes interesting to query a binary image. If the image resolution is below 512^2, 16-bit precision is sufficient. This also holds for $1,024^2$ textures when using the origin-centering strategy. Although an overflow could theoretically occur if the entire image is filled with ones, in practice, one can easily account for this particular case. On newer cards, unsigned short or, for higher-resolution textures, integer textures are the best choice. On older cards, integer textures are not available. Consequently, 16-bit fixed-point values (GL_LUMINANCE16) can be used instead; for higher precision, one can also rely on 32-bit floating-point numbers. The latter leads to an effective precision of 24 bits—the size of the mantissa. Consequently, it is possible to deal with textures up to a $4,096^2$ resolution.

D.3.2   Filtering

The filtering with summed-area tables is of very high quality. As indicated initially, lookups at the four corners can be used to directly compute the sum of all pixels in the corresponding rectangle. One interesting observation is that SATs are compatible with linear filtering. Even windows that overlap pixels partially result

Method	Construction	Quality	Memory	Min/max
Mipmap	⊕⊕	○	⊕⊕	yes
N-buffer	○	⊕	⊖	yes
Y map	⊕	⊕	⊕	yes
SAT	○	⊕⊕	○	no

Table D.1. Filtering method overview: construction performance, filtering quality, memory consumption, and compatibility with min/max computation.

in a correct response. Consequently, SATs are the optimal choice for high-quality results.

D.4   Summary

Depending on the application, all three filtering methods presented in this chapter can prove useful. For accurate computations, there is no way around summed-area tables, but they often imply a relatively high cost. This performance drop is mostly related to two issues: the higher bit precision and the fact that four lookups are needed, which is more than for mipmaps or N-buffers. N-buffers turn out to be a very good tradeoff if some accuracy loss is acceptable. In particular, the extension to Y maps deals with the overwhelming memory consumption of the original N-buffer definition. In practice, this representation provides very good results and still enables high efficiency. Mipmaps, on the other hand, prove very useful when memory usage is the main concern, but gives significantly coarser approximations. For example, an average occluder might not have to be very precise, as the result itself might be used in an approximate formula. Here, mipmaps can be the representation of choice. Table D.1 shows an overview of the methodological consequences.

Even though we only addressed the computation of the maximum or minimum value in a rectangular area briefly, it should be mentioned that mipmaps, N-buffers, and Y maps are all naturally compatible with this task, while summed-area tables are not. Actually, N-buffers and Y maps are even able to deliver the accurate result for an arbitrarily sized square region with only four lookups by superposing the lookup windows.

More For Less: Deferred Shading and Upsampling

This chapter introduces the principle of deferred shading and upsampling. These techniques are useful, not only in the context of shadow computations, but can be advantageous whenever algorithms are pixel-shader bound. In other words, if per-pixel computations have a high cost, these methods often increase the overall performance.

Deferred shading only affects the way a result is computed, but not its appearance.[1] Contrarily, upsampling strategies might lead to some loss of accuracy. In the following, we will analyze the principle of both techniques, which can lead to an impressive speed-up when applied in practice. Especially, deferred shading has become a useful addition to the toolbox of game developers (Stalker [Shishkovtsov06] is an example that well illustrates this fact).

E.1 Deferred Shading

E.1.1 Definition

In the standard graphics pipeline, the color of a pixel is computed before it is sent to the framebuffer. This fragment (a color and a depth) is then tested against the depth buffer. Only if it is closer than the previously stored depth value, the color is actually stored. In other words, any pixel value that is computed for a hidden part of the scene can incur a complex and unnecessary shader evaluation. This

---

[1]Supersampling and multisampling techniques do not work any longer, though, so antialiasing and also transparency are known to be problematic.

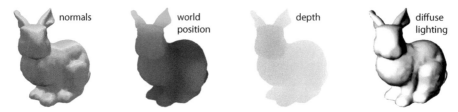

Figure E.1. G-buffers capture surface information in the form of images. Normals, world position, depth, lighting, or material properties are typical choices.

performance overhead might have been negligible when shading operations were cheap, but with today's hardware, complex material and illumination computations have become the standard. The goal of deferred shading is to avoid calculations on hidden fragments and to evaluate illumination in screen space without involving the actual geometry.

The idea is relatively simple. If you have ever seen painting by numbers, you should grasp the principle immediately. Imagine a fictional rendering problem: All surfaces in the scene have a material number which, when executed with an expensive pixel shader, can be converted into an actual pixel color. When using the standard graphics pipeline, many surfaces will execute this costly conversion operation, although their pixels might ultimately be hidden behind another surface. Instead, deferred shading avoids this issue by deferring (or delaying) the shading operation. In practice, it means that we first render the scene, but output the material number instead of the color. The resulting image will finally contain in each pixel the material number of the underlying visible surface. Hence, it resembles a painting-by-number picture. The expensive conversion shader can then be executed on this material-number image, which ensures that the shader is only executed on image pixels that are actually present in the rendered image. Consequently, the costly conversion is only applied to visible surfaces and never to hidden ones. Furthermore, this second rendering pass does not involve the scene geometry any longer; the cost is directly related to the pixels.

In a "real-world" case, such a material ID might actually be attributes (e.g., shadow map coordinates, normals) that are extracted and stored in so-called *G-buffers*, originally called geometric buffers [Saito90]. Basically, a G-buffer is a snapshot of the scene that recovers surface attributes. Figure E.1 shows some typical examples. The necessary condition is that the extracted values allow us to evaluate the expensive pixel shader in the second pass.

E.1.2   Practical Considerations

In practice, deferred shading is useful from Shader Model 3.0 onwards, where the so-called multiple render targets (MRTs) were introduced (compare Appendix A).

MRTs allow the user to write not only a single color value in the framebuffer, but several ones. This property is crucial, as it allows to collect a set of values (e.g., normals, position, color) without having to perform several render passes.

Nonetheless, the more values are output in parallel, the more costly the creation and storage of the attribute collection, in the form of G-buffers, becomes. Bandwidth is a big issue with this technique. Hence, it can make sense to store results of cheap computations instead of attributes (e.g., one might directly compute and collect diffuse illumination instead of a reflectance and a normal value) if these values are not needed for any other purpose. Optimizing for such attributes can be complex and the search for a good tradeoff between memory consumption and shader performance cannot be avoided. It is not easy to give general advice on how to optimize one's code. In some situations, even complex strategies, such as the packing of different information in bit patterns of a color can prove useful. As a rule of thumb for today's hardware, one can rely on four 16-bit buffers which leads to reasonable performance on many systems.

E.1.3   Examples

The practical impact of deferred shading can be impressive. As an example, the algorithm in [Eisemann08b] benefits from a 50% speed-up when using deferred shading over an on-surface evaluation.

The reason for the performance increase is actually two-fold. We mentioned before that hidden pixels are not evaluated, but there is another advantage that is slightly more technical. When evaluating pixel shaders, the graphics hardware needs to process groups of several pixels. The reason is linked to the existence of a derivative operator in shaders. The derivative commands (`ddx`, `ddy`) can compute the derivative of an arbitrary value in a shader program. In hardware, this operation is computed by differentiating neighboring pixel values. In consequence, groups of at least four pixels are always evaluated in parallel (potentially even more).

Unfortunately, this choice has negative implications too. If one renders a very small triangle—of the size of one pixel—still four shader computations are performed and, basically, 75% of the computation is wasted. In deferred shading, evaluating neighboring pixels do not incur this penalty because all pixels are actually processed. Hence, the work can benefit from coherent computations and data exchange between neighboring pixels. Nonetheless, when using derivatives, the result can be less accurate.

E.2   Upsampling

The idea of upsampling is to take advantage of pixel coherence in the final image. For example, soft shadows often exhibit low-frequency variations and, therefore, many neighboring pixels show similar shading results. Consequently, one should aim at exploiting this coherence in screen space by only computing the correct shadow response for a subset of pixels and then reconstructing the remaining information. In practice, such a reconstruction operation can be as simple as a filter, but we will see that better solutions take the geometric information of the scene into account. Finally, we will give a quick outlook on the possibility of integrating computations over time by exploiting temporal coherence. Unfortunately, making such attempts work in practice is a difficult issue and, especially for quickly varying lighting conditions, many solutions fail. Nevertheless, it is a particularly interesting venue of future work, which is the reason why we will discuss this topic briefly.

E.2.1   Spatial Methods and Geometry-Aware Blur

Let's motivate the idea behind upsampling with a simple example. Imagine one wants to illuminate a scene with many light sources and even with deferred shading, we would need to evaluate every single of the, say, 1,000 light sources. The cost of such an evaluation would be very high and is particularly frustrating when one realizes that the energy contribution of a single light source might be very similar for a given group of neighboring pixels. Much of the computation seems redundant.

To exploit this coherency, a solution is to evaluate only a subset of light sources per pixel and produce an average incoming light contribution. This contribution could then be propagated to the neighboring pixels instead of accurately evaluating all sources per pixel. One should notice that the propagated light is the *incoming* radiance (i.e., the contribution coming from the light before it is modulated by the surface reflectance). Only then is it possible to spread this information to neighboring pixels. Otherwise, a red surface lit with a white light would bleed its red color into the surrounding pixels.

Such a decomposition of the light set is useful. Imagine that we consider 2×2-pixel groups and for each pixel in such a group we evaluate a distinct set of 250 light sources out of the overall 1,000. Thus, the per-pixel cost is reduced by a factor of four. Unfortunately, using a different set of light sources per pixel results in a clearly visible noise (Figure E.2, left). To get rid of this artifact, the noisy image is filtered in order to improve its appearance. This filtering can be as simple as an averaging process and any of the techniques in Appendix D can be used, but there is a catch. When averaging neighboring pixels, the light contributions might leak across depth discontinuities and induce visible halos around objects. A better solution is to rely on a particular filtering process that takes the underlying geometry into account because shading discontinuities often coincide with geometric discontinuities.

In the following, we will discuss geometry-aware filtering which is a technique that has recently received much attention. An example of its effectiveness is the

interleaved radiance   geometry-aware blur + textures

Figure E.2. Instead of evaluating a large set of light sources in each pixel, it is more efficient to select a suitable subset of light sources per block of pixels. Choosing different sets will increase performance but will also lead to noise in the final image (left). This noise can often be removed by filtering the information (right).

high-quality image (Figure E.2, right) that was computed from a noisy input (Figure E.2, left).

E.2.2 Advanced Filtering

We have analyzed in Appendix D how to average a set of pixel values $I(\mathbf{t})$ in the image I from a neighborhood $\mathcal{K}(\mathbf{t})$ around a pixel position $\mathbf{t}$. Here, we will see that it is sometimes beneficial to consider the underlying structure of the image (e.g., in order to preserve discontinuities). This filter modification is enabled by a weighting function ω. Mathematically, the result of the filtering process for a pixel location $\mathbf{t}$ is

$$f_{\text{filter}}(\mathbf{t}) = \frac{\sum_{\mathbf{t}_i \in \mathcal{K}(\mathbf{t})} \omega(\mathbf{t}, \mathbf{t}_i) I(\mathbf{t}_i)}{\sum_{\mathbf{t}_i \in \mathcal{K}(\mathbf{t})} \omega(\mathbf{t}, \mathbf{t}_i)}, \tag{E.1}$$

where ω is a function that compares the two pixel locations $\mathbf{t}$ and $\mathbf{t}_i$ and decides on a corresponding weight. Because the weighting function does not have to rely on the original image I, but can be defined using other images, such a filtering is usually referred to as joint [Petschnigg04] or cross [Eisemann04] bilateral filtering. We will soon see possible definitions for ω, but first, let's look at another interesting element of Equation (E.1), which is the denominator $\sum_{\mathbf{t}_i \in \mathcal{K}(\mathbf{t})} \omega(\mathbf{t}, \mathbf{t}_i)$. It assures energy conservation (the image does not become darker or brighter when the filter is applied several times). In other words, each pixel in the sum is weighted, such that the sum of all weights equals one.

The definition of the weighting function ω can depend on the wanted filtering effect. A simple choice is to use the distance between the two pixel locations. For example, $\omega(\mathbf{t}, \mathbf{t}_i) = G(\sigma, \|\mathbf{t} - \mathbf{t}_i\|) := \exp(-\|\mathbf{t} - \mathbf{t}_i\|^2/\sigma^2)$ results in a *Gaussian blur*. Often, the function ω will fall off quickly in image space and distant pixels tend to receive very low weights. Hence, it is usually possible to clamp ω to zero as soon as it falls below some small threshold. In the case of a Gaussian, one can clamp it between 2σ or 3σ pixels. The direct advantage is that the filtering at a pixel position $\mathbf{t}$ only needs to involve a small neighborhood.

Geometry-Aware Filtering

In the following, we extend Equation (E.1) to take the geometry of the underlying scene into account. We have previously seen in Section E.1 that it is possible to retrieve image buffers containing properties of the underlying surface, the G-buffers. We will now make use of these buffers in order to control the filtering process. This extension will allow us, for example, to avoid blurring across depth discontinuities, or across strong normal changes.

In the context of our initial problem of evaluating thousands of light sources, this solution will allow us to evaluate different sets of lights in each pixel and remove the resulting noise without introducing artifacts. Basically, only similar pixels—that would have resulted in similar illumination anyway—will share their values.

A good solution for a geometry-aware filtering is to rely on a weighting function that considers the projected position (screen position and depth), as well as the normal orientation. By relying on the previously defined Gaussian kernel G, a good choice is

$$\omega(\mathbf{t}, \mathbf{t}_i) = G(\sigma_n, \text{normal}(\mathbf{t}) \cdot \text{normal}(\mathbf{t}_i))G(\sigma_p, \|\text{position}(\mathbf{t}) - \text{position}(\mathbf{t}_i)\|),$$

where $\text{position}(\cdot)$ and $\text{normal}(\cdot)$ are the image buffers of the extracted position and surface normals, respectively. The two values σ_n, σ_p are chosen empirically and depend on the scene. Two pixels with strongly differing normals result in a very low weight, meaning that our confidence that these two pixels would receive a similar full illumination is relatively low. On the contrary, if both pixels share the same normal and are at a similar position, it is very likely that both receive a similar illumination—accordingly the weight is high.

Instead of the world position, many approaches use only the depth of a pixel. In this case, it is very common to also add an image-based distance (the projected distance on the screen) and to apply it to a falloff function k. Consequently, the examined neighborhood can be restricted to only contain pixels that receive a sufficient spatial weight. These modifications result in the following definition:

$$\omega(\mathbf{t}, \mathbf{t}_i) = k(\mathbf{t} - \mathbf{t}_i)G(\sigma_n, \text{normal}(\mathbf{t}) \cdot \text{normal}(\mathbf{t}_i))G(\sigma_p, \|\text{depth}(\mathbf{t}) - \text{depth}(\mathbf{t}_i)\|).$$

One should notice that especially for distant scene elements such choices might prove insufficiently accurate. Due to the camera perspective, two distant elements might appear to be in close proximity on the screen while being very distant in the scene, which in turn would imply that their shading is likely to be very different too. Often, this is not a big issue because users tend to pay more attention to nearby elements. In general, only similar pixels can benefit from the process and some isolated pixels can always persist.

The only clean correction for the artifacts for distant objects would be to avoid filtering in these regions altogether. Consequently, one would need to rely on a full evaluation of the original shader, which is costly, but possible. A good solution to estimate the confidence in the result of the filtering process is given by the expression $\sum_{t_i \in \mathcal{K}(t)} \omega(\mathbf{t}, \mathbf{t}_i)$ [Durand02, Herzog10]. Basically, this is the sum of all weights attributed to surrounding pixels. If no pixels are similar, the weight is low, and consequently, the pixel under consideration is rather unique and cannot benefit from any coherence.

Geometry-Aware Upsampling

We have previously seen that pixels can share values via filtering. In the following, we will push this idea even further. One can compute shading values only for a subset of all pixels and then upsample this information. In other words, computing shading of a small set of pixels can be enough to derive a high-quality full-resolution image [Yang08]. In practice, one can imagine rendering a low resolution image with, say, 960×540 pixels for which the shading is evaluated accurately. This low-resolution image is then upsampled into a full-HD $1{,}920 \times 1{,}080$ high-resolution version.

One way to define such an upsampling would be to simply mix neighboring pixels. Unfortunately, doing so would result in a blurry image. Instead, we will exploit the same observation as before; shading discontinuities often coincide with geometric discontinuities. Consequently, we will again make use of deferred shading to extract G-buffers. The insight is that by using a high-resolution G-buffer, accurate confidence values can be computed that allows for a far superior resolution increase than if one would rely only on low-resolution images. Furthermore, the creation of the G-buffers is cheap because they do not involve complex computations. This resolution heterogeneity between cheap-to-compute high-resolution attributes and expensive low-resolution shading leads to an excellent tradeoff.

The upsampling itself looks similar to the filtering process previously described:

$$\text{Upsample}(\mathbf{t}) = \frac{\sum_{\mathbf{t}_i^l \in \mathcal{K}(\mathbf{t}^l)} \omega(\mathbf{t}, \mathbf{t}_i) I(\mathbf{t}_i^l)}{\sum_{\mathbf{t}_i^l \in \mathcal{K}(\mathbf{t}^l)} \omega(\mathbf{t}, \mathbf{t}_i)}, \tag{E.2}$$

where $\mathcal{K}(\mathbf{t})$ is again a pixel neighborhood and $\mathbf{t}^l, \mathbf{t}_i^l$ are the corresponding positions of $\mathbf{t}, \mathbf{t}_i$ in the low resolution image I. It is important to notice that the above

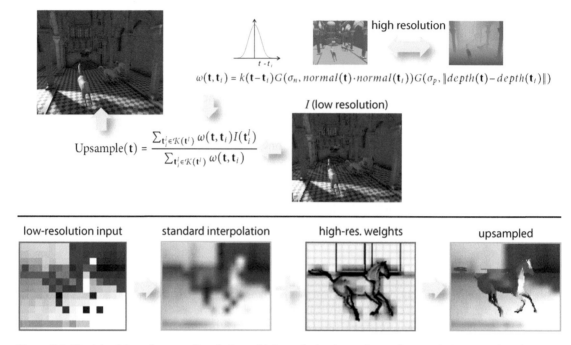

Figure E.3. The joint-bilateral upsampling derives a high-resolution image from a low-resolution input by relying on additional high-resolution buffers that determine the reconstruction weights (top). The quality improvement is striking when compared to standard interpolation (bottom).

equation defines high-resolution pixels. While the G-buffers (used by the ω function) are of high resolution the shading image I itself is of low resolution. In other words, the only modification with respect to the previously explained filtering is that for each high-resolution pixel position $\mathbf{t}$, several low-resolution shading pixels $\mathbf{t}_i$ are tested for similarity. Still they use weights that are derived from the corresponding positions in the high-resolution G-buffers. This process of joint-bilateral upsampling [Kopf07] is illustrated in Figure E.3, based on the previously mentioned joint/cross-bilateral filter [Petschnigg04, Eisemann04].

Upsampling is an effective solution that can be realized very efficiently on current GPUs without much implementation effort. It is not perfect though. Very detailed information cannot be captured accurately. Recently, spatiotemporal approaches aim at addressing this shortcoming by relying on previously computed values [Nehab07, Sitthi-amorn08, Herzog10]. Although very efficient and often superior in quality, the exploitation of temporal coherence is not straightforward and we refer the interested reader to [Scherzer11]. In the future, such upsampling algorithms might become increasingly important as they seem a promising possibility for efficient remote-rendering applications in client-server systems [Pajak11].

E.3 Summary

We have seen various ways of accelerating computations completely independently of the underlying algorithm. The two main strategies were deferred shading and filtering/upsampling. Deferred shading is extremely effective for expensive fragment processing and avoids evaluating the costly shader for hidden geometry. Consequently, if a process is shader bound, one should definitely test a deferred-shading version.

Aside from issues concerning antialiasing, deferred shading delivers a virtually equivalent image. When it is possible to accept a slight degradation, one can achieve further performance increases by relying on filtering and upsampling. The assumption behind these processes is that similar pixels will also receive similar shading. Consequently, it becomes possible to share information between similar pixels, thereby reducing the shader workload. For filtering, all pixels compute a degraded version and similar pixels mix their results. For upsampling, only a subset computes the full shader solution and the process then propagates this result to neighboring pixels. While the latter is always possible, filtering assumes that a shader can easily be broken down to yield simpler approximations. Depending on the algorithm, this may or may not be possible.

In many cases the advice in this chapter helps achieve a much higher frame rate with only little deviation from the full solution. Furthermore, it is relatively easy to apply these suggestions and they are compatible with almost any shadow algorithm. Hence, it is good advice to consider the here-presented approaches in practical applications.

APPENDIX F
Symbols

Symbol	Description
$\mathcal{L}$	Light
$\mathcal{B}$	Blocker, occluder, shadow caster
$\mathbf{p}$	Scene point, receiver point, view sample
$\mathbf{l}$	Light (sample) point
$\mathbf{t}$	Texel, texture coordinates
$\mathbf{p}^{\mathrm{L}}$	Light-space coordinates of point $\mathbf{p}$
$\mathbf{p}^{\mathrm{LC}}$	Light-clip–space coordinates of point $\mathbf{p}$
$\mathbf{p}^{\mathrm{s}}$	Shadow-map texture coordinates for point $\mathbf{p}$
$\mathbf{M}_{\mathrm{v}}$	View matrix (world $\rightarrow$ eye space)
$\mathbf{M}_{\mathrm{p}}$	Projection matrix
$\mathbf{M}_{\mathrm{c}}$	Camera matrix (world $\rightarrow$ clip space)
$\mathbf{M}_{\mathrm{v}}^{\mathrm{L}}$	Light-view matrix (world $\rightarrow$ light space)
$V(\mathbf{p}, \mathbf{q})$	Mutual (binary) visibility of points $\mathbf{p}$ and $\mathbf{q}$
$V_{\mathcal{L}}(\mathbf{p}), V(\mathbf{p})$	Fraction of light ($\mathcal{L}$) visible from $\mathbf{p}$; visibility factor
$z(\mathbf{t})$	Light-space depth value from shadow map
$\tilde{z}$	Light-space depth value of fragment
$\mathbf{p}_{\tilde{z}}^{\mathrm{L}}$	Light-space depth of point $\mathbf{p}$
$s(z, \tilde{z})$	Shadow-test function
$f(\mathbf{t}, \tilde{z}) = s(z(\mathbf{t}), \tilde{z})$	Shadow-mapping function
$H(x)$	Heaviside/step function

Symbol	Description
$\mathcal{R}$	Region
$\mathcal{K}$	Filter kernel region
$k(x)$	Filter kernel function
L	Radiance
$f_{\mathrm{r}}(\mathbf{p}, \omega, \omega')$	BRDF

Bibliography

[Agrawala00] Agrawala, M., Ramamoorthi, R., Heirich, A., and Moll, L. 2000. Efficient image-based methods for rendering soft shadows. In *Proceedings of ACM SIGGRAPH 2000*, pp. 375–384.

[Aila04a] Aila, T. and Akenine-Möller, T. 2004. A hierarchical shadow volume algorithm. In *Proceedings of Graphics Hardware 2004*, pp. 15–23.

[Aila04b] Aila, T. and Laine, S. 2004. Alias-free shadow maps. In *Proceedings of Eurographics Symposium on Rendering 2004*, pp. 161–166.

[Akenine-Möller02] Akenine-Möller, T. and Assarsson, U. 2002. Approximate soft shadows on arbitrary surfaces using penumbra wedges. In *Proceedings of Eurographics Workshop on Rendering 2002*, pp. 297–306.

[Akenine-Möller08] Akenine-Möller, T., Haines, E., and Hoffman, N. 2008. *Real-Time Rendering*. 3rd ed. A K Peters.

[Aldridge04] Aldridge, G. and Woods, E. 2004. Robust, geometry-independent shadow volumes. In *GRAPHITE '04: Proceedings of the 2nd international conference on Computer graphics and interactive techniques in Australasia and South East Asia*, pp. 250–253.

[Anderson] Anderson, S. E. Bit twiddling hacks. http://graphics.stanford.edu/~seander/bithacks.html.

[Annen07] Annen, T., Mertens, T., Bekaert, P., Seidel, H.-P., and Kautz, J. 2007. Convolution shadow maps. In *Proceedings of Eurographics Symposium on Rendering 2007*, pp. 51–60.

[Annen08a] Annen, T., Dong, Z., Mertens, T., Bekaert, P., Seidel, H.-P., and Kautz, J. 2008. Real-time, all-frequency shadows in dynamic scenes. *ACM Transactions on Graphics*, 27, 3 (Proceedings of ACM SIGGRAPH 2008), 34:1–34:8.

[Annen08b] Annen, T., Mertens, T., Seidel, H.-P., Flerackers, E., and Kautz, J. 2008. Exponential shadow maps. In *Proceedings of Graphics Interface 2008*, pp. 155–161.

[Appel67] Appel, A. 1967. The notion of quantitative invisibility and the machine rendering of solids. In *Proceedings of ACM '67*, pp. 387–393.

[Appel68] Appel, A. 1968. Some techniques for shading machine renderings of solids. In *AFIPS '68 (Spring): Proceedings of the April 30–May 2, 1968, spring joint computer conference*, pp. 37–45.

[Arvo04a] Arvo, J. 2004. Tiled shadow maps. In *Proceedings of Computer Graphics International 2004*, pp. 240–246.

[Arvo04b] Arvo, J., Hirvikorpi, M., and Tyystjärvi, J. 2004. Approximate soft shadows with an image-space flood-fill algorithm. *Computer Graphics Forum*, 23, 3 (Proceedings of Eurographics 2004), 271–280.

[Arvo05] Arvo, J. and Hirvikorpi, M. 2005. Compressed shadow maps. *The Visual Computer*, 21, 3, 125–138.

[Arvo07] Arvo, J. 2007. Alias-free shadow maps using graphics hardware. *Journal of Graphics Tools*, 12, 1, 47–59.

[Assarsson03a] Assarsson, U. and Akenine-Möller, T. 2003. A geometry-based soft shadow volume algorithm using graphics hardware. *ACM Transactions on Graphics*, 22, 3 (Proceedings of ACM SIGGRAPH 2003), 511–520.

[Assarsson03b] Assarsson, U., Dougherty, M., Mounier, M., and Akenine-Möller, T. 2003. An optimized soft shadow volume algorithm with real-time performance. In *Proceedings of Graphics Hardware 2003*, pp. 33–40.

[Assarsson04] Assarsson, U. and Akenine-Möller, T. 2004. Occlusion culling and z-fail for soft shadow volume algorithms. *The Visual Computer*, 20, 8-9.

[Aszódi06] Aszódi, B. and Szirmay-Kalos, L. 2006. Real-time soft shadows with shadow accumulation. In *Eurographics 2006 Short Papers*, pp. 53–56.

[Atherton78] Atherton, P., Weiler, K., and Greenberg, D. 1978. Polygon shadow generation. *Computer Graphics*, 12, 3 (Proceedings of ACM SIGGRAPH 78), 275–281.

[Atty06] Atty, L., Holzschuch, N., Lapierre, M., Hasenfratz, J.-M., Hansen, C., and Sillion, F. X. 2006. Soft shadow maps: Efficient sampling of light source visibility. *Computer Graphics Forum*, 25, 4, 725–741.

[Baran10] Baran, I., Chen, J., Ragan-Kelley, J., Durand, F., and Lehtinen, J. 2010. A hierarchical volumetric shadow algorithm for single scattering. *ACM Transactions on Graphics*, 29, 6 (Proceedings of ACM SIGGRAPH Asia 2010), 178:1–178:10.

[Barzel97] Barzel, R. 1997. Lighting controls for computer cinematography. *Journal of Graphics Tools*, 2, 1, 1–20.

[Batagelo99] Batagelo, H. C. and Júnior, I. C. 1999. Real-time shadow generation using bsp trees and stencil buffers. In *SIBGRAPI '99: Proceedings of the XII Brazilian Symposium on Computer Graphics and Image Processing*, p. 93.

[Bavoil06] Bavoil, L. and Silva, C. T. 2006. Real-time soft shadows with cone culling. In *ACM SIGGRAPH 2006 Sketches and Applications*, p. 105.

[Bavoil08a] Bavoil, L. 2008. Advanced soft shadow mapping techniques. Presentation, *Game Developers Conference 2008*. http://developer.download.nvidia.com/presentations/2008/GDC/GDC08_SoftShadowMapping.pdf.

[Bavoil08b] Bavoil, L., Callahan, S. P., and Silva, C. T. 2008. Robust soft shadow mapping with backprojection and depth peeling. *Journal of Graphics Tools*, 13, 1, 19–30.

[Bavoil08c] Bavoil, L., Sainz, M., and Dimitrov, R. 2008. Image-space horizon-based ambient occlusion. In *ACM SIGGRAPH 2008 Talks*, pp. 22:1–22:1.

[Behrens98] Behrens, U. and Ratering, R. 1998. Adding shadows to a texture-based volume renderer. In *Proceedings of the 1998 IEEE symposium on Volume visualization*, VVS '98, pp. 39–46.

[Benthin09] Benthin, C. and Wald, I. 2009. Efficient ray traced soft shadows using multi-frusta tracing. In *Proceedings of High Performance Graphics 2009*, pp. 135–144.

[Bergeron86] Bergeron, P. 1986. A general version of crow's shadow volumes. *IEEE Computer Graphics and Applications*, 6, 9, 17–28.

[Bestimt99] Bestimt, J. and Freitag, B. 1999. Real-time shadow casting using shadow volumes. *Gamasutra*. http://www.gamasutra.com/features/19991115/bestimt_freitag_01.htm.

[Billeter09] Billeter, M., Olsson, O., and Assarsson, U. 2009. Efficient stream compaction on wide simd many-core architectures. In *Proceedings of High Performance Graphics 2009*, pp. 159–166.

[Billeter10] Billeter, M., Sintorn, E., and Assarson, U. 2010. Volumetric shadows using polygonal light volumes. In *Proceedings of High Performance Graphics 2010*, pp. 39–45.

[Bilodeau99] Bilodeau, W. and Songy, M. 1999. Real time shadows. Creativity 1999, Creative Labs Inc. Sponsored game developer conferences, Los Angeles, California, and Surrey, England.

[Biri06] Biri, V., Arquès, D., and Michelin, S. 2006. Real Time Rendering of Atmospheric Scattering and Volumetric Shadows. *Journal of WSCG*, 14, 1, 65–72.

[Bittner11] Bittner, J., Mattausch, O., Silvennoinen, A., and Wimmer, M. 2011. Shadow caster culling for efficient shadow mapping. In *Proceedings of ACM SIGGRAPH Symposium on Interactive 3D Graphics and Games 2011*, pp. 81–88.

[Blinn82] Blinn, J. F. 1982. Light reflection functions for simulation of clouds and dusty surfaces. *Computer Graphics*, 16, 3 (Proceedings of ACM SIGGRAPH 82), 21–29.

[Blinn88] Blinn, J. F. 1988. Me and my (fake) shadow. *IEEE Computer Graphics and Applications*, 8, 1, 82–86.

[Blinn93] Blinn, J. 1993. A trip down the graphics pipeline: The homogeneous perspective transform. *IEEE Computer Graphics and Applications*, 13, 75–80.

[Blinn98] Blinn, J. F. 1998. Ten more unsolved problems in computer graphics. *IEEE Computer Graphics and Applications*, 18, 5, 86–89.

[Blythe06] Blythe, D. 2006. The Direct3D 10 system. *ACM Transactions on Graphics*, 25, 3 (Proceedings of ACM SIGGRAPH 2006), 724–734.

[Bouknight70] Bouknight, J. and Kelley, K. 1970. An algorithm for producing half-tone computer graphics presentations with shadows and movable light sources. In *AFIPS '70 (Spring): Proceedings of the May 5-7, 1970, spring joint computer conference*, pp. 1–10.

[Brabec02a] Brabec, S., Annen, T., and Seidel, H.-P. 2002. Practical shadow mapping. *Journal of Graphics Tools*, 7, 4, 9–18.

[Brabec02b] Brabec, S., Annen, T., and Seidel, H.-P. 2002. Shadow mapping for hemispherical and omnidirectional light sources. In *Advances in Modeling, Animation and Rendering (Proceedings Computer Graphics International 2002)*, pp. 397–408.

[Brabec02c] Brabec, S. and Seidel, H.-P. 2002. Single sample soft shadows using depth maps. In *Proceedings of Graphics Interface 2002*, pp. 219–228.

[Brabec03] Brabec, S. and Seidel, H.-P. 2003. Shadow volumes on programmable graphics hardware. *Computer Graphics Forum*, 25, 3 (Proceedings of Eurographics 2003).

[Brennan02] Brennan, C. 2002. Shadow volume extrusion using a vertex shader. In *ShaderX: Vertex and Pixel Shaders Tips and Tricks* (edited by W. Engel), pp. 188–194. Wordware Publishing, Plano, TX. ISBN 1-55622-041-3.

[Brotman84] Brotman, L. S. and Badler, N. 1984. Generating soft shadows with a depth buffer algorithm. *IEEE Computer Graphics and Applications*, 4, 10, 71–81.

[Bunnell06] Bunnell, M. 2006. Dynamic ambient occlusion and indirect lighting. In *GPU Gems 2: Programming Techniques for High-Performance Graphics and General-Purpose Computation* (edited by M. Pharr), pp. 223–233. Addison-Wesley Professional, Reading, MA. ISBN 0-321-33559-7.

[Buntin07] Buntin, S. and Stamminger, M. 2007. Instanced shadow maps. In *Proceedings of CGAMES'07, La Rochelle, France*, pp. 135–142. http://www9.informatik.uni-erlangen.de/get/457.

[Burley06] Burley, B. 2006. Shadow map bias cone and improved soft shadows. In *ACM SIGGRAPH 2006 Courses*, course 25 (RenderMan for Everyone).

[Cai06] Cai, X.-H., Jia, Y.-T., Wang, X., Hu, S.-M., and Martin, R. R. 2006. Rendering soft shadows using multi-layered shadow fins. *Computer Graphics Forum*, 25, 1, 15–28.

[Carmack00] Carmack, J. 2000. Z-fail shadow volumes. Internet Forum.

[Cavanagh05] Cavanagh, P. 2005. The artist as neuroscientist. *Nature*, 434, 7031, 301–307.

[Cerezo05] Cerezo, E., Perez-Cazorla, F., Pueyo, X., Seron, F., and Sillion, F. 2005. A survey on participating media rendering techniques. *The Visual Computer*, 21, 5, 303–328.

[Chajdas10] Chajdas, M. G., Eisenacher, C., Stamminger, M., and Lefebvre, S. 2010. Virtual texture mapping 101. In *GPU Pro: Advanced Rendering Techniques* (edited by W. Engel), pp. 185–195. A K Peters, Wellesley, MA. ISBN 978-1-56881-472-8.

[Chan03] Chan, E. and Durand, F. 2003. Rendering fake soft shadows with smoothies. In *Proceedings of Eurographics Symposium on Rendering 2003*, pp. 208–218.

[Chan04] Chan, E. and Durand, F. 2004. An efficient hybrid shadow rendering algorithm. In *Proceedings of Eurographics Symposium on Rendering 2004*, pp. 185–196.

[Chen08] Chen, Y.-C. and Chang, C.-F. 2008. A prism-free method for silhouette rendering in inverse displacement mapping. *Computer Graphics Forum*, 27, 7 (Proceedings of Pacific Graphics 2008), 1929–1936.

[Chen11] Chen, J., Baran, I., Durand, F., and Jarosz, W. 2011. Real-time volumetric shadows using 1d min-max mipmaps. In *Proceedings of ACM SIGGRAPH Symposium on Interactive 3D Graphics and Games 2011*, pp. 39–46.

[Chin89] Chin, N. and Feiner, S. 1989. Near real-time shadow generation using BSP trees. *Computer Graphics*, 23, 3 (Proceedings of ACM SIGGRAPH 89), 99–106.

[Chong03] Chong, H. Y.-I. 2003. *Real-time perspective optimal shadow maps*. Senior thesis, Harvard University.

[Chong04] Chong, H. Y. and Gortler, S. J. 2004. A lixel for every pixel. In *Proceedings of Eurographics Symposium on Rendering 2004*, pp. 167–172.

[Chong07] Chong, H. Y. and Gortler, S. J. 2007. Scene optimized shadow mapping. Tech. Rep. TR-07-07, Harvard Computer Science, Harvard University, Cambridge, MA.

[Chrysanthou95] Chrysanthou, Y. and Slater, M. 1995. Shadow volume BSP trees for computation of shadows in dynamic scenes. In *Proceedings of ACM Symposium on Interactive 3D Graphics 1995*, pp. 45–50.

[Clark76] Clark, J. H. 1976. Hierarchical geometric models for visible surface algorithms. *Communications of the ACM*, 19, 10, 547–554.

[Cohen85] Cohen, M. F. and Greenberg, D. P. 1985. The hemi-cube: A radiosity solution for complex environments. *Computer Graphics*, 19, 3 (Proceedings of ACM SIGGRAPH 85), 31–40.

[Cohen93] Cohen, M. F. and Wallace, J. R. 1993. *Radiosity and Realistic Image Synthesis*. Academic Press Professional, New York, NY. ISBN 0-12-178270-0.

[Cook84] Cook, R. L., Porter, T., and Carpenter, L. 1984. Distributed ray tracing. *Computer Graphics*, 18, 3 (Proceedings of ACM SIGGRAPH 84), 137 145.

[Crassin09] Crassin, C., Neyret, F., Lefebvre, S., and Eisemann, E. 2009. Gigavoxels : Ray-guided streaming for efficient and detailed voxel rendering. In *Proceedings of ACM SIGGRAPH Symposium on Interactive 3D Graphics and Games 2009*.

[Crassin10] Crassin, C., Neyret, F., Sainz, M., and Eisemann, E. 2010. Efficient rendering of highly detailed volumetric scenes with gigavoxels. In *GPU Pro: Advanced Rendering Techniques* (edited by W. Engel), chap. X.3, pp. 643–676. A K Peters, Wellesley, MA. ISBN 978-1-56881-472-8.

[Crow77] Crow, F. C. 1977. Shadow algorithms for computer graphics. *Computer Graphics*, 11, 2 (Proceedings of ACM SIGGRAPH 77), 242–248.

[Crow84] Crow, F. C. 1984. Summed-area tables for texture mapping. *Computer Graphics*, 18, 3 (Proceedings of ACM SIGGRAPH 84), 207–212.

[Dai08] Dai, Q., Yang, B., and Feng, J. 2008. Reconstructable geometry shadow maps. In *ACM SIGGRAPH Symposium on Interactive 3D Graphics and Games 2008: Posters*, p. 4:1.

[deBoer06] de Boer, W. H. 2006. Smooth penumbra transitions with shadow maps. *Journal of Graphics Tools*, 11, 2, 59–71.

[Décoret05] Décoret, X. 2005. N-buffers for efficient depth map query. *Computer Graphics Forum*, 24, 3 (Proceedings of Eurographics 2005), 393–400.

[DeCoro07] DeCoro, C., Cole, F., Finkelstein, A., and Rusinkiewicz, S. 2007. Stylized shadows. In *Proceedings of NPAR (Symposium on Non-Photorealistic Animation and Rendering)*, pp. 77–83.

[Diefenbach96] Diefenbach, P. J. 1996. *Multi-pass pipeline rendering: interaction and realism through hardware provisions.* Phd thesis, University of Pennsylvania.

[Dietrich99] Dietrich, S. March 1999. Using the stencil buffer. *Game Developers Conference.*
http://developer.nvidia.com/content/using-stencil-buffer.

[Dietrich01] Dietrich, S. 2001. Practical priority buffer shadows. In *Game Programming Gems 2* (edited by M. DeLoura), pp. 481–487. Charles River Media, Hingham, MA. ISBN 1584500549.

[Dmitriev07] Dmitriev, K. 2007. Soft shadows. White Paper WP-03016-001_v01, NVIDIA Corporation.
http://developer.download.nvidia.com/whitepapers/2007/SDK10/SoftShadows.pdf.

[Dobashi02] Dobashi, Y., Yamamoto, T., and Nishita, T. 2002. Interactive rendering of atmospheric scattering effects using graphics hardware. In *Proceedings of Graphics Hardware 2002*, pp. 99–107.

[Dong04] Dong, Z., Chen, W., Bao, H., Zhang, H., and Peng, Q. 2004. Real-time voxelization for complex polygonal models. In *Proceedings of Pacific Graphics 2004*, pp. 43–50.

[Dong10] Dong, Z. and Yang, B. 2010. Variance soft shadow mapping. In *ACM SIGGRAPH Symposium on Interactive 3D Graphics and Games 2010: Posters*, p. 18:1.

[Donnelly06] Donnelly, W. and Lauritzen, A. 2006. Variance shadow maps. In *Proceedings of ACM SIGGRAPH Symposium on Interactive 3D Graphics and Games 2006*, pp. 161–165.

[Drettakis94] Drettakis, G. and Fiume, E. 1994. A fast shadow algorithm for area light sources using backprojection. In *Proceedings of ACM SIGGRAPH 94*, pp. 223–230.

[Duda72] Duda, R. O. and Hart, P. E. 1972. Use of the Hough transformation to detect lines and curves in pictures. *Communications of the ACM*, 15, 1, 11–15.

[Durand02] Durand, F. and Dorsey, J. 2002. Fast bilateral filtering for the display of high-dynamic-range images. *ACM Transactions on Graphics*, 21, 3 (Proceedings of ACM SIGGRAPH 2002), 257–266.

[Eisemann04] Eisemann, E. and Durand, F. 2004. Flash photography enhancement via intrinsic relighting. *ACM Transactions on Graphics*, 23, 3 (Proceedings of ACM SIGGRAPH 2004), 673–678.

[Eisemann06a] Eisemann, E. and Décoret, X. 2006. Fast scene voxelization and applications. In *Proceedings of ACM SIGGRAPH Symposium on Interactive 3D Graphics and Games 2006*, pp. 71–78.

[Eisemann06b] Eisemann, E. and Décoret, X. 2006. Plausible image based soft shadows
using occlusion textures. In *Proceedings of SIBGRAPI 2006*, pp. 155–162.

[Eisemann07] Eisemann, E. and Décoret, X. 2007. Visibility sampling on GPU and applications. *Computer Graphics Forum*, 26, 3 (Proceedings of Eurographics 2007), 535–544.

[Eisemann08a] Eisemann, E. 2008. *Optimized representations for the acceleration of display-
and collision queries.* PhD thesis, Grenoble Universities.

[Eisemann08b] Eisemann, E. and Décoret, X. 2008. Occlusion textures for plausible soft
shadows. *Computer Graphics Forum*, 27, 1, 13–23.

[Eisemann08c] Eisemann, E. and Décoret, X. 2008. Single-pass gpu solid voxelization for
real-time applications. In *Proceedings of Graphics Interface 2008*, pp. 73–80.

[Eisemann09] Eisemann, E., Assarsson, U., Schwarz, M., and Wimmer, M. 2009. Casting
shadows in real time. In *ACM SIGGRAPH Asia 2009 Courses*.

[Eisemann10] Eisemann, E., Assarsson, U., Schwarz, M., and Wimmer, M. 2010. Shadow
algorithms for real-time rendering. In *Eurographics 2010 Tutorials*.

[Enderton10] Enderton, E., Sintorn, E., Shirley, P., and Luebke, D. 2010. Stochastic transparency. In *Proceedings of ACM SIGGRAPH Symposium on Interactive 3D Graphics
and Games 2010*, pp. 157–164.

[Engel01] Engel, K., Kraus, M., and Ertl, T. 2001. High-quality pre-integrated volume
rendering using hardware-accelerated pixel shading. In *Proceedings of Workshop on
Graphics Hardware 2001*, pp. 9–16.

[Engel06] Engel, W. 2006. Cascaded shadow maps. In *ShaderX⁵: Advanced Rendering
Techniques* (edited by W. Engel), pp. 197–206. Charles River Media, Hingham, MA.
ISBN 978-1-58450-499-3.

[Engelhardt10] Engelhardt, T. and Dachsbacher, C. 2010. Epipolar sampling for shadows
and crepuscular rays in participating media with single scattering. In *Proceedings of
ACM SIGGRAPH Symposium on Interactive 3D Graphics and Games 2010*, pp. 119–
125.

[Everitt01] Everitt, C. 2001. Interactive order-independent transparency.
http://www.nvidia.com/object/Interactive_Order_Transparency.html.

[Everitt02] Everitt, C. and Kilgard, M. J. 2002. Practical and robust stenciled shadow volumes for hardware-accelerated rendering.
http://developer.nvidia.com.

[Everitt03] Everitt, C. and Kilgard, M. J. 2003. Optimized stencil shadow volumes. Presentation, *Game Developers Conference 2003*.
developer.nvidia.com/docs/IO/8230/GDC2003_ShadowVolumes.ppt.

[Fernando01] Fernando, R., Fernandez, S., Bala, K., and Greenberg, D. P. 2001. Adaptive
shadow maps. In *Proceedings of ACM SIGGRAPH 2001*, pp. 387–390.

[Fernando02] Fernando, P. R. 2002. *Adaptive techniques for hardware shadow generation.*
Master's thesis, Cornell University.

[Fernando05] Fernando, R. 2005. Percentage-closer soft shadows. In *ACM SIGGRAPH
2005 Sketches and Applications*, p. 35.

[Foley00] Foley, J. 2000. Getting there: The ten top problems left. *IEEE Computer Graphics and Applications*, 20, 1, 66–68.

[Forest06] Forest, V., Barthe, L., and Paulin, M. 2006. Realistic soft shadows by penumbra-wedges blending. In *Proceedings of Graphics Hardware 2006*, pp. 39–47.

[Forest08] Forest, V., Barthe, L., and Paulin, M. 2008. Accurate shadows by depth complexity sampling. *Computer Graphics Forum*, 27, 2 (Proceedings of Eurographics 2008), 663–674.

[Forest09] Forest, V., Barthe, L., Guennebaud, G., and Paulin, M. 2009. Soft textured shadow volume. *Computer Graphics Forum*, 28, 4 (Proceedings of Eurographics Symposium on Rendering 2009), 1111–1120.

[Forest10] Forest, V., Barthe, L., and Paulin, M. 2010. Real-time hierarchical binary-scene voxelization. *Journal of Graphics, GPU, and Game Tools*, 14, 3, 21–34.

[Forsyth06] Forsyth, T. 2006. Making shadow buffers robust using multiple dynamic frustums. In *ShaderX⁴: Advanced Rendering Techniques* (edited by W. Engel). Charles River Media, Hingham, MA. ISBN 1-58450-425-0.

[Forsyth07] Forsyth, T. 2007. Shadowbuffers. Presentation, *Game Developers Conference 2007*.
http://home.comcast.net/~tom_forsyth/papers/Tom_Forsyth_Shadowbuffers_GDC2007_small.ppt.zip.

[Fortes00] Fortes, T. 2000. Tetrahedron environment maps. Tech. rep., Chalmers Univ. of Technology, Gothenburg, Sweden.

[Fuchs85] Fuchs, H., Goldfeather, J., Hultquist, J. P., Spach, S., Austin, J. D., Brooks, F. P., Jr., Eyles, J. G., and Poulton, J. 1985. Fast spheres, shadows, textures, transparencies, and image enhancements in pixel-planes. *Computer Graphics*, 19, 3 (Proceedings of ACM SIGGRAPH 85), 111–120.

[Gascuel08] Gascuel, J.-D., Holzschuch, N., Fournier, G., and Peroche, B. 2008. Fast non-linear projections using graphics hardware. In *Proceedings of ACM SIGGRAPH Symposium on Interactive 3D Graphics and Games 2008*, pp. 107–114.

[Gautron09] Gautron, P., Marvie, J.-E., and François, G. 2009. Volumetric shadow mapping. In *ACM SIGGRAPH 2009 Talks*, pp. 49:1–49:1.

[Giegl07a] Giegl, M. and Wimmer, M. 2007. Fitted virtual shadow maps. In *Proceedings of Graphics Interface 2007*, pp. 159–168.

[Giegl07b] Giegl, M. and Wimmer, M. 2007. Queried virtual shadow maps. In *Proceedings of ACM SIGGRAPH Symposium on Interactive 3D Graphics and Games 2007*, pp. 65–72.

[Glassner94] Glassner, A. S. 1994. *Principles of Digital Image Synthesis*. Morgan Kaufmann Publishers, San Francisco, CA, USA. ISBN 1558602763.

[Gobbetti08] Gobbetti, E., Marton, F., and Iglesias Guitián, J. A. 2008. A single-pass GPU ray casting framework for interactive out-of-core rendering of massive volumetric datasets. *The Visual Computer*, 24, 7, 797–806.

[Gooch99] Gooch, B., Sloan, P.-P. J., Gooch, A., Shirley, P., and Riesenfeld, R. 1999. Interactive technical illustration. In *Proceedings of ACM Symposium on Interactive 3D Graphics 1999*, pp. 31–38.

[Gouraud71] Gouraud, H. 1971. Continuous shading of curved surfaces. *IEEE Transactions on Computers*, 20, 6, 623–629.

[Govindaraju03] Govindaraju, N. K., Lloyd, B., Yoon, S.-E., Sud, A., and Manocha, D. 2003. Interactive shadow generation in complex environments. *ACM Transactions on Graphics*, 22, 3 (Proceedings of ACM SIGGRAPH 2003), 501–510.

[Greene93] Greene, N., Kass, M., and Miller, G. 1993. Hierarchical z-buffer visibility. In *Proceedings of ACM SIGGRAPH 93*, pp. 231–238.

[Guennebaud06] Guennebaud, G., Barthe, L., and Paulin, M. 2006. Real-time soft shadow mapping by backprojection. In *Proceedings of Eurographics Symposium on Rendering 2006*, pp. 227–234.

[Guennebaud07] Guennebaud, G., Barthe, L., and Paulin, M. 2007. High-quality adaptive soft shadow mapping. *Computer Graphics Forum*, 26, 3 (Proceedings of Eurographics 2007), 525–533.

[Gumbau11] Gumbau, J., Szirmay-Kalos, L., Sbert, M., and Sells, M. C. 2011. Improving Shadow Map Filtering with Statistical Analysis. In *Eurographics 2011 Short Papers*, pp. 33–36.

[Hadwiger06] Hadwiger, M., Kratz, A., Sigg, C., and Bühler, K. 2006. Gpu-accelerated deep shadow maps for direct volume rendering. In *Proceedings of Graphics Hardware 2006*, pp. 49–52.

[Haeberli90] Haeberli, P. and Akeley, K. 1990. The accumulation buffer: Hardware support for high-quality rendering. *Computer Graphics*, 24, 4 (Proceedings of ACM SIGGRAPH 90), 309–318.

[Haines01] Haines, E. 2001. Soft planar shadows using plateaus. *Journal of Graphics Tools*, 6, 1, 19–27.

[Hammersley64] Hammersley, J. M. and Handscomb, D. 1964. *Monte Carlo Methods*. Methuen & Co Ltd., London, UK. ISBN 0-416-52340-4.

[Hasenfratz03] Hasenfratz, J.-M., Lapierre, M., Holzschuch, N., and Sillion, F. 2003. A survey of real-time soft shadows algorithms. *Computer Graphics Forum*, 22, 4, 753–774.

[Hasselgren05] Hasselgren, J., Akenine-Möller, T., and Ohlsson, L. 2005. Conservative rasterization. In *GPU Gems 2: Programming Techniques for High-Performance Graphics and General-Purpose Computation* (edited by M. Pharr). Addison-Wesley Professional, Reading, MA. ISBN 0-321-33559-7.

[Hasselgren07] Hasselgren, J. and Akenine-Möller, T. 2007. Textured shadow volumes. *Journal of Graphics Tools*, 12, 4, 59–72.

[Heckbert87] Heckbert, P. 1987. Ten unsolved problems in rendering. In *Workshop on Rendering Algorithms and Systems, Graphics Interface '87*.

[Heckbert89] Heckbert, P. S. 1989. Fundamentals of texture mapping and image warping. Tech. Rep. UCB/CSD-89-516, EECS Department, University of California, Berkeley.

[Heckbert97] Heckbert, P. S. and Herf, M. 1997. Simulating soft shadows with graphics hardware. Tech. Rep. CMU-CS-97-104, Carnegie Mellon University.

[Heidmann91] Heidmann, T. 1991. Real shadows real time. *IRIS Universe*, 18, 28–31.

[Heidrich98] Heidrich, W. and Seidel, H.-P. 1998. View-independent environment maps. In *Proceedings of Workshop on Graphics Hardware 1998*, pp. 39–45.

[Heidrich99a] Heidrich, W. 1999. *High-quality shading and lighting for hardware-accelerated rendering.* PhD thesis, University of Erlangen-Nuremberg.

[Heidrich99b] Heidrich, W. and Seidel, H.-P. 1999. Realistic, hardware-accelerated shading and lighting. In *Proceedings of ACM SIGGRAPH 99*, pp. 171–178.

[Hensley05] Hensley, J., Scheuermann, T., Coombe, G., Singh, M., and Lastra, A. 2005. Fast summed-area table generation and its applications. *Computer Graphics Forum*, 24, 3 (Proceedings of Eurographics 2005), 547–555.

[Herf96] Herf, M. and Heckbert, P. S. 1996. Fast soft shadows. In *ACM SIGGRAPH 96 Visual Proceedings*, p. 145.

[Herf97] Herf, M. 1997. Efficient generation of soft shadow textures. Tech. Rep. CMU-CS-97-138, Carnegie Mellon University.

[Herzog10] Herzog, R., Eisemann, E., Myszkowski, K., and Seidel, H.-P. 2010. Spatio-temporal upsampling on the GPU. In *Proceedings of ACM SIGGRAPH Symposium on Interactive 3D Graphics and Games 2010*, pp. 91–98.

[Hoberock07] Hoberock, J. and Jia, Y. 2007. High-quality ambient occlusion. In *GPU Gems 3* (edited by H. Nguyen), pp. 257–274. Addison-Wesley Professional, Reading, MA. ISBN 978-0-321-51526-1.

[Hornus05] Hornus, S., Hoberock, J., Lefebvre, S., and Hart, J. C. 2005. ZP+: correct z-pass stencil shadows. In *Proceedings of ACM SIGGRAPH Symposium on Interactive 3D Graphics and Games 2005*, pp. 195–202.

[Hourcade85] Hourcade, J.-C. and Nicolas, A. 1985. Algorithms for antialiased cast shadows. *Computers & Graphics*, 9, 3, 259–265.

[Huang11] Huang, J., Boubekeur, T., Ritschel, T., Holländer, M., and Eisemann, E. 2011. Separable approximation of ambient occlusion. In *Eurographics 2011 Short Papers*, pp. 29–32.

[Igehy99] Igehy, H. 1999. Tracing ray differentials. In *Proceedings of ACM SIGGRAPH 99*, pp. 179–186.

[Imagire07] Imagire, T., Johan, H., Tamura, N., and Nishita, T. 2007. Anti-aliased and real-time rendering of scenes with light scattering effects. *The Visual Computer*, 23, 9, 935–944.

[Immel86] Immel, D. S., Cohen, M. F., and Greenberg, D. P. 1986. A radiosity method for non-diffuse environments. *Computer Graphics*, 20, 4 (Proceedings of ACM SIGGRAPH 86), 133–142.

[Isidoro06] Isidoro, J. 2006. Shadow mapping: GPU-based tips and techniques. Presentation, *Game Developers Conference 2008*.
http://developer.amd.com/media/gpu_assets/Isidoro-ShadowMapping.pdf.

[Itkis06] Itkis, M., Kniss, J., Lefohn, A., and Hansen, C. 2006. Volume rendering techniques. In *GPU Gems 2: Programming Techniques for High-Performance Graphics and General-Purpose Computation* (edited by M. Pharr). Addison-Wesley Professional, Reading, MA. ISBN 0-321-33559-7.

[Jähne05] Jähne, B. 2005. *Digital Image Processing*. 6th ed. Springer-Verlag, New York, NY. ISBN 978-3-540-24035-8.

[James03] James, R. 2003. True volumetric shadows. In *Graphics programming methods* (edited by J. Lander), pp. 353–366. Charles River Media, Rockland, MA. ISBN 1-58450-299-1.

[Jansen10] Jansen, J. and Bavoil, L. 2010. Fourier opacity mapping. In *Proceedings of ACM SIGGRAPH Symposium on Interactive 3D Graphics and Games 2010*, pp. 165–172.

[Johnson63] Johnson, T. E. 1963. Sketchpad III: a computer program for drawing in three dimensions. In *AFIPS '63 (Spring): Proceedings of the May 21-23, 1963, spring joint computer conference*, pp. 347–353.

[Johnson05] Johnson, G. S., Lee, J., Burns, C. A., and Mark, W. R. 2005. The irregular z-buffer: Hardware acceleration for irregular data structures. *ACM Transactions on Graphics*, 24, 4, 1462–1482.

[Johnson09] Johnson, G. S., Hunt, W. A., Hux, A., Mark, W. R., Burns, C. A., and Junkins, S. 2009. Soft irregular shadow mapping: Fast, high-quality, and robust soft shadows. In *Proceedings of ACM SIGGRAPH Symposium on Interactive 3D Graphics and Games 2009*, pp. 57–66.

[Jordan87] Jordan, C. 1887. *Cours d'analyse*. l'École Polytechnique, pp. 587–594. Available online at:
http://www.maths.ed.ac.uk/~aar/jordan/jordan.pdf.

[Kajiya84] Kajiya, J. T. and Von Herzen, B. P. 1984. Ray tracing volume densities. *Computer Graphics*, 18, 3 (Proceedings of ACM SIGGRAPH 84), 165–174.

[Kajiya86] Kajiya, J. T. 1986. The rendering equation. *Computer Graphics*, 20, 4 (Proceedings of ACM SIGGRAPH 86), 143–150.

[Kautz04] Kautz, J., Lehtinen, J., and Aila, T. 2004. Hemispherical rasterization for self-shadowing of dynamic objects. In *Proceedings of Eurographics Symposium on Rendering 2004*, pp. 179–184.

[Keating99] Keating, B. and Max, N. 1999. Shadow penumbras for complex objects by depth-dependent filtering of multi-layer depth images. In *Proceedings of Eurographics Workshop on Rendering 1999*, pp. 197–212.

[Keller01] Keller, A. and Heidrich, W. 2001. Interleaved sampling. In *Proceedings of Eurographics Workshop on Rendering 2001*, pp. 269–276.

[Kersten96] Kersten, D., Knill, D. C., Mamassian, P., and Bülthoff, I. 1996. Illusory motion from shadows. *Nature*, 379, 31.

[Kilgard99] Kilgard, M. 1999. Improving shadows and reflections via the stencil buffer. In *Advanced OpenGL Game Development course notes, Game Developer Conference 1999*, pp. 204–253.

[Kilgard00] Kilgard, M. J. March 2000. More advanced hardware rendering techniques. *Game Developers Conference*.
http://developer.nvidia.com.

[Kilgard01] Kilgard, M. J. 2001. Robust stencil shadow volumes. Presentation, *CEDEC 2001*.
http://developer.nvidia.com/object/cedec_stencil.html.

[Kim01] Kim, T.-Y. and Neumann, U. 2001. Opacity shadow maps. In *Proceedings of Eurographics Workshop on Rendering 2001*, pp. 177–182.

[Kim08] Kim, B., Kim, K., and Turk, G. 2008. A shadow volume algorithm for opaque and transparent non-manifold casters. *Journal of Graphics Tools*, 13, 3, 1–14.

[Kircher09] Kircher, S. and Lawrance, A. 2009. Inferred lighting: fast dynamic lighting and shadows for opaque and translucent objects. In *Proceedings of the 2009 ACM SIGGRAPH Symposium on Video Games*, pp. 39–45.

[Kirsch03] Kirsch, F. and Döllner, J. 2003. Real-time soft shadows using a single light sample. *Journal of WSCG*, 11, 255–262.

[Kontkanen05] Kontkanen, J. and Laine, S. 2005. Ambient occlusion fields. In *Proceedings of ACM SIGGRAPH Symposium on Interactive 3D Graphics and Games 2005*, pp. 41–48.

[Kopf07] Kopf, J., Cohen, M. F., Lischinski, D., and Uyttendaele, M. 2007. Joint bilateral upsampling. *ACM Transactions on Graphics*, 26, 3 (Proceedings of ACM SIGGRAPH 2007), 96:1–96:5.

[Kozlov04] Kozlov, S. 2004. Perspective shadow maps - care and feeding. In *GPU Gems: Programming Techniques, Tips, and Tricks for Real-Time Graphics* (edited by R. Fernando), pp. 217–244. Addison-Wesley Professional, Reading, MA. ISBN 0-321-22832-4.

[Kwoon03] Kwoon, H. Y. 2003. The theory of stencil shadow volumes. In *ShaderX²: Introduction & Tutorials with DirectX 9* (edited by W. Engel), pp. 587–593. Wordware Publishing, Plano, TX. ISBN 1-55622-902-X. Short version available online: http://www.gamedev.net/reference/articles/article1873.asp.

[Lagae08] Lagae, A. and Dutré, P. 2008. A comparison of methods for generating Poisson disk distributions. *Computer Graphics Forum*, 27, 1, 114–129.

[Laine05a] Laine, S. 2005. Split-plane shadow volumes. In *Proceedings of Graphics Hardware 2005*, pp. 23–32.

[Laine05b] Laine, S. and Aila, T. 2005. Hierarchical penumbra casting. *Computer Graphics Forum*, 24, 3 (Proceedings of Eurographics 2005), 313–322.

[Laine05c] Laine, S., Aila, T., Assarsson, U., Lehtinen, J., and Akenine-Möller, T. 2005. Soft shadow volumes for ray tracing. *ACM Transactions on Graphics*, 24, 3 (Proceedings of ACM SIGGRAPH 2005), 1156–1165.

[Landis02] Landis, H. 2002. Production-ready global illumination. In *ACM SIGGRAPH 2002 Course Notes*, RenderMan in Production.

[Lauritzen07] Lauritzen, A. 2007. Summed-area variance shadow maps. In *GPU Gems 3* (edited by H. Nguyen), pp. 157–182. Addison-Wesley Professional, Reading, MA. ISBN 978-0-321-51526-1.

[Lauritzen08] Lauritzen, A. and McCool, M. 2008. Layered variance shadow maps. In *Proceedings of Graphics Interface 2008*, pp. 139–146.

[Lauritzen11] Lauritzen, A., Salvi, M., and Lefohn, A. 2011. Sample distribution shadow maps. In *Proceedings of ACM SIGGRAPH Symposium on Interactive 3D Graphics and Games 2011*, pp. 97–102.

[Lee09] Lee, S., Eisemann, E., and Seidel, H.-P. 2009. Depth-of-Field Rendering with Multiview Synthesis. *ACM Transactions on Graphics*, 28, 5 (Proceedings of ACM SIGGRAPH Asia 2009), 134:1–134:6.

[Lefohn05] Lefohn, A., Sengupta, S., Kniss, J., Strzodka, R., and Owens, J. D. 2005. Dynamic adaptive shadow maps on graphics hardware. In *ACM SIGGRAPH 2005 Sketches and Applications*, p. 13.

[Lefohn07] Lefohn, A. E., Sengupta, S., and Owens, J. D. 2007. Resolution matched shadow maps. *ACM Transactions on Graphics*, 26, 4, 20:1–20:17.

[Lefohn08] Lefohn, A., Houston, M., et al. 2008. Beyond programmable shading. In *ACM SIGGRAPH 2008 Classes*, pp. 9:1–9:21.

[Lehtinen06] Lehtinen, J., Laine, S., and Aila, T. 2006. An improved physically-based soft shadow volume algorithm. *Computer Graphics Forum*, 25, 3 (Proceedings of Eurographics 2006), 303–312.

[Lehtinen08] Lehtinen, J., Zwicker, M., Turquin, E., Kontkanen, J., Durand, F., Sillion, F. X., and Aila, T. 2008. A meshless hierarchical representation for light transport. *ACM Transactions on Graphics*, 27, 3 (Proceedings of ACM SIGGRAPH 2008), 37:1–37:9.

[Lengyel00] Lengyel, E. 2000. Tweaking a vertex's projected depth value. In *Game Programming Gems* (edited by M. DeLoura), pp. 361–365. Charles River Media, Hingham, MA. ISBN 1-58450-049-2.

[Lengyel02] Lengyel, E. 2002. The mechanics of robust stencil shadows. *Gamasutra*. http://www.gamasutra.com/features/20021011/lengyel_01.htm.

[Lengyel05] Lengyel, E. 2005. Advanced stencil shadow and penumbral wedge rendering. Presentation, *Game Developers Conference 2005*. http://www.terathon.com/gdc_lengyel.ppt.

[Liao07] Liao, H.-c. 2007. Mapping and drawing method for a tetrahedron map. U.S. Patent Application 20070159479. http://www.freepatentsonline.com/y2007/0159479.html.

[Liao10] Liao, H.-C. 2010. Shadow mapping for omni-directional light using tetrahedron mapping. In *GPU Pro: Advanced Rendering Techniques* (edited by W. Engel), pp. 455–475. A K Peters, Wellesley, MA. ISBN 978-1-56881-472-8.

[Lichtenbelt98] Lichtenbelt, B., Crane, R., and Naqvi, S. 1998. *Introduction to volume rendering*. Prentice Hall, Upper Saddle River, NJ. ISBN 0-13-861683-3.

[Lischinski98] Lischinski, D. and Rappoport, A. 1998. Image-based rendering for non-diffuse synthetic scenes. In *Proceedings of Eurographics Workshop on Rendering 1998*, pp. 301–314.

[Liu06] Liu, B., Wei, L.-Y., and Xu, Y.-Q. 2006. Multi-layer depth peeling via fragment sort. Tech. Rep. MSR-TR-2006-81, Microsoft Research.

[Lloyd04] Lloyd, D. B., Wendt, J., Govindaraju, N. K., and Manocha, D. 2004. CC shadow volumes. In *Proceedings of Eurographics Symposium on Rendering 2004*, pp. 197–205.

[Lloyd06a] Lloyd, B., Govindaraju, N. K., Tuft, D., Molnar, S., and Manocha, D. 2006. Practical logarithmic shadow maps. In *ACM SIGGRAPH 2006 Sketches and Applications*.

[Lloyd06b] Lloyd, D. B., Tuft, D., Yoon, S., and Manocha, D. 2006. Warping and partitioning for low error shadow maps. In *Proceedings of Eurographics Symposium on Rendering 2006*, pp. 215–226.

[Lloyd07a] Lloyd, B. 2007. *Logarithmic perspective shadow maps*. PhD thesis, University of North Carolina.

[Lloyd07b] Lloyd, D. B., Govindaraju, N. K., Molnar, S. E., and Manocha, D. 2007. Practical logarithmic rasterization for low-error shadow maps. In *Proceedings of Graphics Hardware 2007*, pp. 17–24.

[Lloyd08] Lloyd, D. B., Govindaraju, N. K., Quammen, C., Molnar, S. E., and Manocha, D. 2008. Logarithmic perspective shadow maps. *ACM Transactions on Graphics*, 27, 4, 106:1–106:32.

[Lokovic00] Lokovic, T. and Veach, E. 2000. Deep shadow maps. In *Proceedings of ACM SIGGRAPH 2000*, pp. 385–392.

[Loop06] Loop, C. and Blinn, J. 2006. Real-time GPU rendering of piecewise algebraic surfaces. *ACM Transactions on Graphics*, 25, 3 (Proceedings of ACM SIGGRAPH 2006), 664–670.

[Loos10] Loos, B. J. and Sloan, P.-P. J. 2010. Volumetric obscurance. In *Proceedings of ACM SIGGRAPH Symposium on Interactive 3D Graphics and Games 2010*, pp. 151–156.

[Luft06] Luft, T. and Deussen, O. 2006. Real-time watercolor illustrations of plants using a blurred depth test. In *Proceedings of Symposium on Non-Photorealistic Animation and Rendering 2006*, pp. 11–20.

[Malmer07] Malmer, M., Malmer, F., Assarsson, U., and Holzschuch, N. 2007. Fast pre-computed ambient occlusion for proximity shadows. *Journal of Graphics Tools*, 12, 2, 59–71.

[Mamassian98] Mamassian, P., Knill, D. C., and Kersten, D. 1998. The perception of cast shadows. *Trends in Cognitive Sciences*, 2, 8, 288–295.

[Martin04] Martin, T. and Tan, T.-S. 2004. Anti-aliasing and continuity with trapezoidal shadow maps. In *Proceedings of Eurographics Symposium on Rendering 2004*, pp. 153–160.

[Mattausch08] Mattausch, O., Bittner, J., and Wimmer, M. 2008. CHC++: Coherent hierarchical culling revisited. *Computer Graphics Forum*, 27, 2 (Proceedings of Eurographics 2008), 221–230.

[Max86a] Max, N. 1986. Light diffusion through clouds and haze. *Computer Vision, Graphics, and Image Processing*, 33, 3, 280–292.

[Max86b] Max, N. L. 1986. Atmospheric illumination and shadows. *Computer Graphics*, 20, 4 (Proceedings of ACM SIGGRAPH 86), 117–124.

[Max95] Max, N. 1995. Optical models for direct volume rendering. *IEEE Transactions on Visualization and Computer Graphics*, 1, 99–108.

[McCool00] McCool, M. D. 2000. Shadow volume reconstruction from depth maps. *ACM Transactions on Graphics*, 19, 1, 1–26.

[McGuire03] McGuire, M., Hughes, J. F., Egan, K., Kilgard, M., and Everitt, C. 2003. Fast, practical and robust shadows. Tech. rep., NVIDIA Corporation, Austin, TX.

[McGuire04a] McGuire, M. 2004. Efficient shadow volume rendering. In *GPU Gems: Programming Techniques, Tips, and Tricks for Real-Time Graphics* (edited by R. Fernando), pp. 137–166. Addison-Wesley Professional, Reading, MA. ISBN 0-321-22832-4.

[McGuire04b] McGuire, M. 2004. Observations on silhouette sizes. *Journal of Graphics Tools*, 9, 1, 1–12.

[McGuire07] McGuire, M. 2007. Single-pass shadow volumes for arbitrary meshes. In *ACM SIGGRAPH 2007 Posters*, p. 177.

[McGuire10a] McGuire, M. 2010. Ambient occlusion volumes. In *Proceedings of High Performance Graphics 2010*, pp. 47–56.

[McGuire10b] McGuire, M. 2010. Hardware-accelerated colored stochastic shadow maps. Tech. Rep. NVR-2010-003, NVIDIA Corporation, Santa Clara, CA.

[McGuire10c] McGuire, M., Enderton, E., Shirley, P., and Luebke, D. 2010. Real-time stochastic rasterization on conventional GPU architectures. In *Proceedings of High Performance Graphics 2010*, pp. 173–182.

[Méndez-Feliu09] Méndez-Feliu, À. and Sbert, M. 2009. From obscurances to ambient occlusion: A survey. *The Visual Computer*, 25, 2, 181–196.

[Merriam-Webster09] Merriam-Webster. 2009. Merriam-webster online dictionary. http://www.merriam-webster.com/dictionary/.

[Mikkelsen07] Mikkelsen, M. S. 2007. Separating-plane perspective shadow mapping. *Journal of Graphics Tools*, 12, 3, 43–54.

[Miller94] Miller, G. 1994. Efficient algorithms for local and global accessibility shading. In *Proceedings of ACM SIGGRAPH 94*, pp. 319–326.

[Miller07] Miller, K. 2007. The emblem of earthly vanities. *Tate ETC*, 9.

[Mitchell04a] Mitchell, J. 2004. Light shafts: Rendering shadows in participating media. Presentation, *Game Developers Conference 2004*. http://developer.amd.com/media/gpu_assets/Mitchell_LightShafts.pdf.

[Mitchell04b] Mitchell, J. L. 2004. Poisson shadow blur. In *ShaderX^3: Advanced Rendering with DirectX and OpenGL* (edited by W. Engel), pp. 403–409. Charles River Media, Hingham, MA. ISBN 1-58450-357-2.

[Mitra09] Mitra, N. J. and Pauly, M. 2009. Shadow art. *ACM Transactions on Graphics*, 28, 5 (Proceedings of ACM SIGGRAPH Asia 2009), 156:1–156:7.

[Mo07] Mo, Q., Popescu, V., and Wyman, C. 2007. The soft shadow occlusion camera. In *Proceedings of Pacific Graphics 2007*, pp. 189–198.

[MohammadBagher10] MohammadBagher, M., Kautz, J., Holzschuch, N., and Soler, C. 2010. Screen-space percentage-closer soft shadows. In *ACM SIGGRAPH 2010 Posters*, p. 133:1.

[Nagy00] Nagy, G. 2000. Real-time shadows on complex objects. In *Game Programming Gems* (edited by M. DeLoura), pp. 567–580. Charles River Media, Hingham, MA. ISBN 1-58450-049-2.

[Nehab07] Nehab, D., Sander, P. V., Lawrence, J., Tatarchuk, N., and Isidoro, J. R. 2007. Accelerating real-time shading with reverse reprojection caching. In *Proceedings of Graphics Hardware 2007*, pp. 25–35.

[Newell77] Newell, M. E. and Blinn, J. F. 1977. The progression of realism in computer generated images. In *Proceedings of ACM '77*, pp. 444–448.

[Ngan04] Ngan, A., Durand, F., and Matusik, W. 2004. Experimental validation of analytical BRDF models. In *ACM SIGGRAPH 2004 Sketches and Applications*, p. 90.

[Ni04] Ni, R., Braunstein, M. L., and Andersen, G. J. 2004. Interaction of optical contact, shadows and motion in determining perceived scene layout. *Journal of Vision*, 4, 8, 615–615.

[Nichols10] Nichols, G., Penmatsa, R., and Wyman, C. 2010. Interactive, multiresolution image-space rendering for dynamic area lighting. *Computer Graphics Forum*, 29, 4 (Proceedings of Eurographics Symposium on Rendering 2010).

[Nishita87] Nishita, T., Miyawaki, Y., and Nakamae, E. 1987. A shading model for atmospheric scattering considering luminous intensity distribution of light sources. *Computer Graphics*, 21, 4 (Proceedings of ACM SIGGRAPH 87), 303–310.

[Nishita96] Nishita, T., Dobashi, Y., and Nakamae, E. 1996. Display of clouds taking into account multiple anisotropic scattering and sky light. In *Proceedings of ACM SIGGRAPH 96*, pp. 379–386.

[Nowrouzezahrai09] Nowrouzezahrai, D. and Snyder, J. 2009. Fast global illumination on dynamic height fields. *Computer Graphics Forum*, 28, 4 (Proceedings of Eurographics Symposium on Rendering 2009), 1131–1139.

[Oat07] Oat, C. and Sander, P. V. 2007. Ambient aperture lighting. In *Proceedings of ACM SIGGRAPH Symposium on Interactive 3D Graphics and Games 2007*, pp. 61–64.

[Oh07] Oh, K. and Park, S. 2007. Realtime hybrid shadow algorithm using shadow texture and shadow map. In *Proceedings of ICCSA 2007, Part I*, Lecture Notes in Computer Science, pp. 972–980.

[Oliveira05] Oliveira, M. M. and Policarpo, F. 2005. An efficient representation for surface details. Tech. Rep. RP-351, Universidade Federal do Rio Grande do Sul.

[Overbeck07] Overbeck, R., Ramamoorthi, R., and Mark, W. R. 2007. A real-time beam tracer with application to exact soft shadows. In *Proceedings of Eurographics Symposium on Rendering 2007*, pp. 85–98.

[Pagot04] Pagot, C. A., Comba, J. L. D., and de Oliveira Neto, M. M. 2004. Multiple-depth shadow maps. In *Proceedings of SIBGRAPI 2004*, pp. 308–315.

[Pajak11] Pajak, D., Herzog, R., Eisemann, E., Myszkowski, K., and Seidel, H.-P. 2011. Scalable remote rendering with depth and motion-flow augmented streaming. *Computer Graphics Forum*, 30, 2 (Proceedings of Eurographics 2011), 415–424.

[Pan07] Pan, M., Wang, R., Liu, X., Peng, Q., and Bao, H. 2007. Precomputed radiance transfer field for rendering interreflections in dynamic scenes. *Computer Graphics Forum*, 26, 3 (Proceedings of Eurographics 2007), 485–493.

[Pan09] Pan, M., Wang, R., Chen, W., Zhou, K., and Bao, H. 2009. Fast, sub-pixel antialiased shadow maps. *Computer Graphics Forum*, 28, 7 (Proceedings of Pacific Graphics 2009), 1927–1934.

[Paris06] Paris, S. and Durand, F. 2006. A fast approximation of the bilateral filter using a signal processing approach. In *Proceedings of ECCV 2006, Part IV*, Lecture Notes in Computer Science, pp. 568–580.

[Parker98] Parker, S., Shirley, P., and Smits, B. 1998. Single sample soft shadows. Tech. Rep. UUCS-98-019, University of Utah.

[Patney10] Patney, A., Tzeng, S., and Owens, J. D. 2010. Fragment-parallel composite and filter. *Computer Graphics Forum*, 29, 4 (Proceedings of Eurographics Symposium on Rendering 2010), 1251–1258.

[Pegoraro09a] Pegoraro, V., Schott, M., and Parker, S. 2009. Reduced dual-formulation for analytical anisotropic single scattering. In *High Performance Graphics 2009 Posters*.

[Pegoraro09b] Pegoraro, V., Schott, M., and Parker, S. G. 2009. An analytical approach to single scattering for anisotropic media and light distributions. In *Proceedings of Graphics Interface 2009*, pp. 71–77.

[Pegoraro10] Pegoraro, V., Schott, M., and Parker, S. G. 2010. A closed-form solution to single scattering for general phase functions and light distributions. *Computer Graphics Forum*, 29, 4 (Proceedings of Eurographics Symposium on Rendering 2010), 1365–1374.

[Petschnigg04] Petschnigg, G., Szeliski, R., Agrawala, M., Cohen, M., Hoppe, H., and Toyama, K. 2004. Digital photography with flash and no-flash image pairs. *ACM Transactions on Graphics*, 23, 3 (Proceedings of ACM SIGGRAPH 2004), 664–672.

[Pickett00] Pickett, J. P. et al. (eds.). 2000. *The American Heritage Dictionary of the English Language*. 4th ed. Houghton Mifflin Company, Boston, MA.

[Popescu06] Popescu, V. and Aliaga, D. 2006. The depth discontinuity occlusion camera. In *Proceedings of ACM SIGGRAPH Symposium on Interactive 3D Graphics and Games 2006*, pp. 139–143.

[Pranckevičius06] Pranckevičius, A. 2006. Soft projected shadows. In *ShaderX⁴: Advanced Rendering Techniques* (edited by W. Engel), pp. 279–288. Charles River Media, Hingham, MA. ISBN 1-58450-425-0.

[Princeton University09] Princeton University. 2009. WordNet 3.0. http://wordnet.princeton.edu/.

[Ramamoorthi09] Ramamoorthi, R. 2009. Precomputation-based rendering. *Foundations and Trends in Computer Graphics and Vision*, 3, 4, 281–369.

[Reeves87] Reeves, W. T., Salesin, D. H., and Cook, R. L. 1987. Rendering antialiased shadows with depth maps. *Computer Graphics*, 21, 4 (Proceedings of ACM SIGGRAPH 87), 283–291.

[Reinbothe09] Reinbothe, C. K., Boubekeur, T., and Alexa, M. 2009. Hybrid ambient occlusion. In *Eurographics 2009 Annex (Area Papers)*, pp. 51–57.

[Ren06] Ren, Z., Wang, R., Snyder, J., Zhou, K., Liu, X., Sun, B., Sloan, P.-P., Bao, H., Peng, Q., and Guo, B. 2006. Real-time soft shadows in dynamic scenes using spherical harmonic exponentiation. *ACM Transactions on Graphics*, 25, 3 (Proceedings of ACM SIGGRAPH 2006), 977–986.

[Revelles00] Revelles, J., Ureña, C., and Lastra, M. 2000. An efficient parametric algorithm for octree traversal. *Journal of WSCG*, 8, 2, 212–219.

[Ritschel09] Ritschel, T., Grosch, T., and Seidel, H.-P. 2009. Approximating dynamic global illumination in image space. In *Proceedings of ACM SIGGRAPH Symposium on Interactive 3D Graphics and Games 2009*, pp. 75–82.

[Robison09] Robison, A. and Shirley, P. 2009. Image space gathering. In *Proceedings of High Performance Graphics 2009*, pp. 91–98.

[Rong06] Rong, G. and Tan, T.-S. 2006. Utilizing jump flooding in image-based soft shadows. In *Proceedings of ACM Symposium on Virtual Reality Software and Technology 2006*, pp. 173–180.

[Röttger02] Röttger, S., Irion, A., and Ertl, T. 2002. Shadow volumes revisited. *Journal of WSCG*, 10, 2, 373–380.

[Saito90] Saito, T. and Takahashi, T. 1990. Comprehensible rendering of 3-D shapes. *Computer Graphics*, 24, 4 (Proceedings of ACM SIGGRAPH 90), 197–206.

[Salvi08] Salvi, M. 2008. Rendering filtered shadows with exponential shadow maps. In *ShaderX^6: Advanced Rendering Techniques* (edited by W. Engel), pp. 257–274. Charles River Media, Hingham, MA. ISBN 978-1-58450-544-0.

[Salvi10] Salvi, M., Vidimce, K., Lauritzen, A., and Lefohn, A. E. 2010. Adaptive volumetric shadow maps. *Computer Graphics Forum*, 29, 4 (Proceedings of Eurographics Symposium on Rendering 2010), 1289–1296.

[Scherzer07] Scherzer, D., Jeschke, S., and Wimmer, M. 2007. Pixel-correct shadow maps with temporal reprojection and shadow test confidence. In *Proceedings of Eurographics Symposium on Rendering 2007*, pp. 45–50.

[Scherzer09] Scherzer, D., Schwärzler, M., Mattausch, O., and Wimmer, M. 2009. Real-time soft shadows using temporal coherence. In *Proceedings of ISVC 2009, Part II*, Lecture Notes in Computer Science, pp. 13–24.

[Scherzer11] Scherzer, D., Yang, L., Mattausch, O., Nehab, D., Sander, P. V., Wimmer, M., and Eisemann, E. 2011. A survey on temporal coherence methods in real-time rendering. In *Eurographics 2011 State of the Art Reports*, pp. 101–126.

[Schlick94] Schlick, C. 1994. A survey of shading and reflectance models. *Computer Graphics Forum*, 13, 2, 121–131.

[Schröder93] Schröder, P. and Hanrahan, P. 1993. On the form factor between two polygons. In *Proceedings of ACM SIGGRAPH 93*, pp. 163–164. ISBN 0-89791-601-8.

[Schüler05] Schüler, C. 2005. Eliminating surface acne with gradient shadow mapping. In *ShaderX⁴: Advanced Rendering Techniques* (edited by W. Engel), pp. 289–297. Charles River Media, Hingham, MA. ISBN 1-58450-425-0.

[Schüler06] Schüler, C. 2006. Multisampling extension for gradient shadow maps. In *ShaderX⁵: Advanced Rendering Techniques* (edited by W. Engel), pp. 207–218. Charles River Media, Hingham, MA. ISBN 978-1-58450-499-3.

[Schwarz07] Schwarz, M. and Stamminger, M. 2007. Bitmask soft shadows. *Computer Graphics Forum*, 26, 3 (Proceedings of Eurographics 2007), 515–524.

[Schwarz08a] Schwarz, M. and Stamminger, M. 2008. Microquad soft shadow mapping revisited. In *Eurographics 2008 Annex to the Conference Proceedings (Short Papers)*, pp. 295–298.

[Schwarz08b] Schwarz, M. and Stamminger, M. 2008. Quality scalability of soft shadow mapping. In *Proceedings of Graphics Interface 2008*, pp. 147–154.

[Schwarz09] Schwarz, M. 2009. *Soft shadows, curved surfaces and perceptual sensitivity: Advanced methods for improving realism in real-time rendering*. PhD thesis, University of Erlangen-Nuremberg.

[Schwarz10] Schwarz, M. and Seidel, H.-P. 2010. Fast parallel surface and solid voxelization on GPUs. *ACM Transactions on Graphics*, 29, 6 (Proceedings of ACM SIGGRAPH Asia 2010), 179:1–179:9.

[Schwärzler09] Schwärzler, M. 2009. Real-time soft shadows with adaptive light source sampling. In *Proceedings of CESCG 2009*. http://www.cescg.org/CESCG-2009/papers/VUT-Schwaerzler-Michael.pdf.

[Sen03] Sen, P., Cammarano, M., and Hanrahan, P. 2003. Shadow silhouette maps. *ACM Transactions on Graphics*, 22, 3 (Proceedings of ACM SIGGRAPH 2003), 521–526.

[Sen04] Sen, P. 2004. Silhouette maps for improved texture magnification. In *Proceedings of Graphics Hardware 2004*, pp. 65–73.

[Shade98] Shade, J., Gortler, S., He, L., and Szeliski, R. 1998. Layered depth images. In *Proceedings of ACM SIGGRAPH 98*, pp. 231–242.

[Shanmugam07] Shanmugam, P. and Arikan, O. 2007. Hardware accelerated ambient occlusion techniques on GPUs. In *Proceedings of ACM SIGGRAPH Symposium on Interactive 3D Graphics and Games 2007*, pp. 73–80.

[Shishkovtsov06] Shishkovtsov, O. 2006. Deferred shading in S.T.A.L.K.E.R. In *GPU Gems 2: Programming Techniques for High-Performance Graphics and General-Purpose Computation* (edited by M. Pharr), pp. 143–166. Addison-Wesley Professional, Reading, MA. ISBN 0-321-33559-7.

[Shreiner09] Shreiner, D. 2009. *OpenGL Programming Guide: The Official Guide to Learning OpenGL, Versions 3.0 and 3.1*. 7th ed. Addison-Wesley, Boston, MA. ISBN 0321552628.

[Sigg06] Sigg, C. and Hadwiger, M. 2006. Fast third-order texture filtering. In *GPU Gems 2: Programming Techniques for High-Performance Graphics and General-Purpose Computation* (edited by M. Pharr). Addison-Wesley Professional, Reading, MA. ISBN 0-321-33559-7.

[Sillion94] Sillion, F. X. and Puech, C. 1994. *Radiosity and Global Illumination*. Morgan Kaufmann Publishers, San Francisco, CA. ISBN 1558602771.

[Sintorn08a] Sintorn, E. and Assarsson, U. 2008. Fast parallel gpu-sorting using a hybrid algorithm. *Journal of Parallel and Distributed Computing*, 68, 1381–1388.

[Sintorn08b] Sintorn, E., Eisemann, E., and Assarsson, U. 2008. Sample based visibility for soft shadows using alias-free shadow maps. *Computer Graphics Forum*, 27, 4 (Proceedings of Eurographics Symposium on Rendering 2008), 1285–1292.

[Sintorn09] Sintorn, E. and Assarsson, U. 2009. Hair self shadowing and transparency depth ordering using occupancy maps. In *Proceedings of ACM SIGGRAPH Symposium on Interactive 3D Graphics and Games 2009*, pp. 67–74.

[Sitthi-amorn08] Sitthi-amorn, P., Lawrence, J., Yang, L., Sander, P. V., Nehab, D., and Xi, J. 2008. Automated reprojection-based pixel shader optimization. *ACM Transactions on Graphics*, 27, 5 (Proceedings of ACM SIGGRAPH Asia 2008), 127:1–127:11.

[Sloan07] Sloan, P.-P., Govindaraju, N. K., Nowrouzezahrai, D., and Snyder, J. 2007. Image-based proxy accumulation for real-time soft global illumination. In *Proceedings of Pacific Graphics 2007*, pp. 97–105.

[Smith95] Smith, S. M. and Brady, J. M. 1995. SUSAN – A new approach to low level image processing. Tech. Rep. TR95SMS1c, Chertsey, Surrey, UK.

[Snyder08] Snyder, J. and Nowrouzezahrai, D. 2008. Fast soft self-shadowing on dynamic height fields. *Computer Graphics Forum*, 27, 4 (Proceedings of Eurographics Symposium on Rendering 2008), 1275–1283.

[Soler98a] Soler, C. 1998. *Représentations hiérarchiques de la visibilité pour le contrôle de l'erreur en simulation de l'éclairage*. PhD thesis, Université Joseph Fourier (Grenoble).

[Soler98b] Soler, C. and Sillion, F. X. 1998. Fast calculation of soft shadow textures using convolution. In *Proceedings of ACM SIGGRAPH 98*, pp. 321–332.

[St-Amour05] St-Amour, J.-F., Paquette, E., and Poulin, P. 2005. Soft shadows from extended light sources with penumbra deep shadow maps. In *Proceedings of Graphics Interface 2005*, pp. 105–112.

[Stamminger02] Stamminger, M. and Drettakis, G. 2002. Perspective shadow maps. *ACM Transactions on Graphics*, 21, 3 (Proceedings of ACM SIGGRAPH 2002), 557–562.

[Steiner06] Steiner, C. 2006. *Shadow volumes in complex scenes*. Master's thesis, Institute of Computer Graphics and Algorithms, Vienna University of Technology, Favoritenstrasse 9-11/186, A-1040 Vienna, Austria.

[Stewart94] Stewart, A. J. and Ghali, S. 1994. Fast computation of shadow boundaries using spatial coherence and backprojections. In *Proceedings of ACM SIGGRAPH 94*, pp. 231–238.

[Stich07] Stich, M., Wächter, C., and Keller, A. 2007. Efficient and robust shadow volumes using hierarchical occlusion culling and geometry shaders. In *GPU Gems 3* (edited by H. Nguyen), pp. 239–256. Addison-Wesley Professional, Reading, MA. ISBN 978-0-321-51526-1.

[Stoll06] Stoll, C., Gumhold, S., and Seidel, H.-P. 2006. Incremental raycasting of piecewise quadratic surfaces on the GPU. In *Proceedings of IEEE Symposium on Interactive Ray Tracing 2006*, pp. 141–150.

[Sun05] Sun, B., Ramamoorthi, R., Narasimhan, S. G., and Nayar, S. K. 2005. A practical analytic single scattering model for real time rendering. *ACM Transactions on Graphics*, 24, 3 (Proceedings of ACM SIGGRAPH 2005), 1040–1049.

[Sutherland66] Sutherland, I. E. 1966. Ten unsolved problems in computer graphics. *Datamation*, 12, 5, 22–27.

[Szirmay-Kalos10] Szirmay-Kalos, L., Umenhoffer, T., Tóth, B., Szécsi, L., and Sbert, M. 2010. Volumetric ambient occlusion for real-time rendering and games. *IEEE Computer Graphics and Applications*, 30, 70–79.

[Tadamura99] Tadamura, K., Qin, X., Jiao, G., and Nakamae, E. 1999. Rendering optimal solar shadows using plural sunlight depth buffers. In *Proceedings of Computer Graphics International 1999*, pp. 166–173.

[Tadamura01] Tadamura, K., Qin, X., Jiao, G., and Nakamae, E. 2001. Rendering optimal solar shadows with plural sunlight depth buffers. *The Visual Computer*, 17, 2, 76–90.

[Takashi06] Takashi, I. 2006. Dynamic global illumination using tetrahedron environment mapping. In *ShaderX^4: Advanced Rendering Techniques* (edited by W. Engel), pp. 157–169. Charles River Media, Hingham, MA. ISBN 1-58450-425-0.

[Tamura06] Tamura, N., Johan, H., Chen, B.-Y., and Nishita, T. 2006. A practical and fast rendering algorithm for dynamic scenes using adaptive shadow fields. *The Visual Computer*, 22, 9–11, 702–712.

[Thibieroz09] Thibieroz, N. 2009. Deferred shading with multisampling anti-aliasing in DirectX 10. In *ShaderX^7: Advanced Rendering Techniques* (edited by W. Engel), pp. 225–242. Charles River Media, Hingham, MA. ISBN 978-1-58450-598-3.

[Thompson98] Thompson, W. B., Smits, B., Shirley, P., Kersten, D. J., and Madison, C. 1998. Visual glue. Tech. Rep. UUCS-98-007, University of Utah.

[Tomasi98] Tomasi, C. and Manduchi, R. 1998. Bilateral filtering for gray and color images. In *Proceedings of the Sixth International Conference on Computer Vision*, pp. 839–846.

[Tóth09] Tóth, B. and Umenhoffer, T. 2009. Real-time volumetric lighting in participating media. In *Eurographics 2009 Short Papers*.

[Uralsky05] Uralsky, Y. 2005. Efficient soft-edged shadows using pixel shader branching. In *GPU Gems 2: Programming Techniques for High-Performance Graphics and General-Purpose Computation* (edited by M. Pharr), pp. 269–282. Addison-Wesley Professional, Reading, MA. ISBN 0-321-33559-7.

[Valient04] Valient, M. and de Boer, W. H. 2004. Fractional-disk soft shadows. In *ShaderX^3: Advanced Rendering with DirectX and OpenGL* (edited by W. Engel), pp. 411–423. Charles River Media, Hingham, MA. ISBN 1-58450-357-2.

[Valient08] Valient, M. 2008. Stable rendering of cascaded shadow maps. In *ShaderX^6: Advanced Rendering Techniques* (edited by W. Engel), pp. 231–238. Charles River Media, Hingham, MA. ISBN 978-1-58450-544-0.

[vanWaveren05] van Waveren, J. M. P. 2005. Shadow volume construction. Intel Software Network. http://cache-www.intel.com/cd/00/00/29/37/293752_293752.pdf. Id Software, Inc.

[Vlachos02] Vlachos, A. and Card, D. 2002. Computing optimized shadow volumes for complex data sets. In *Game Programming Gems 3* (edited by D. Treglia), pp. 367–371. Charles River Media, Cambridge, MA. ISBN 9781584502333.

[Wan07] Wan, L., Wong, T.-T., and Leung, C.-S. 2007. Isocube: Exploiting the cubemap hardware. *IEEE Transactions on Visualization and Computer Graphics*, 13, 4, 720–731.

[Wang94] Wang, Y. and Molnar, S. 1994. Second-depth shadow mapping. Tech. Rep. TR 94-019, University of North Carolina at Chapel Hill.

[Weiler77] Weiler, K. and Atherton, P. 1977. Hidden surface removal using polygon area sorting. *Computer Graphics*, 11, 2 (Proceedings of ACM SIGGRAPH 77), 214–222.

[Weiskopf03] Weiskopf, D. and Ertl, T. 2003. Shadow Mapping Based on Dual Depth Layers. In *Eurographics 2003 Short Papers*, pp. 53–60.

[Whitted80] Whitted, T. 1980. An improved illumination model for shaded display. *Communications of the ACM*, 23, 6, 343–349.

[Williams78] Williams, L. 1978. Casting curved shadows on curved surfaces. *Computer Graphics*, 12, 3 (Proceedings of ACM SIGGRAPH 78), 270–274.

[Wimmer04] Wimmer, M., Scherzer, D., and Purgathofer, W. 2004. Light space perspective shadow maps. In *Proceedings of Eurographics Symposium on Rendering 2004*, pp. 143–152.

[Wimmer06] Wimmer, M. and Scherzer, D. 2006. Robust shadow mapping with light-space perspective shadow maps. In *ShaderX⁴: Advanced Rendering Techniques* (edited by W. Engel), pp. 313–330. Charles River Media, Hingham, MA. ISBN 1-58450-425-0.

[Wolberg94] Wolberg, G. 1994. *Digital Image Warping*. 1st ed. IEEE Computer Society Press, Los Alamitos, CA. ISBN 0818689447.

[Woo90] Woo, A., Poulin, P., and Fournier, A. 1990. A survey of shadow algorithms. *IEEE Computer Graphics and Applications*, 10, 6, 13–32.

[Woo92] Woo, A. 1992. The shadow depth map revisited. In *Graphics Gems III* (edited by D. Kirk), pp. 338–342. Academic Press, Boston, MA. ISBN 0-12-409673-5.

[Wylie67] Wylie, C., Romney, G., Evans, D., and Erdahl, A. 1967. Half-tone perspective drawings by computer. In *AFIPS '67 (Fall): Proceedings of the November 14-16, 1967, fall joint computer conference*, pp. 49–58.

[Wyman03] Wyman, C. and Hansen, C. 2003. Penumbra maps: Approximate soft shadows in real-time. In *Proceedings of Eurographics Symposium on Rendering 2003*, pp. 202–207.

[Wyman08] Wyman, C. and Ramsey, S. 2008. Interactive volumetric shadows in participating media with single scattering. In *Proceedings of the IEEE Symposium on Interactive Ray Tracing 2008*, pp. 87–92.

[Wyman10] Wyman, C. 2010. Interactive voxelized epipolar shadow volumes. In *ACM SIGGRAPH ASIA 2010 Sketches*, pp. 53:1–53:2.

[Xie07]   Xie, F., Tabellion, E., and Pearce, A. 2007. Soft shadows by ray tracing multilayer transparent shadow maps. In *Proceedings of Eurographics Symposium on Rendering 2007*, pp. 265–276.

[Yang08] Yang, L., Sander, P. V., and Lawrence, J. 2008. Geometry-aware framebuffer level of detail. *Computer Graphics Forum*, 27, 4 (Proceedings of Eurographics Symposium on Rendering 2008), 1183–1188.

[Yang09] Yang, B., Feng, J., Guennebaud, G., and Liu, X. 2009. Packet-based hierarchal soft shadow mapping. *Computer Graphics Forum*, 28, 4 (Proceedings of Eurographics Symposium on Rendering 2009), 1121–1130.

[Yang10a] Yang, B., Dong, Z., Feng, J., Seidel, H.-P., and Kautz, J. 2010. Variance soft shadow mapping. *Computer Graphics Forum*, 29, 7 (Proceedings of Pacific Graphics 2010), 2127–2134.

[Yang10b] Yang, J., Hensley, J., Gruen, H., and Thibieroz, N. 2010. Dynamic construction of concurrent linked-lists for real-time rendering. *Computer Graphics Forum*, 29, 4 (Proceedings of Eurographics Symposium on Rendering 2010), 1297–1304.

[Zhang98] Zhang, H. 1998. Forward shadow mapping. In *Proceedings of Eurographics Workshop on Rendering 1998*, pp. 131–138.

[Zhang06a] Zhang, F., Sun, H., Xu, L., and Lun, L. K. 2006. Parallel-split shadow maps for large-scale virtual environments. In *Proceedings of ACM International Conference on Virtual Reality Continuum and Its Applications 2006*, pp. 311–318.

[Zhang06b] Zhang, F., Xu, L., Tao, C., and Sun, H. 2006. Generalized linear perspective shadow map reparametrization. In *Proceedings of ACM International Conference on Virtual Reality Continuum and Its Applications 2006*, pp. 339–342.

[Zhang07a] Zhang, F., Sun, H., and Nyman, O. 2007. Parallel-split shadow maps on programmable GPUs. In *GPU Gems 3* (edited by H. Nguyen), pp. 203–238. Addison-Wesley Professional, Reading, MA. ISBN 978-0-321-51526-1.

[Zhang07b] Zhang, L., Chen, W., Ebert, D. S., and Peng, Q. 2007. Conservative voxelization. *The Visual Computer*, 23, 9–11, 783–792.

[Zhang09] Zhang, F., Zaprjagaev, A., and Bentham, A. 2009. Practical cascaded shadow maps. In *ShaderX^7: Advanced Rendering Techniques* (edited by W. Engel), pp. 305–330. Charles River Media, Hingham, MA. ISBN 978-1-58450-598-3.

[Zhou05] Zhou, K., Hu, Y., Lin, S., Guo, B., and Shum, H.-Y. 2005. Precomputed shadow fields for dynamic scenes. *ACM Transactions on Graphics*, 24, 3 (Proceedings of ACM SIGGRAPH 2005), 1196–1201.

[Zinke08] Zinke, A., Yuksel, C., Weber, A., and Keyser, J. 2008. Dual scattering approximation for fast multiple scattering in hair. *ACM Transactions on Graphics*, 27, 3 (Proceedings of ACM SIGGRAPH 2008), 32:1–32:10.

[Zioma03] Zioma, R. 2003. Reverse extruded shadow volumes. In *ShaderX^2: Shader Programming Tips & Tricks with DirectX 9* (edited by W. Engel), pp. 587–593. Wordware Publishing, Plano, TX. ISBN 1-55622-988-7.

Index

T - #0486 - 071024 - C400 - 235/191/18 - PB - 9780367659264 - Gloss Lamination